W9-CCM-702

100 YEARS
OF
NOTRE DAME
FOOTBALL

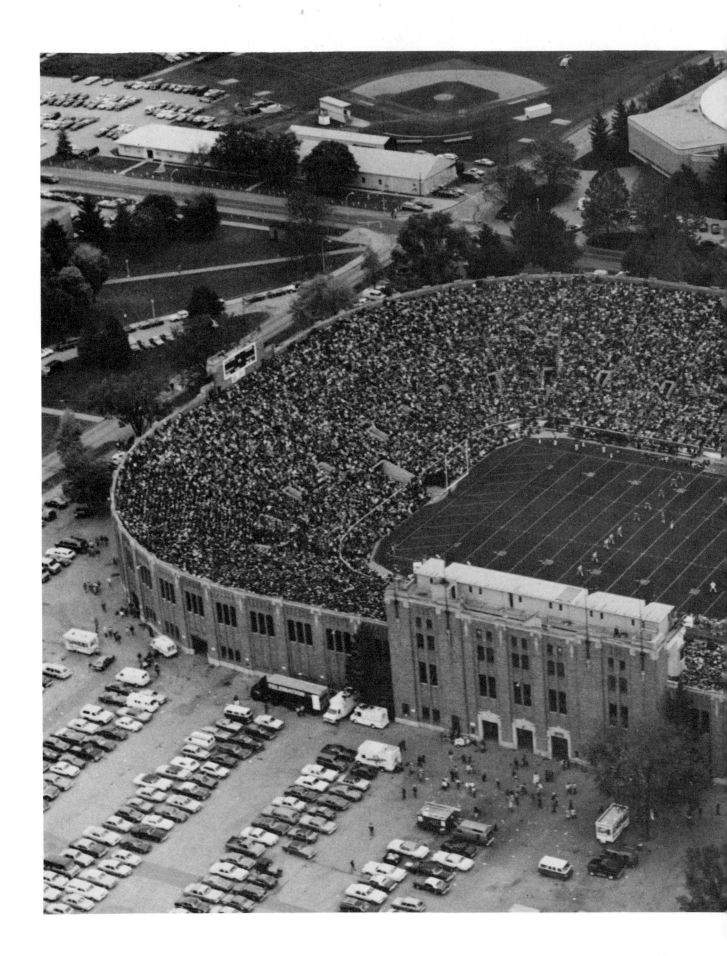

100 YEARS OF NOTRE DAME FOOTBALL

GENE SCHOOR

WILLIAM MORROW AND COMPANY, INC.
NEW YORK

This book is dedicated
to the greatest football family
in the history of intercollegiate football:

THE SEVEN MILLERS OF NOTRE DAME

Harry "Red" Miller, 1906–9; captain, 1908
Ray Miller, 1912; substitute for Knute Rockne; mayor of
Cleveland
Walter Miller, 1916–17; teammate of George Gipp
Gerry Miller, 1922–24
Don Miller, 1922–24; one of the immortal Four Horsemen
Tom Miller, 1941–42
Creighton Miller, 1941–43; All-American; College Hall of
Fame; organizer, NFL Players' Association
And a very special debt of gratitude to
Creighton Miller,
who was always available with his wise counsel
and endless supply of Notre Dame anecdotes.

Copyright © 1987 by Gene Schoor

All rights reserved. No part of this book may be reproduced
or utilized in any form or by any means, electronic or mechanical, including photocopying, recording or by any information storage and retrieval system, without permission in
writing from the Publisher. Inquiries should be addressed to
Permissions Department, William Morrow and Company, Inc.,
105 Madison Ave., New York, N.Y. 10016.

Library of Congress Cataloging-in-Publication Data

Schoor, Gene.
  One hundred years of Notre Dame football.
  Includes index.
  1. University of Notre Dame—Football—History.
I. Title.   II. Title: 100 years of Notre Dame football.
GV958.N6S29 1987   796.332'63'0977289   87-11116
ISBN 0-688-07218-6

Printed in the United States of America

First Edition

1 2 3 4 5 6 7 8 9 10

BOOK DESIGN BY M 'N O PRODUCTION SERVICES, INC.

FOREWORD
BY JOHNNY LUJACK

When the Notre Dame football team takes the field to start the 1987 season, the second under Coach Lou Holtz, the players will be participating in what will be the most memorable year in their football lives, one that promises to be one of the most exciting in the history of Notre Dame football—for 1987 will mark the one-hundredth anniversary of Notre Dame football.

To commemorate this unique anniversary, an outstanding sportswriter, Gene Schoor, has written a book I believe is one of the most interesting, most comprehensive books on Notre Dame football ever written.

In *100 Years of Notre Dame Football*, Schoor re-creates in dramatic style the entire story of those fabled hundred years.

Brought together in this outstanding book is the story of a number of the most exhilarating individuals and events our great nation has produced. Their magic and the mystique they contributed to Notre Dame football are hard to define but unmistakable.

The immortal Knute Rockne wanted to study medicine. Instead he taught chemistry, coached track and football, and walked around the campus, hustling football tickets, which he carried around in a shoe box. Jesse Harper coached Rockne and Gus Dorais to their great victory over the championship Army team of 1913, in what experts consider Notre Dame's greatest victory. Harper bargained with Army about expense money for the team trip in 1913. Army offered $600. Harper held out for and got $1,000—otherwise the team could not have made the trip. In that Army game Notre Dame was so poor that when Harper put in a substitute, the player coming out of the game had to take his shoes off and give them to the sub. The Irish had but eleven pairs of shoes.

The names of the great players roll off the tip of one's tongue; Knute Rockne, Gus Dorais, George Gipp, the Four Horsemen, Hunk Anderson, Frank Leahy, Frank Carideo, Ziggy Czaroboski, Leon Hart, Jim Martin, Creighton Miller, John Lattner, George Connor, Angelo Bertelli, Rocky Bleier, Joe Montana, Allen Pinkett, and many more. . . .

Schoor's book, then, is not a history of dates, of all-inclusive events, of encyclopedic completeness; rather it is a celebration of certain marvelous lives and events and of their power to move us.

Above all, the book is a tribute to the heroic tradition of Notre Dame football as a domain of the American imagination.

It is a book that every Notre Dame alumnus, every Notre Dame fan, and every football fan will treasure, for it should be on your must-read list.

PHOTO SOURCES

From scrapbooks of players named . . . ; Creighton Miller and the Miller family; Bagby Photo Studio, South Bend; University of Southern California; U.S. Military Academy, West Point; Associated Press Photos and Wide World Photos; Dayton University; Kent State University; Northwestern University; Jethrow Kyles of the University of Notre Dame Sports Library; University of Notre Dame; United Press Photos; Helms Foundation; *The Irish Eye*; *Notre Dame* magazine; Bill Moor, sports editor, *South Bend Tribune*; *Chicago Tribune* Sports Department; *Blue & Gold*'s Louie Somogyi; *Sport* magazine; *Sports Illustrated*; *The Sporting News*; *New York Journal-American*; *New York Daily Mirror*; *Brooklyn Eagle*—Bob Farrell; New York Jets; University of Arkansas; North Carolina State University; and Miami University, Ohio.

ACKNOWLEDGMENTS

It would be impossible to list all the Notre Dame players, coaches, assistant coaches, and sportswriters, editors, and athletic directors across the country who have contributed their efforts to this mammoth project, but there are an especial few I must single out:

So heartfelt thanks to: the family of Knute Rockne; Jesse Harper's son and grandaughter; Harry "Red" Miller, captain of the 1908 team, the brilliant Paul Castner, whose injury in 1923 paved the way to the development of the immortal Four Horsemen, and to those gallant Four Horsemen, Jim Crowley, Elmer Layden, Don Miller, and Harry Stuhldreher, who supplied me with personal anecdotes in anticipation of this project; to the Seven Mules, Adam Walsh, Chuck Collins, Joe Bach, John Weibel, Noble Kizer, Edgar Miller, and Ed Hunsinger; to Calumet High School, for some interesting George Gipp material; and to Chet Grant, a teammate of Gipp.

To the Notre Dame coaches: Hunk Anderson, Frank Leahy, Elmer Layden, Hugh Devore, Joe Kuharich, Terry Brennan, Dan Devine, Ara Parseghian, Gerry Faust, Lou Holtz, Tom Pagna, Moose Krause, Joe Boland, Bill Fischer, John Druze, John Lujack, Fred Miller, Wayne Millner, Marchy Schwartz, Hank Stram . . .

To the players: George Connor, Leon Hart, Paul Hornung, Tom Gatewood, Creighton Miller, Ray Miller, Monty Stickles, Christie Flanagan, Jack Cannon, Marty Brill, Joe Savoldi, Joe Benoir, Milt Piepul, John Mastrangelo, Angelo "Duke" Bertelli, Frank Tripucka, Phil Sheridan, Bill Fischer, Ziggy Czarobski, Bob Williams, Al Ecuyer, Frank Carideo, Nick Buoniconti, Frank Pomarico, Dick Lynch, Rusty Leach, Terry Hanratty, Bill Shakespeare, John Law, Dr. Paul "Bucky" O'Connor, Dr. Bob Williams, Jim Mello, Judge Roger Kiley, Tom Carey, Bronko Nagurski, Jr., Andy Pilney, Mike Layden, Jim Martin, Rockey Bleier, and numerous others. . . .

To the sportswriters: Francis Wallace, Arch Ward, Jimmy Breslin, Jerry Brondfield, Al Silverman, Ed Fitzgerald, Jim Beach, Dick Schaap, Wells Twombly, "Red" Blaik, Tim Cohane, Jimmy Powers, Max Kase, Chet Grant, Eugene Young, Dave Condon, Bob Best, and to Sean Hallinan of Cosida. . . .

To the more than one hundred sports information directors of the various colleges who responded to my inquiries on Notre Dame football.

A very special tribute to Julian Bach, simply the greatest literary agent in the nation and a great guy. To Morrow's lovely Mary Ellen Curley, who was always there when needed . . . and to Adrian Zackheim . . . the best Editor in town. . . .

CONTENTS

INTRODUCTION
ARA PARSEGHIAN

Few schools in the nation can boast as many tales of victory, valor, drama, and glory as Notre Dame. The penchant of the "Fighting Irish" for pulling upsets on the football field and winning despite the most incredible odds has endeared the school and its football team to fans across the nation.

The year 1987 marks the one-hundredth anniversary of Notre Dame football, and I am delighted to write briefly about this new book that tells the marvelous story of this great school and its wonderful teams. To celebrate the anniversary Gene Schoor, one of the nation's top sportswriters, has created an unforgettable volume, *One Hundred Years of Notre Dame Football*.

This book tells the complete and engrossing story, from the first game, against Michigan, in 1887, then tracing Irish football fables and fortunes to the present in a most colorful, exciting, and dramatic narrative style that would satisfy any follower of Notre Dame football.

There are wonderful, human-interest stories of the fabled coaches: Harper, Rockne, Anderson, Layden, Brennan, Leahy, Devine, Faust, Holtz, and, yes, this writer, too; and dozens of personal stories told by Angelo Bertelli, Johnny Lujack, Creighton Miller, Don Miller, Harry Stuhldreher, Jack Chevigny, Frank Leahy, Leon Hart, Paul Hornung, Joe Montana, Rocky Bleier, and others, and hundreds of dramatic photographs that make this a book you will treasure forever.

CHAPTER 1

NOTRE DAME'S BIGGEST GAME

Early in the spring of 1913, an item of sports intelligence sparked consternation among the cadets at West Point. Yale University was not on this season's football schedule. For the first time in twenty years, Old Eli, famed for the great teams coached by the immortal Howard Jones and in fiction as the alma mater of Frank Merriwell, had filled the date of or near Saturday, November 1, with Lehigh University as their opposition. That was the annual date Army had held open for the Yalies.

There would be no trip this year to New Haven, with pennant-waving Old Blues answering, cheer for cheer, the gray-clad corps, five hundred strong. The cadets would not see All-American Henry Ketchum and great Yale halfback Forrester Ainsworth in action. And heads would roll at West Point for this.

There was simply no excuse for this tragic blunder. Or so went the grumbles among the cadets.

The Army coach was Lieutenant Charlie Daly, a former All-American quarterback at Harvard and later recognized as one of Army's all-time great football coaches. It was Daly's job to make up the schedule, but he took little interest in filling the Yale spot because he knew that the other major teams in the East were already booked. Daly turned to second classman Hal Loomis, cadet manager of football.

"Hal, send out some letters. Find any team anywhere that will give us some decent opposition. We've got to fill that open date."

Cadet Loomis, proceeding in the most practicable manner, consulted the *Spalding Football Guide* of 1912. He wrote to any number of colleges with football teams, most of them unknown to him. One of the most prompt replies came from a small midwestern school that had trouble getting games in its own sector because of its winning teams. The school was Notre Dame, in South Bend, Indiana.

Neither name rang a bell with Loomis, but he noted with mild satisfaction that Notre Dame had been undefeated in 1912 and had beaten such teams as St. Viator by a 116–7 score, then came back in the following weeks to trounce Adrian, 74–7; Morris Harvey, 39–0; and a strong Wabash team, 41–6. At least, thought Loomis, Notre Dame ought to be able to give Army a midseason test. And soon letters were shooting back and forth between Army and Notre Dame's new coach, Jesse Harper.

Army authorities offered Harper $600 to bring the team to West Point, but Jesse said that was not enough expense money for a squad of fourteen men. Harper held out for more money and finally agreed on $1,000, and the date was set and game firmly scheduled.

Decades later, the Army-Notre Dame game was to be called off for the very reason of the frenetic enthusiasm it created, unprecedented in football. There would even be reports that a pair of fifty-yard-line tickets at Yankee Stadium would bring enough money to finance Notre Dame's entire first football expedition.

When it was announced by Army that Notre Dame had agreed to play at West Point, there were a few shrugs. They'd lost Yale and scheduled an unknown with a name that could not even be pronounced.

The cadets' contempt was readily understandable. Football had begun in the East, and the East still was the game's stronghold. Even the few well-known teams from the West were beaten in the few intersectional games with eastern colleges. Veteran sportswriters were indifferent. How could anybody get excited about Army playing a tiny, unknown western school with a strange name?

But in the West, storms were brewing that were to revolutionize the game of football. New ideas were being tried. The East, in football as well as everything else under the sun, went its proud, conservative way.

The game centered around massive center rushes, cyclonic end sweeps, bone-crushing line plays, and field goals: Those were the things football was made of, and it was unthinkable to try anything else.

This football revolution was to break out in full fury at West Point on the afternoon of November 1, 1913, and the military would be unable to suppress it. It would go on to topple the proud and haughty East off its football pedestal and turn the gridiron world upside down.

In the summer of 1913, the coming struggle was just a dangerous idea in the brain of a young revolutionist named Charles Emile Dorais, better known as Gus. Dorais and his fellow conspirator, Knute Rockne, were inseparable. They roomed together in Sorin Hall on the campus, participated in practically every campus activity, and had played together on the Irish football team for three years.

The wispy, 150-pound Dorais, a star hurler on the baseball team and quarterback on the Irish eleven, was a shrewd field general. Rockne, sturdy, tough, with a bashed-in nose, was the acknowledged leader of the team as captain. Together they developed a relationship that was to last a lifetime.

Rockne, a brilliant science student, was slated to become a chemistry instructor upon graduation and then go on to study medicine. Dorais was studying law. Both were handy do-it-yourself men. They rigged up a hinge on the bars over their basement window and charged admission to students sneaking into the dorm after hours. Later they operated a "radiator concession." They would show up in freshman quarters, Rockne with a huge Stilson wrench in hand, and would threaten to remove the radiator unless the monthly 50-cent fee for it was paid to Rock and Gus. The faculty eventually stamped out this unique enterprise.

In the summer of 1913 Rockne and Dorais got jobs in a restaurant at Cedar Point, an Ohio resort, and started scheming up new tactics for the fall. In their leisure hours, Gus and Rockne practiced an aerial act. Gus would spiral a football and pass to Rockne twenty, thirty, and forty yards away, and Rockne would gather the ball in his outstretched fingertips. Gus had developed a new technique in throwing the football. He gripped the ball, much fatter than it is now, at one end, and cocked it behind his ear. Then, with split-second timing, he spiraled the ball to Rock, who meanwhile would run certain pass patterns agreed on beforehand.

The forward pass itself was not new. It had been legalized in 1906, and that year the Carlisle Indians

Jesse Harper, Notre Dame's head coach, 1913–17, transformed the Irish into a national collegiate football power by defeating Army, 35–13, in his first season. His teams lost but five games in five years.

Rare photo of Knute Rockne as a player at left end vs. South Dakota in 1913 game at South Bend.

had used short underhand passes to humble Minnesota's Golden Gophers, 17–5. Minnesota's coach, Dr. Harry Williams, promptly seized on the idea of tossing the ball overhand and worked out a number of successful pass plays for his players. At St. Louis University, coach Eddie Cochems began to use the forward pass to batter his opposition. But those passers used to lay the ball on the palm of their hand and sling a spiral. Dorais, by gripping the ball, had superior control, and since he had been a strong right-handed hurler for the baseball team, could grip and throw the football accurately.

"Rock kept repeating a phrase," Dorais was to say. "Mobility. Mobility and change of pace. That's what we need. They're not going to know where we're going or when we get there."

What Rockne meant was that there'd be no camping out under a pass, waiting for the ball to arrive. He'd grab the ball on a run in full stride, if possible, and with open, relaxed hands. No more catching the pass against the chest or stomach. Rock later admitted that he was possibly the first receiver to use his hands in that manner.

The two roommates worked tirelessly, establishing pass routes and timing the patterns so that Dorais could lead Rock or hurl the ball over his shoulder, or toss the ball short, so that Rock could cut back for the ball.

By the time September rolled around, Dorais' arm and Rockne's hands were primed for an aerial circus that would astound the entire world of football. Coach Jesse Harper met his favorite duo at the train at South Bend, shouting, "Boys, we're gonna play Army at West Point. We're gonna give them a surprise November first."

Notre Dame opened the 1913 season with a smashing 87–0 victory over Ohio Northern. South Dakota was the next victim, 20–7. Alma College was swamped by the ferocious line smashes of Ray Eichenlaub and the marvelous quarterbacking of Gus Dorais as the Irish swamped Alma, 62–0.

> Daly's a Wonder . . .
> He is, by thunder . . .
> And this is the Army's day.

So sang the Corps of Cadets in Lieutenant Charlie Daly's heyday as a player. Daly was a five-time All-American—first at Harvard, then at West Point. Now, as head football coach, he had raised Army football to soaring heights, and in 1913, it looked as though he might be coaching the Cadets through their first undefeated season in history. The Cadets had romped over five eastern opponents, and as they prepared to face an unknown midwestern eleven, Notre Dame, Daly had sent a former teammate, now an assistant, Captain Tom Hammond, to South Bend to scout Notre Dame against Alma College.

However, in the game against Alma, Coach Jesse Harper of Notre Dame kept his superb forward-passing combination under cover and ordered quarterback Dorais to restrict his offense to running plays.

Thus Hammond reported back to West Point that the Irish had a magnificent quarterback and ball-handler in Charles Dorais and a powerful line smasher in Ray "Iron Eich" Eichenlaub, but that all their plays were power plays.

So Army prepared a defense against power and was primed with an offense based on superior strength blasting a path through opponents with the surging force of the wedge and a line that outweighed the Irish by as much as twenty to twenty-five pounds per man.

"Meanwhile, in secret practice sessions when we were certain that no Army scouts were around," said Rockne, "we sharpened our passing attack. And as the days went by, the entire student body became so excited about the 'big game' they began to cut classes to watch practice.

"The morning we left South Bend—that was on a Thursday, two days before the game—every student and professor was out of bed long before breakfast and marched downtown accompanying the team to the railroad station," said Rockne. "It was the first time I'd ever seen anything like this mass hysteria generated on the Notre Dame campus over a football game, and it made every one of the players so excited they wanted to march on to West Point. It was marvelous. The fellows sang all the college songs, cheered and applauded each individual player, the coaches. Even the townspeople joined in the tribute as we left the depot."

With its limited travel budget, the Notre Dame entourage of some eighteen players and coaches took along sandwiches and fruit packed by the kitchen ladies in the refectory, to save money for dinner aboard the train. It took an entire day to get to Buffalo, where at about 11:00 P.M. they gawked at the luxury of a transfer to Pullman berths—lowers for the regulars, uppers for the subs.

"It struck me," Rockne said, "as a rather reasonable form of discrimination. It remained so fixed in my mind that I used it for later Notre Dame trips when I became head coach."

The Notre Dame team en route to the biggest game in Irish history, against Army at West Point, pauses for a photo.

It was also the first time anyone in the Notre Dame group had ever slept on a train, and the players were so awed that few of them got any kind of the sleep that coach Harper always prescribed for the week of a game. Harper worried about this when the Irish scrambled off the train at West Point at 8:00 A.M. He needn't have. Irish adrenaline was at a boiling point.

On arriving at West Point, the Irish were quartered at Cullom Hall and given every sample of the hospitality that has existed in Notre Dame-Army relations since that day when the game's oldest and finest intersectional feud began.

The Notre Dame team, led by Captain Knute Rockne on that day that will live forever in the hearts and minds of all Notre Dame men, was the finest football team the Irish had put together.

Gus Dorais, the ex-baseball hurler, ran the team from his quarterback post like an Army general. Six-foot, three-inch, 225-pound Ray Eichenlaub, the biggest man on the squad, was a crashing type at fullback: Joe Pliska and Sam Finegan were a pair of flashy halfbacks who could run with the ball. At the ends, Captain Knute Rockne and Fred Gushurst were a pair of speedy flankers who could catch any ball thrown at them and once they were in possession of the ball could run with the speed of a halfback. Deak Jones and Ralph Lathrop were the tackles; Freeman Fitzgerald and Emmett Keefe were the guards, while Al Feeney was at the center post.

Army, with five consecutive victories over the strongest teams in the East, included such outstanding stars as All-American Vern Prichard at quarterback, Benny Hoge and Leland Hobbs at the halfback spots, and Paul Hodgson at fullback. Cadet Dwight Eisenhower, a flashy halfback in the running for All-American honors, had injured his knee in a game against Tufts the previous week, and although he suited up for the Notre Dame game, Ike was unable to play. As a matter of fact, the injured knee would prevent Ike from ever playing football again, and for a period of time it even threatened to end his Army career.

Only three thousand spectators were on hand to witness the sensational exhibition of offensive football by the midwestern eleven. A number of fans had come to the Point merely for the day's outing, watching the dress parade in the morning, and their pass admitted them free to the game in the afternoon. But among the crowd was a young fellow from nearby Haverstraw, James A. Farley, reporting the game for a local paper. Mr. Farley later became postmaster general of the United States in the cabinet of President Franklin D. Roosevelt. After that first game, Farley never missed a Notre Dame game and became one of the leading supporters of Irish football.

The game got under way as Johnny McEwan, plebe center for Army, kicked off to Gus Dorais, and Gus scampered to the twenty-five-yard line before he was

"During halftime," said Ray Eichenlaub, Irish fullback, "we just threw a blanket over our shoulders and sat right down on the sidelines and talked over our game strategy."

smothered by a host of huge Army tacklers. Eichenlaub fumbled on the second running play, and Army recovered. Notre Dame held Army, and after an exchange of punts, the tense Notre Dame team again fumbled the ball. Once again they held the tough Army eleven without a significant gain.

"The Cadets and most of the spectators seemed to regard the game as a quiet, friendly engagement," said Rockne. "A little workout for Army; and for the first quarter it looked that way. Army knocked our guys around. They were bigger and so confident and were giving us a physical beating, until we suddenly overcame the notion that we were actually playing the great Army team."

Army tacklers crashing in to stop line charges suddenly began to find Dorais calmly fading back to pass to Pliska, Finegan, and Eichenlaub, and now Notre Dame had three first downs in succession and Army was bewildered.

Now Rockne, the campus actor, went into his football routine, which still is effective today. Rock pretended to be hurt, affected a limp, until "the Army halfback covering me almost yawned in my face. Suddenly I feinted to my left, left him flat-footed, and raced down the field as Dorais whipped a forty-yard toss to me and I took the ball over my shoulder for a touchdown. There was a roar of surprise from the five hundred cadets massed in the west stands, and at that moment, the moment I caught the ball,

life for me was complete. And we proceeded to make it more complete."

Army, stung by the ease with which the Irish scored, came fighting back. Hodgson and Hobbs smashed through tackle for huge gains and battered their way into Notre Dame territory. Prichard connected for a pass to Jouett for a first down on the Irish fifteen-yard line, and then big Leland Hobbs smashed over for an Army score. Spike Woodruff missed a left-footed try for the extra point and it was 7–6 Notre Dame.

After the kickoff and an exchange of punts, Notre Dame fumbled and Army recovered. Army drove to the Irish three-yard line and the crowd settled down, confident now that Army would begin to roll up points. A holding penalty against the Irish placed the ball on the six-inch line. Hodgson smashed into the line but was held for no gain.

Now the Irish settled down and turned back another smash. A third Army drive into the line was stopped, and now the crowd was up and screaming for an Army touchdown. On fourth down, Prichard faked a lateral pass to Hoge, wheeled, and smashed in for the score.

The extra point was kicked and Army led, 13–7.

"We still felt we could win," Rockne recalled, "but we honestly didn't think we could do it with our running game, good as we thought it was. Army was just too big and too strong. So we decided we'd hit them with our air attack. We didn't think Army was quick enough or smart enough to adjust its defenses. It was time for us to outsmart Army."

West Point supporters soon were on their feet clamoring in dismay as Notre Dame went on the attack. Rockne returned the Army kickoff to the fifteen-yard line and then Dorais faked a forward pass, ducked under two big Army tacklers, and skipped through the line for fifteen yards. On the next play Rockne sped downfield and three Army backs converged on him, so Dorais calmly flipped a short pass over center to Pliska, and Joe ripped off thirty yards before he was downed. Dorais now tossed two successive passes to Rockne, and Knute sped to the Army five-yard line. With the Cadets now thoroughly bewildered by the Irish strategy and completely off-balance, Pliska drove through for the second Notre Dame touchdown. At the half it was Notre Dame 14, Army 13.

Between the halves, Charlie Daly, the Army coach, improvised a floating defense to contend with Notre Dame's clever mixing of passes and drives off-tackle. He played a five-man line and instructed his ends to drift back to cover receivers if Dorais faded back to pass.

It was an admirable effort and it worked for a short time during the third period as the Irish, unable to gain, tried a field goal from midfield that went wide of the mark.

Army then took over and, with Frank Millburn replacing Hoge at halfback, promptly proceeded to tear huge holes in the outweighed Irish line. At ten, twelve, and fifteen yards at a clip, Army crunched down to the Notre Dame ten-yard stripe, moving like a well-oiled machine.

Then Rockne tackled Hodgson for a loss. Millburn was stopped on the three-yard line, and then dramatically, Vern Prichard took the ball on fourth down, faded to his right, and flipped a short pass to Lou Merrilat, racing into the end zone. It looked like a certain Army touchdown. Suddenly a streak named Dorais cut in front of Merrilat, intercepted the sure Army touchdown pass, and drove on to the ten-yard line.

"Stick around," Dorais yelled over to Prichard, "and I'll show you how to throw the ball!"

From that moment on, the picture was one that was etched forever in the memories of knowledgeable critics of the game.

The interception just about broke Army's combative spirit, and from that point, Dorais and Rockne

unleashed the full beauty and precision of their passing game. Thirteen times in the last half Dorais put the ball in the air. There was seven passes to Rockne, and one each to Pliska, Gushurst, and Finegan. The West Pointers were reeling. When Army spread their defense to stop the passing attack, Pliska and Eichenlaub ripped the huge Army line to shreds as the Irish pounded out three more touchdowns.

When it was all over, it was 35–13. Ray Eichenlaub spearheaded the ground attack, scoring the final two touchdowns after passes had set the stage. Spectators and Army players alike left the field shaking their heads in wonderment that the forward pass could play such a dominant role.

One legend that persists to this day is that Harper, Rockne, and Dorais stayed over the weekend at West Point to teach the Cadets the Notre Dame passing game. This, however, is not true, for the entire team, including Harper, Rock, and Dorais, left West Point late Saturday afternoon, after the game, and arrived in Buffalo Sunday morning. The team spent Sunday at Niagara Falls.

In this first game against Army, Notre Dame made just one substitution, and that as a result of a broken shoe lace.

It seems that Irish halfback Sam Finegan, who played a superb game against the Cadets, broke his shoe lace in the last five minutes of the game. Harper ordered Bunny Larkin, who was sitting on the bench the entire game, to remove his shoes and give them to Finegan. Larkin flatly refused. After all, he didn't come nine hundred miles to sit on the bench.

Harper had no choice and sent Larkin in at right halfback, replacing Finegan.

The next day, the Sunday edition of *The New York Times* headlined the story, "Notre Dame Open Play Amazes Army." The follow-up included this note: "The Westerners flashed the most sensational football ever seen in the East."

Head Umpire Bill Roper, one of the most respected football men in the nation, concluded: "I've always believed such a style of play was possible under the new rules, which legalized the forward pass and opened the game. [The new rules were adopted in 1906 by the Collegiate Rules Committee after Coach John Heisman and Walter Camp led the fight to "open and to streamline" the game.] But I have never known the forward pass to be employed with such marvelous perfection," said Roper.

Notre Dame teams have had many a homecoming since that first Army game in 1913, but on Monday,

The undefeated 1913 team. Front row (left to right): Mal Elward, end; Al Bergman, halfback; Bill Cook, tackle; Art Larkin, tackle. Middle row: Ralph Lathrop, tackle; Keith Jones, tackle; Joe Pliska, halfback; Captain Knute Rockne, end; Gus Dorais, quarterback; Fred Gushurst, end; Al Fee-ney, center. Back row: Joe Edwards (street clothes); Emmett Keefe, guard; Ray Eichenlaub, fullback; Hollis King, guard; Freeman Fitzgerald, guard; Charles "Sam" Finegan, back; Jesse Harper, head coach.

November 3, 1913, when the team arrived back in South Bend, the entire populace turned out to greet the boys who had upheld western football against the East in such sensational style. There were brass bands and a huge torchlight parade and speeches. The players themselves had had the most enjoyable trip of their lives. When the team departed from their Pullman in Buffalo on the return ride, they were greeted by a railroad official who asked them if they were the football team. Upon discovering that they were, he told them a special breakfast was ready in the station house. As the team devoured a magnificent meal and were ready to board their special day coach for South Bend, they noticed another group of husky young men singing the blues about breakfast . . . the one they did not eat. It turned out they were the Syracuse team, who were just returning home from a 43–7 trouncing at the hands of Michigan. The bountiful repast that Notre Dame's players had devoured had been intended for Syracuse.

Years later, in his autobiography, Rockne would write: "That victory over Army gave the greatest impetus yet to the development of the Notre Dame spirit. Among other things, it brought out more boys for varsity football—and began attracting high school players who might very well have gone elsewhere. It was," said Rock, "the biggest game in Notre Dame history."

Here is how the teams lined up:

ARMY—13		NOTRE DAME—35
Jouett	LE	Rockne (captain)
Wynne	LT	Jones
Meacham	LG	Keefe
McEwan	C	Feeney
Jones	RG	Fitzgerald
Weyand	RT	Lathrop
Merrilat	RE	Gushurst
Prichard	QB	Dorais
Hoge (captain)	LH	Pliska
Hobbs	RH	Finegan
Hodgson	FB	Eichenlaub

Touchdowns: Army, Hodgson, Prichard; Notre Dame, Rockne, Pliska (2), Eichenlaub (2)
Conversions: Army, Hoge; Notre Dame, Dorais (5)

Notre Dame	7	7	0	21—35
Army	6	7	0	0—13

Substitutes: Army, Britton, Packard, Goodman, Huston, Ford, Waddell, Hess, Woodruff, Lamphier, Millburn; Notre Dame, Larkin

CHAPTER 2

THE EARLY DAYS: 1887–1907

A LETTER TO WALTER CAMP

James Kivlan, popular instructor in the Notre Dame machine shop and part-time "coacher" of Notre Dame football, was most unhappy. He had noted the great interest students had shown in several meetings with him concerning the football situation and he had done everything he possibly could to improve the team, yet they had lost several games during the past years.

"There must be something radically wrong with my coaching methods," he said to a colleague. "Surely we can, we *must* do better if we ever expect to defeat the hated Michigan Wolverines. The lads here have shown marvelous interest and an affinity for the game. I've got to think of something."

And so Coacher Kivlan sent the following letter to a man who was known throughout the nation as the Father of American Football, Yale's Walter Camp.

September 20, 1893

Dear Mr. Camp:

I want to ask you a special favor.

Will you kindly furnish me with some fine points on the best way to develop a good football team. I am an instructor connected with the University of Notre Dame and have been asked to help coach the team. I do know something of the old Rugby game, but would like to find out the best manner to handle the young men.

I have seen a good many Yale games that you played (as I do come from New Haven, you can find out about me from Dr. Seaver). And knowing you are the authority on the game, I would welcome any points you might give me. Hoping that I am not asking too great a favor of you.

Your sincere admirer,

James H. Kivlan
University of Notre Dame

Kivlan's letter was typical of the hundreds Walter Camp received, and being the kind of understanding man he was, he undoubtedly helped Kivlan, for the Notre Dame teams of 1892 and 1893 won five of the seven games played, with but one loss, to Chicago, by 8–0.

Indian villages and fur trading posts dotted the Indiana prairie in 1842 when the young Reverend Edward Sorin traveled from France to found the University of Notre Dame. Together with a small band of clerics, he took possession of a log building in bad repair, dedicated the land and their efforts to the Mother of God, and began the arduous task of establishing an educational program suitable for the needs of the frontier dwellers.

Oddly enough, registration increased rapidly, and by the end of the Civil War, Notre Dame was a bustling institution of more than five hundred students, all housed and taught in a new "huge" five-story building.

There was a need to organize and develop sports to engage the spirited young men on campus, and soon there were clubs and class teams competing in a number of sports activities.

At that time football was a form of soccer played by as many as forty players on a side. Class teams competed with each other for side bets that usually included a keg of cider or a barrel of apples.

So when Michigan students suggested that its team drop in at Notre Dame for a game of football, the Irish eagerly accepted but said the visitors would first have to show them how the new game was played.

Michigan, "champions of the West," arrived on the morning of Wednesday, November 23, 1887, was met by a committee of students, taken on a tour of the campus, and then two teams were formed, each composed of Michigan and Notre Dame players.

After "some minutes" of this demonstration, the real game began, with eleven men on a side; there was time for just "one inning," and Michigan won, 8–0. After a hearty dinner, President Walsh thanked the visitors, who departed for Chicago, where the next day they defeated an eleven picked from alumni of Yale and Harvard, 26–0.

The following April the Wolverines came back for two more games and defeated the Irish in both. The first was played at the Green Stocking Ball Park in South Bend before a crowd of more than four hundred spectators, with the Wolverines winning, 26–6. The following afternoon the Michigan team came to the campus for a noon dinner and after a "short ride on the lake" took to the playing field again, but with a change in the lineup. R. S. Babcock, a Michigan player who had been injured the previous day, exchanged jobs with Edward Sprague, the referee, who had officiated the previous day.

Then the first dispute between the two schools erupted.

Notre Dame Scholastic reported:

"The University of Michigan was held scoreless by a sturdy Notre Dame eleven and they could not score until the final two minutes of play. Then, while the players were settling a dispute over a play, Sprague of Michigan snatched the ball out of the referee's hands and dashed for a touchdown." Notre Dame claimed the touchdown was illegal, asserting that Sprague had tricked them and that he also stepped out of bounds near the goal line. Referee Babcock, however, ruled the play legal, and once again Michigan had a win, this time 10–4. This was the first of a series of controversies that kept the two teams apart for nine years.

Notre Dame's first victory ever, over the Harvard School of Chicago by 20–0 on December 6, 1888, brought forth a tremendous burst of undergraduate

The first team, 1887: H. B. Luhn, Hal Jewett, Joe Hepburn, George Houck, Ed Hawkins, Frank Fehr, Pat Nelson, Gene Melady, Frank Springer, Joe Cusack, Ed Prudhomme.

enthusiasm, and all over the campus the football players were singled out for cheers whenever they were noticed.

In the spring of 1889, Notre Dame, resplendent in new gold and blue uniforms, which were padded along the shoulders, challenged Michigan, hoping to defeat the Wolverines for the "championship of the West." But according to *Notre Dame Scholastic's* editor, "Michigan backed squarely out of the game, alleging that their best men had left school and the team is in a weak state." At any rate, whatever the excuse, the fine camaraderie between the two schools had dissipated and the teams did not play each other for nine years.

The first great game that was to develop into a Notre Dame tradition was against Northwestern in 1889. Captain Ed Prudhomme led his Irish to a hard-fought 9–0 victory. According to Brother Hugh, one of the team's advisers, the Notre Dame players still were being brought back to the campus—in ambulances—a week later. The inference, of course, was

that any man able to return to Notre Dame after the game and under his own power was not considered to have done his full duty to the university.

In 1894 the need for a full-time "coacher" was realized, and James L. Morison, a star player with the Michigan Wolverines, was brought in. Morison promptly developed a most ambitious schedule of five games, and the team got off to an auspicious start, with a 14–0 victory over Hillsdale. Albion played an aggressive game, and the result was a 6–6 tie. A strong Wabash team was trounced, 30–0, and Rush Medical was defeated by an 18–6 score. The lone defeat was to Albion, by a 19–12 score in a return game.

H. G. Hadden succeeded James Morison after Morison left to coach at Hillsdale in 1895, and the Irish won three of four games played.

Frank E. Hering had been a star quarterback under Coach Amos Alonzo Stagg at Chicago but came to Notre Dame to study law, play on the team, and coach the Irish. He was elected captain, played several

The 1893 team, led by Captain Frank Keough (with ball), won four games and lost one (there was no head coach in 1893).

positions, and was an inspiration to everyone on the team. Hering was an outstanding student and fine speaker, and after graduation he became associated with the Order of Eagles as the editor of their magazine. In 1930, after the entire nation had adopted the custom of Mother's Day, the Mother's Day Committee traced the observance's source and credited the original impetus to Frank Hering, who advocated the idea in a speech he gave on February 7, 1904, at an Eagles' convention at the English Opera House in Indianapolis. A commemorative tablet now marks the spot.

Hering, who took over as player, captain, and coach of the team in 1896, organized a most ambitious schedule. Seven games were played. The most difficult one was with Purdue University, and the boilermakers defeated the Irish in a grueling struggle by a 28–22 score. The Irish won four and lost three games in Hering's first year.

In 1897 three major games were scheduled—with Chicago, DePauw, and Michigan State. And Notre Dame's Fighting Irish won out over Michigan State by a whopping 34–6 score, lost to the formidable Chicago eleven by 34–5, and beat DePauw, 4–0.

Hering served as head football coach for three years and was succeeded in the next several years by a transitory group, most of whom seem to have been players brought in from other schools—players who coached the team, played on the team, and sometimes continued their studies. This was a fertile period for the tramp athlete, muscular fellows who spent more time on the football field than in the classroom.

In 1900 Pat O'Dea, an Australian football star, took over as Notre Dame's fifth head football coach. Widely known as the "Kangaroo Kicker" for his incredible kicking feats, Pat came to the University of Wisconsin in 1896 from Melbourne University to join brother Andy, who at that time was the Badgers' crew coach.

Old-time Wisconsin football men who played with O'Dea say Pat's kicking abilities will never be equaled. Copies of an old *New York Sun* sports article describe

Frank Hering (with ball), coach and captain of the 1896 Irish eleven, became involved with the Eagles organization after graduation from Notre Dame. His talk on the role of American mothers before an Eagles' convention in 1904 later became the basis for the founding of Mother's Day.

a game in which one of O'Dea's punts traveled 117 yards. In another tussle, against Yale, the Badger halfback kicked a ball that traveled 110 yards. Against the Minnesota Gophers, O'Dea, ready to punt, saw a horde of Minnesota tacklers charging in at him and began to run toward the sidelines to evade them. Suddenly he stopped in his tracks and kicked an unbelievable sixty-yard field goal to win the game.

Led by O'Dea, the Irish met and defeated such bitter rivals as Indiana and Purdue, in 1901, and lost a bitter tussle to Northwestern, 2–0. The loss to Northwestern marred what could have been Notre Dame's first undefeated season as they closed with a remarkable record of eight victories and one loss, and a tie against the South Bend A.C.

Under O'Dea's skillful coaching, several of Notre Dame's greatest heroes emerged. There was Louis "Red" Salmon, who played four years and became head coach in 1904. Red was the first great legendary hero of Irish football. A fullback of the Nagurski type, although he was only five-ten and weighed 175 pounds, he nevertheless was a savage line plunger and was selected on Walter Camp's All-America team—the first Notre Dame star to be thus honored.

Frank Shaughnessy won a baseball scholarship to Notre Dame and made the football team in 1901 simply by asking the coach for a football suit. Shag was a hard-driving end during the four years he played, and in 1904 he captained the Irish eleven, a team that won five and lost three games.

The 1903 team, captained by Red Salmon, was the first undefeated Notre Dame eleven. The Irish won eight games, with a 0–0 tie against a strong Northwestern team. The tie was the only blemish in a nine-game schedule as the Irish ran up a total of 292 points to none for their opponents, a most remarkable record.

After he graduated from Notre Dame in 1904, Shaughnessy played minor-league baseball, then got a contract with the Washington Senators in 1905. In 1908 Shag joined the Philadelphia Athletics, then managed the Reading club; he passed his bar examination in Reading. Shag was one of the men who introduced the American style of football into Canada. In 1925 Shag was named president of the International Baseball League and is credited with saving the very nature of minor-league baseball with his great organizational and managerial skills. He served the league for more than thirty-five years before he retired in 1960.

Jim Faragher, a Youngstown, Ohio, native, was one of the most colorful characters ever to don the Irish moleskins. Jim loved to play football and followed a vagabond trail that included stops at Nebraska, Duquesne, and West Virginia. At West Virginia, Jim played under Coach Fielding Yost, who also played with the team. Yost later became an outstanding head coach at the University of Michigan and one of Knute Rockne's bitterest foes.

Faragher, who lost an eye in a football game, came to Notre Dame and played under Pat O'Dea during the seasons of 1900 and 1901. He then took over as head coach in 1902 after Pat left Notre Dame.

A strange and unruly man, Faragher knew his football and was a good teacher. When he left his football job at Notre Dame, Faragher became a cop on the Notre Dame campus and was a favorite with the students for years.

Tom Barry graduated from Brown University, where he was an honor student and was captain of its 1902 football team. He studied law at Harvard but was unwilling to give up football, and he took the post as Notre Dame's football coach in 1906. His two-year reign was one of the most spectacular periods in Irish football. In 1906 Notre Dame won six games, losing only to a strong Indiana eleven by a 12–0 score. In 1907 Indiana again was the stumbling block to an unblemished record as they played the Irish to a 0–0 tie. When he left Notre Dame Barry coached at Tulane, Bowdoin, and Wisconsin before he finally settled down to the practice of law. He was secretary of the National Metal Trades Association for more than thirty years and became an important adviser to a number of leading national corporations.

The 1907 Irish squad was most unusual. The team was big by ordinary standards of the time: The line averaged 214 pounds, while the pony backfield averaged about 170 pounds. Outstanding players included the first of the seven marvelous Millers; Harry "Red" Miller, lightest man on the squad, weighed 165, while the biggest man, Pat Beacom, topped the scales at 235 pounds.

A quarterback on the team was shifty Allan Dwan, who graduated in 1907, then drifted to Hollywood, where he began an illustrious career that started as a stagehand, then camera aide, and then he broke in as an assistant director and finally as a full-fledged director. As a director, Dwan developed into one of Hollywood's finest. Over a span of over fifty years in Hollywood, Dwan directed more than four hundred feature films and directed such Hollywood greats as Doug Fairbanks, Sr., Charlie Chaplin, Rudolph Valentino, Gloria Swanson, Clark Gable, Robert Taylor, John Wayne, and most of Hollywood's other male and female stars. Dwan passed away in 1978 at age ninety-three in a Hollywood nursing home.

Red Miller won his first Notre Dame monogram as the regular halfback on the 1906 Irish squad. In 1907 Miller led Notre Dame to an undefeated season and in 1908 was elected captain of the team, which lost but one game, that to Michigan by a 12–6 margin. Of course, Red did not know then that he was to be the first ruler of what is undoubtedly the greatest football dynasty in the archives of Notre Dame football.

Red Miller was followed by brother Ray, who made the Irish team in 1912. However, aggressive as he was, Ray Miller was edged out of a regular position on the Irish varsity by a tough, hard-nosed, aggressive football player who was an absolute wizard at catching forward passes at a dead run. His name was Knute Rockne.

Upon graduation from Notre Dame, Ray Miller became nationally known in several other fields of endeavor. A heroic World War II captain and leader of a rugged machine-gun battalion, Ray opened a law office in Cleveland and entered politics. He was elected mayor of Cleveland for several terms and became a leading member of the national Democratic Party and a close friend of Presidents John F. Kennedy and Lyndon B. Johnson.

Walter Miller, third of the famous Millers, was a hard-running fullback and teammate of the great George Gipp and played with Gipp on Coach Rockne's undefeated teams of 1919 and 1920.

Notre Dame listed still two more Millers in the 1922–24 period. Gerry Miller, injured early on, served as a substitute halfback, ofttimes replacing brother Don, who, of course, was to become one of the famous members of the "Four Horsemen," Notre Dame's greatest backfield.

In 1942 Red Miller's two sons, Tom, a fine halfback, and Creighton, were outstanding varsity performers as the Irish lost to Michigan, 32–20. Creighton scored two sensational touchdowns in a losing effort. A year later Tom had graduated, but Creighton, now in his third and final season as a varsity halfback, was again outstanding, scoring two touchdowns in a magnificent display of broken-field running to spark Notre Dame to a spectacular 35–12 win. It was Notre Dame's first win over the Michigan Wolverines since 1909.

The advent of Red Miller at Notre Dame in 1906 coincided with a number of revolutionary changes in football's code of rules. The new rule changes permitted the use of the forward pass, eliminated the flying tackle, hurdling, and the crushing "flying wedge play," which caused so many serious injuries. The new rules also stipulated that a team had to gain ten yards instead of five for a first down.

Notre Dame began using the forward pass immediately. At first it was either a short shovel pass or an end-over-end toss. The season of 1907 saw Notre Dame backs using the spiral pass play consistently, and by the time the 1908 season rolled around, the spiral as used for forward passing was fully developed. Notre Dame's fullback, Pete Vaughan, became specially skillful and could throw a fifty-yard pass like a baseball. Red Miller developed a low, accurate pass at forty yards, and quarterback Don Hamilton became one of the finest short passers in the Midwest.

In that 1906–10 era, the field of play was 110 yards long; the goal posts were in the goal lines; the ball was much fatter and larger than it is now; the game had no quarters but was composed of two thirty-five-minute halves; and there were no free substitutions. It was quite common for the same eleven men to play through an entire game.

The 1906–10 period also witnessed a number of radical changes in football paraphernalia and the dawn of better protection against injuries. Shinguards and noseguards had not appeared. Throughout the next several years, the union suit with vest attached to the pants gave way to just the pants. The union suit, as well as the pants with their thick padding of splints and papier-mâché, were heavy and became more so with perspiration and rain.

Shoulder and elbow pads sewed on the jerseys offered poor protection as compared with the present pads. Headguards were made of felt and were of little use. Shoes were much heavier, and no attention was paid to the cleats once they wore out.

In 1909 Frank "Shorty" Longman, an end on Michigan's "point a minute" team, became Notre Dame's new coach. He was a fiery orator, and his speeches rang through the locker room like thunder. Longman's idea to show he was the boss, was to thrash every man on the football squad. His main ambition, however, was to defeat his former coach, Fielding Yost of Michigan.

The game that year between Notre Dame and Michigan was a classic. Played at Ann Arbor on November 6 and with a huge Michigan crowd on hand, the faster, lighter, and shiftier Irish team completely outplayed Michigan's cumbersome eleven. Red Miller, Pete Vaughan, and Don Hamilton starred as the Irish defeated Michigan 11–3 and claimed the title of "champions of the West."

"FOOTBALL AT NOTRE DAME WHEN I PLAYED"
BY HARRY "RED" MILLER,
1908 CAPTAIN

"I had been brought up knowing that I would go to Notre Dame. My parents had filled me with romantic tales of the school. I was extremely ambitious to make the football team even though my father despised the game. He called all football players 'tramp athletes—all muscle and no brains.' He was a baseball man and had been a famous catcher on the Defiance Blue Stockings team about 1887–88 and was credited with inventing the catcher's glove and the chest protector. The inventions were the butt of jokes and cracks by opposing players. Later on, of course, all the catchers wore the chest protector and glove.

"Father forbade my playing football at Notre Dame, and until I had been elected captain in 1908, he did not know that I had been playing with the team for two years. I had bruised my leg in a game and it became infected and I had to go to the infirmary. The injury was quite serious and I almost lost the leg. A story appeared in the *Chicago Tribune* about my injury, and Father dashed up to school to investigate. But Dad fell into the hands of Father John Cavanaugh, president of Notre Dame. Father Cavanaugh charmed Dad and from then on he was a fervent football man.

"I was probably the happiest young man on the campus in 1908 when the players elected me as their captain. It was pure ecstasy, and I was on cloud nine all year long.

"Vic Place of Dartmouth was the new head coach in 1908. He was a great strategist and line coach who brought in a wealth of power and deceptive plays. However, he believed in the old theory that iron men could be produced by hours and hours of practice. Practice under Coach Place began ten days before the opening of school, and when school started, we had practice in the morning and about three and a half hours in the afternoon, with the exception of Sunday, when we practiced only two and a half hours.

"We lost a bitter game to Michigan on October 17, 12–6. Allerdice of Michigan kicked three magnificent field goals of four points each. We scored a great touchdown as MacDonald sped through and around Michigan for a forty-yard run in the second half, but the referee declared that MacDonald had stepped out of bounds during his run. Mac did not go out of bounds. We protested the decision, but it was of no use. Michigan won.

"The Indiana game, which at the time was traditionally more important than the Michigan game, was a tough, hard-fought battle from start to finish. Indiana had a fine team led by halfback Paddock, but I think we had a bit of an edge. Howie Edwards at fullback played a marvelous game and we scored twice to beat Indiana, 11–0. It was a great victory for us.

"The following year, 1909, we had a new coach, Shorty Longman of Michigan. Longman's system was entirely different from Place's. His plays were simple and we had just a few of them, but they were more than enough to give us one of Notre Dame's greatest seasons. We defeated Pittsburgh 6–0 in Notre Dame's first visit to an eastern team. The following week we defeated a tough, aggressive, but slow-footed Michigan eleven by an 11–3 score. It was our first win over the heralded, 'champions of the West,' and the entire student body met the team as we detrained from the Michigan game and paraded us through the town.

"Miami (Ohio) and Wabash were easily beaten during the next two weeks, but injuries to key members of the team cost us the game with Marquette. It was the last game of the season, played on

Thanksgiving Day in Milwaukee, and injuries hurt us. Sam Dolan, our great linebacker, fractured a collarbone in the first period but played the entire game without telling anyone of the injury. And so we were lucky to get a 0–0 tie.

"However, in spite of the tie game. the sportswriters awarded Notre Dame the title 'champions of the West.' "

Harry "Red" Miller (right), captain of the 1908 team, and teammate Sam "Rosy" Dolan, an outstanding tackle on the same Irish team, after a tough game.

CHAPTER 3

THE ROCKNE ERA

"I DREAMED THAT I, TOO, WOULD BE A HERO"
BY KNUTE ROCKNE

"The first time I learned a football was something to think with, and not merely something to kick," said Knute Rockne, "was when I saw a great football player in action for the first time . . . the intersectional game between the eastern high-school champions, Brooklyn Prep, and the western champions, the Hyde Park team of Chicago. I lived in the area—the Logan Square Park area of Chicago—with Momma, Poppa, and four sisters, and since the game was the biggest of the year, I just had to see the game and crashed the gate—a habit I was forced into because money was always so tight in our large family.

"I sat utterly spellbound before the brilliant play of Hyde Park's clever quarterback, a boy named Walter Eckersall. The smooth, machinelike way he handled his teammates . . . like an orchestra leader. After the game was over everybody was shouting and cheering Eckersall, for he led his team to an incredible 105–0 victory, I tried to get close to him. I wanted to shake his hand, but so did two or three thousand other kids, so I had to go home without that handshake. Yet I felt that I had met with a real American hero. I thought that someday I would want to be just like Eckersall, a great football hero. And for years they were nothing . . . nothing but empty dreams. I began my life working as a grubby mail dispatcher for the Chicago Post Office, working at night for more than four years.

"But there came a day when the Notre Dame squad ran out on the field in 1913 and there I was, the former sandlotter, ex-mail dispatcher, captain of the Notre Dame football team. The referee was Walter Eckersall. In his smart white uniform, he looked scarcely a day older than when he led Hyde Park to its victory over Brooklyn Prep. Grasping his hand, I said:

" 'I've been waiting years for this.'

" 'For what?' said Eckersall.

" 'To shake your hand,' I said, recounting how his brilliant performance for Hyde Park High turned my mind from track to football. 'I was gonna be as much like you as I could.'

" 'Stop, stop,' said Eckersall in the middle of my recital, 'or Notre Dame will be penalized five yards for speechmaking.'

"How a youngster from Voss, a hamlet in Norway that lies between Bergen and Oslo, could find himself, in his midtwenties, captain of a typical midwestern American football team may require explaining. Perhaps it's sufficient explanation to say that this evolution is a typical American story—in business, athletics, and politics. It has occurred so often that it's quite ordinary. The breaks came my way when I had sense enough to take them; and while that's an unromantic way of explaining a career, it has the advantage of being the truth.

"The World's Fair [the World's Columbian Exposition] of 1893 was to be held in Chicago. Dad, by profession a stationary engineer and carriage builder, wanted to show his design for a new carriage at the Fair and went to America. Later he sent for the rest of the family. My mother took her three girls and me, her only son, to New York.

"How my mother ever managed that tedious voyage; how she guided us through the intricacies of entry, knowing nothing of English, took us into the heart of a new, strange, bewildering country from our town—how, in brief, she achieved the first step in our Americanization, unaided by anybody, is one of the millions of minor miracles that are the stuff and fabric of America.

"Chicago in the era B.C.—Before Al Capone— was a spacious city, with its endless corner lots and tolerant police, and was a great place for a boy to grow up in. We lived in the Logan Square neighborhood, chiefly inhabited by Swedes and Irish, and that's where I got my first real baptism of fire on a corner lot. I was an end on the Tricky Tigers— historic rivals of the Avondales—so called because we had a great triple pass back of the line that always was good for a big gain. Our equipment was meager. No helmets, one shinguard per player. *We tied our ears with tape to prevent an opponent from pulling at them.*

"Most of our team returned home after the game with blackened eyes, cut lips, scratched faces, and clothes ripped to a frazzle. After one of the games where we all got beat up badly, my parents refused to allow me to play football. Baseball was OK.

"The following week in a baseball game against Maplewood a red-hot argument broke out and punches were thrown all over the field. I was in the middle of the battle and all of a sudden some wise guy swung a bat right across the bridge of my nose. I went home full of blood and with a bashed-in nose that was to be my most recognizable facial characteristic for the rest of my days."

The quick mind that was to distinguish Rockne's later years revealed itself as early as his grade-school days at the Brentano School in Logan Square. As a result, Knute became one of the shining lights of the area. He was an avid and eager reader, a happy faculty he retained throughout his life. After he entered Northwest High School his marks fell in proportion to his interests in all sports. Of these he soon began to make quite a name for himself in track, where his great speed earned him a place on the varsity team as a halfmiler and where his own urge to excel in other fields established him as a very good pole vaulter. In football, Rock made the scrub team. At thirteen years of age he weighed but 110 pounds but was the team's fullback.

"After I left high school, I had my heart set on going to college. I wanted to go to Illinois and to that end saved every dime I could get. I got a job cleaning our high-school windows, but the other kids, jealous that I got the job, broke a good many of the windows. I was blamed and was fired.

"But that incident drove me to take a civil-service exam, which I easily passed and was then appointed a mail dispatcher at the princely salary of six hundred dollars per year.

"The job at the post office taught me little save its unevenness and unfairness," said Rockne. "And I was soon on my way to developing into the smartest shirker of all time. I did have a couple of goals in mind. One of my sisters kept at me to save my money and go to college. She insisted that a college education would mean more to me and the family than anything else and so I saved and scrimped in every way that I could. I wanted to go to the University of Illinois and I needed about a thousand dollars."

Two former teammates from the Illinois Athletic Club, John Devine and Johnny Plant, both trackmen, suggested that Rock go with them to Notre Dame.

"What swung me to Notre Dame," said Rockne, "was that my thousand dollars would go a longer way than at Illinois and that I could get a job very easily at South Bend. And so I went down to South Bend with a cheap suitcase and my thousand dollars."

Rockne passed the exacting special examination that his lack of a prep-school diploma made necessary and was sent to a dormitory in the very lowest floor of Brownson Hall. There he was met by a husky, compact, smiling eighteen-year-old.

"Hi," said the younger man. "My name's Dorais. Gus Dorais. I guess you're my new roommate. Where do you want to put your trunk?"

"I haven't any trunk," said Rock.

"Neither have I," replied Dorais. "Let's shake on that. I guess we're starting all even."

Dorais' home was in Chippewa Falls, Wisconsin, where he had made quite a reputation as a pitcher with the baseball team as well as a fine quarterback on the high-school football squad.

Dorais recalled his first talk with Rockne: "You gonna play football. Everybody here plays at least hall football. But I'm going to play varsity ball."

"Hall football? Phooey," said Rock. "Don't think so. I'll try for the big team, myself. Only weigh a hundred and fifty pounds, though."

"I sort of sensed that the old guy—and that's what he looked like to me, a much older guy—was annoyed by my questions," said Gus. "But I really liked him at first sight. There was something about Rock, a kind of smartness, quick, bright eyes, that made you forget his battered face."

The four- or five-year difference between Rockne and his younger classmates didn't prevent him from having as much fun as they did.

"There was a lot of the little boy in Rock," said Gus. "Breaking a rule was never a sign of rebellion or a mark of disrespect for the established order. Rock just acted on impulse. Yet as poor as we were, we did have our fun," said Dorais. "Rock came to school with but one suit, two shirts. When he earned his first monogram sweater, he wore it till it fell apart. In the winter, he'd borrow a coat from a friend. It was so big, Rock looked like a circus clown. But he would only use the coat when we went into town. Rock would walk the two miles to save the nickel fare.

"Once a month," said Dorais, "to really earn some spending money, we'd sneak off to town to attend a club smoker. A feature presentation at these monthly smokers was a prize fight between local boxers, and since Rock was a very good boxer, we would try to line up a bout each month for him. I was Rock's partner and would second him in the corner. I handled all the business and we got as much as twenty-five dollars each time Rock fought. Knute was a very good fighter and most of the time won his fights without too much trouble. And thank heavens for those bouts. It helped us through many rough times during our undergraduate days.

"At that time forward passing was frowned on and teams used the pass only when they were hopelessly behind in the score," said Dorais. "Standard practice was to throw the ball either underhand or end over end.

"But I was a very good baseball pitcher," said Gus, "and I adapted the overhand throw of the diamond to football. When I first tried to throw the ball overhand, Coach Longman pulled me out of a scrimmage and yelled that I could not throw a football that way.

" 'What in hell are you gonna do on a rainy day?' said Longman. 'You're not gonna be able to control the ball.' "

To prove his point, Longman placed a ball in a bucket of water for an hour and then presented it to Dorais. Gus continued to throw the ball with uncanny accuracy. Longman's neck became fiery red, and a few weeks later Dorais was promoted and became the regular quarterback of a Notre Dame

team that was to lose only one game that season and none in the next three years.

"The university gave me a chance to work for my room and board as the janitor of the chemical lab, cleaning out the slop buckets and doing other minor chores," Rock said. "Somebody stole a gallon of experimental wine from the pharmacy lab; I was blamed and was almost expelled. So I was walking a tightrope and my reputation was not glamorous. When Joe Collins, a varsity end for three years, a big man on the campus, recommended me for a chance with the varsity, Coach Shorty Longman was not too enthusiastic.

"But he gave me a chance. Longman sent me

Knute Rockne did not impress Coach Longman in his first tryout for football in 1910, so he was determined to show the coach he could outrun any varsity ends. He went out for the Irish track team and in a meet in 1910 entered the 440-yard run; the 880-yard dash, and the mile, and he set a meet pole-vault record. Longman was impressed, and in 1911 Rock was a varsity end.

out with the scrubs in a practice game with the varsity. He put me at fullback. And never was there so dismal a flop. I fumbled the first punt. Then tried again and fumbled again. Nothing seemed to work for me. I was paralyzed with fright. Finally on a play, a big two-hundred-pound tackle crashed into me, knocked me for a fifteen-yard loss, and then Longman pulled me out and sent me back to Brownson Hall with the hall team.

"I was discouraged, but decided if I could prove to Longman that I could run—could outrun—his ends, I might have another chance. So I went out for the track team; made the team, made my varsity letter. Now I had some prestige—enough to warrant another tryout for the football team."

Twenty-three-year-old Knute Rockne made a wise decision in returning as an end for the 1910 season; for even Coach Longman finally had to admit that Rock was tough enough to play varsity ball, even though he then weighed only 145 pounds. He was the fastest man on the squad and managed to play in enough games to earn his first varsity football letter as Notre Dame managed victories over Olivet, Butchel (Akron), Rose Poly, and Ohio Northern, lost to Michigan State, and wound up the season with a 5–5 tie with a rugged Marquette eleven.

Longman left after the 1910 season, and a stronger, heavier Knute Rockne reported to the new coach, John Marks, a former Dartmouth halfback.

"Marks made us over from a green, aggressive squad into a slashing, driving outfit," said Rock. "The first time Marks looked over Ray Eichenlaub, the two-hundred-twenty-pound fullback, Marks said, 'Jones, Feeney, and the rest will make the holes. Ray, you're gonna tear through them.' And Eichenlaub ripped and tore at the Northern Ohio line for three touchdowns as we beat them thirty-two to six," said Rock.

"Marks even gave some attention to the forward pass, and Dorais and I scored a couple of times that year. We were a faster, shiftier team than our opponents and won six games. We tied Pittsburgh and Marquette and had one of our best seasons.

"I won a regular berth as an end under Marks and had the pleasant surprise of seeing myself discussed as an All-American possibility toward the end of the 1912 season. Then it was the end of football for the year, and it was almost the end of my college career.

"My father died, and it seemed imperative that I quit school to help out my family. But once again my smart sister intervened with her arguments:

" 'If you quit now, especially with your *cum laude* grade in chemistry, it would be a crime. Knute, you remember, you may earn a living, but it won't be in chemistry. It will be as a mail dispatcher, and you'll regret it all of your life.'

"So I went back to school and was elected captain of the 1913 football team. I was hardly off the train that autumn when I was greeted by a friendly voice.

" 'You're Rockne?' a man asked.

" 'Well,' the man went on, 'I'm grabbing you football men off the trains as fast as I can. I'm Jesse Harper, Notre Dame's new coach. And we've got to work our heads off this year.'

" 'What's the special excitement?' I said calmly.

" 'They're letting us play in the East,' he said. 'Army has agreed to play Notre Dame. How about that?' "

His balding captain grinned. It was the first time Harper was to see that famous lopsided grin on Rockne's face.

"Army, eh?" Rock shouted and dashed off to spread the word to his teammates, especially to his roommate and quarterback, Gus Dorais.

"We play Army," mused Rockne.

Well, that was something. Here was little Notre Dame, which for years had played such teams as the Illinois Cycling Club, the Indianapolis Artillery, and even South Bend High School, drawing a game against Army, one of the citadels of eastern football. The Irish had played Wabash, Marquette, and Indiana (big games) but they had never played east of Pittsburgh. Now they were to play the big guns at Army—with stars such as McEwan, Merrilat, Eisenhower, Prichard, and their coach, Daly, one of the smartest in football. Now they were to play in the "big leagues." This was a job—a crusade to prove that Notre Dame could play with the best of them. Now he and Gus would show the boys on the plains above the Hudson a bit of fancy middle-western football.

JESSE HARPER NAMED FOOTBALL COACH

Jesse Harper, a former University of Chicago quarterback, was appointed head football coach at Wabash College in Indiana in 1909 and built his offense around the forward pass. In his second season at Wabash, his eleven were undefeated.

In 1911 Harper brought Wabash to South Bend and nearly scored a major upset over the Irish, losing a fierce contest by a 6–3 score. That game against Notre Dame practically clinched the Notre Dame post for Jesse, and in 1913 he was named director of athletics and head football coach at Notre Dame.

Harper inherited a team of experienced, crafty veterans led by Captain Knute Rockne, a brilliant end, and an excellent quarterback in Charles Dorais. Despite his own short coaching career, Harper saw an opportunity that would make him a coaching immortal, and from the beginning he was smart enough to appreciate the abilities of Rockne and Dorais. And he allowed Rock and Dorais to go off on their own and practice their own pet plays.

Rock and Dorais were to work that summer of 1913 at Cedar Point, a popular summer resort, as checkers in a restaurant. The two players borrowed a football so they could practice some new and unique pass plays that would revolutionize the game of football and bring national fame to Notre Dame, to Harper, and to Rockne and Dorais.

Suddenly it was all over—the four years of college that had been so wonderful, so enlightening, so eminently successful for Knute Rockne. Graduation Day, June 15, 1914, had provided him with the most marvelous memories. He had really crammed at his studies after the football season had ended. He put everything into his work the last six months, and when it was over, Rock, always an outstanding student, graduated with a four-year average of 93, *magna cum laude*, with honors in chemistry, biology, and bacteriology.

And now Rock knew that more than anything else in the world, he wanted to become a doctor. Notre Dame had no medical school, so he got in touch with St. Louis University, and they accepted him. And Jess Harper helped him line up a job as a high-school coach to help support himself.

But suddenly the St. Louis officials decided that Rockne could not carry a full medical course while earning his living as a football coach. So he returned to Chicago, confused and disappointed. He was immediately contacted by Harper. There was a coaching job at St. Joseph's College, and Rock and Gus Dorais were the prime candidates for the job. The roommates looked at each other:

"There was only one thing to do," Rock recalled. "I don't remember whether it was Gus's idea or mine, but we decided to flip a coin for the job."

Dorais won, and Rockne began to explore other jobs.

Jess Harper knew what he wanted: Rockne as his assistant. He liked Rock's analytical mind, his knowledge of the game. Finally it was settled: Knute was to return to Notre Dame as head track coach, assistant football coach, and instructor in chemistry. The key, of course, was the job coaching football, and it was Jesse Harper who made it possible. The coaching position, the chemistry job, and the track post would pay him a total of $2,500 per year. That was enough for Rock to take one of the most important steps in his life.

At Cedar Point he had met and fallen in love with a woman who was to be the supreme influence through the remainder of his life. She was Bonnie Skiles of Kenton, Ohio, a tall, slim, sweet-mannered woman of the Catholic faith, who was to provide Rock with the only type of home he could have lived in—one that was almost a dormitory for the students and players he loved.

They were married in the parish church of Sts. Peter and Paul in Sandusky, Ohio, on July 15, 1914. Rev. William Murphy, who married them and forever remained a close friend, spoke knowingly of the two people when he said: "She was a devout young lady, modest in her ways and manners, capable of winning the hand and heart of the staid and judicious Rockne. Her womanly qualities were of a superior kind. Certainly, Miss Bonnie Skiles had no small part in forming the character of the peerless Rockne."

Burdened now by debts, by a new life, and by the knowledge of a fatherless family back home in Chicago, Rock plunged into his several jobs at Notre Dame. He taught chemistry, worked in the lab, and coached football and track. Necessity was driving him to greatness.

Coaching the football team was a hard, driving, tiring, thankless job. The poverty-ridden budget of the football left only bare necessities. Rock had to work with and instruct every player on the squad— backs, ends, tackles, guards, and centers. He doubled in brass as trainer-ticket seller, a man of all jobs who somehow had to turn out a football team that would challenge the world.

Once when he had instructed a husky lineman that he wanted a certain kind of blocking on a certain play, the lineman ignored Rock's orders and played the position the way he wanted.

Rock walked onto the field.

"Turn in your suit. You're through."

The team was astonished: an assistant coach firing a top-notch varsity player. The big lineman appealed to Coach Harper, only to meet stony silence. There was an immediate apology on the field before the entire squad, and Rock reinstated the player.

An assistant coach in 1914, Rockne personally drilled his players, often using himself as the target for tackles.

The shabby uniforms, jerseys, and headgear were handed down from year to year. When one player came off the field, his feet in agony where the cleats had broken through, he looked at Rock, saw the hurt on Rock's face, and hopped back into the lineup.

Afterward, Rock said of this period:

"If the sportswriters had really known how little we had at Notre Dame, the poverty of our equipment, they would have made us All-Americans on guts alone."

Technically, the thing that made Notre Dame players the greatest in football under Rockne was the perfecting of every known aspect of the game. If, in the dusty old records, others invented aspects of the game, Rockne perfected them. Under him the forward pass reached its height. Under him the Notre Dame shift turned the game into one of speed and deception. Under Rock the open game became exactly what the term implied, a game in which quick thinking and strategy, instead of mass power, became the keys to success.

Hour after hour, day after day, he schooled his men. Ofttimes he would work on a single play until darkness forced him to stop. Errorless performances were demanded of every player.

"I can't play the game from the bench," he told his players. "Only the quarterback can discover the weakness of an opposing team. But all of you can watch, study your opponents. Think out there! Think! Think! Outsmart! Use your head all the time!"

The fact that he'd been comparatively small as a player helped Rock discover a new system of blocking. In practice as a player, Rock had to block a huge tackle, 6-foot, 3½-inch, 235-pound George Philbrook. On every play Philbrook would demolish Rockne with ease. It was evident that Rock had to come up with a solution or someone else would take over his post.

The system of blocking taught by every coach in those early days was for a blocker to lunge directly at the man he was to block out of the play.

But Rock had learned that it wouldn't work when a smaller man like himself had to block out a huge opponent. Each day he pondered the situation and tried new methods, but nothing seemed to work.

So in his analytical mind he set to work using an old math formula, one that included balance, position, speed, surprise, and leverage—and it worked. It worked so well that *later every head coach in the nation copied the Rockne method.*

To develop the leverage or brush block, Rock faced big Philbrook on the line of scrimmage. Rockne crouched low, hands extended, and when he came at George, he bobbed and weaved like a boxer looking for an opening; then, as Philbrook hesitated, not knowing where Rock would move at him, Rock hit big George who was off-balance, and pushed him aside, thereby opening a hole big enough for a halfback to crash through. The strategy worked every time.

Eventually this was to become the foundation for the Rockne System: single-man blocking. In all other systems of coaching at that time, the blocking was done by double-teaming: two men blocking a single opponent. Rockne's new system made possible the long, spectacular gains, even the "perfect play."

"Our big game in 1914 was with the Yale Bulldogs," recalled Rockne. "I sat on the sidelines at New Haven and saw a fine Yale team captained by Bud Talbott and with halfback Harry Legore lead the Yale attack, and they made us look like a bunch of high-school kids. We were overconfident with a winning streak that had stretched over four seasons, and Yale beat our ears off. They lateral-passed us out of the park and beat us to the turn of twenty-eight to nothing. It was the most valuable lesson Notre Dame ever had in football. It taught us never to be cocksure. Modern football at Notre Dame can be dated from that game, as we made vital use of every lesson we learned.

"The following Monday, back at South Bend, Harper decided to install a new type of offense. Jess decided to use Stagg's backfield shift combined with my idea of shifting both ends, and it worked very well in a couple of games. That was the beginning of what later became known as the Notre Dame Shift," said Rockne.

Head coach in 1918, Rockne carefully details a defensive play.

On a December night in 1917, during a farewell dinner party he had arranged for a number of Notre Dame players about to leave for Europe and World War I, Rockne revealed to his players that he had grown weary of his job as an assistant coach and was about to accept a post as head coach at Michigan State. Rock felt that his jobs as assistant football coach, chemistry instructor, head track coach, and football scout left little time for himself and his growing family. He felt there were better opportunities and more money in the position offered him at Michigan State. But the unexpected death of a relative of Harper's led to Jess's resignation to return home to Sitka, Kansas, to run the family cattle ranch.

"When I resigned early in 1918," said Jess, "I insisted that Rockne should be given the job, and for weeks I argued with Father Cavanaugh that Rock could do the job better than anyone else. Besides," said Harper, "I promised Rockne the job more than two years ago."

"Well," said Father Cavanaugh, "if you promised it to him, I will give it to him."

The wartime season of 1918, Rockne's first as head coach, was necessarily abbreviated. Notre Dame scheduled only six games, but the new head coach lost only to a strong Michigan State eleven and held mighty Nebraska to a scoreless tie.

During the summer of 1919, Rock approached his former roommate, Gus Dorais, to assist him in coaching the backfield. Dorais had coached at Columbia College, Iowa, and immediately accepted the opportunity to team up once more with his ex-roommate.

And in 1919 the two were so successful and worked so well together that Notre Dame swept on through victories over Kalamazoo, Mountain Union College, a strong Nebraska team, Western Michigan, Indiana, Army, Michigan State, Purdue, and Morningside in an unbroken skein of nine straight victories. When the season ended, Park Davis, a noted football historian and writer and his aides, who had started a national football ranking system, voted Notre Dame national champions. (Davis and his aides selected the ratings for the *Spalding Official College Football Guide*.)

THE BRIEF AND SPECTACULAR CAREER OF GEORGE GIPP

Although he was to become a gridiron immortal, George Gipp never made the first team on his high-school eleven. He was an outstanding baseball and basketball star and played on the town YMCA team in Laurium, Michigan. Laurium, a small mining town in the northern part of the state, "was too cold for football," said Gipp. George was good enough at baseball to be scouted and later signed by the Chicago White Sox, but he never won a baseball monogram at Notre Dame, despite the fact that he received a baseball scholarship there.

Yet old-timers around Laurium still recall him as a gangling schoolboy who was one of the finest batters against the leading semiprofessional pitchers in the area. In one crucial four-game series against Iron Mountain, Gipp drove out seven hits in twelve at-bats. News stories point to his batting: he hit .494 one year and won a crucial game with one of the longest home runs ever seen in the Laurium ball park.

In the summer of 1916, Bill Gray, a fine catcher for Notre Dame's baseball team who lived in nearby Calumet, returned home after being signed to a big-league contract by the White Sox. Bill told Gipp that he could easily arrange a scholarship if George would play ball at Notre Dame.

Thus, at age twenty-one, George Gipp quit his taxi-driving job in Laurium, packed his suitcase, and set out for Notre Dame and immortality.

It was shortly after a practice session on a September afternoon in 1916, and Notre Dame's young assistant football coach, Knute Rockne, started to walk across the campus when he was attracted by a young man kicking a football. Suddenly he stopped short in his tracks and followed the next kick, which traveled more than fifty yards and straight as an arrow. He looked once again at the rangy, good-looking boy who had kicked the ball and gasped. The boy drove his foot savagely into the ball for another tremendous boot. But this time Rock did a double-take, for the *boy had drop-kicked the ball*—and it flew straight as an arrow once more, at least sixty yards.

Rock hustled over to the kicker.

"My name's Rockne, Knute Rockne. I'm an assistant football coach. What's your name?"

"Name's Gipp. George Gipp. Yeah, I know who you are. See you around all the time." He spoke easily, casually, and was not impressed with the coach.

"What about football? Interested in playing? Did you ever play much? You sure can kick 'em."

Rock urged the youngster to come out for the freshman football team.

"I don't know." He seemed indifferent.

Three days later, he reported for practice.

Harper suggested that Gipp kick a few. After a couple of sixty-five-yard punts and a couple of fifty-yard drop kicks, all practice came to a halt. Now the varsity players were staring at this gangling newcomer who easily outkicked every player on the squad.

A few days later, Gipp was inserted into the lineup against a scrub team and repeatedly ripped through their line for ten- and fifteen-yard gains. And three times he punted clear over the safetyman's head.

Three weeks later he started the game on the freshman team against Western State at Kalamazoo, Michigan. In the fourth quarter of the game, one that saw Gipp rip through the line for repeated gains, the score was tied 7–7.

On fourth down, quarterback Frank Thomas called for a punt, with Gipp back in kicking formation.

As the ball was snapped by the center, Notre Dame's left end, Dave Hayes, raced downfield to cover the ball. Suddenly the crowd roared. Hayes stopped running, turned around, and asked, "What happened?"

"That sonofabitch kicked a field goal."

Gipp, not wanting to settle for a tie, calmly drop-kicked a sixty-two-yard field goal to win the game. The record still stands in the books.

Freshman were not eligible for varsity play at Notre Dame, so Gipp's real debut was a year away. Meanwhile, he had come to Rockne for a job. He was broke.

"I want to work," he said. "How about a job waiting on tables?"

Rockne was startled. He would learn to expect the unexpected from Gipp. Work in the kitchen of the cafeteria and dining rooms was tedious and dirty. But Gipp didn't seem to mind, took the job, and held it for two years, earning his room and board.

"I came to know a lot—and very little—about George Gipp," said Rockne. "He lived quietly, had no single class buddy nor even a circle of good friends.

He was a loner, seemed to live for the moment."

George spent the summer of 1917 playing semipro baseball with a host of collegians who played under assumed names to protect their scholarships. It was common practice in those early days for entire college ball clubs to play semipro games in that manner. A few college players were detected playing pro ball and their scholarships were canceled. The most prominent case—one that had international repercussions—was that of Jim Thorpe, who played ball in the East Carolina League in 1910 and 1911. Jim did not play under an assumed name—he was "too proud," he later said. Thorpe's name in an East Carolina League lineup was ferreted out by a New York newspaperman, Francis Albertanti, who brought the matter to the attention of officials of the AAU, and Jim was declared a professional and had to forfeit all of the medals he won in the 1912 Olympics.

But the business of playing pro ball did not bother Gipp very much, and he continued the practice all summer long. When the Irish squad assembled for football practice in the fall, Gipp was not on hand.

Rockne tracked him down, found he was still playing ball with the Simmons Baseball Club in Wisconsin, and finally was able to talk Gipp into coming back to school.

In 1917, Gipp showed signs of fulfilling his promise of greatness. He was hampered by a soggy, muddy field in a "big game," against Nebraska, and the Irish suffered a 7–0 loss. It was to be their lone defeat of the year. South Dakota was trounced a week later by a 40–0 score as Gipp ran, passed, and kicked his team to an easy win. Then on November 3 at West Point, George Gipp was the whole show as he ripped the big Army line to shreds with savage drives off-tackle. When Army bolstered the line, Gipp passed the Cadets dizzy. Army was led by one of their greatest stars, halfback Elmer Oliphant, and it was Gipp vs. Oliphant in a remarkable display of individual play as the Irish eked out a 7–2 victory over a strong Army eleven that went on to win seven in a row over some of the finest teams in the East. Oliphant ended his career after playing four years of baseball, football, basketball, and track. In addition to earning twelve varsity letters in the four major sports, Oliphant won the heavyweight boxing championship, was a swimming star, and was one of West Point's finest hockey players. But on this day against Army it was George Gipp whose star shone brighter.

When the Notre Dame squad arrived back at South Bend after the Army victory, hundreds of cheering students and townies mobbed the smiling Gipp and his mates. After flashing a wry smile, George hurriedly left the celebration. He had bet a good deal of money for himself and his cronies and wanted to deliver the winnings. Part of the money was his commission for handling the deal, and he wanted to collect his share of the purse.

Gipp's first varsity season almost ended his football career. In a game against tiny Morningside College, one week after the Army game, George was gang-tackled and thrown against an iron post near the sidelines. He was carried from the field and went directly to the hospital, where further examination showed he had suffered a broken leg. Gipp spent a restless week at the infirmary at South Bend, then he went home to Laurium on crutches to recuperate.

Because of the exigencies of World War I, the 1918 college football season was declared an "unofficial year" by university officials, and most schools played an abbreviated schedule. It was a year that did not count against a player's eligibility.

In his first year as head coach in 1918, Rockne fielded a team that showed a great deal of promise,

though they lost to Michigan State and tied Great Lakes and Nebraska. George Gipp sparked the team with his long-distance kicking, marvelous passing and running. He led the Irish in touchdowns, points scored, and yards gained, showed flashes of the form that would make him the greatest player in college ball during the next two years.

The following year the war was over, and all the great stars were back at Notre Dame. Bernie Kirk and Roger Kiley and Eddie Anderson were the ends, Buck Shaw and Cy DeGrew were the tackles, Hunk Anderson and John Smith were the guards. George Trafton was the center. Captain Pete Bahan was the quarterback, George Gipp and Dutch Bergman the halfbacks, while Fritz Slackford was at fullback.

In the opening game, against Kalamazoo, Gipp scored twice on two long runs. When the first run was called back, Gipp took it in stride. But when the second touchdown was also called back, Gipp objected: "Next time give me one whistle to stop or two to keep going!" he shouted at the official.

In the third game of the season against a strong Nebraska team, a game that Rockne described as one

In 1919, with George Gipp (back row, third from left) starring in every game, Rockne guided the Irish to an undefeated season and their first national championship.

of the "most grueling Notre Dame ever played," the Irish led by a slim 14–9 margin. But several first-line players had been injured, and few good substitutes were available. Rock called time, called Gipp over, and said, "George, we need to stall. Take time on every play. Our best guys are hurt."

The situation appealed to Gipp, who conceived and directed a gem of scientific stalling as the clock finally ran out and Notre Dame won 14–9.

Four weeks later, Gipp led the Irish to their seventh consecutive victory, over a tenacious Michigan State eleven, by a 13–0 score. The game featured an all-around performance by Gipp—his great booming kicks plus some incredible running that time and time advanced the Irish out of danger.

The next week another bitter rival fell before the Gipp magic. This time it was Purdue by a 33–13 score as Gipp ran through the line, around the ends, and passed for three touchdowns as the Irish played their finest game of the season. A week later, Morningside College gave the Irish a real scare, but once more in the waning moments it was Gipp, Gipp, and more Gipp and a victory for Notre Dame in the season's finale, by a 14–6 score.

Rockne now had his first undefeated season and a strong claim to the national championship, with nine straight victories. And he couldn't wait for 1920.

An instinctive master of improvisation on the field, the versatile, naturally gifted "Gipper" was by now perhaps the best all-around player of his time. He threw a soft, arching ball: The last of his career was a dramatic fifty-five-yard completion to Norm Barry against Northwestern that shattered all previous Notre Dame aerial distance records. But he lacked just one Rockne quality: the punishing ingredient of disciplined determination. The "Gipper" was only as good as he had to be. And few before or after him have been as good as he had to be in 1920—his last year on earth.

It was a year of heavy decision (with Fate a hollow victor) that marked Gipp's unanimous election as captain of the team by a unit that included: Hunk and Ed Anderson, Roger Kiley, Buck Shaw, Harry Mehre, John Mohardt, Norm Barry, Clipper Smith, Paul Castner, and Chet Grant. But before the season opened, the news spread like wildfire through the Notre Dame campus: *George Gipp, captain-elect of the football team, had been bounced out of college for missing too many law classes.*

Confronted by a furious Rockne, Gipp explained he had been ill on at least three of the cuts mentioned.

"Listen, Rock, I know the material that I missed. Why not let the professor give me an oral exam, as tough as they want to make it, and I'll prove that I can pass the courses."

Rockne pleaded with Father James Burns, president of Notre Dame, to give Gipp the oral exam, and Father Burns agreed.

The entire campus held their collective breath as Gipp sweated away the exam before a corps of law professors.

Rockne, waiting outside the building, grabbed Gipp as he came out after two tough hours.

"How'd you do, George?"

"Made it," Gipp said quietly. "Thanks for your help, Rock."

Gipp was reinstated to the team. But not as captain.

Gipp hated to practice. Ofttimes he would stand around on the field and watch the tough scrimmages in street clothes.

(Right) George Gipp at the height of his career in 1920. At six-two and 190 pounds, he could run like a deer. He was the finest all-around player in college football.

Good Luck from Gipp

In 1920 Gipp led the Irish to a 9–0 season and their second consecutive undefeated season. Every player on this team, except Gipp, later coached football at a major college. Front row (left to right): Dave Coughlin, Chet Grant, Chet Wynne, John Mohardt. Second row: Joe Brandy, Dave Hayes, Maurice Smith, Captain Frank Coughlin, Hunk An-derson, Norm Barry, Ed Anderson. Third row: Coach Rockne, Earl Walsh, Paul Castner, Fred Larson, Art Garvey, Jim Dooley, Jim Phelan, George Halas. Back row: Buck Shaw, Harry Mehre, Bill Voss, George Gipp, Roger Kiley, Ed DeGree, Glenn Carberry.

The season began with an easy 39–0 win over Kalamazoo. The following week Western Michigan fell by a 42–0 score, and then the Huskies of Nebraska lost to the Irish by a 16–7 count.

And through it all it was Gipp's running, his incredible kicking, his forward passing, and his uner-ring gambling instincts that put him in the center of every game.

And then it was October 30 against Army at West Point.

Army, after two straight defeats by Notre Dame, had one of its truly great teams, led by Walt French, the former Rutgers All-American; French was a break-away sprinter who was a threat to score every time he carried the ball.

As the game began, French carried the ball on every play, and in successive bursts through the Irish line sped to Notre Dame's twenty-five-yard line. Then Walt faked an off-tackle burst, stopped, spun around, and handed off to Chick Lawrence. Lawrence re-versed his field and sped across the left side of Notre Dame's line and across the goal line. The kick for the extra point made the score 7–0, Army.

Gipp took Army's kickoff and carried to the Notre Dame twenty-eight-yard line. George then cracked the middle of the Cadets' line and went to the fifty-yard stripe before he was stopped as fistfights broke out all over the field. Gipp tossed his helmet to the turf and challenged the entire Army team. He was furious at Army's slugging tactics, and although he seldom allowed any enemy action on the field really to bother him in a game, this time he was livid.

When play resumed, Gipp sped for ten yards. Then Joe Brandy, the Irish quarterback, picked up ten more yards, and the Irish were on a roll. Gipp faked a line buck, then flipped a short pass to Mohardt, and big John drove to the Army thirty-five. Gipp again ran to his right, stopped, wheeled, and heaved a long pass to Roger Kiley, who made a spectacular one-handed catch, outjumping three Army men to put the ball down on the five-yard line. On the next play, Mo-hardt blasted through for a touchdown. The kick was good, and the score was 7–7.

Army failed to gain ground after the kickoff, and French booted a superb fifty-five-yard punt to Gipp, who caught the ball on the dead run and burst his way upfield for fifteen yards. Then George took a shovel pass from Brandy and slashed his way through the Army line for twenty-five yards. On the next play, Gipp tossed a bullet pass to Kiley, and the play was good for another thirty-yard gain and an Irish score. Gipp kicked the extra point and Notre Dame was out in front by a 14–7 margin.

On the kickoff, Walt French took Gipp's kick, evaded three Irish tacklers, and sped through the entire Notre Dame team for a magnificent sixty-five-yard touchdown run. Army's extra-point try was good, and the Army fans on the sidelines went wild as the Cadets tied the Irish at 14–14.

Just before halftime, Gipp got off his only poor kick and the ball slithered out of bounds on the Irish fifteen-yard line. The Irish defense, however, tightened, and then French calmly kicked a field goal and it was Army in front 17–14 at halftime.

Between the halves, sportswriters covering the game wired their papers for additional space, for they were witnessing one of the great football battles of all time; they had never seen a dual, a personal struggle between two great stars as they were now seeing between George Gipp and Walter French. It was a classic.

As the third quarter began, Gipp took the kickoff and zigzagged to the Irish forty-five-yard line before he was tackled. He was fighting mad as he ran back into position. Chet Wynne bucked for ten yards. Army held the Irish offense, and then Gipp tried a forty-five-yard field-goal kick. But the ball went wide.

Army took over, failed to gain, and Notre Dame had the ball.

Gipp took over. He was now a slashing fury of a runner and unstoppable. He picked up ten yards, then fifteen more. Another carry by Gipp, another gain; again and again he picked up yardage.

In the fourth quarter the entire Army team bunched to stop Gipp. He was the decoy now; he faked and handed the ball off to Mohardt, who blasted through for a score. Gipp kicked the extra point and now it was Notre Dame 21, Army 17.

Army took the kick but failed to gain, and French kicked to Gipp. George took the ball on the dead run and sped fifty yards before he was brought down at midfield. On the next play Gipp passed to Roger Kiley, who sped to the Army twenty-yard line. Gipp faked handing off to Wynne, kept the ball, and drove for seven yards. On the next play George faked to Joe Brandy and handed off to Wynne, who smashed over the goal line for a touchdown. Gipp kicked the extra point, and the game ended with Notre Dame the victors by a 27–17 score. As the contest ended the small crowd of Irish rooters at the game dashed onto the field and carried Gipp off on their shoulders.

The following day, headlines and stories across the nation's sports pages heralded Gipp's performance:

"George Gipp was equal to the greatest in all of football."

"Many Notre Dame stars have climbed the glory ladder of raw courage to greatness, but none further than George Gipp on this single day. Something had touched him deeply and he became a flaming spirit on the field—a one-man team that did it all. It was a show of immortality," wrote Bill Corum of the *New York Journal-American*.

Back at South Bend the students marched through the downtown streets, chanting, "Gipp, Gipp, Gipp—we want Gipp."

The following week at South Bend Gipp sped eighty-five yards to set the stage for a 28–0 victory over a powerful Purdue team.

On November 13 at Indianapolis, the Hoosiers of Indiana University were just minutes away from achieving their first win in thirty years over Notre Dame as they led the Irish 10–7 going into the final minutes of the third period.

Gipp had injured his left shoulder during a drive into the line, and Rockne had personally taped George's arm and shoulder during the halftime. Now Gipp squirmed on the bench, his shoulder racked with pain; he worried about the outcome of the game as the Hoosiers seemed about to score once more. But the Irish defense stiffened, held, and Notre Dame took over the ball and on the first series of plays started to march downfield—toward the Indiana goal line.

Quarterback Joe Brandy playing brilliantly, now mixed his plays beautifully and had the Hoosiers off-balance as Chet Wynne and Norm Barry took turns pounding the line, smashing off-tackle for big gains.

Now the Irish were down to the Indiana five-yard line, and Rockne called Gipp to his side: "Now, listen to me, George. I want you to get in there and act as a decoy. Don't carry the ball. Indiana will expect you to get the ball. But I don't want to take any chances on that shoulder. Understand?"

Gipp nodded and sped onto the field as the crowd began to chant, "Gipp . . . Gipp . . . Gipp."

On the very first play, injured shoulder and all, Gipp took the ball from Brandy, faked a pass, then bent low and charged right through the Hoosier line for the winning touchdown. The crowd went wild as the Irish took the game, 13–10.

The next day the team's physician examined Gipp and announced that George had a broken collarbone and would be out for the rest of the season.

The following Saturday, November 20, was a game against Northwestern at Evanston, Illinois, in a resumption of a series that was to go almost continuously for the next twenty-nine years and would become the Army-Notre Dame game of the Midwest.

Gipp was there and in uniform. He was through for the season except that he still could drop-kick if the team needed him. Before the game started, injured shoulder and all, he gave an exhibition from the fifty-yard line that had the twenty-five thousand spectators gasping. Gipp kicked ten field goals in rapid succession and then to thunderous applause took a seat on the bench.

Notre Dame had complete control of the game and took a commanding 26–0 lead going into the final period. Suddenly the crowd, largest ever to witness a Notre Dame game, began to chant,

"Gipp . . . Gipp . . . Gipp . . . we want Gipp . . . we want Gipp!"

Rockne was a dramatist and very human. Here was his Golden Boy, now on his feet, pleading to go into the game. And as the crowd noise swelled into a tremendous roar, Rock walked over to Gipp.

"Now, George, get in there—and don't carry the ball. Understand? Just take it nice and easy."

George did take it easy. And on the very next play he took the pass from center, faded back, and threw a long, arching pass. The ball traveled some fifty-five yards in the air to halfback Norm Barry, who took the ball with one hand, guided it to his chest, and scored a touchdown. The crowd went berserk. And Rockne walked out to meet George and led him back to the bench.

Two weeks after the final game of the year, Notre Dame's annual football dinner was held at the Oliver Hotel. Nobody present thought it unusual when Gipp excused himself and left early. He was a loner and would just as soon be off by himself, shooting pool or playing poker.

But what they didn't know and George certainly did not tell anyone was that he was ill. He had not felt well for days. He didn't know what was wrong, just that he was so tired and faint and with a terrible cough that was racking his very soul.

A day later he was taken to the hospital with pneumonia.

Soon his condition became critical as the poison spread.

There was gloom over the entire campus he had kept so brightly lit through the years.

The drama mounted when *Collier's* magazine announced that Gipp had been named to the All-America team, the first Notre Dame man named. Two days later, the Chicago White Sox announced that George Gipp had signed a contract to play for them.

And in the quiet hospital room, a frail, wispy-voiced Gipp made a request to his coach:

"Rock, I know I'm going to die. I'm not afraid. But someday, Rock, when things on the field are going against us, tell the boys, Rock, to go out and *win just one for the Gipper*. Now, I don't know where I'll be then, coach. But I'll know about it, and I'll be happy."

The tired, sick eyes closed once more.

Rockne brushed away a tear, then reached out a hand to soothe the sick boy's brow.

The dying boy smiled, a thin smile.

"Rock, one more thing, please. I'd like to see a priest."

A memorial service was held for Gipp at Sacred Heart Church on the campus, and the entire student body escorted the body to the station at South Bend for shipment home. They trudged in grief-stricken array through a blinding snowstorm. The varsity team walked as a unit, the left-halfback spot vacant.

He was buried at Laurium, Michigan.

As author Francis Wallace wrote so movingly: "The snows of Christmas powdered the grave of Thanksgiving's Hero."

"OUTLINED AGAINST A BLUE-GRAY OCTOBER SKY, THE FOUR HORSEMEN RODE AGAIN."

Rockne was profoundly shaken by the death of the Gipper. It is even possible that the seeds of his own conversion were planted then, although he never discussed the subject and kept everything about it locked in his secret heart.

To him George Gipp was another son. His death filled him with a sense of uneasiness, a dread that something similar might even happen to his family. He could stand pain and sickness like the Spartan that he was. But the slightest thing that went wrong with any member of his family threw him into a panic after Gipp's passing.

However, the everyday affairs of the world go on despite sorrow and fear, and so Rockne pulled himself together and reluctantly tackled another football season.

Over the years the Hawkeyes had been no threat to the members of the Big Ten, for the Hawks had enjoyed only one winning season in twenty-one years. But under the direction of Coach Howard Jones, the Hawkeyes had won the last three games of the 1920 season, and with such fine backs as Aubrey Devine, his brother Glenn, and Gordon Locke, Les Belding, and a big, tough slashing tackle, Duke Slater, all potential All-Americans, the Hawkeyes would put together two undefeated seasons, back to back.

In Notre Dame's first meeting with the Hawks, on October 7, 1921, Rockne fielded a team consisting of Johnny Mohardt, Chet Wynne, Chet Grant at the quarterback spot, and at fullback, Frank Coughlin. On the line Rock started Eddie Anderson and Roger Kiley at the end posts, Art Garvey and Buck Shaw were the tackles, Hunk Anderson and Jim Dooley the guards, and Harry Mehere at center. It was a power-packed squad that had wracked up Kalamazoo 57–0 in the opening game of the season, then shellacked DePauw 57–10, and it appeared to all the experts that Rock had a team that would come through with his third straight undefeated season.

It was a classic case of a good football team that would not be intimidated by a super team. Iowa's line outcharged and outfought the Notre Dame line in the first period, and Aubrey Devine sliced through the Irish line for short but consecutive gains, then flipped several short passes to Belding for a touchdown. Then, after Notre Dame failed to gain ground, the Hawkeyes kicked a field goal and it was 10–0 Iowa.

In the second period, Johnny Mohardt fired a long pass to Roger Kiley for an Irish score and it was 10–7. Another series of downs and Notre Dame was on the Iowa five-yard line, but could not score.

In the final period it was all Notre Dame. Four times the Irish were inside the ten-yard line, but failed to score, and the game ended as a Mohardt pass intended for Kiley was intercepted by Belding on the five-yard line and the twenty-game Notre Dame winning streak was over as Iowa won, 10–7.

Nobody smiled on the campus for a week. As compensation for having their two-year winning streak broken, the Irish trounced Purdue 33–0. Nebraska was much tougher, but the Irish managed to score a lone touchdown and a 7–0 victory.

The following week, Ocotber 29, the Indiana Hoosiers were easily defeated, 28–7, and then within the next eight days the Irish were to play three major games: against Army at West Point; then on the eighth of November versus Rutgers at the Polo Grounds, New York City, then to be followed on November 12 against the tough Haskell Indians, back home at South Bend.

Against Army, Johnny Mohardt ran and passed and passed to Roger Kiley and Eddie Anderson for a couple of touchdowns. Paul Castner and Chet Wynne also scored, and it was a 28–0 rout for the Irish.

The Irish, responding to the cheers of their New York rooters, soundly trounced Rutgers 48–0, and then it was back to South Bend on November 12 for the Haskell Indians. The subs played practically the entire game and easily defeated the Indians, 42–7. Marquette was beaten in a game played at Milwaukee by a 21–7 score, and then, in the season's final game at South Bend, the Irish had a field day at the expense of the Michigan Aggies and easily romped, 48–0.

"That 1921 team with a 10–1 season was one of my greatest teams," recalled Rockne. "One of the things that impressed me most about that group was our defense. They didn't allow any of the eleven teams we played, to score more than a single touchdown against us. The highest total of points was the 10 points that Iowa scored in beating us. But the most amazing thing about that bunch was that every one of the boys became a head coach or an assistant coach after leaving Notre Dame."

The spirit of George Gipp had barely begun to tap Notre Dame on the shoulder when the "Four Horsemen" became a living legend at South Bend. No backfield unit, before or since, has captured a football nation's imagination like this pony quarter.

Thirty games—from 1922 through 1924-embraced their career, which included twenty-seven victories, a scoreless tie with Army, and two successive defeats by Nebraska.

Grantland Rice ensured the immortality of this stirring array on October 18, 1924, when he studied the keys of his typewriter in the press box of the Polo Grounds in New York and then pecked away at his "lead" of Notre Dame's stirring 13–7 conquest of Army that day.

"Outlined against a blue-gray October sky, the Four Horsemen rode again. In dramatic lore they are known as Famine, Pestilence, Destruction, and Death. But these are only aliases. Their real names are Stuhldreher, Miller, Crowley, and Layden. They formed the crest of the South Bend Cyclone before which another Army football team was swept over the precipice at the Polo Grounds yesterday afternoon as 55,000 spectators peered down on the bewildering panorama spread on the green plain below."

Stuhldreher, Miller, Crowley, and *Layden . . .* where did they come from, and why to Notre Dame?

Harry Stuhldreher was influenced in his teens when he carried Rockne's football suit to the Massillon, Ohio, ball park as a means of admission to the stadium where Rockne started his pro football career and functioned as a weekend player to pick up some extra money.

Don Miller, from Defiance, Ohio, was a younger brother of Red Miller, star of the 1909 Irish team, and of Ray and Walter, who preceded him to Notre Dame. Don, a leading high-school back, came to Notre Dame to carry on the family tradition.

Jim Crowley, all 164 pounds, had been a star at Green Bay High School and was persuaded to go to Notre Dame by Curly Lambeau, who had played a year at Notre Dame but who had dropped out and was organizing the Packers at Green Bay.

Elmer Layden, a 162-pound halfback, was delivered by his Davenport, Iowa, coach, Walter Halas (brother of George), who joined Rock as an assistant coach.

It was not until the ninth game of their sophomore season, against Carnegie Tech in 1922, that these coming "Horsemen" were to be branded as a unit. Heretofore, Rockne had Stuhldreher subbing for Frank Thomas, the veteran quarterback and teammate of Gipp in his last year; Crowley and Layden divided the left-halfback position; Don Miller held down the

right-halfback post; and Paul Castner, a triple-threat star, was at fullback. But a week before the Carnegie Tech game, Paul suffered a broken hip against Butler University and Rockne shifted Layden from halfback to fullback.

Layden was outstanding in the Carnegie Tech game, playing the position as though he had been born to it. It was a memorable game—the first time, the first game in which the Four Horsemen worked together as a complete unit, and they devastated Tech, 19–0. It was the seventeenth straight game without a defeat for the Irish, and they came to Lincoln, Nebraska, for the final game of the season.

It didn't upset Rockne too much when the underdog Nebraska team handed the Irish their only defeat of the season, 14–6. It was a bigger, heavier Nebraska eleven that outweighed the Irish by more than fifteen pounds per man, but Rockne was thrilled with the excellent game of his "pony backfield."

An era was launched. Only Rockne himself was fully aware of it.

As they prepared for the 1923 season, Rock knew he had something special in the Four Horsemen. He went to work with a vengeance on making the unit even better. Stuhldreher and Crowley were a bit slower than Layden and Miller. Rock designed lighter silk pants with less padding, lighter shoes, stockings, and thigh pads. It worked for Crowley but not for Stuhldreher. So Harry dropped the pads entirely. It

made him just a bit faster. Eventually, the pony backfield (Layden, 162 pounds; Miller, 162 pounds; Crowley, 164 pounds; Stuhldreher, 154 pounds) became so fast off the quarterback's signal that Rockne had to move their lining-up positions farther back from the line.

The Horsemen lined up in the traditional T formation. When the signal to shift was given, they'd move into the new Notre Dame shift. Crowley would be the tailback. Miller would be a wingback. Stuhldreher would line up between guard and tackle, while Layden would line up behind the tackle.

Stuhldreher did most of the passing, and his chief targets were the other backfield men. This was another case of Rockne devising another weapon—for until Rock came along, forward passes were thrown only to the ends.

The 1923 schedule was one of the toughest in Notre Dame history. It included a visit to Princeton and a game with Army. The Army game was set in old Ebbets Field, home of the Brooklyn Dodgers, and the biggest crowd in Notre Dame history—some thirty-five thousand—witnessed the game.

The opening game of the season was a romp over Kalamazoo, 74–0. A win over Lombard was next, a 14–0 squeaker. It was, however, just the tonic against overconfidence that Rock would prescribe. The Irish then left South Bend on two successive weekends, defeating Army 13–0 and trouncing the strong Prince-

Fullback Paul Castner slashed through the Rutgers line for two touchdowns in the game between the Irish and Rutgers in 1921. Note that many Rutgers players did not wear helmets. Final score: Notre Dame 48, Rutgers 0.

The Four Horsemen, aptly named by sportswriter Grantland Rice in 1924. Elmer Layden, Jim Crowley, Harry Stuhldreher, and Don Miller, bound together by that sobriquet, became the most famous college backfield of all time.

After twenty consecutive victories, from 1919 to 1921, Notre Dame was defeated by Iowa in 1921. Captain Eddie Anderson (with ball).

A relaxed Rockne, comfortably seated, looks over his squad on the first day of practice, 1923.

ton Tigers, 25–2. Georgia Tech fell, 35–7, and the rugged Purdue Boilermakers were beaten by 34–7.

Once again the young, talented Irish squad came up to the Nebraska game with an undefeated record. And once more the bigger, heavier Nebraska Cornhuskers, who had defeated the highly touted Illinois led by the immortal Red Grange, outplayed and outfought the lighter Notre Dame squad by a 14–7 score.

"That defeat, the only one in 1923, was probably the best thing," said Stuhldreher. "It made us promise each other that we would beat Nebraska in 1924, even if we lost every game of the season."

In 1924, the Four Horsemen and the Seven Mules (the Notre Dame line)—with Ed Hunsinger and Chuck Collins at the ends, Rip Miller and Joe Bach at tackle, Nobel Kizer and John Weibel at guard, and Captain Adam Walsh at center—became household words as the Irish swept Lombard, Wabash, Army, Princeton, Georgia Tech (for Notre Dame's two-hundredth football victory), Wisconsin, and, on November 15, blasted Nebraska, 34–6, with a devastating attack that gave them their tenth straight victory, extending back to 1923. Northwestern and Carnegie Tech were swept, and the Irish were on their way to the national

The 1924 Notre Dame team that defeated an unbeaten Stanford eleven on January 1, 1925, in the Rose Bowl. This game marked the final collegiate appearance of the Four Horsemen and the Seven Mules.

championship with a 9–0 record for the regular season.

By this time Rockne was the most famous football coach in the nation, and the Four Horsemen, with their split-second timing, speed, and dexterous ball handling, were a thing of beauty; opponents would stare in awe at the swiftness and precision of their backfield play.

As a result of that undefeated season, Notre Dame was invited to meet the great Glen "Pop" Warner's superb Stanford University team in the annual Rose Bowl game on New Year's Day 1925.

Out on the West Coast, unbeaten Stanford, led by one of the greatest fullbacks of all time, Ernie Nevers, was primed for the invasion of the Irish.

With the exception of Knute Rockne, Pop Warner was the most publicized college coach in football. One of the patriarchs of the game (he died at age eighty-three in 1954, after coaching from 1895 to 1939), Warner was a contemporary of Amos Alonzo Stagg, who went from Yale to Springfield to Chicago University, where he coached for forty-one years.

Warner won national recognition as a coach of rare talent during his years at Carlisle Indian School at the start of the century, and even more so with his mighty Pittsburgh teams prior to the First World War. But it was not until Rockne usurped the national spotlight that Warner attained his greatest fame, at Stanford.

During the twenties, when million-dollar football stadiums sprang up all over the nation, Warner and Rockne were the two magic names of the coaching fraternity. Theirs were the two systems of play that set the example for coaches throughout the country. The other coaches jumped on the Warner bandwagon, with its double wingbacks and unbalanced line, tricky reverses, single-wing formation, and the off-tackle play; or they jumped aboard the Rockne T formation.

The rivalry between the two coaches and their systems stood without parallel in football until approached by that between another Notre Dame coach, Frank Leahy, a Rockne protégé, and Earl "Red" Blaik of West Point in the 1940s and 1950s.

Pop Warner was the first coach to use an unbalanced line. He also emphasized "possession" ball, since forward passing had not been so well developed at the time because of the big ball, so different from the smaller one of the present era. Pop was the first coach to get line interference in front of the ball carriers.

As a player at Cornell in 1893, Warner was familiar with the shortcomings of the game of beef and brawn and dangerous mass plays. His was one of the more intelligent and visionary minds that helped bring about the evolution of football from a mere physical test to a contest of skill in which the college players were given a chance to show that there was more to the game than brawn.

The Rose Bowl was the only bowl game in existence at the time, so national attention was focused on the two competing teams, for the game would clearly determine the undisputed national champions.

The imagination of the entire country was gripped

by the prospect of this battle between two undefeated football teams and two of the nation's greatest football coaches.

Coach Rockne started his second team—or shock troops, as he called them—just to see the kind of attack he would have to face from Warner's Stanford eleven. But the Indians quickly drove the ball down to the Irish fifteen-yard line and then Cuddleack kicked a seventeen-yard field goal after Johnson recovered Don Miller's fumble, and Stanford had a 3–0 lead.

The Four Horsemen then went to work on the big Stanford line. Jim Crowley, Miller, and Elmer Layden broke through for several first downs that brought the ball to midfield. Jim Crowley, aided by the blocking of Miller and Layden, broke out into the open for a thirty-seven-yard gain before Ernie Nevers and Ted Shipkey stopped Jim. On succeeding bursts through the line, the Irish penetrated to the Stanford nine-yard stripe. Just when it seemed that Notre Dame would score, Stanford's line held and the Irish gave up the ball on downs.

But Stanford failed to gain against the determined Irish line. A bad punt by Stanford and Notre Dame took over on the Indians' forty-yard line.

Crowley sped off-tackle for fifteen yards. Miller and Layden crashed through to the seven-yard line. Then Layden broke through the middle of the Stanford line for a touchdown, and the score was Notre Dame 6, Stanford 3.

Big Ernie Nevers smashed through the Irish line again and again. He was simply unstoppable. At six feet, three inches and weighing 235 pounds, Nevers never stopped running, and it took two and even three Irish tacklers to bring him down. It was Stanford with the ball on the Irish thirty-yard line as Nevers flipped the ball to quarterback Fred Solomon. Solomon heaved a long pass intended for Ted Shipkey, Stanford's great end. Out of nowhere flashed Elmer Layden to snare the pass, and then he was off like a streak. Elmer got some excellent blocking and sped through the entire Stanford team for seventy-eight yards and a touchdown as the Irish fans shook the earth with their cheers.

At halftime Notre Dame was in the lead, 13–3.

In the third quarter Elmer Layden, whose tremendous punting kept Stanford continually in a hole, booted a sixty-five-yard punt to Solomon on the Indians' twenty-five-yard line. Solomon, eager to take the ball on the run, fumbled, and Hunsinger picked up the loose ball and raced over for another Irish score. Crowley kicked the extra point and the score was now a comfortable 20–3 for the Irish.

But Stanford wasn't through. Big Ernie Nevers faked a run and tossed a long pass to Shipkey for a Stanford touchdown. The score was now 20–10.

It was Stanford's turn once again, and Ernie Nevers was equal to the task. Time after time he smashed at the Irish line. It was three yards . . . then five yards . . . then four more, and down the field he pounded

Elmer Layden scored three touchdowns for the Irish as they posted a 27–10 victory over Stanford in the 1925 Rose Bowl.

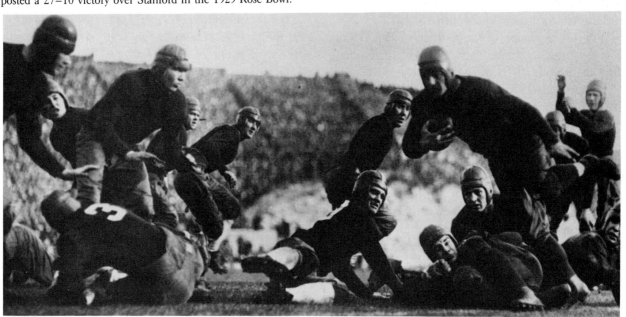

and crashed until he had moved the ball to the Notre Dame two-yard line. Another touchdown and the game would be up for grabs.

Now Stanford had two more downs to put the ball across.

Nevers once more smashed that line—for one yard.

The ball was two feet away from the goal.

The Rose Bowl goal-line stand of 1925 is now history, for it is one of the great peaks of Notre Dame football.

Nevers smashed the Irish line on fourth down. It was a mighty effort, and Ernie gave it his all. And when the referee dug everybody out, there was Nevers—four inches from the goal.

"It was one the greatest plays in football history," said Rockne. "The greatest goal-line stand any team ever made because the toughest line smasher in the world was coming at us. If he'd scored, it would have given Stanford terrific momentum and quite possibly the ball game. But then on the next play, Elmer Layden gave us the greatest kick of his lifetime. From far back in the end zone he kicked hell out of the ball—some seventy-five yards in the air. It finally rolled out of bounds on the Stanford seventeen."

But Stanford wasn't through—and neither was Notre Dame.

There were but five minutes left to play, and the Indians once again were on the warpath. They drove to the Irish thirty-five-yard line. With just one minute left to play, Ed Walker of Stanford threw a short pass to Shipkey. But Elmer Layden raced in and took the ball right out of Shipkey's hands, then sprinted seventy yards for the final score and it was all over.

After the game Stuhldreher revealed that he had played most of the game with a broken foot. Jim Crowley went to the hospital suffering from total exhaustion.

"We were completely spent," said Rockne, "emotionally and physically. It had been a very warm day. Stanford was used to that kind of weather, but we suffered."

"That 1924 team," reminisced Rock, later on, "the Four Horsemen and Seven Mules, would always be my favorite team. I think I sensed that that backfield was to be a great one. They were a product of destiny. At times they caused me a certain amount of pain and exasperation, but mainly they brought me great joy. I suppose they'd been brought together by accident, but it was no accident that made them into one great unit. That was design and hard work."

Considering the fact that Rockne lost every member of the starting varsity from the 1924 national championship team—the Four Horsemen, the Seven Mules, and some thirteen of the leading substitutes—the 1925 season had to be recognized as an outstanding one. But by the time it was over and the Irish had compiled a 7–2–1 record with losses to Army and Nebraska and a 0–0 tie with Penn State, Rock was beginning to show signs of terrific strain. Several varsity players had talked about the "difference in Rock."

And now there were extra pressures. Acclaimed as the finest coach in the land, he attracted the attention of other colleges, and then suddenly the bombshell.

On the evening of December 11, 1925, sports pages throughout the nation front-paged a story to the effect that Knute Rockne had signed a contract to coach Columbia University's football team. It appeared unbelievable that Rock, with eight more years remaining on his Notre Dame contract, would leave Notre Dame. Notre Dame alumni throughout the nation were stunned. But it was true.

While in New York City, Rockne had met with Joe Knapp, an official at Union Carbide and trustee at Columbia. Knapp painted a glowing picture of the future. Rock could coach at Columbia and also could work with Union Carbide as a chemist. Impulsively Rockne agreed and actually signed a contract with Columbia officials until it was learned that Notre Dame had a clause in their contract with Rock that stated that Rockne would have to get a written release from Notre Dame to take a post at any other school. Since Notre Dame officials never released Rock, his deal with Columbia was just so much paper.

In an interview with Grantland Rice, Rock said: "I felt myself going downhill about three weeks after practice started, and for some reason or other I couldn't pull myself together. I've been taught a lesson and I'm going to look after my health first. I'm going to Europe for a long vacation. Tom Lieb will handle the track team. But understand this. Don't ever pay any attention to talk about my going elsewhere to coach. Notre Dame took me in as a poor boy years ago. It gave me the opportunity for an education. It enabled me to make good in the field I have chosen for my own. I am indebted to the university as long as I live, and nothing will ever tear me away, no matter what the inducements. When I quit coaching Notre Dame, I am through with football."

THE MOST FAMOUS COACH

After the 1925 season Notre Dame and Rockne had become the most famous football bywords in the land. Rockne was more than a football coach now. He was a national celebrity. He was invited to address sports groups throughout the nation. He conducted coaching clinics, wrote magazine articles, and developed a syndicated column with the aid of a noted sportswriter, Christy Walsh. And Rockne became one of the most sought-after after-dinner speakers in the nation, addressing business groups and sports organizations throughout the country.

But his coaching efforts never stopped. Even when his players had graduated, he wanted them to come to him with their personal or business problems. He would go out of his way to write letters of recommendation and to contact other schools for Notre Dame players who were looking for a coaching assignment.

He was particularly kind to young coaches—and not necessarily his own. The late Lou Little, Columbia's great coach, wrote: "It was my pleasure to have known him during my years of coaching at Georgetown. He was a great help to me and also gave me great inspiration."

Bill Cerney, who was one of Rock's coaches at the time, tells this story: "Howard Jones had left Iowa and had taken over the football post at Duke University. He lost the first eight games of a nine-game schedule and decided that Duke was not the place for him. He called Rock and explained the situation.

"At just about the same time, a two-man committee from the University of Southern California offered Rock the USC job on his own terms. Rock declined the offer but suggested Jones for the Southern Cal job. And when Rockne praised Jones highly, the Southern California committeemen signed a ten-year contract with Jones.

"There was another deal that Rock set up," said Cerney. "Fred Dawson, coach of the great Nebraska teams of 1922–23, was looking for another post. Rockne contacted the University of Virginia and suggested Dawson. And it was Rock's recommendation that clinched the job for Dawson."

In 1926 Rock went to work with a new weapon in his attack. He added a split buck formation as a device for striking to the weakside. Because the Notre Dame shift invariably went to the strong side, the defenses were massing there, and Rock always believed in keeping his attack at least one step ahead of the defense.

Christy Flanagan and Butch Niemiec were the stars of the team that year.

Christy Flanagan had attended Culver Military Academy and had been a star with their fine football team. He could have enjoyed a free ride at any college in the nation, but Rockne's flaming personality and his winning ways attracted Flanagan to Notre Dame.

Butch Niemiec was a tough product of one of Ohio's fine football schools. Three years older than the average student, Butch was an all-around star and was offered scholarships at numerous colleges. But he also selected Notre Dame because of Rockne's great impact and the Notre Dame reputation.

The Irish juggernaut flattened Beloit, 77–0, in the opening game of the season, then proceeded to grind down such opposition as Minnesota, Penn State, and Northwestern. It was 12–0 over Georgia Tech and 26–0 over Indiana. Then, waiting for Notre Dame at Yankee Stadium in New York, was Army.

In 1926 Army, with much of the same manpower who roughed up the Irish in 1925 by a 27–0 score, was ready to make it two in a row, and a crowd of more than 65,000 was on hand for the battle.

The key Notre Dame play—the bread-and-butter play that ground out huge yardage all year long—was called Old 51, an off-tackle smash that the Irish practiced every day for at least an hour. It depended on the ability of the Notre Dame halfback to take the opposing end to the outside. The Irish end then would drive the opposing tackle inside. If the two players handled their blocking assignments, a big hole would be opened, possibly resulting in a touchdown play. It was "the perfect play."

As the second half of a brutal battle began with the score 0–0, Harry O'Boyle, a tough competitor who had gained ground consistently with this play during the first half, opened with the same play off tackle, but was held for no gain. On the next play, O'Boyle took the ball from center, faked a run, then handed it to Flanagan, and Christy was off and running. He sped sixty-two yards without an Army hand on him for the only score of the game before the extra point was kicked.

The Army game was the big one, and when Drake was beaten 21–0 there remained only a routine game against Carnegie Tech and the final game of the season against Southern California.

Elated and superconfident after the unbeaten string of eight straight victories over the best teams in the nation, Rock decided not to go with the team to Pittsburgh for the game with Carnegie Tech. So he sent Hunk Anderson and Tommy Mills, his assistants, to Pittsburgh to handle the Tech game.

Rock got the shock of his life in the press box of the Army-Navy game he was watching in Chicago.

The final score: Carnegie Tech 19, Notre Dame 0.

It was one of the greatest upsets in football history, and most of the nation's coaches and sports editors were laughing at Rock up their sleeves.

Rock had taken what looked like a reasonable gamble. He had a game scheduled with Navy the next year and thought it would be a good opportunity to scout both Navy and Army. He accepted full responsibility for the defeat and made no excuses.

At a special Sunday practice, that week, Rockne told the players: "Look, it was all my fault. No one is to blame—not Hunk or Tommy. Now let's be glad that we have another opportunity. We've got to give it all we've got if we want to redeem ourselves this week against Southern California. Let's do it."

And Notre Dame went into the final period of the Southern California game leading 7–6. But the terrific heat was taking its toll. Several first-string players had been injured, and a number were exhausted by the frantic pace of the game.

The Trojans scored with but four minutes to go and led, 12–7.

Then the old master pulled a rabbit out of his hat.

There was little spark left in the players who had been putting up a brutal game against Southern California for almost four quarters. They were spent. But there was a nifty, 160-pound, left-handed quarterback, Art Parasien, who had come through six weeks before with a great pass to Butch Niemiec in the Northwestern game to give Notre Dame a 6–0 win.

Art was fretting on the bench when the call came: "Art, how about those two plays, eighty-three and eighty-four? You think you can do it?"

"It's a cinch, coach. You know I can deliver."

And on the very first play, Parasien passed thirty-five yards to end Chili Walsh. Another pass picked up fifteen more yards, and now Notre Dame had a first down on the Southern California twenty-four-yard line.

On the next play, Parasien faded back, back and then tossed a soaring pass to Butch Niemiec, who caught the ball on a dead run, stumbled, and fell over the goal line, and Notre Dame had the winning score as the game ended: Notre Dame 13, USC 12.

The Frank Merriwell finish was one of the great thrills of a thrill-packed season, and it gave Notre Dame a 9–1–0 year. The only defeat was the Carnegie Tech disaster.

THE COACH, A FAMILY MAN

Knute Rockne had reached the pinnacle of success. At age thirty-six he was the most famous and most successful football coach in the land.

The trouble with that, however, is that a football coach has to keep proving it over and over, year after year. And Rock knew that rough days were ahead. His dream team had graduated, and each fall he had to start from scratch.

Even though Rock now faced the difficult prospect of trying to stay on top as coach, football was hardly his chief concern. Despite the general impression that Rock's only love in life was football and that his every waking moment was concentrated on the sport, it actually ran a very poor second to his family.

Rock was a devoted husband and father. Most coaches bring their football problems home with them and keep them with them twenty-four hours a day. But Rock had the unique quality of being able to leave them behind in the Notre Dame athletic office.

To him, his home was his castle, and there was no room in the castle for anything but love and laughter. The children raced joyously to embrace him whenever he entered the house. Rock played with them and read them nursery rhymes or told them stories just before bedtime. It was the mother, though, who heard their prayers, because she was Catholic and Rock was not.

A dedicated family man, Rockne was never happier than when he was surrounded by his sons (left to right): Billy, Jackie, and Knute, Jr.

Yet he faithfully observed all the Catholic days of fasting and abstinence with the rest of the family.

He had a good-humored way of handling children. In many respects it was not unlike the way he handled his football players, with a lightness that brought home a message.

As a birthday present he promised Mary Jeanne "something for your neck," presumably a necklace. One day she came running into the house after scuffling outdoors with her brothers. Rock looked her over carefully with twinkle-eyed merriment.

"Now I know what to give you for your neck," he said. "It will be a nice cake of soap."

Most of Rock's friends would have said that his family and football were his only concerns, but unknown to almost everyone, another interest began to loom largely in his life. Ever since the tragic death of George Gipp, he had occasionally slipped into a rear pew of the chapel at Notre Dame and just sat there in the semidarkness, absorbing the peace and comfort that seemed to flicker toward him from the candles on the altar. Now his visits were more frequent. That restless, inquiring mind was asking questions his soul couldn't answer.

After the end of a football season, followed by speechmaking through the winter, coaching clinics, guest appearances, and then the supervision of spring practice drills, Rock looked forward most eagerly to the summer. That was when he and his brood would vacation together at the beach on the shores of Lake Michigan—the same beach where he and Gus Dorais had perfected their forward passing and where he had met his beloved Bonnie.

Once the children were in bed, after a long day of family picnics and beach games, Knute plunged into his reading. He was a greedy reader, absorbing every word with swiftness and understanding. He first read newspapers from metropolitan centers such as New York, Chicago, and Los Angeles. Not only did this keep him informed, but it also enabled him to keep track of his sportswriter friends. Thus he could mention at the next meeting with each writer something recently in print. No wonder he was admired and respected by one and all.

With much more regularity, however, he read a certain number of pages from three different books at the same sitting. One would be a detective story; another would be a classic; the third would be a book on biography, science, history, or psychology.

Few persons could follow a reading program as odd as Rock's. But his mind was so sharp, his memory so keen, that he could perform this feat without hesitation or backtracking.

He seemed to forget nothing that he read. Furthermore, his mind was so nimble and flexible that he could take a humorous moment or incident from a book and bring it up to date by converting it into a football joke that he used in his talks.

With a summer of almost complete rest and relaxation behind him, Rock returned for the 1927 campaign, one that produced a record of but one defeat—to Army by an 18–0 score—and a national championship. A solid segment of upperclassmen led by Captain John Smith, an All-American center, Christy Flanagan, Jack Elder, Chet Wynne, Charley Riley, and Butch Niemiec, was augmented by a fine group of sophomore linemen including Ike Voedisch, Fred Miller, Joe Nash, Chili Walsh, and John Law.

As the season began, however, there were unimpressive victories over Coe College and the University of Detroit. Then the Irish took their first big game of the year in style, with a 19–6 win over an aggressive and tough Navy eleven.

On successive weeks it was 19–6 over Indiana and 26–7 over Georgia Tech. But there was something missing; there were no big runaway scores, and every team seemed to be able to score against Notre Dame. Minnesota, with the great Herb Joesting at fullback

Rock and one of his favorite players, Captain John "Clipper" Smith, a 1927 All-America guard.

The 1927 Notre Dame eleven shared national championship honors with Illinois and Yale.

and Bronko Nagurski at tackle, provided the biggest test. It was late in the fourth quarter, and the Irish led, 7–0. A Notre Dame fumble and Nagurski, the Gophers' All-American star, recovered. Three plays later, Joesting crashed to the Irish ten-yard line. Then a pass to Eddie Walsh gave Minnesota a touchdown. The kick was good, and the bruising battle ended in a 7–7 tie.

Notre Dame had always responded brilliantly after a defeat, and so everyone expected Notre Dame to run roughshod over Army the next week in New York's Yankee Stadium.

The Army varsity squad of 1927 boasted some of the greatest players ever to wear the uniform of the Cadets. Such All-Americans as Chris "Red" Cagle, Moe Daly, Bud Sprague, and Blondy Saunders already had played out three years of varsity ball at other schools prior to their appointment to West Point, and they were gunning for the Irish.

The game was but a few minutes old when Cagle took the ball from his center, cracked inside his own left end, and was in the clear. The crowd of more than sixty-five thousand spectators roared as Red shook off one Notre Dame tackler after another. They tried

to bring him down, but Red kept on his feet and crossed the goal line after a fifty-five-yard dash. The extra-point try was blocked, but Army had a 6–0 lead.

Cagle kept the huge crowd on its feet with his spectacular runs, but each time he was downed by a horde of Irish tacklers, and the half ended without further scoring.

In the third period, Army intercepted an Irish pass at midfield. On the first play, Cagle sped over for the second Cadet score. And in the final period Red broke loose once more for his third touchdown as Army racked up its second straight victory over the Irish, by an 18–0 score.

The following week, a rejuvenated Irish squad ran roughshod over a strong Drake eleven by a 32–0 score, and now the Irish were ready for their annual struggle against another bitter rival, the Trojans of Southern California, at Soldier Field, Chicago, on November 26.

Butch Niemiec, who had emerged as one of the stars of the Irish backfield that season along with Christy Flanagan, had been injured in the Drake encounter and was on the sidelines for the USC battle. And a battle it was before the largest crowd ever to witness a football game in modern times: The crowd was estimated at 120,000.

Going into the final period of a desperate struggle, Notre Dame was holding on to a 7–6 lead. USC punted, and safetyman Charlie Riley of Notre Dame tried for a running catch but juggled the ball, and while doing so crossed into the end zone. Here he was hit hard, and the ball bounced out of bounds. The officials ruled a touchback and no score. But USC coaches and players charged on the field, and a wild melee halted play. USC claimed Riley had possession of the ball and that the play should have been ruled a safety. That would have given USC two points and an 8–7 victory.

It was strictly the official's judgment, and the ruling was official. And Notre Dame took a disputed 7–6 victory to close out a successful season, with seven victories, a tie with Minnesota, and a loss to Army.

"WIN ONE FOR THE GIPPER"

As long as Notre Dame plays football—as long as any shred of drama remains of the Rockne legend—wherever Notre Dame men gather to talk of old times, they still talk of the 1928 football season in hushed tones, for in turn it was one of the poorest seasons on record, yet one of the greatest in terms of dramatic impact.

On paper the Irish looked as formidable as any recent Notre Dame eleven. Their captain, at tackle, was Fred Miller (later to become president of Miller Beer). The other tackle was a husky, fierce-tackling six-footer, Frank Leahy. Tim Moynihan was at the center post. Johnny Law and Jack Cannon were the guards, a substitute was the 145-pound Bert Metzger. Jimmy Brady, a 145-pound speedster, was the quarterback. Butch Niemiec and Jack Chevigny were the halfbacks, and at fullback, Fred Collins, understudied by Larry "Moon" Mullins. Subs included sophomores Joe Savoldi, a powerhouse fullback, and at quarterback, Fred Carideo.

Yet the Irish had a good deal of trouble eking out a 12–6 victory over Loyola in the opening game of the season. The game was tied at 6–6 with a few minutes to go in the last period, and Butch Niemiec finally scored to wrap it up.

All-America tackle Fred Miller captained the 1928 Irish eleven. A number of years after he graduated from Notre Dame, Miller was named president of Miller Brewing Company.

The following week, a fast-moving Wisconsin eleven defeated a fumble-prone Irish squad, 22–6. Three Notre Dame fumbles led to Wisconsin scores. The Badgers were the first Big Ten team to defeat the Irish in eight years.

A scrappy Navy eleven coached by Captain Bill Ingram played Notre Dame to a standstill until the final five minutes, when Butch Niemiec hurled a desperate pass to left end Johnny Colrick, who made one of those unbelievable, one-handed catches and stepped over the goal line for the touchdown. The kick was good, and the Irish had pulled out another game, by a 7–0 score.

Just one week later, in a complete reversal of form, Notre Dame dropped a lackluster game to Georgia Tech by 12–0, and now the sports wags began their messages: The old master was through, he had lost his touch, he might even be fired!

However, in the next two weeks, an easy win over Drake by a 32–6 score and a 9–0 victory over a solid, highly rated Penn State team and the sun began to shine once more in South Bend as the annual battle against a crack Army team, rated as one of the best in Army history, approached.

In an interview with Paul Gallico of New York's *Daily News*, Rockne called this Irish team his "minute men."

"They'll be right in the game one minute," he said with a laugh, "and then the other team will score." Rock's humorous interview was widely quoted in sports pages across the country. It was good copy everywhere but in South Bend.

Army had defeated Notre Dame in 1927, and a score of those Army stars were back for the 1928 season. Led by Chris Cagle, one of Army's most brilliant backs, quarterback Doyle Nave, Harry Wilson, Johnny Murrell, and a solid, aggressive group of veteran linemen, Army had piled up six straight victories and was headed for the national championship—if they beat Notre Dame.

The game began, with both teams playing aggressively. Cagle almost broke loose in the first period but was downed just as he seemed out in the clear, headed for a touchdown. On the next series of plays, Fred Collins and Jack Chevigny smashed into Army's great line and slowly but surely gained ground. Then Chevigny dashed for fifteen yards and Collins smashed the line for five yards, then five more, and the crowd of more than seventy-eight thousand was standing and screaming as Notre Dame had a first down on the Army five-yard line.

The Notre Dame machine was a whirling dervish. Chevigny picked up two yards. Then Collins took the ball and was hit by three Army tacklers—and the ball popped out of his hand and across the goal line. And Murrell of Army pounced on the ball for a touchback.

In the second period the ball changed hands frequently, but neither team had the advantage. But the blocking and tackling were so savage that high in the stands, spectators cringed at the impact of flying bodies.

The teams were scoreless as the first half ended.

The Notre Dame players slowly filed into their locker room, and the trainers attended to the injuries. There was a steady hum of voices as players and assistant coaches talked. Then suddenly Rockne ordered the attendants to clear out all visitors except three, and Rock introduced them to his team.

"Mayor Jimmy Walker . . . former heavyweight champion Jack Dempsey . . . and New York's greatest cop, John Broderick."

Now, with the locker room cleared, Rockne began to talk.

The machine-gun-fire voice had disappeared. He acted like a man who could not find the proper words easily. He looked up at the ceiling, gripping a cigar. He seemed like a man who had seen a vision.

Then he quickly spoke in a hushed voice that was barely heard.

"Boys, it will be eight years next month since I visited a sick young Notre Dame man in St. Joe's Hospital," he said. "He was breathing his last few breaths in this world. He was a fine young man, a man who contributed so much to the university they named for Our Lady.

"There he was, on his deathbed, and he had just become a Catholic. He wanted so badly to be a complete part of Notre Dame. But boys, he had already brought glory to our school as the greatest football player in the nation. His name is George Gipp. Remember that name. Never forget it.

"You know, boys, just before he died, George Gipp called me over close to him and in phrases that were barely whispers, he said, 'Someday, Rock, when things on the field are going against us, tell the boys, Rock, to go out and *win just one for the Gipper*. Now, I don't know where I'll be then, coach. But I'll know about it, and I'll be happy.'

"Boys, within a few minutes, that great Notre Dame gentleman George Gipp had died."

Tears flowed down Frank Leahy's cheeks. He looked around the locker room. Everybody was crying. Some

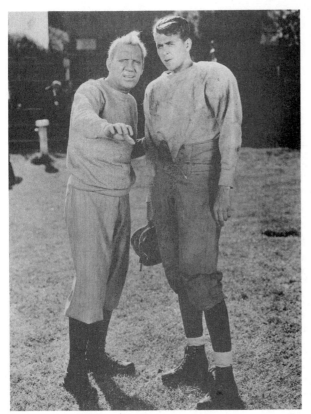

In 1940 Warner Brothers produced *Knute Rockne of Notre Dame*. Pat O'Brien played Rockne. The part of George Gipp was given to a Hollywood newcomer, Ronald Reagan.

over the Army goal line with the ball and cried, "There's one for the Gipper! Let's get another!"

The fourth quarter was about over when Rockne sent in Frank Leahy's roommate, gangling, six-foot, three-inch Johnny O'Brien, at end. On the next play, Niemiec took the ball from center and whirled as though handing it to Chevigny, who carried out his faking role perfectly. Niemiec then continued to move backward, finally sighting O'Brien way down the field. Butch threw the ball as far as he could. O'Brien caught the ball on the tips of his fingers on the ten-yard line. The next few seconds seemed an eternity to the players and to Rockne on the Irish bench. O'Brien, off balance when he caught the ball, juggled it as he struggled and staggered toward the end zone. Finally he clutched it and dived across the goal line as two big Cadets drove into him.

That single, heroic catch earned O'Brien immortality as "One-Play O'Brien," for Rockne hauled him out of the game immediately. Rock was so affected that he came off the bench to hug the big end as he came off the field. And it was Rockne himself who draped the boy's blanket around him.

The next morning Frank Wallace, in New York's *Daily News*, wrote the headlines on the front page:

GIPP'S GHOST BEATS ARMY
IRISH HERO'S DEATHBED REQUEST
INSPIRED NOTRE DAME TO VICTORY

George Gipp beat the Army in 1920 and died that fall, the outstanding football man of the year, mourned by the entire nation. Saturday, what was thought to be the weakest Notre Dame team in fifteen years, completely outplayed the Cadets, stopped the great player of this season and provided the biggest upset of the current college football campaign.

Notre Dame people regard the 12–6 victory over the Army as the most glorious in the entire history of the school; and the eleven men who played almost the entire game will forever be honored with George Gipp, the Four Horsemen, Rockne, Dorais, Al Feeney, Jack Chevigny, Cap't Fred Miller and the rest.

Those boys overcame physical strength, pure form, theory and bad breaks. They played as few teams have ever played.

The Pulitzer Prize-winning writer Paul Gallico wrote in the press box after the game:

Long after the people struggled off the playing field, the waves of play kept surging through the brain like heavy disturbing swells, uprooting all logical thought and still carrying the emotions on their curling crests. When football becomes a near-tragic race against time there is nothing like it for thrill, excitement or suspense. The game exerts a strange magic and you forget that it is just football and that one mustn't overemphasize. . . . Hells bells and gongs of inferno. Let us overemphasize while we may. Tomorrow it will be too late.

of the boys were sobbing. Up against the wall, Jack Dempsey and Jimmy Walker and New York's greatest cop, John Broderick, were all wiping the tears.

"Boys," said Rockne, "I'm convinced that this is the game George Gipp would want us to win.

"Okay, let's go and get 'em."

The battered survivors of the first half charged out on the field with a grimness that boded no good for Army. A couple of sophomores sobbed as they trailed after the varsity, now in a huddle in the middle of Yankee Stadium.

Notre Dame electrified the huge crowd by taking the kickoff and driving eighty yards. However, with third down and two yards to go, fullback Fred Collins, who had been playing an inspired game despite a broken wrist encased in splints, fumbled the ball, and Army recovered. Cagle and Murrell cracked through the Irish line for big gains and finally Cagle scored an Army touchdown. The kick was blocked and Army led 6–0.

Then it was that Jack Chevigny, Collins, and Niemiec, and Brady outdid themselves. They drove eighty yards, and in one smashing charge Chevigny drove

The enchantment which holds me still enthralled will be lifted. It will have been but a football game between two institutions which prepare for months for these hippodromes. . . . As this is written the spell of Collins and Niemiec and Chevigny and Cagle is still on this mundane spot and one regrets that they have gone and that they are not still charging over the turf and flinging their bodies like living scythes through the air. . . . I'm very glad Notre Dame won the way they did. Do I mind being a boob on my prediction story? Gee no. It would have been heartbreaking to see the Irish lose after so much gallant effort. And I'm personally delighted they "Won One For The Gipper."

The Irish lost their last two games that season. The first was to an outstanding Carnegie Tech team, 27–7, as Moon Mullins, Notre Dame's fine fullback, scored the only Irish touchdown. It was Notre Dame's first loss at home since 1905, when Wabash whipped the Irish, 5–0. An open date gave Notre Dame two weeks to recover from the Tech defeat; then they headed for Los Angeles to meet the Southern California Trojans in their annual tussle.

Southern California was loaded with an array of all-stars, including Russ Saunders, Marsh Duffield, and Marger Apsit, and they ran up a 20–0 lead over Notre Dame in the first half.

But again the Irish made one of their traditional stands. They scored twice in the third quarter and four times stopped the Trojans within the five-yard line before USC finally pushed over a fourth touchdown for a 27–14 victory. It was one of the hardest-fought struggles in the series between the teams.

Three Notre Dame players were carried from the field, and the victors knew they had been in a battle.

The defeat by Southern California climaxed the poorest campaign a Notre Dame team had waged since 1905. But somehow it didn't seem to bother Rockne that much. The emotionally charged win over Army had almost salvaged the season. He had predicted he'd lose four games that year—and he did.

But he was not depressed. Ground was now being broken for a new stadium at South Bend. It was a dream that Rock had fought over with the administration for a number of years. Now it was coming true. The Irish would have one of the most modern stadiums in the country.

When asked about the future, Rock said:

"This is the worst season Notre Dame football ever has seen. It's the worst for me, too. There are a lot of folks throughout the country who think I'm through. The team and coaches made a lot of mistakes this year. But I tell you, we're not through. After all, a football team should be conducted like any business organization. What happens when the salesmen of a firm find their merchandise isn't selling? Do they quit? No, they analyze their product for weaknesses they might not have suspected, they change their personnel, they adjust the faults on their product. That's what Notre Dame is going to do. In next spring practice, we'll incorporate a lot of new stuff. Probably work on some new spinner plays. And don't let anyone tell you we're through!"

THE "GREATEST FIGHT OF HIS LIFE"

By 1929, the start of the greatest depression the nation had ever known, the crowds at football games had grown from hundreds to swollen thousands. People began to travel hundreds of miles by car and train to see a game. Highways were clogged for miles before any big contest. Exuberant alumni were demanding bigger and bigger stadia. Football had become the greatest financial asset in college life.

Rock had been planning, scheming, and promoting the development of a new multimillion-dollar dream stadium that would be able to accommodate fifty thousand to sixty thousand fans, and finally in 1929 his dream had come true. Notre Dame would finally get its new stadium. Excavation had started at old Cartier Field, and so every game of the 1929 season was played away from Notre Dame.

Rock made good his promise that his 1929 team would show the nation's football fans a few new tricks. It was slow going at first, this incorporation of an entirely new kind of Irish offense. He stressed spinners, reverse plays, and tricky pass plays that were more deceptive than ever.

And in 1929 Rockne had the players to fit his new system of play.

Captain John Law, who hailed from Yonkers, New York, teamed with Jack Cannon at the guard position to give the Irish two potential All-Americans at the center of the line. Frank Leahy and Ted Twomey were two of the most aggressive tackles Rock had ever seen, and Tim Moynihan was a three-year veteran at center. In the backfield, Frank Carideo, a triple-threat quarterback, directed the team.

"Frank is another coach on the field," said Rockne. Jack Elder, an intercollegiate sprint champion who

John Law, captain of the 1929 national championship team, took a post as football coach at Sing Sing Prison, New York, after he graduated from Notre Dame.

(Above, right) "He could run, pass, and kick," said Rockne of his All-American quarterback Frank Carideo. "He was my coach on the field in 1928 and 1929."

The performance of the 1929 undefeated Irish team is considered one of the most remarkable in college football history. Because the new stadium at South Bend was under construction, the team played every one of the nine scheduled games away from their home field. The national champions: Front row (left to right): Tom Conley, Frank Leahy, Captain John Law, Tim Moynihan, Jack Cannon, Ted Twomey, John Colrick. Back row: Frank Carideo, Marty Brill, Larry Mullins, Jack Elder.

could run the hundred-yard dash in 9.7 seconds, and Marty Brill, a marvelous blocking back, were the halfbacks. "Jumping" Joe Savoldi and Larry Mullins were the fullbacks as the season started at Indiana.

Shortly before the Indiana game, Rockne began the greatest fight of his life when he was stricken with phlebitis. Doctors advised him to give up active coaching—the excitement or mere activity might dislodge the clot that had formed in his leg and send it racing through the bloodstream, where it could pass into his heart or the big artery at the base of the brain—causing a heart attack or a complete stroke.

But Rock wouldn't give up.

Instead he brought back Tom Lieb, a husky tackle who had played with the Four Horsemen and Seven Mules team of 1921–22, as his line coach and first assistant. Tom handled most of the spring practice and actually served as coach's faithful valet, and personal medical attendant for Rockne during most of the season—one that saw Rock in bed for most of the year.

In the Indiana game, Jack Elder scored both touchdowns in a 14–0 Irish victory to open the season. A week later, the Irish traveled to Baltimore for the Navy game and took up residence at the Gibson Island Country Club. In the morning Lieb, in charge of the team since Rock was confined to his bed back at South Bend, ordered the starting eleven to line up in the clubhouse near the phone booth. In a special phone hookup Rock spoke to each of his players. "Don't try to break in, just let him do all the talking, because he's pretty sick," said Lieb.

Then followed the strangest procession of young men taking their turns at entering the phone booth to talk with the man who was their coach, who was laid up in bed at South Bend. A few of the players came away with moist eyes. Others bounced out as though they couldn't wait for the kickoff.

When Frank Leahy went into the booth, Rock said: "This is an important game, Frank. You're relatively inexperienced, but you're going to start. Remember, I'm depending on you and the rest of the juniors. Go on out there and fight."

That was it. Only a minute or so on a telephone with the man who was his idol, but it left a vivid impression on his mind. Well, Leahy thought, if I have anything to do about it, Rockne will never have to call me inexperienced again. I'm going to show him what I can do at tackle.

Navy scored first when Joe Clifton broke through and raced fifteen yards for a touchdown. The extra-point kick was good, and Navy led 7–0.

Notre Dame evened the score as Marty Brill drilled a twenty-two-yard pass to Elder and Jack sprinted across the Navy goal line. Carideo kicked the extra point and it was 7–7.

Late in the battle, Navy tried a pass on the Notre Dame seven-yard line, but Carideo intercepted and ran it back to the Navy thirty-three-yard line. Brill sped through a hole and went down to the Navy twenty-eight. Elder drove for nineteen yards, and then Marchy Schwartz and Moon Mullins alternated in taking the ball across for an Irish touchdown. The game ended Notre Dame 14, Navy 7.

The following week, ninety thousand spectators packed Soldier Field, Chicago, and roared approval as Joe Savoldi smashed across for touchdown sprints of forty and seventy-one yards and Wisconsin was sent home with a 19–0 defeat. The following week, Elder and Savoldi sparked a lone touchdown drive in the third quarter for the only score of the game, and Carnegie Tech was defeated by a 7–0 margin. Then a visit to Georgia Tech and Elder, Carideo, Schwartz, and Tom Conley had a field day whipping Georgia Tech, 26–6. Then two fourth-quarter touchdowns gave the Irish their sixth straight win, a 19–7 decision over Drake.

Frank Leahy had dislocated an elbow in the Navy game, and he had to be carried into the dressing room and was given a hypodermic injection. Later, back at South Bend, doctors encased the arm in a cement cast for three weeks.

One afternoon, Leahy decided to visit Rockne, who was at home in bed.

"Too bad about the elbow, Frank," Rock greeted him. "The docs tell me you won't be able to play against Southern California Saturday."

"Why, coach, I'll be ready," Leahy answered. "The arm feels perfect right now."

"Well, what's this the doctors been telling me?" Rock said. "Let's see you extend that elbow."

Frank promptly thrust out his left, or good arm. It was a gamble, and it succeeded. Rockne never blinked as he began a tirade against the doctors, ending up by telling Frank that he would start the game.

The USC contest was in the best tradition of the long series between the Irish and the Trojans. Before a jam-packed Soldier Field crowd of more than 112,000 fans, USC opened the scoring early in the game. Marsh Duffield, USC's fine back, tossed a twenty-five-yard pass to end Marger Aspit, who dashed for another forty yards and a USC touchdown. The extra-point kick was blocked, and USC led 6–0.

In the second period Notre Dame tied the score

on a forty-two-yard pass from Jack Elder to Tom Conley, but Carideo failed to convert the point-after-touchdown, and the score was tied at 6–6.

At halftime, a tired Irish squad trudged back to the dressing room with the knowledge that they were up against a team as good as they were, a team who would fight them to the last minute.

Tom Lieb spoke to the team for a few minutes. Then Paul Castner, one of the great Irish halfbacks, who played with Gipp in 1920, talked to the team:

"Fellows, who do you go to when you're in trouble? It's Rock, isn't it? Who do you regard as your best friend at Notre Dame? It's Rock again. Who is—"

The door opened. . . .

The players, accustomed to seeing Rockne as a perfect picture of health and vigor, were shocked at the sight. Two managers guided Rock's wheelchair into the locker room. He had watched from the sidelines as the team played, and the strain was obvious. He was thin and gray, and he looked around the room for a full minute before he spoke, but when he finally did, the familiar Rockne voice was heard:

"Boys, I want you to get out there and play them hard in the first five minutes. They aren't going to like it, but you just play them hard! Rock will be watching you. Now go ahead, play them hard!"

Play them hard. The Irish did just that. In a brilliant march down the field, Savoldi cracked through for an Irish score, Carideo made good on the extra point, and Notre Dame had a 13–6 lead.

Russ Saunders, USC's great back, scored on a sensational ninety-two-yard dash for USC's second touchdown. But Jim Musick failed to convert the extra point, and the game ended with Notre Dame ahead by a single point, 13–12.

The next week Northwestern went down as the Irish stormed to a 26–6 triumph for their eighth straight win. And now they were ready for Army at Yankee Stadium in New York.

The Notre Dame-Army game that year was played on turf that was frozen solid. It was about eight degrees at game time, and a biting wind cut across the field as the players dashed onto it to start the game.

The first period was scoreless as neither team could make any headway in the icy weather.

The second period began as Red Cagle attempted to pass to his end, Carl Carlmark, as Army threatened the Irish goal line. Carlmark was set, ready to catch a pass that looked like a certain Army score, when out of nowhere, Jack Elder snared the ball right out

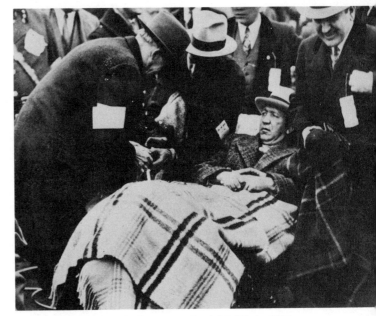

A severe phlebitis attack almost cost Rock his life in 1929, but he insisted on coaching the team from the sidelines in a wheelchair.

of Carlmark's fingers and sprinted some ninety-three yards for the only touchdown of the game. Carideo added the extra point, and the Irish had won their ninth straight game—and a clear-cut claim to the national championship.

Rockne had made good on his promise after the 1928 season to prove to the nation's football fans that neither he nor Notre Dame were through.

Happiest of all the players were Frank Leahy and his friends Moon Mullins and Johnny (One-Play) O'Brien. Leahy felt that his three years of effort at Notre Dame were now repaid. He had set out as a teenager from Winner, South Dakota, with the thought vaguely set in his mind to return to his hometown high school as its football coach. But now he was convinced that he could go beyond Winner in the coaching field . . . perhaps at a small college? Well, there was plenty of time to think about that. The Notre Dame team had been given tickets to a Broadway show, *Showboat*, with Helen Morgan, and they thoroughly enjoyed the performance. In the lobby of their hotel after the show, Leahy and Mullins found a group of people gathered around a husky, sandy-haired man who was giving his account of the Notre Dame-Army game. Frank and Mullins joined the group, and Frank realized that the speaker was the University of Illinois football coach, Bob Zuppke. Zup didn't think that Mullins or Leahy were football players. The two players, despite their battered appearances, restrained themselves as Zup went on to say that the Irish were very lucky to win and that Cagle was the greatest player on the field and that Army had no business to try that last-minute pass in Elder's territory.

Glancing at Leahy, Zuppke finally said, "Young fellow, if there's anything else you want to know about football, I'll be happy to tell you."

Frank Leahy eyed the coach for a second, then said, "Perhaps you can tell me which one of those great Army players gave me this black eye and cut lip and busted arm."

The astounded Zuppke could only say, "Did you play in the game?"

HIS LAST SEASON

At the beginning of the 1930 season, Rockne seemed happier than at any time in his life. He had learned to live with the phlebitis that almost cost him his life. His tonsils had been taken out, and Mayo Clinic doctors had gone over him from head to foot and given him a clean bill of health.

He had his new stadium, the construction of which, in characteristic fashion, he had supervised in every minute detail. Rock even went to the trouble to visit the new University of Michigan Stadium, to check some of the extraordinary details in that structure and to incorporate those details in his new fifty-nine-thousand-seat stadium.

Most of the 1929 squad, including Carideo, Savoldi, Schwartz, Brill, Moon Mullins, Jack Elder, Tom Conley, and Frank Leahy were back, and such new stars as Bert Metzger, Ed Kosky, Al Culver, and Tom Yarr were ready and able to perform up to Rockne's standards. He also had a full-time equipment manager, a trainer, a doctor who traveled with the team, a business manager, several secretaries, and a staff to handle the complex sale and distribution of tickets. At long last he was completely free to devote himself to the task of turning out another championship team.

A major setback occurred on an afternoon just two

The 1930 team won ten straight games and another national championship. It was the sixth national title for Knute Rockne and his last. He died shortly after the year ended. The National Champions: Front row (left to right): Captain

Tom Conley, Joe Kurth, Burt Metzger, Tommy Yarr, Tom Kassis, Art McManmon, Johnny O'Brien. Back row: Frank Carideo, Marty Brill, Larry Mullins, Marchy Schwartz, Rock's assistant Dan Halpin.

NOTRE DAME NATIONAL CHAMPIONS
1930

days before the opening game of the season against a pass-crazy Southern Methodist team.

Rockne had put the varsity through a rugged scrimmage on October 2, one of the longest veteran players had ever known. Finally, after two hours, Rock dismissed the team and they trooped wearily to the locker room. A number of players had already passed into the room when they heard Rock's voice, "C'mon back, boys. I want to try that off-tackle play to the right. Schwartz, let's see that once more."

Back they went. The play was not a new one, and it had done quite well in the past.

Frank Leahy had played varsity ball for three seasons and was gearing up for his senior year—what he thought would be his finest year in football. A rugged, aggressive, hard-driving tackle, Leahy was the epitome of what Notre Dame football was all about. He would play this season, perhaps well enough to get himself some kind of All-American recognition and then be off to a coaching job. It was a dream he had nurtured since he entered Notre Dame. And he had played well enough to gain Rockne's personal attention and approval.

On this off-tackle play, Leahy's assignment was to break out from his tackle post, dash ahead of the ball carrier (Schwartz), and lead the interference for Marchy if he seemed headed for a long run.

Carideo called the signal.

Leahy never did get down the field. Just as he started to move back, pivot, and lead the play, the cleats on his right shoe dug into the turf and he severely twisted a cartilage in his right knee. The accident terminated Frank's playing career. He faithfully visited a South Bend osteopath for special treatment and made several dogged efforts to get the knee back into shape, but it was plain that his days as a player were over.

Rockne called Leahy aside one evening and said, "Frank, I've been watching you and that knee. And if there's one thing I admire in a player, it is stick-to-itiveness. You've got plenty of that, but I'm going to give you some advice. Give up playing now. Come out and watch the team all you want, but don't try to play. You might injure yourself permanently. I'll see that you're part of the team, and you can travel with us."

Not play football? It was the emptiest feeling Leahy had ever experienced. It was the end of the world. Now he would never make his mark in coaching.

Shortly after Rock's advice to drop football, Leahy sat in his room in Sorin Hall, analyzing the situation.

At first he thought all his opportunities for a coaching career had ended the moment he turned in his suit. Then the thought suddenly came to him that even if he could not play, he could still be among the players—among one of the greatest teams ever turned out by the greatest football coach in the land.

Why not take a sideline course in Rockne's coaching methods? His psychology in the treatment of his players? Here, day after day, he could watch and study the master at work.

Frank Leahy became the most faithful attendant at every practice session, every drill, every team meeting. Every afternoon he could be found wandering from one group of players to another. He watched Hunk Anderson, one of the Irish's greatest linemen, coach the linemen. He studied every move Hunk made, and made copious notes himself. He studied the way Ike Voedisch worked with the ends. Frank was all over, yet bothered no one.

He forgot everything else on the field as he began to study Rockne from the sidelines. Leahy noted that the great coach made a deliberate effort to mask his emotions. He remained calm and cool and invariably smiled to a player when sending in a substitute. He played no favorites at any time. His eyes never left the field of play, and he was aware of every activity on the field at all times.

Came October 4 and the first game ever played at the spanking new Notre Dame Stadium, a game against the razzle-dazzle offense of Southern Methodist University.

The SMU team, sparked by half a dozen tricky pass plays, scored after the first four minutes on a forty-eight-yard pass play from Bob Mason to Doug Kattman.

But exactly a minute later, SMU kicked off to Notre Dame and Joe Savoldi took the ball on his own two-yard line and bulled and twisted and turned his way up the field for a spectacular ninety-eight-yard touchdown dash, and the score was 7–7. Frank Carideo ran back an SMU punt for forty-five yards and another Irish score, but SMU tied the game at 14–14 when they passed their way to another touchdown as the half ended.

A marvelous catch by Ed Kosky from quarterback Carideo in the final period moved the Irish in front by 20–14. And that's the way the game ended.

October 11, 1930, was a red-letter day in Notre Dame history, for on that day the new stadium was dedicated and the Navy game was the highlight of the dedication ceremonies.

A crowd of more than forty thousand was on hand. There were parades, bands, and a five-block-long ceremonial parade with all participants roaring the "Victory March." All of South Bend turned out.

Rockne spoke briefly. Admiral Sam Robison told about Navy's friendly relations with Notre Dame. Rev. Charles O'Donnell told the story of George Gipp, and then the game began with the kickoff against Navy.

Jumping Joe Savoldi exploded for three touchdowns as the Irish romped to a 26–2 triumph over Navy. Carnegie Tech was the next victim, being downed by a 21–6 score, and now the Irish were on a roll as they easily defeated a strong Pittsburgh team, 35–19.

"You have one of the greatest teams I've ever seen, Rock," said Coach Jock Sutherland of Pittsburgh. "Thanks for being so nice to us. I can see that you could have scored a hundred points."

On November 1, Indiana fell by the wayside, 27–0.

The Notre Dame steamroller moved on next to Franklin Field, Philadelphia, for the second appearance in the East that season for a Notre Dame team, against the University of Pennsylvania.

A crowd of over seventy-five thousand, many of them Notre Dame alumni, went wild as Marty Brill, hitherto a blocking back for two seasons, seldom carrying the ball, was the star of the game.

Marty Brill had come to Notre Dame from the University of Pennsylvania, where the coaching staff either overlooked him or did not rate his ability up to their standards. Marty left Penn, transferred to Notre Dame, and this was his homecoming party. And a party it was indeed, for Marty and for the Irish as Brill, playing the greatest game of his career, sprang loose for three touchdown runs of forty-five, fifty-two and sixty-five yards as the Irish pounded out a 60–20 rout of the Quakers.

Fullback Joe Savoldi gave Rockne a brilliant season that year. But with two games left to play, news leaked to the press that the recently married Savoldi

Joe Savoldi, star fullback.

Marty Brill, All-America halfback, 1930.

had filed for a separation. And under the regulations, Rockne's best fullback was immediately expelled from school.

A legendary meeting took place in Rockne's office:

"Joe, I'm sorry about all this. Nothing I can do. You're a good man and you did your best. Now you have to go out and make a living for yourself. Here's some money to tide you over. Pay me back when you can. Good luck in whatever you do, Joe. Keep in touch."

Savoldi left Rock's office, tore open the envelope, and counted the money Rock had given him. There was $1,500, a fortune in those days.

Joe played out the season with the Chicago Bears football team, turned to professional wrestling, and became the heavyweight champion of the world. And he made a great deal of money.

During World War II, as a member of General Donovan's OSS unit, Savoldi operated behind enemy lines in Sicily and mainland Italy and performed much valuable and heroic service for his country.

Savoldi's departure left Rockne with one proven fullback, Moon Mullins, and a sophomore, Dan Hanley. With both Hanley and Mullins operating, the Irish crushed Drake, 28–7, and then prepared to face the Northwestern Wildcats. This was a grim, relentless battle. The Irish gained plenty of ground during the first half but could not push across the goal line. The half ended at 0–0, and an upset seemed on its way.

Two quick last-period touchdowns, one by Marchy Schwartz, another by Carideo, made the final score 14–0, and the Irish had gained their eighth straight victory that season in their quest for a second straight national championship. Still left, though, were Army and Southern California.

At Soldier Field, Chicago, on November 29, more than 110,000 spectators jammed the stadium for the annual Notre Dame-Army battle.

It was a cold, miserable day. The rain beat down steadily and turned the field into a swamp. Then the rain chilled and came pelting down as sleet. Players slipped and skidded. Neither team could do a thing, and the game soon resembled a dreary tug-of-war. No score, and worse, still no prospect of a score.

Then suddenly there were two touchdowns within minutes of each other. They came with the blinding speed of the lightning that flashed intermittently beyond the concrete oval.

Marchy Schwartz, brilliant all season long, broke off-tackle on the Old 51 play. It appeared that Marchy would pick up some five yards on the slant, but all of a sudden Irish blockers sprung into action and Army players were strewn all over the field. Marchy tore through for five yards, ten, and suddenly he was in the clear for a fifty-four-yard touchdown sprint that had spectators screaming with every yard he gained. Carideo kicked the extra point and it was Notre Dame 7, Army 0.

In the fourth period, Carideo attempted to punt, Army blocked the kick, and Dick King of Army fell on the ball behind the goal line. Now the score was Notre Dame 7, Army 6.

A frail, blond cadet, Chris Broshus, Army's outstanding drop-kicker, set himself for the all-important extra-point try. He opened his hand as a signal for the center snap. The ball was centered to him but he was swarmed under by a host of Irish tacklers and the kick was blocked. The game ended two plays later with the score Notre Dame 7, Army 6.

In the Army dressing room after the game, Rockne visited the watery-eyed Broshus. He put his arm around the cadet's shoulder and told him not to allow one failure in a football game to get him down.

"Thank you, sir," said Broshus. The tears stopped flowing from his eyes. The Rockne personality had melted his grief. He smiled. The other cadets smiled and thanked Rockne for his visit. Before he left, Rockne shook the hands of every cadet and congratulated the Army coach, Major Ralph Sasse, on his team's showing. Rock had captivated them all, completely.

Then Southern California was given a lesson in Rock's applied psychology. Moon Mullins had injured his knee in the Drake game and again in the Army battle, and Dan Hanley was the only remaining fullback on the squad. Two days before the Southern California game, Rockne decided to make a first-string fullback out of Bucky O'Connor, a second-string halfback. It was a typical Rockne psychological ploy. He had O'Connor trade jerseys with Hanley, and visiting newspapermen never suspected the switch. Several sportswriters interviewed O'Connor thinking he was Hanley.

That December afternoon stands out as one of the brightest chapters in all Notre Dame football history. For sixty minutes Notre Dame pushed the high-scoring USC team all over the field. This was precision football born of months of precise training and a week of psychology by the master of them all. And the star in the 27–0 rout that brought the Irish their

The Irish third-string fullback, Bucky O'Connor, was Rockne's choice to start against USC in the final game of the 1930 season. All Bucky did that day was score twice on sensationally long runs, and another run by O'Connor paved the way for a third score as Notre Dame defeated USC, 27–0. Bucky O'Connor is still scoring today: in Montclair, New Jersey, as one of the state's leading doctors.

New York Mayor Jimmy Walker presented Rockne with an auto at City Hall in New York after the Irish won the 1930 national championship. Seen here (left to right): Frank Carideo; Award Chairman Bill McGeehan; Mayor Walker; and Hugh O'Donnell, president of the Notre Dame Alumni Association.

second successive national championship was little Bucky O'Connor, who scored twice, once on a brilliant eighty-yard dash.

Rockne and the team gathered for the huge victory banquet after the game. And Rock beamed with pride as he looked about the room to see the Four Horsemen—Don Miller, Harry Stuhldreher, Elmer Layden, and Jim Crowley—the Seven Mules, and so many other Irish heroes of the past.

And what a past it had been. In thirteen years under Rockne, a total of 122 games had been played. Notre Dame won 105, lost twelve, and tied five of them. No coach in the entire history of football had ever compiled such a record.

ROCKNE AND FRANK LEAHY

"After the Southern California game," said Frank Leahy, "Rockne told all the players they could break training for a few days. It was a fantastic time. There were so many parties for us it was difficult to attend them all. But we tried. There was wine, women, and a great deal of song.

"The night before we were to head back to Notre Dame, the team went to a party at Moon Mullins' home in Pasadena. The odd thing was that I got into the only real trouble at Moon's house. I was playing tiddleywinks on the floor with Leona Martin. She

was Johnny O'Brien's girlfriend and suddenly when I tried to get up, my knee locked. The pain shot up and down my entire right side and I couldn't move. Johnny and a couple of players helped me to the car, drove back to the hotel, and we immediately called the house physician. The good doctor packed my knee in ice, but nothing seemed to make it feel any better.

"The next morning a couple of the players carried me on board the train and I draped my leg over a couple of seats.

"We were about an hour out of Los Angeles when Rock came through, stopping to joke with the players. Rock was about to pass when he noted that I was lying flat on my back with my leg extended."

Diagnosing the situation immediately, the coach said, "Same old trouble, eh, Frank? Well, we're going to have to do something about that leg one of these days." He turned to go on again, then swung around and fired a question.

"Say, Frank, what are you doing around the Christmas holidays?"

"I don't have any plans, Coach."

"Well, you just see me when we get back to school. I've got to go on up to the Mayo Clinic in Rochester, Minnesota, to have my bad leg operated on. And you know how I hate to travel alone. Now, you plan to come along with me and get your knee fixed up. We can share a room and I'll have somebody to talk to. Maybe I can give you a course in football coaching while we're both recuperating?"

Leahy was bewildered by this incredible invitation. Nevertheless, he accepted quickly, and a day later the coach and his pupil set out for the Mayo Clinic.

"On the morning when the train was set to pull out of the South Bend Station, I was a wreck," recalled Leahy. "I was about to make a trip with Knute Rockne, the greatest football coach in America. I arrived at the station more than two hours early after not being able to sleep a wink. I was so excited about being with Rock that I couldn't eat breakfast. I had been fairly close to Rockne, but only as a member of the football team. Now I was about to be his friend and companion for two weeks or more."

During the journey to Rochester, Leahy used every ruse he could so he would not interfere with Rock's reading or chats with other passengers. Leahy thought that the great coach had arranged for separate rooms at the Kahler Hotel, Rochester, where they were to stay before entering the hospital. Instead, Rockne had taken a large double suite, which coach and former player were to share.

"When we arrived at the hotel suite," said Leahy, "I was in an actual state of panic. I was scared stiff."

Finally Rockne said, "Please, Frank, I'd really appreciate it you'd forget about me being 'the Great Rockne' and you just a member of my team. I'm not so great and you've got a fine football head. I admire you. And who knows, someday you may make them forget old Rock. You're my friend and I hope I'm yours. Now how about looking at things the way they really are? You and I are a couple of broken-down football folks up here at the clinic trying to get all fixed up so we can get to work again. How's that sound?"

Leahy had no time to express his appreciation for the gentle, friendly manner in which his coach had put him at ease before Rockne went on, "Watch that phone there, Frank. I'll bet it's going to be mighty busy from this minute on."

He had no sooner spoken than the first barrage of calls came in. The calls came from townpeople who knew Rock, inviting him out to dinner, from clubs and civic organizations asking him to make speeches. It hadn't taken long for Rock's public in Rochester to discover that he was in town.

Out of the four days Leahy spent in the room with Rockne prior to the operation on his knee, the fact that struck him most forcibly was the manner in which Rockne treated everyone who came into contact with him—doctors, nurses, politicians, manufacturers, chambermaids, bellhops. He showed an equal interest in the health and doings of all, a trait that made all remember him kindly. It is likely that Frank's kindred talent for understanding people began to mature during the days of this close relationship with Rockne. Leahy was also blessed with Rock's marvelous memory for names and for connecting persons with the source of his original meetings with them.

Another Leahy trait was his unfailing courtesy. A particular instance occurred just before the 1943 Notre Dame-Iowa Pre-Flight game, which the Irish won, 14–13, after one of the most stirring battles of the year. A half hour before the kickoff, Lieutenant Commander Larry Mullins, who was one of the Seahawks' coaches, decided to pay a last pregame visit to his old friend Leahy, then Notre Dame's head coach. Standing near Mullins as he headed for the Notre Dame dressing room was a sailor named Pat Pederson, yeoman to the late Captain David Hanrahan, commanding officer of the Iowa Pre-Flight base. Mullins thought that Pederson, a football fan, might like to meet Leahy and invited the sailor to join him.

Pederson shook hands with Frank and then stepped aside while Mullins and Leahy chatted. Moon and Frank wished each other luck, and the two Navy men started to leave. They hadn't gone ten steps when the Notre Dame coach said, "Pederson!" They turned, and there was Leahy, with hand outstretched to the sailor, saying, "Mighty glad to have met you, Pat." Another coach, confronted with the problem of sending his team out to fight the team that was vieing with them for number-one national recognition, might well have overlooked such a gesture, but not Leahy.

Once he and Rockne were established at the Mayo clinic in that 1930 visit, Leahy underwent several tests and preliminary examinations before Dr. Melvin S. Henderson operated on his knee. He rejoined Rockne in their comfortable suite, and in the following days he and the coach talked football from A to Z, with Rockne giving the younger man the most thorough educational sessions of his football career. Rockne was amazed at the keenness and football knowledge his pupil revealed, a discovery that may have been the reason for a remark he made to Fritz Crisler. Crisler, then head football coach at the University of Minnesota, dropped in to visit Rockne during his Rochester stay. Rock introduced Fritz to Leahy; later, in the corridor, when Crisler was leaving, Rock said, "Fritz, that boy Leahy is going to make a great coach someday."

When he returned to the room, Rock told Leahy of his talk. "I just told Crisler that someday you're going to have everybody in the country talking about you, Frank. You're going to be a great coach."

"I'm very grateful, coach. But I just can't seem to get rid of this down feeling I've had ever since my leg went out."

"Frank, you have no reason to feel this way. I thought our Notre Dame players were taught to fight back against adversity. At least that's what I'm telling you to do. Are you still fretting that you won't be able to play ball? It could be the very best thing that ever happened to you. Now, it's a damned foolish attitude."

"Can't help it, coach," said Frank. "This knee injury cost me every opportunity I ever thought I had. I figured if I played well this last year, I could line up a coaching job. Now they've all but forgotten me."

A few minutes later, Rockne dropped some letters on Leahy's lap.

"What are these, coach?"

"Those are letters from athletic directors and coaches wanting to know who I could recommend for a job. Do you know, Frank, that ever since we beat Stanford in the Rose Bowl, I have letters from the biggest schools in the country? Imagine Yale University wanting a Notre Dame man to coach football? I must have at least thirty-five requests on my desk right now for job offers, and I've helped a number of our players get those jobs. I recommended Adam Walsh to Yale, Rip Miller went to Indiana; Harry Stuhldreher went to Villanova; and Rex Enright, Chuck Collins, and Bill Cerney are all at North Carolina. Joe Bach is at Duquesne, Clipper Smith at Trinity. Jim Phelan went to Purdue, while Hunk Anderson and Charlie Walsh went to St. Louis, Frank Thomas to Alabama, and Harry Mehre is at Georgia.

"That's about all I can remember, Frank. Now if you'll stop feeling sorry for yourself, I'll recommend you for any job that you like. Now stop acting like a hurt schoolboy. Why, you've got your entire life before you and it's going to be a fine one and I'm backing you all the way."

Frank went through each of the letters Rockne had given him and found that the position that really appealed to him was a chance to become an assistant to Tommy Mills at Georgetown. It was the same Tommy Mills who had befriended Leahy when he first came to Notre Dame. Mills was now a successful head coach at Georgetown, and Frank immediately called Tommy and discussed the post with him. After discussing the situation with Mills, Frank was told that the job was his. He would replace another Notre Dame man, John "Clipper" Smith, who was leaving.

Frank immediately went back to Rockne and with tears in his eyes started to thank his coach.

"Now cut that all out," said Rockne.

"You wouldn't get the job if I didn't think you would be a fine coach. You're going to do a great job at Georgetown and you'll go on from there. And then maybe someday you'll have a head coaching job of your own. Good luck, Frank."

As Christmas approached, Leahy once again became increasingly lonely and depressed.

On the afternoon of December 24, he was alone in his hospital room, feeling very low. Then a huge package arrived.

The package was addressed to Mr. Frank Leahy. He unwrapped the package and found a handsome Alaska lamb overcoat, the gift of his old Chicago friend Eddie Dunigan. A flock of wires and cards followed the receipt of the coat. They came not only from his family but from players and professors at Notre Dame as well.

When Rockne saw the coat he said, "Better hurry up and get on your feet, Frank. That coat will earn you a lot of dates with the nurses around here."

Leahy's most indelible memory of that hospital stretch was of Christmas Day. He knew that Rockne had a dinner engagement with friends but was unaware that the coach's host was his own physician, Dr. Clifford Barborka. Frank wished Rock a good time and then settled back in his bed, resigned to solitary contemplation of the coat he couldn't wear. He was wondering how the folks back in Winner and in Omaha were celebrating the Yule when a knock sounded on the door.

"Come in," he called. Probably one of the nurses, he thought. The door opened, and there stood Dr. Barborka, bearing a huge tray with a homecooked Christmas dinner of turkey with all the trimmings, wishing him a Merry Christmas. The Leahy appetite needed no further urging, and his spirits soared to unbelievable heights.

"That man Rockne," Frank said aloud to himself, "is the kindest, most thoughtful, and the greatest coach in the world."

On his return to the campus, Leahy found the going tough. He had to navigate around the campus on crutches at first, but after several weeks was able to walk with the aid of a cane. His regular class was to graduate in June 1931, but the knee condition prevented him from carrying out his practice teaching assignments in the South Bend grammar and high schools. This was a compulsory requirement as part of the physical education degree at Notre Dame. He was short several additional study units but completed the work in six weeks of summer school and finally received his degree early in August 1931. A modest ceremony was held in Washington Hall on August 28, as a number of other students received their belated degrees. The next morning, Frank Leahy took a train to Washington, D.C., for his assignment with the Georgetown eleven, and for ten years did not set foot on the campus at Notre Dame.

The Golden Age of Sports was rapidly coming to an end, the glorious decade from 1920 to 1930. It had produced supermen—the incomparable Babe Ruth in baseball, Jack Dempsey and Gene Tunney in boxing, Bobby Jones in golf, Big Bill Tilden and Helen Wills in tennis, Paavo Nurmi in track, Red Grange and Jim Thorpe in football, and George Gipp, the Four Horsemen, and Knute Rockne.

Rockne was one of the best-known men in the United States and unquestionably the most popular. The demands on his time were incredible. He chose his extra jobs with care so that the returns would bring in the most security for his loved ones. The job that appealed most to him was serving as sales promotion director for Studebaker, the huge automobile concern whose main offices were in South Bend.

The job was ideal because it would entail inspirational talks to Studebaker salespeople and he would receive a handsome fee of some $10,000 for six talks.

In March 1931 a new opportunity for greater financial security developed. Hollywood was about to make a motion picture, *The Spirit of Notre Dame*. Lew Ayres, at that time one of the most popular leading men in Hollywood, was to be the star, and Rock agreed to take a leading part in the production. Rock was to receive the princely sum of $75,000 for his work, and he was most anxious to make the trip, for it was more money at one time than he had ever received in his entire coaching career.

On his way out to the Coast, Rockne stopped in Chicago for dinner with his financial adviser, Christy Walsh, and several other friends. Then he was to take a train for Kansas City, where he would board a plane for Los Angeles.

"Soft landing, coach," said Walsh in a laughing farewell.

"You mean a happy landing, don't you?" said Rockne with a laugh.

In Kansas City he sent his wife, Bonnie, a wire. It read:

LEAVING RIGHT NOW . . . STOP . . . WILL BE AT BILTMORE . . . STOP . . . LOVE AND KISSES. . . .

KNUTE.

A STUNNED NATION

Ed Baker, a rancher, was feeding cattle in the Flint Hills when he heard the sound of the regular mail plane between Kansas City and Wichita on that fateful day, Tuesday, March 31, 1931. It was his habit to gaze overhead at the silver gleam of the trimotored Fokker plane. Airplanes were rarities in those early days. But Baker saw nothing. Gray clouds hung low in the skies, so low that the limestone points of the distant hills seemed to be part of the clouds.

Baker shifted uneasily, gripped by a sense of foreboding. It was almost as if the banshees were wailing their warning of impending doom. The hum of the hidden plane faded, then resumed. But it resumed in stuttering fashion. Something was wrong.

There was a sudden flash of silver as the Fokker broke through the bottom of the clouds, fluttering like a huge, wounded bird. Behind it trailed a wing, severed from the main body.

Down it plunged, motors roaring. In horror, Baker watched. Behind a hill the plane crashed into the earth with a sickening thud. The Kansas farmer leaped onto his horse and rushed over. One look at the smoking wreckage and he knew that all those aboard were beyond help. Nevertheless, he raced to nearby Cottonwood Falls to tell the world of the plane crash and get ambulances and doctors out to the Flint Hills.

Ranchers and farmers from every direction rode their horses to the crash scene. Automobiles raced in from every part of the area. Planes flew overhead, chartered by newspapers. The Fokker never burned or exploded. It just buried its nose in the hilltop. In the pilot's pocket was a passenger list. Eight men died in the crash. But one of the eight was Knute Rockne, who was found still holding in his hand the rosary one of his players had given him.

"ROCKNE DEAD" screamed front-page headlines all over the country in the biggest, blackest type available.

The entire nation was shocked, jolted to the core at news of the death of this onetime immigrant boy from Norway, for he was more than just a most successful football coach. He was also one of the most beloved figures in America. Now he was gone forever at the height of his career, at age forty-three.

The news was so sudden and so shocking to the millions of Americans to whom Rockne's name stood for the highest in football that it was doubly so to those young men who had been most recently associated with him in the two most successful seasons of his brilliant career.

As the student body and faculty of the university kneeled in Sacred Heart Church on the campus that evening, they prayed for a man who only a day before had been among them, wisecracking with his players, telling them to study extra hard while he was gone.

Thousands of messages of condolence poured into the Rockne home on East Wayne Avenue. They came from the great, the near great, and the humble. President Hoover wired Mrs. Rockne, "I know that every American grieves with you. Mr. Rockne so contributed to the cleanness and high purpose of sportsmanship in athletics that his passing is a national loss." Secretary of War Patrick Hurley; General Douglas MacArthur, then Chief of Staff of the Army; the king of Norway, land of Rockne's birth; and scores of his coaching rivals over the years followed with tributes.

Probably the most spontaneous demonstration of Americans' affection for Rock was witnessed early in the evening of April 1, when the train bearing his remains rolled into Chicago's grimy Dearborn Street station. More than ten thousand citizens jammed the old structure and the streets surrounding it. A few blocks away, a flag flew at half mast over Soldier Field, the scene of so many Notre Dame triumphs under his direction. It was an impressive and respectful tribute from the huge throng who had constituted the most loyal legion of Rockne's followers: the sort of vigorous farewell that Rock, who died as he lived—in action—would have wanted.

The funeral services were held in the afternoon of April 5, 1931. Six of Rock's greatest pupils—Frank Carideo, Marchy Schwartz, Marty Brill, Larry Mullins, Tom Conley, and Tommy Yarr—acted as pallbearers. Only fourteen hundred of the huge crowd that came to the church could be accommodated within, but loudspeakers carried the organ music and the voice of Father Hugh O'Donnell, C.S.C., president of the university, outdoors. Uncounted thousands of others heard the service over a national radio network to which Father O'Donnell had given permission to broadcast.

Father O'Donnell, a close personal friend of Rockne for more than twenty years, delivered the sermon from a pulpit draped in black.

"In this Holy Week of Christ's Passion," he said, "there has occurred a tragedy which accounts for our presence here today. Knute Rockne is dead.

"And who was Knute Rockne? Ask the president of the United States, who dispatched a personal message of tribute to his memory and comfort to his bereaved family. Ask the king of Norway, who sends a special delegation to this solemn service.

"Was he, perhaps, a martyr who laid down his life for some great cause, a patriot who laid down his life for country, a statesman, a soldier, admiral of a fleet, or captain of industry or finance?

"No," and here Father O'Donnell's voice fell to a whisper, "he was none of these. He was a football coach and athletic director of Notre Dame. I find myself in this piteous hour of loss recalling the words of Christ 'Thou shalt love thy neighbor as thyself.' I think that supremely he loved his neighbor."

The last blessing then was invoked and the pallbearers, blinking hard to keep the tears from their eyes, bore their coach's body to Highland Cemetery, hard by the old Indian portage where La Salle and his lieutenant, Tonti, had blazed the trail into Indiana for Marquette, Joliet, and Allouez.

CHAPTER 4

AFTER ROCKNE

HUNK ANDERSON (1931—33)

Deep gloom hung like a cloud over the Notre Dame campus as the days slowly passed after the tragic death of Knute Rockne. Students, players, and even faculty members who were close to Rock did little else but talk about him, his great teams, his players, and the personal loss everyone felt.

As the days slowly drifted by and the first warm days of April appeared, there was a call for spring football practice for the 1931 season. That first drill attracted a record 320 candidates for the team, and the practice drills were handled by members of Rockne's 1930 staff headed by Hunk Anderson, Jack Chevigny, and Ike Voedisch.

It was assumed that Rockne's successor would come from the ranks of the sixty to seventy Rockne-schooled players who were now coaching at a number of the leading schools. All of them had returned to South Bend for Rockne's funeral. Most of the coaches were much too young for the Notre Dame post and the older ones would have difficulty being released from their present assignments with the new season just five months away.

The selection, when it was made by Father O'Donnell, was Hunk Anderson, a star lineman and an assistant to Rockne as the head coach.

Anderson, an outstanding guard for the championship teams of 1919 and 1921, was named to the All-America team in 1921. Hunk aided Rockne for several seasons, played professional football, and had been the head coach at St. Louis University for two seasons.

Rockne had called Anderson "the best line coach in America," and he was to be aided by Jack Chevigny, a fiery and competitive halfback who starred for the 1926—28 Irish. It was Chevigny who in the 1928

Notre Dame-Army battle scored the tieing touchdown and as he dashed over the goal line cried, "There's one for the Gipper!"

Jesse Harper, former head coach and athletic director, was brought back from his farm in Kansas to oversee the football program and to act as athletic director.

Hunk Anderson led a veteran team against the Indiana Hoosiers in the opening game of the 1931 season. It was the first Notre Dame eleven without Knute Rockne at the helm since 1917, but the Anderson-led Irish upheld Notre Dame's finest tradition by trouncing the strong Indiana team by a 25—0 score.

The Irish eleven functioned as a well-oiled machine in trouncing the Hoosiers, with such veterans as Ed Kosky, Hugh Devore, and Dick Mahoney handling the end posts; Al Culver and Joe Kurth at tackle; Nordy Hoffman, Moose Krause, and Jim Harris as the guards, and Captain Tom Yarr at center. Chuck Jaskwich ran the team at quarterback, Marchy Schwartz and Joe Sheeketski were at the halfback posts, and at fullback was George Melinkovich. It was the twentieth consecutive win for Notre Dame, a win streak that started back in 1929 and that brought the Irish national championship honors in 1929 and 1930.

A week later, Notre Dame was held to a 0—0 tie by Northwestern. Then Drake was demolished, 63—0. Pitt, the next opponent, was looked upon as a significant test for the new coach, for the Panthers had a fine team. But halfback Marchy Schwartz, playing brilliantly all afternoon, led the Irish to a well-earned 25—12 victory. This was also the game that saw a mean, aroused Irish tackle named Hugh Devore throw an open-field block that took out three

(Above, right) After Rockne's death in 1931, Hunk Anderson (second from left) was named head coach. Jesse Harper (left) was named athletic director. Jack Chevigny was named Hunk's assistant. Tom Yarr (extreme right) was captain of the 1931 team.

(Above, left) William Shakespeare (left) and Al Smith were outstanding candidates for freshman football in 1932.

(Right) Coach Hunk Anderson with his assistants in 1933 (left to right): All-America tackle Nordy Hoffman; Anderson; Ike Voedich; and Tom Conley, captain in 1930.

Pitt players, enabling Schwartz to score a touchdown.

Then in rapid succession, like a huge, tidal wave, the Irish rolled over Carnegie Tech, 19–0; Pennsylvania, 49–0; and Navy, 20–0.

Hunk Anderson was now sitting tall in the saddle. Only one opponent had scored against the Irish in the first seven games, a close approximation to Rockne's record in 1926, when only one touchdown had been scored against the Irish in their first eight games.

In 1931 Coach Howard Jones brought his USC Trojans to the new Notre Dame Stadium for the first time, bent on avenging a humiliating 27–0 beating the Irish had inflicted the previous year. USC had won six straight games after an upset loss to little St. Mary's and was headed for the Rose Bowl—if they could defeat Notre Dame. Jones had drilled his team behind closed gates for ten days. They were fit and ready for the battle of the year.

For the first time, five Los Angeles radio stations broadcast the game. By one estimate, more than ten million football fans coast to coast heard the broadcast—it was the largest listening audience in broadcast history. And they heard one of the great games in collegiate football history.

Notre Dame scored first as Marchy Schwartz and Steve Banas cracked the Trojan line for huge gains. Schwartz scored and Chuck Jaskwich kicked the extra point for a 7–0 halftime lead. In the third quarter Schwartz and Banas again punched the line for gains, and Schwartz pounded across from the ten-yard line. Jaskwich kicked the extra point, and it was 14–0 Notre Dame.

Then something happened. That something was one of the greatest come-from-behind victories in college football.

Irv Mohler, the Trojan quarterback, playing the game of his life, inspired the rest of his teammates with his play, and they responded. Gus Shaver and Mohler pounded the Irish line for a touchdown, but John Baker missed the extra point. The score was now 14–6 Notre Dame with about six minutes to play, and the huge crowd was up and screaming as the action became furious.

Shaver drove over the Irish goal line and once again Baker tried the extra point. This time he made it. The score was Notre Dame 14, USC 13 with four minutes to play.

USC took possession of the ball after Notre Dame's drive stalled. Shaver tossed a fifty-yard pass and Ray Sparling made a spectacular catch and took the ball to the Irish seventeen-yard line. Time was running out, and with sixty seconds left to play John Baker kicked a twenty-three yard field goal for a 16–14 upset victory over Notre Dame.

With the victory, USC won the Dickinson Trophy and the Knute Rockne Memorial Trophy, symbolic of the national championship.

At the presentation ceremony of the Rockne Trophy after the game, Coach Jones accepted the award and suddenly asked Jack Rissman, donor of the trophy, "Jack, do you know where Rockne is buried?"

"I'll take you there," said Rissman.

Half an hour later, Howard Jones and the entire USC football team stood bareheaded in Highland Cemetery, South Bend, at the grave of their bitterest adversary on the field, their most respected opponent. In the chill November evening they paid silent tribute to the fallen Irish warrior.

The Notre Dame streak of twenty-six undefeated games had been broken.

"The streak got to be too much," said Marchy Schwartz. "We just couldn't take the pressure, and I guess we were relieved when we finally got beat."

The big question was whether the Irish could recoup against a big, tough Army eleven. Many thought the Cadets would be the victim of a Notre Dame rebound, but many others were just as sure the Irish had lost a spark never to be regained.

A snowstorm whirled across Yankee Stadium as the Irish took the field against Army, yet more than seventy-eight thousand fans jammed every inch of the huge ball park in the Bronx. It was the last game for such stars as Marchy Schwartz, Nordy Hoffman, Chuck Jaskwich, George Melinkovich, and Captain Tom Yarr, the last time they would ever wear the blue and gold.

On the Friday night before the game, Army's twenty-one-year-old star halfback, Ray Stecker, was suddenly taken ill with a high fever. He was rushed to a doctor in New York City at six o'clock Saturday morning, and with his illness Army just about gave up on the game. However, when the team arrived at Yankee Stadium, Stecker was there in full uniform, and his touchdown run of sixty-five yards in the fourth quarter clinched the game for Army as they romped over the Irish by a 12–0 score.

In 1944 Colonel Ray Stecker was the squad leader of a Thunderbolt P-47 fighter group, and his unit was one of the first two fighter groups to be based in Germany during World War II.

THE TIDE TURNS

The 1932 season opened with the colorful Haskell Indian School opposing Notre Dame at South Bend on October 8. The Indians had previously played the Irish back in 1921, and Rockne had scheduled this game to give his friend, Coach Dietz of Haskell, an opportunity to play against a major opponent. But the game turned into an utter rout as the Irish ran up a 73–0 score against the light and undermanned Indians. Anderson tried to keep the score down and inserted every man on his squad, but the substitutes, eager to make an impression before the home crowd, played their best game, and it was no contest. The following week Drake University fell before a thundering herd from South Bend by a 62–0 score, and when Carnegie Tech, always a tough opponent, was easily defeated, 42–0, it looked as if Coach Anderson had one of Notre Dame's great teams.

Then it was Pittsburgh on October 29, and the Panthers, already victorious over a strong Army eleven, surprised the Irish by the fury of their attack. In the first period, Notre Dame's fine halfback Mike Koken attempted to pass and it looked as if Captain Paul Host would catch the ball, but Bud Hogan of Pitt intercepted the pass. On the very next play, Izzie Weinstock, Pitt's great fullback star, bulled his way across the Irish goal line for a 6–0 lead. Again an Irish pass went awry as Al McGuff, a substitute Irish halfback, lofted the ball right into the arms of Ted Dailey, who sped thirty-five yards for a score. Pitt, with a 12–0 win, had "the year's greatest upset." Kansas was beaten 24–6 after the Jayhawks sped to a 6–0 lead in the first quarter, but the Irish team effort was far from impressive. The next week, on November 12, with the temperature near zero and a light snow falling, George Melinkovich took the opening kickoff against Northwestern, twisted and turned his way ninety-eight yards for a spectacular touchdown, and Notre Dame then went on to score twice more to win over the Wildcats, 21–0.

At Cleveland on November 19 two formidable foes awaited the Irish: Navy and Navy weather. And looking across the field, Hunk Anderson saw some familiar faces wearing the Navy coaches' official jackets: Head Coach "Rip" Miller, one of the famous Irish Seven Mules, who played with the Four Horsemen; Christy Flanagan, whose sixty-five-yard dash beat Army in 1926; and Johnny "One-Play" O'Brien, who caught the winning pass against Army in the great victory of 1928. The weather, according to *The New York Times*, was "the worst . . . rain and then windstorms . . . across the field, turning it into a quagmire."

But the Irish had the better footing, and big Joe Sheeketski scored two touchdowns to give Notre Dame a hard-fought 12–0 victory before a crowd of over sixty-one thousand in that frozen stadium at Cleveland.

The following week, reporting for the *New York Sun*, sportswriter George Trevor wrote, "This Notre Dame team, beaten by Pittsburgh was out for Army blood today [November 26] and proved this from the first move when every man in green hit Army with a rush and crash that meant open warfare. Melinkovich, Banas, Lukats and Mike Koken were like a 4,000 horsepowered machine as they battered the Cadets 21–0.

"The clash," continued Trevor, "between Notre Dame and Southern California on December 10 will decide which is the greatest football team in America."

The Trojans had won eighteen games in a row, but the gamblers had a standing order in those days, "never bet against the Yankees or Notre Dame," and made the Irish the favorites. But the play of the Trojans' Cotton Warburton led to two Trojan touchdowns and another great upset victory for the University of Southern California by a 13–0 score.

And now there were alumni voices all across the land, voices that cried for the head of Hunk Anderson, for under Hunk, they said, "Notre Dame was learning to lose."

In reply, Anderson said:

"I want to give all credit to those teams that have

In his first season as head football coach, 1931, Hunk Anderson's team won six, lost two, and tied one.

beaten us—Pittsburgh, Southern California, and any other team which may beat us from time to time. There was lots of talk after the Pitt game that indicated that Notre Dame lost heart. The talk was dispelled with the showing in subsequent contests, especially in the Army game. No team is great until it has lost a game—and Notre Dame this year has shown its greatness by bouncing back."

Now it was another year, 1933, and Anderson still had a nucleus of Rockne leftovers and a highly regarded group of sophomores he had personally recruited. But in the home opener on October 7 against Kansas, the Irish were stunned as they were held to a 0–0 tie in a drab game that attracted only 9,221 spectators at South Bend.

As Anderson had said they would, the Irish bounced back and defeated a sturdy Indiana team by a 12–2 score the following week, and it seemed that the Irish were on their way back. But then Carnegie Tech ran through them on October 21 and scored a stunning 7–0 upset victory. Pittsburgh did the very same thing a week later at South Bend and trounced Notre Dame 14–0, and so did Navy by a 7–0 score. Then it was Purdue's turn, and the Boilermakers smashed out a 19–0 victory. Now the wolves were howling for Anderson's scalp.

The Irish had lost four in a row and had been held scoreless in those four games, and Anderson and Flanagan and all the other coaches worked tirelessly with the players during the week, trying to develop new strategy, new plays, a new spirit—something to put new life into the team.

Against Northwestern on November 18, Notre Dame came to life briefly and scored one touchdown, but that was just enough to gain a 7–0 victory over the Wildcats. Now the harried Irish prepared to face Howard Jones and the great Southern California eleven.

This time it wasn't even close. Cotton Warburton was once again the standout star as he scored twice in a 19–0 defeat of the once-proud Irish. Now a lone enemy was left.

The last chance for redemption was against Army on December 2 in Yankee Stadium, with a crowd of over seventy-three thousand looking on.

The huge crowd that had come to the game to witness a marvelous spectacle, Notre Dame vs. Army, still believed in the magic of Notre Dame. They could not or would not accept the stories they had read in the sports pages describing the wretched showing of Notre Dame in the previous games. But by the end of the first half, they were willing to believe

A new candidate for the team in 1933 was Knute Rockne, Jr. Assistant Coach Larry Mullins (right) is giving young Rockne some pointers on passing.

anything, for they had seen a great Army team drive and punch and fight through Notre Dame for two touchdowns, and Army backs headed by the brilliant Jack Buckler and Joe Stancook pounded the Irish line at will for huge gains.

Almost three periods rolled by and Army continued to outplay Notre Dame. And then, as if by magic, something happened. Slowly at first, Fred Carideo, cousin of the great Notre Dame quarterback Frank Carideo, began to yell, "C'mon Irish, let's get 'em. Army, we're coming to get you. We're gonna get you." And then Nick Lukats, a fine three-year veteran fullback, playing his final game for the blue and gold, began to move the team. He spun and drove off-tackle for fifteen yards, then made ten more. A pass gained ten yards. Then with the Irish up and fighting mad now, Lukats and Wayne Millner tried an end-around play, and Millner, an All-American end, sped to the Army twenty-five yard line.

The fourth quarter had just started when Lukats smashed to the Army five-yard line. Then on the next play, he bulled his way through five Army defenders to score Notre Dame's first TD. Bud Bonar, the Irish quarterback, kicked the extra point and the score was now Army 12, Notre Dame 7. The spectators were up and screaming as the Irish kicked to Army. With but three minutes to play the action became a sea of fury as the two teams battled up and down the field. Ed "Moose" Krause, Notre Dame's six-foot, three-inch, 225-pound tackle, had been charging Army kickers throughout the game, vowing to block the next punt. On the next play Ozzie Simmons, Army's kicker, tried to punt. Krause slammed in, but three Army blockers took him out of the play; that left Simmons completely without any protection, and Millner, the Irish's great end, tore in, blocked the kick, and pounced on the ball for a Notre Dame touchdown. The noise of the Irish rooters was deafening as Bonar dropped back for the extra-point try. They groaned as he missed, but the Irish had a one-point edge.

The score as the game ended was Notre Dame 13, while the clock ran down. Army 12 in one of the wildest, most exciting games in the great rivalry.

In the locker room after the game, Army's fine young head coach, Gar Davidson, congratulated Anderson and the Notre Dame squad, then added ruefully, "But I don't know why in hell you fellows from Notre Dame always save your best for us!" Davidson, who wound up his Army career years later as Lieutenant General Gar Davidson, was a first lieutenant in the Army, and his salary for coaching football at West Point in 1933 was $166.50 per month.

THE LAYDEN ERA
BY ELMER LAYDEN

"After graduation, I was torn between coaching football and getting my law degree. That summer, which I spent as a playground supervisor in my hometown, Davenport, Iowa, I received a call from Columbia College in Dubuque, Iowa. It seemed that Eddie Anderson, an end and captain of the 1921 Notre Dame team, had been coaching Columbia and had decided to attend Rush Medical College and become a doctor. Columbia wanted a coach and sweetened their offer to me with a chance to study for the Iowa bar while working in the law office of Frantzen, Benson, and Gilloon.

"I called Rockne, asked his advice. He told me that I was making a very smart move and so I had a chance to coach and to study law.

"Anybody who has ever coached football remembers his first day on the job. My first day at Columbia College was something that no football coach had ever experienced.

"At the appointed hour for the first drill, I walked out onto the practice field dressed in my football outfit, and there were *only two players out on the field.*

" 'Where's the rest of the team? Or are you two the entire team?' I asked.

" 'The rest of the team is at choir practice,' one of the boys answered.

" 'At choir practice?' I screamed.

" 'Sure,' the boy answered, 'most of the guys are planning to enter the seminary, and choir practice is required.'

"He was right. Many of the boys going to Co-lumbia did enter the seminary, and a number of the boys who played for me in the time I was there became priests.

"My contract called for me to coach football, basketball, and track. A priest coached the baseball team.

"We had a rainy autumn in 1925. Mud was everywhere, and that helped my lightweight team. Our conference record was three wins, one loss, one tie, and we beat Luther in the final game for the conference title.

"One of the candidates for my basketball team in 1926 was a pretty fair ballplayer, Don Ameche. Later on Don made it big in the movies and when the All-America Conference was formed in 1945, Don bankrolled the Los Angeles Dons team.

"In the summer of 1926, I was married to Edythe Davis and also received the great news that I had passed the Iowa bar exams and then when news that a little Layden was due, I began to scout around for a better coaching job.

"On August 20, 1927, I signed a two-year contract to become athletic director and head football coach at Duquesne University for the then munificent salary of $6,500 per annum.

"For the first time, I had some great help. Duquesne allowed me an assistant, and I immediately hired John Weibel. John had been an outstanding guard on our 1924 team at Notre Dame. He was studying medicine and was an assistant coach at Vanderbilt University before he came back to assist me. John worked with me for a while and then tragically died of a ruptured appendix before finishing his internship. Bob Reagan succeeded Johnny, and Joe Bach later replaced Reagan, who left for a head coaching job.

"We opened the season by losing to St. Bonaventure and ended by beating Ashland College. Our record: four wins, four losses, and one tie.

"By 1928 Duquesne had reached a point in its football history where we had games scheduled with a real power in eastern football, Washington & Jefferson University, and if ever a team had prepped for a game, it was our team. I had the team fighting mad, and they went out and beat W&J by a 12–7 score, a tremendous upset. We got so much press out of beating W&J that we finally were able to schedule Pittsburgh and other major elevens.

"The season's record was a tremendous one, with eight wins and just one loss. It was one of Duquesne's outstanding years.

"Through the next few years we managed to play most of the leading teams and win our fair share of ball games, and by the time in 1933 that I was ready to make another move, Duquesne had become an important factor in eastern football circles. When I took over as head coach it was considered a compliment to the team and to the coach if Duquesne drew a crowd of five thousand to the games. When I was ready to leave, we had drawn crowds of forty thousand to fifty thousand spectators, and it was time for me to go on to a new challenge.

"When I was coaching football, the only place to coach, at least for me, was Notre Dame. Every alumnus dreamed of the day he would be tapped for the post. Even today, when the job is open, it is still the cream of the crop. I'm told that Ara Parseghian actively pursued the job, and certainly his record shows that he was magnificently qualified.

"When Terry Brennan abruptly was dismissed, there were rumors that he had been considering another coaching job. John Carmichael, sports editor of the *Chicago Daily News*, quashed them all in his column by writing: 'This would be like President Ike Eisenhower running for the House of Representatives.' For a college coach, Notre Dame is the zenith, or it certainly was in 1933, when I was hired.

"Duquesne's season ended and I was able to get down to New York for the Army-Notre Dame game, December 2. I checked into the old Commodore Hotel on Forty-second Street in New York,

and I immediately received a phone call from Father John O'Hara. Father John was the vice-president of the university and directly in charge of the athletic board, and he invited me to dinner.

"There was no fuss or beating-about-the-bush discussion. Father John put it right to me. Would I consider becoming head football coach and athletic director at Notre Dame?

"The answer jumped in my throat. But I would not say 'Yes' until I found out more about the situation. Hunk Anderson, the head coach, was an old friend. Jesse Harper, another great friend, was athletic director.

"Hunk Anderson had had a dismal season to that point in 1933, winning but two games, tying one, and losing five. This Army-Notre Dame game was his last game. But even before the results of the game were known, Father O'Hara told me that the administration had decided that a change was necessary.

"Duquesne still had two postseason games ahead, and after the first of these games—a charity affair in St. Louis against a team of Purdue All-Stars—I dropped off and met Father O'Hara in Indianapolis, where I signed a contract that Notre Dame had prepared for me.

"I signed the Notre Dame contract, then left for Miami, where Duquesne was scheduled to meet the University of Miami at the Orange Bowl. We went into the game with a record of nine wins and one defeat, by Pittsburgh, but we had little trouble defeating a struggling Miami team, 33–7.

"A major and immediate task for me was the selection of a corps of assistant coaches, and I immediately signed Chet Grant as my backfield coach. Chet had played in 1916 and had been a good quarterback. Next was Tom Conley, captain of the last Rockne team, of 1930. Tom was my selection as end coach, and then I went back to the Four Horsemen of my day and appointed Joe Boland and Bill Cerney to my staff of coaches.

"Boland had been an outstanding tackle on the 1924 and '25 teams; Cerney had been playing behind me as a fullback, and he liked to call himself 'the Fifth Horseman.'

"I ran across a story in the *South Bend Tribune* about Bill that marked the twenty-fifth anniversary of the Four Horsemen. The story began: 'Outlined against a gray-blue sky, the Fifth Horseman rode the bench again today.' And the story continued to

New staff members assisting Coach Layden in 1936 included (left to right): Joe Boland, Bill Cerney, Tim Monahan, and Chet Grant. Layden is at the far right.

Elmer Layden, one of the immortal Four Horsemen, was named head coach in 1934 to succeed Hunk Anderson.

describe how Cerney rode the bench waiting to substitute for me.

"During the late summer of 1934 the entire school was in mourning as John 'Tex' Young, a first-string fullback, died of a blood infection. Then, a year later, just as we were getting ready for spring practice, the captain-elect of the 1935 team, Joe Sullivan, a great-looking, husky, six-foot, 195-pound tackle, became ill and died of pneumonia. The 1935 team dedicated each game that season to his memory.

"Our first opponent in 1934 was the University of Texas. Their new head coach, Jack Chevigny, was a Notre Dame immortal. Now he had his young, tough Texas squad primed for us. The final score of the game was 7–6 in favor of Texas, and it was one of the year's great upsets. Later one critic of mine said that if I did not substitute so freely and play practically every member of the team, we would have easily beaten Texas.

"But as I saw it, the only way I could find out the kind of players I had was to play as many of the boys as I could and see their reaction under fire. I also didn't think it proper for a coach to have the substitutes take a battering each week from the varsity and never get a chance to play in a real game. That's my theory of coaching.

"Incidentally, Jack Chevigny's team was well

coached and in marvelous condition, and it was just that a Notre Dame man should defeat his alma mater in his first big coaching post. Jack Chevigny was a great football player, a superb coach, and a credit to Notre Dame and to his country.

"During World War II, Lieutenant Jack Chevigny led his Marine company in a charge against the Japanese in the terrible battle at Iwo Jima and was killed in that action.

"The following week in that 1934 season, October 13, in another battle at South Bend, we barely edged out a tough bunch of football players from Purdue by an 18–7 score. Then in rapid succession we won over rugged Carnegie Tech, 13–0, defeated the Wisconsin Badgers, 19–0, and for a couple of weeks at least it looked as if we would have a pretty good season, with a backfield that included one of the finest kickers I've ever seen in Bill Shakespeare. When I first started to meet with individual players, I had a great shock to learn that Shakespeare was having problems passing his English courses. But we were able to have a couple of tutors work with Bill, and soon that was taken care of. Bill could and did kick the ball sixty to seventy yards when we needed it most and got us out of a good deal of trouble with his punts as well as his great all-around play. We also had my kid brother Mike at halfback, as well as Andy Pilney, Don Elser, and Frank Carideo's kid cousin Fred. Wally Fromhart was my varsity quarterback and a fine one; Wayne Millner at end was to go on to win All-America honors. Then we had Captain Dom Vairo at the other end, Ken Stilley and John Mishuta were my tackles, Bill Smith and Rocco Schiralli were the guards, and Jack Robinson my starting center."

The game with Pittsburgh was another story as Coach Jock Sutherland had one of his finest teams, and before a hometown crowd of more than fifty-six thousand bug-eyed Panther rooters, Pitt trounced Layden's Irish gridsters by a 19–0 score. The following week it was another loss, to Navy by 10–6.

The season's record was now back to 3 and 3, and it looked as if the Irish were about to suffer another defeat in the annual battle against Northwestern, on November 17. The Wildcats had the edge by a 7–6 score going into the last period, and it looked as if Notre Dame was faced with another losing season and perhaps another wrong coaching selection. Then with time running out the Irish magic struck with devastating effect, and they poured across two quick touchdowns for an inspiring come-from-behind victory, 20–7.

On November 24 at Yankee Stadium the Irish prepared to face another fine Army team before a jam-packed crowd of more than seventy-eight thousand frenzied fans. And they witnessed one of the most grueling, hard-fought gridiron battles ever waged between the two schools.

In the first period Bill Shakespeare faded back from two Army tacklers and fired a forty-yard pass to Captain Dom Vairo. Vairo was completely surrounded by several Army defenders, including Whitey Grove and Ralph King, but somehow outjumped both Army man, took the ball right out of their hands, and raced to the Army goal line for the first Notre Dame touchdown. The play covered fifty-two yards. The try for the extra point was blocked, and Notre Dame led 6–0.

Army's Jack Buckler picked up yardage on three successive plays, then passed sixteen yards to Bill Shuler, who raced over for an Army touchdown. The extra point was blocked, and the score was 6–6 as the half ended.

The third period saw both teams locked in battle, hammering away at each other but failing to score as the play raged up and down the gridiron.

With but four minutes to play in the final period, Andy Pilney fired a long pass to the six-foot-three halfback Dan Hanley, who bulled his way for the final ten yards to score the winning touchdown. It was a brilliant 12–6 victory for Notre Dame.

The intersectional battle between USC and Notre Dame had been marked by some of the greatest games between two bitter rivals, and since USC had won three in a row over Notre Dame, Layden was irritated beyond belief and wanted and needed badly to win this ninth game between them.

On the other hand, Coach Howard Jones had won four and lost five games that season, and a loss to Notre Dame would scar the 1934 season as the worst in his career.

"I don't know what we can do against Notre Dame," said Jones. "Some of our boys are hurt, some played badly last week. It looks very bad for us."

Coach Layden's father, who would drop in on Notre Dame's practice sessions, was always free with advice for his son. One of his best tips was, "Elmer, if you want a winning team, play your ten best players . . . and your brother."

After USC missed a field goal, the Irish took over. Bill Shakespeare fired a long pass from his forty-yard line to Mike Layden, who dashed twenty-five yards through the entire USC defense for the Irish touchdown. Wally Fromhart kicked the extra point and it was 7–0.

In the second period Shakespeare heaved another long pass, this time to Wayne Millner, who made a diving catch on the two-yard line. On the next play, Mike Layden crashed through for his second touchdown and once more Fromhart kicked the extra point for a 14–0 victory.

"A bit of luck against Texas," said Layden, "and against Navy and we would have had a nine-and-one season. As it turned out, we won six games and lost three. It was not the best of years."

THE GAME OF THE CENTURY:
NOTRE DAME VS. OHIO STATE, 1935

During the first three years of Elmer Layden's regime he still had quality players recruited by Hunk Anderson, and the 1935 squad certainly was one of the finest. Returning for another year was the entire backfield of Bill Shakespeare, Andy Pilney, and Mike Layden, with Wally Fromhart at quarterback. Substitutes in the backfield included Frank Gaul, Andy Puplis, Fred Carideo, Don Elser, Steve Miller, Larry Danbom, and Tony Mazziotti. In the line were such stars as All-American end Wayne Millner, Dick Pfefferle, John Lautar, Marty Peters, and Joe Kuharich.

After opening victories over Kansas, Carnegie Tech, and Wisconsin, the team dug in for battle with a mighty Pittsburgh team that had defeated Notre Dame three straight years while holding the Irish scoreless over that period.

It was a fight to the football death. The Panthers scored first and were fighting for another score as they backed Notre Dame to the Irish five-yard line. Notre Dame had the ball, but Pitt was threatening to down Notre Dame with its back to the wall. But Bill Shakespeare came through with one of the greatest punts in college football history—from his own end zone some ninety yards in the air, a kick that changed the entire course of the game.

From that moment on, the Irish were the Irish of the Rockne tradition. With the score 6–6 in the late moments of the fourth quarter, Marty Peters, a six-foot, three-inch, 215-pound veteran end, tried to kick a field goal for the first time in his career. The kick looked like it hit the crossbar, then veered slightly, then came back and went over. No doubt it was the wind and a "Hail Mary" that brought the ball beautifully over for a three-pointer. With their 9–6 triumph the Irish had crushed Pitt's hopes for an undefeated year. It was the only Notre Dame win over Pitt in a six-year period and the only time Layden won over Jock Sutherland.

"But the one game that stands out over all—the game with Ohio State in 1935—was the most exciting college football game ever played," said Layden. "When the nation's sportswriters were polled back in 1951 to select the most thrilling college football game of the first half of the twentieth century, they chose our game with Ohio State. It was a game that taught Hollywood writers how to put a thrilling finish to the rash of 1930s football movies. It was a game that most of the Hollywood writers would not have dared to dream up. It was too unbelievable to be true.

"Andy Pilney had always been an exceptional player for our 1933 and '34 teams but had never been able to beat out triple-threat star Bill Shakespeare for the first-string post at left halfback. In practice Andy was so eager to get the big play, that he was inclined to stumble, and fumble the ball. But in the Navy game, a week before the Ohio State game, Andy came into his own with an incredible display of broken-field running that set up the two touchdowns that led to a 14–0 victory over the Midshipmen." Now it looked like Coach Layden had a secret weapon all set for the Buckeyes.

"Francis Schmidt had been selected as the new head coach of Ohio State," said Layden. "He came to State with a most impressive record as coach at Texas Christian University. Were he alive today he would be considered way ahead of his time. One of

In 1960 the nation's sportswriters voted the 1935 Notre Dame-Ohio State game "the greatest college game ever played." Notre Dame's starting backfield for that game included (left to right): Wally Fromhart, Fred Carideo, Mike Layden, and Bill Shakespeare.

his former players told me that Schmidt taught his team three hundred different plays running out of seven different formations. By today's standards that is pro teaching, and it would take a bunch of smart pros to learn it all. His Ohio State teams were marvels," said Layden.

"Schmidt brought an undefeated Ohio State team into the game, a team that was touted as the national champions. We had beaten Kansas, Carnegie Tech, Wisconsin, Pitt, and Navy. It was to be a battle between two unbeaten teams. The stage was set for what was billed as the 'game of the century,' and it turned out to be just that."

Parades and pep rallies had been going on all week on both campuses, and tickets were priced, when available, at more than $100.

When Notre Dame arrived in Columbus on the Friday before the game, they traveled to a secluded seminary outside of town in the hope of avoiding all the hysteria going on. But instead they found Buckeye fans by the thousands shouting, "Catholics, go home!"

The next day, November 2, Notre Dame met more than eighty-one thousand screaming fans who had jammed Ohio Stadium. Things got worse for the Irish as Ohio State quickly scored two touchdowns and jumped into a 13–0 lead by the half.

"I had never seen a Notre Dame offense so completely stopped," said Chicago Supreme Court Judge Roger Kiley, an All-America end for the Irish in 1919–21 and a former coach at Loyola and Auburn. "When Notre Dame attempted passes, the ball was intercepted several times and was converted into two touchdowns. We couldn't get a running play started against the Ohio line. It was even tough to get a kick off. One of Bill Shakespeare's kicks was so hurried that it turned into a line drive that hit the Ohio center, Jones, in the chest, bounced off, and Ohio recovered."

There was much speculation down through the years about what Rockne magic Coach Layden worked between halves, what kind of fiery pep talk he had made. Had he called on "the Gipper" again?

Halfback Mike Layden, who was superb in the second half, talked about that recently:

"Coach Layden was analytical. We didn't need to be roused up. That had been our trouble. He calmed us down."

"While we didn't have a 'Gipper story,' said Coach Layden, "we did have a Sullivan. Joe Sullivan, captain-elect of the 1935 team, had died early in the season. He was a marvelous player admired by every-

one, and we dedicated the game to Joe's memory. And so as calmly as possible under the circumstances, I tried to discuss what we hadn't done right and should correct, and then as a clincher I said calmly, 'Gaul's team will start the second half.'

"Frank Gaul quarterbacked the second team, and Pilney was the halfback with this unit this day. Needless to say, this announcement profoundly shocked my first-team players, and they looked as if they were going to go for my throat. They were white with anger."

Frank Gaul's team, charged with the responsibility of winning the ball game, charged onto the field like a human chain of firecrackers and held the bigger Ohio State eleven even for the third period.

"That third period turned into a punting duel as the fourth period began," Coach Layden continued. "Pilney caught an Ohio punt, then turned and twisted and dodged his way thirty-eight yards to the Ohio thirteen-yard line. Then he threw a superb arching pass to Frankie Gaul, who came down on the one-yard line. On the next play Steve Miller crashed over for the touchdown. Fromhart missed the extra point, and the score was now 13–6, Ohio State. The first team came into the game and Pilney tossed another pass to my brother Mike, who scored. But Fromhart missed the extra point again and we were behind, 13–12, with less than two minutes to play.

"Ohio State had the ball with ninety seconds left to play, and up in the stands my wife was sitting near Father O'Hara, who took this moment to console her, saying 'Don't worry, Edythe, Elmer and the boys have done a marvelous job.'

"To which she replied, 'That's easy for you to say. Your job doesn't depend on it.'

"Suddenly Ohio fumbled the ball," said Elmer Layden, "and our center, Hank Pojman, recovered on the forty-five-yard line. Then Pilney faded back for a pass, but finding no one open, started to run. Five tacklers had a shot at him but Andy twisted away from them, and then finally three big Ohio men crashed him out of bounds on Ohio's nineteen-yard line."

But something was wrong, very wrong.

Pilney wasn't getting up. On the last play he had been driven out of bounds by three big Ohio tacklers, and he was knocked unconscious. He was carried to the bench on a stretcher, and with half a minute remaining, Notre Dame's last hope seemed to be going with Andy.

Bill Shakespeare trotted out full of pep and ginger

Bill Shakespeare, one of Notre Dame's great triple-threat halfbacks, was an All-American in 1935.

to replace Pilney, and the crowd just knew that Bill would throw a pass in an attempt to score the winning touchdown.

Bill threw the pass—but it was straight at Dick Beltz, a Buckeye player. Beltz was so surprised he just dropped the ball, and the Irish had one more chance to score.

Shakespeare took the ball from center and faded back for another forward pass. Back, back, back he dodged and twisted, trying to get a look at a Notre Dame man who was free. He found Wayne Millner open and lobbed the ball into the end zone. Millner outjumped three Ohio State defenders to grab the ball and hug it to his chest, and Notre Dame had the winning touchdown.

The point after touchdown was missed, but who cared?

Notre Dame had come from behind in the last two periods of the game to beat one of the greatest college teams of all time in a game that is still considered the most exciting college football game of all time. Final score: Notre Dame 18, Ohio State 13.

Red Barber, broadcasting the game for CBS, told later how a Notre Dame spotter ran screeching from the broadcast booth after the final touchdown, and it took Red ten minutes to find out which Notre Dame player caught the winning pass.

Chances are, if you never heard the name of Jim McKenna before 1935, it's a fair bet that since then you've forgotten just where it was you did hear his name.

Jim was only a fourth-string quarterback for the 1935 Irish team. But Jim McKenna's persistence was for one brief, shining moment to overshadow all the Irish brilliance that made it the great team of the year.

A couple of days before the Ohio State-Notre Dame game, Jim stopped by the locker room at South Bend to see if he would make the trip with the rest of the squad. He looked carefully through the list of players, then looked again. *His name was not on the list.* Coach Layden wasn't counting on Jim for the big game.

Jim dug into his pockets, then borrowed a few dollars from a couple of friends—enough money to buy a ticket on the special students' train to Columbus. He arrived there about noon on the day of the game. The stadium was completely sold out. Only the scalpers had tickets, and Jim couldn't afford to part with a single dollar of his meager amount.

He told his story to the gate guard and asked if he could get in, but the guard had heard all the stories before and it looked as if Jim wouldn't even get into the stadium.

Suddenly Fate smiled on McKenna for, as he was about to turn away, he noticed one of the assistant managers coming through, his arms loaded with equipment. He let Jim carry part of the load and got him through the gates and into the locker room. Coach Layden smiled, greeted McKenna, and told him that as long as he'd come this far, he might as well suit up and sit on the bench.

Jim spent the agonizing moments of a sub sitting on the bench. Then, with time left for only the final play of the game, Coach Layden looked up and down the bench for a messenger to bring it in.

"McKenna," he snapped, "get in there and call that fifty-two pass play. You know the one I mean? Okay—don't forget to report to the ref."

The referee held up the game as McKenna rushed over to report. "McKenna for Puplis," he said. Then he bounced into the Irish backfield and in the shrill voice that only three hours earlier had been wrangling with a gate guard to let him into the stadium, Jim called the long, weak-side winning pass from Shakespeare to Wayne Millner.

McKenna rode home with the regulars.

A joyous crowd of more than thirty-four thousand fans welcomed the Irish stars the following week against Northwestern. But Coach Lynn Waldorf, in his first year at Northwestern, set himself for years to come at the coaching job by pulling off the surprise of the year as his Wildcats stunned the Irish with a 14–7 setback.

By defeating Notre Dame, Coach Waldorf was selected as coach of the year.

Andy Pilney's injury in the final minutes of the Ohio State thriller forced him to give up football. But Andy, who had been a great star with a .450 batting average over four years with the Irish baseball team, signed a contract with the old Boston Bees. Andy received what was then a whopping $15,000 bonus for signing. He appeared in a few games with the ball club in 1936, but despite an operation on his ailing knee, he was never able to maneuver around the diamond as he had prior to the injury. In 1937, after spending a season with Boston's Indianapolis farm club, he called it quits. He took a job with

Andy Pilney, Irish halfback, was one of the great stars of the 1935 Notre Dame–Ohio State game. Pilney later became head football coach at Tulane University.

Washington University's football team as backfield coach, then moved to Tulane University, where he eventually became head football coach.

Bill Shakespeare, who took over the halfback spot after Pilney's injury, was known, naturally, as "the Bard." Bill was elected team captain for the Army game in 1935. His opposing captain was "Monk" Meyer, Army's great 147-pound halfback, who was a terror on the football field.

"Army outplayed us through most of the game," said Coach Layden, "and provided another thrilling finish to a great game." They scored in the first period when Meyer twisted his way past several Irish tacklers and then tossed a fifty-yard pass to Whitey Grove on the five-yard line, and Grove smashed in for an Army touchdown. It was one of the most perfectly executed plays in the history of the Army–Notre Dame series.

Now the Irish took the ball on their own ten-yard line with three minutes left in the game. Shakespeare bulled his way for ten yards. Mike Layden made five more. Then it was Layden and Shakespeare and Wally Fromhart picking up yardage—five, eight, eleven yards as the Irish relentlessly pounded away at Army's line as the clock ran down.

Notre Dame had the ball on Army's thirty-seven-yard line, and the crowd was in a panic of excitement. On the next play Shakespeare tossed a long, long pass to Millner on the two-yard line, and Wayne leaped high into the air for the ball; but as he jumped for it, a Cadet grabbed his arm. There was a whistle on the play, and pass interference was called. Now Notre Dame had the ball on Army's two-yard line.

There were thirty seconds left to play when Coach Layden sent in his fourth-string fullback, Larry Danbom. Larry took the center snap and crashed through a hole between guard and tackle to score the tying touchdown. The score now was Notre Dame 6, Army 6.

The huge stadium at Notre Dame was hushed as the ball was snapped to Bill Shakespeare, holding the ball for Wally Fromhart's extra-point try. Wally booted the ball—and missed the point as the gun signaled the end of the game with the score 6–6.

Danbom was not one of the players selected to make the trip with the team. He "skivved"—an old Notre Dame trick of freeloading on the train with a group of students who have train tickets. He evaded the train conductor by hiding in a berth with a student who had a ticket. Larry arrived in New York late Saturday morning, taxied to Yankee Stadium, and put on his uniform, which had been with the rest of the squad equipment. He figured he would get dressed and have a good seat on the bench so that he could watch the game. Layden saw him on the bench, sent him in, and he made good.

There was a wild scramble for the game ball at the final gun. Shakespeare and Bill Shuler of Army tossed a coin to see who would win it. Shakespeare won the toss and Shuler walked away dejectedly. He was overtaken by a thin man in a gray business suit. It was Elmer Layden.

"Here," said Layden, "you take the ball. He handed Shuler the ball. "Take it with the compliments of Notre Dame because you guys deserve it."

"If there was any team we owed the greatest measure of fame to, it was Army," said Elmer Layden. "Dating back to the very first game in 1913, Army had been a fixture on our schedule and had helped us develop a relationship and reputation among fans all over the East. During the years I coached at Notre Dame, our game with Army in Yankee Stadium was always a sellout, a fact that brought joy to the heart of our business manager. Bill Wood coached Army during most of those years and together we came up with another idea: bringing our teams together for lunch the day before the game. Notre Dame and Army had student bodies from all over the country. Why couldn't they be of help to one another in later years? So each Friday before the game, we'd bring the two squads together for lunch to get acquainted and talk about everything but football. From this practice stemmed many a friendship among our boys after they had left school."

USC had a poor year in 1935 after opening the season with two victories—over Montana by a 9–0 score and then a 19–0 win over Amos Alonzo Stagg's College of the Pacific. Then the Trojans dropped four in a row but managed a 20–0 win over a weak Washington State eleven.

When the Trojans and Irish met at South Bend on November 23, things seemed to be looking up for the Trojans. They quickly jumped into a 6–0 lead as Notre Dame fullback Don Elser fumbled the ball and USC fullback Cliff Propst recovered. Three plays later, quarterback Dave Davis smashed over for the Trojans' first touchdown.

The half ended with Southern California in front by 6–0.

In the third period, quarterback Wally Fromhart, playing his last game for Notre Dame, made a brilliant catch of a pass from Bill Shakespeare to score for the Irish; the extra point made it 7–6. Moments later, after a series of plays, Fromhart passed forty-five yards to Wayne Millner for another Irish score, and it was 14–6 Notre Dame after the extra point. USC scored and converted the extra point and it was Notre Dame 14, USC 13.

In the fourth period, Fromhart, playing his greatest game for Notre Dame, intercepted a pass by quarterback Glenn Thompson and raced all the way to the Trojans' eight-yard line on a play that gained eighty-two yards. On the very next play Shakespeare raced in for the final score to give Notre Dame a 20–13 win and a 7–1–1 season.

After winning the first three games of the 1936 season in rather routine fashion over Carnegie Tech, Washington University of St. Louis, and Wisconsin, Layden brought his Irish eleven to Pittsburgh for what he hoped would be win number four. But Jock Sutherland, Pittsburgh's fine coach, had other ideas. He had no liking for Layden. They had been rather bitter rivals since Elmer's success at Duquesne had taken some of the shine off the Pitt Panthers and Sutherland, and Jock was out for revenge.

When Layden first took over as Notre Dame's coach, he had been told that he could not go off the campus to recruit players, and he lived that rule to the letter. Consequently, Notre Dame lost several outstanding players—players who wanted the head coach to talk personally with them in their homes. But Layden did not budge off campus. One of the great stars who wanted Layden to meet him in Pittsburgh was Marshall Goldberg. When Layden refused, Goldberg accepted a four-year scholarship at Pittsburgh and became one of Pitt's great stars.

On October 24, when the Irish invaded Pittsburgh, Goldberg and company were prepared to greet and beat Layden, and they defeated Notre Dame by a 26–0 score. It was the highest total any opponent would ever score against Layden during his seven years as head coach.

Ohio State traveled to South Bend the following week for the first time, to avenge the 18–13 defeat suffered the previous year, and more than 50,000 delirious fans turned out for the big game. Compared to the thrilling game waged between the two teams in 1935, the 1936 game was rather dull. Notre Dame defeated the Buckeyes 7–2 as Bunny McCormick, a whirling dervish of a halfback, and quarterback Andy Puplis starred in the Irish backfield, while linemen Captain John Lautar and Joe Kuharich were outstanding as Notre Dame squeaked through for the victory.

A hard-nosed Navy team held the Irish scoreless in their battle at Baltimore and just managed a field goal to defeat the Irish, 3–0. However, a week later, a fired-up Irish squad, with halfbacks Bunny Mc-Cormick and Bob Wilke running wild, easily defeated Army, 20–6. Wilke scored two touchdowns for Notre Dame, and the Irish would have scored several more times if not stopped by the great individual efforts of Army's Monk Meyer, Jim Craig, and Jack Ryan. Meyer was a threat all afternoon and scored Army's only touchdown, in the third period, when he took Jack McCarthy's punt and outran every Irish defender into the end zone. The fifty-five-yard sprint was the longest run of the day.

The tremendous spirit Monk Meyer displayed in football was later characteristic of his thirty-five-year Army career. He was a battalion commander in Luzon in the Philippines and was awarded the Distinguished Service Cross for conspicuous gallantry in action. He received this decoration, plus his Silver Star with an oak-leaf cluster, when he personally led an assault against a Japanese pillbox. He climbed the Japanese pillbox three times to set off a demolition charge. The third time he was blown backward some twenty-five feet. He was again decorated in the Vietnam war. General Monk Meyer looks back today on a remarkable career in football and in the armed forces of his country.

The Irish closed out the 1936 season by defeating Northwestern, 26–6, and playing to a 13–13 tie with USC to end the season with a record of six wins, two losses, and a tie.

Coach Layden should have had his finest year, the one in which the freshmen he had recruited were now seniors, in 1937. Among the starters were Joe Thesing, fullback; Bunny McCormick and Jack McCarthy, halfbacks; Andy Puplis, quarterback; and Joe Kuharich, Ed Beinor, Captain Joe Zwers, Len Skoglund, Joe Ruetz, Chick Sweeney, Alex Shellog, and Pat McCarty on the line.

The backs were smart, fast, and shifty; the line, tough and aggressive. The Irish opened the season with an easy 21–0 win over Drake, but Illinois held the Irish to a 0–0 tie. The next three opponents were Carnegie Tech, Navy, and Minnesota. Notre Dame won two of these games by the thinnest of margins—over Navy by a 9–7 score and over Minnesota by 7–6. Carnegie Tech, however, defeated the Irish, 9–7.

There had been only one point difference in the total scores of the Irish and their last four opponents. Yet Notre Dame had won two and tied one of the four, and that is a commentary on a typical Layden team: taut, tough, starless, and determined to win. But against another powerful Pitt team, with one of their greatest backfields that included Marshall Gold-

Led by Captain Joe Zwers; Joe Kuharich, a touch, 150-pound tackle; and All-American Ed Beinor, Elmer Layden's 1937 team won six games, lost two, and tied one.

berg, Dick Cassiano, Bob Chickerno, and Stebbins, the Irish were defeated by a tremendous last-period drive by Goldberg and his cohorts, who scored three touchdowns to defeat the Irish, 21–6.

"We closed out the year in grand style," said Layden about defeating Army, Northwestern, and USC for another 6–2–1 season.

In the Army game, Captain Harry Stella of Army, one of the Cadets' great linemen, greeted Notre Dame's All-American Ed Benoir as they opposed each other

(Below, right) Coach Layden gives tackle Tad Harvey last-minute instructions before sending him into the game against Minnesota in 1938.

(Below, left) In 1939 the Irish won six straight games with this starting backfield (left to right): Lou Zontini, Joe Thesing, Bob Saggau, and quarterback Steve Sitko.

(Bottom) Undefeated Notre Dame rolled into Los Angeles on December 3, 1938, and were upset by USC, 13–0. The photo shows No. 25, Mickey Anderson, a USC halfback, about to score as Irish players No. 75, Ed Beinor; No. 78, Paul Kell; and No. 51, Ed Longhi, try to stop him.

on the line. The two rivals had met previously when they played against each other in the Chicago South Suburban High School League.

"The greatest season I had in my seven years at Notre Dame," recalled Coach Layden, "was in 1938. We started the season by trimming Kansas, 52–0, then squeaked by Georgia Tech and Illinois by identical scores, 14–6. We beat Carnegie Tech, 7–0, then Army, Navy, and the Minnesota Gophers, and got a big scare from Northwestern as we escaped with a 9–7 win. Then we had two weeks to get ready for a Trojan team that had already clinched its first Rose Bowl appearance in six years.

(Below) This starting backfield for the Irish—(left to right), Steve Juzwik, Captain Milt Piepul, Bob Hargrave, and Bob Saggau—run through a few warm-up plays before the big game against Army in 1940.

(Bottom, left) In Hollywood to film the motion picture *The Spirit of Notre Dame* are (left to right): Elmer Layden, Adam Walsh, Frank Carideo, Jim Thorpe, Harry Stuhldreher, Don Miller, and Jim Crowley. (Lew Ayres starred as George Gipp in this picture, produced in 1938.)

(Bottom, right) A tense moment on the sidelines during the game against Iowa in 1939 as Coach Layden shouts some instructions to the players on the bench.

"We arrived in Los Angeles undefeated, and everyone was ready to concede the national championship to us. The L.A. Coliseum was jammed to capacity for the game—97,144 fans were on hand. And as the game began, we were put into an immediate hole. Two of our fine backs, Joe Thesing, fullback, and Benny Sheridan, were injured, and we never got inside the Trojans' fifteen-yard line.

"A key play in the game was when we had the ball on our forty-yard line, fourth down, six yards to go. I signaled for a punt. Bobby Saggau, our halfback, received the center pass, and instead of kicking the ball, Bob started to run. He almost broke away for a long gain, possibly a score. Unfortunately, he was tackled from behind and brought down. The Trojans took over and shortly thereafter scored as Ollie Day, USC's quarterback, passed for forty-eight yards to Al Kreuger for a touchdown. In the third period Mickey Anderson scored another USC touchdown, and that was the ball game. Nothing seemed to work for us that day."

Despite the loss to USC, Notre Dame, with an 8–1–0 record, was voted the number one team in the nation. Tennessee and TCU had 11–0 records, but neither had played opponents of the caliber faced by Notre Dame that year.

"My last two seasons coaching," said Layden, "1939 and '40, would have been great successes if we only played six games. Unfortunately, we played nine games and lost two of the last three games in each of those two years.

"The principal culprit both years was Iowa," said Layden. "Their coach was Eddie Anderson, the same Anderson who had captained the 1921 Notre Dame team. That 1921 team that lost only to Iowa, 10–7, included some of the greatest players to ever play for the Irish: Roger Kiley (later Judge Kiley, Chicago); Glenn Carberry (former Fordham coach and later a judge); Hunk Anderson, who became head coach at Notre Dame after Rockne died and later coached the Chicago Bears; Harry Nehre; Buck Shaw, who became head coach at North Carolina State, Nevada, and Santa Clara, and who was the first head coach at the Air Force Academy; Chet Grant, who later became an assistant coach to Elmer Layden and then became a sportswriter; Frank Thomas, the first Notre Dame player to coach at a major college, Alabama, for fifteen years; Tom Lieb, an assistant to Rockne; Johnny Mohardt; Dutch Bergman; Earl Walsh; Paul Castner; and Chet Wynne. All of the above have

passed on. Chet Grant and Paul Castner died within days of each other in 1986.

"In 1939," said Layden, "Eddie Anderson was in his first year as head coach at Iowa. The great star of the Hawkeyes was their marvelous running back, Nile Kinnick, who went on to win the Heisman Trophy and every award that season. Kinnick was not only a great runner; he was a terrific blocker and a great kicker. It was Kinnick's extra point that beat us 7–6 that year and Anderson was named 'Coach of the Year.'

"In 1940 we won six games in a row, including a smashing 61–0 rouser over one of our bitterest rivals, Carnegie Tech, and it looked good for an unbeaten season. Then perhaps we got a trifle overconfident and dropped games to Eddie Anderson's Iowa team by a 7–0 score and then blew one to Northwestern, 20–0.

"My last game as a Notre Dame coach was on December 7, 1940, against USC in the Los Angeles Coliseum, and in that final game, fullback Milt Piepul, captain of the team, scored all ten points as we beat USC, 10–6.

"At Notre Dame I wore two hats," said Layden, "one as coach, the other as athletic director. If Coach Layden thought his schedule was too tough, or he didn't get enough scholarships for football, he had only one fellow to blame: Athletic Director Layden.

"I was the last coach to wear both hats during my Notre Dame stay. Frank Leahy, my successor, tried it for several years, then turned the athletic directorship to Ed 'Moose' Krause, who continued in the job until 1981, when Gene Corrigan assumed the post.

"Most colleges today recognize that each post is a full-time job in itself. Coaching and being boss of a college athletic department have become far too complex and time-consuming for a single individual to handle both jobs well.

"It came as a shock to everybody connected with Notre Dame football when I announced my resignation on February 4, 1941. I resigned to become the first commissioner of the National Football League. My stated reasons for leaving were the usual ones: more money, a better life for my family. But behind these reasons was a matter of my contract.

"When I came to Notre Dame, I had a three-year contract. After two years, Father O'Hara ripped it up and gave me a new-five year contract. This expired in February 1941. As it neared expiration Father Hugh O'Donnell, president of the university, had the contract made out for one year. I immediately went to see him and complained that I had come under longer terms and expected a contract for longer than a year. He told me that he had decided to give nobody a contract for longer than a year. He then signed the contract and expected me to sign it. I told him I'd have to think about it.

"After giving the matter a great deal of thought, I decided to get some advice. The late Arch Ward was sports editor of the *Chicago Tribune* and very close to the Notre Dame scene. I had come to know Arch and respect him, and we talked about the problem.

"Our discussion ended with Arch suggesting that I should add my name to the list of people who at that time were in the running for the job as commissioner of the National Football League. Ward not only added my name to the list, but he and George Halas pushed me for the job, and on February 2, 1941, I signed a five-year contract at $20,000 a year, nearly double my Notre Dame salary.

"A day later I was back at Notre Dame and talked with Father O'Donnell. He tried to talk me out of my decision, but I had made up my mind, and that was that. I recommended Buck Shaw for the job. Buck had been a teammate of George Gipp's in 1920 and had gone on to become a very successful head coach at Santa Clara College. But my coaching career at Notre Dame was over."

Captain Milt Piepul scored all the points for Notre Dame as they defeated Southern California, 10–6, in 1940. A three-year star at fullback for the Irish, Piepul is currently the director of athletics for American International College, Springfield, Massachusetts.

CHAPTER 5

ENTER FRANK LEAHY

The phone rang in the hallway of the living room of the house at 820 Chestnut Street, Waban, Massachusetts. Floss Leahy was upstairs, tucking Sue and Flossie in bed. Frankie III was in his pajamas, ready for bed after a good-night huddle with his dad. The phone jangled again. Probably it was Charley O'Rourke, or maybe those folks from Norwalk, where he was due to speak at a banquet for Mickey Connolly. The man stepped into the hallway and picked up the phone.

"Is this Mr. Frank Leahy?"

"Yes, this is Frank Leahy."

"I have a person-to-person call for you," the operator replied, "from a Mr. Eddie Dunigan of Palm Beach, Florida. Go ahead Mr. Dunigan, here's your party."

"Hello, Frank. How are you?"

"Fine, Eddie, fine. Bet you haven't any good old northern snow down there in Palm Beach." The receiver shook in Leahy's hand. Why on earth would Eddie Dunigan be calling him from Florida, the same Dunigan who had followed his career at Notre Dame and had befriended him throughout his playing days?

"Frank, I know this much, so do you. The job of head coach and athletic director at Notre Dame is open, and they are talking about you for the job. Just had a call from there and they want to know when it will be convenient for you to meet with Father Frank Cavanaugh at the DeWitt Clinton Hotel in Albany. Can you make it? How about it? I'm not joking, Frank. They have four candidates for the job and you're first on the list. Now, when you get to the hotel, register under an assumed name. Father Frank will meet you there.

"This can't get into the papers. Notre Dame wants you but it can't look like they're stealing a coach, especially from another Catholic school. They're damn sensitive about that, Frank. Are you still there?"

Hours seemed to pass while the compactly built, reddish-haired young man stood there in the doorway. He simply could not believe his ears.

"Yes, I'm here, Edward. Tell me: Why do they want me? I want to know, why me? It's very important to me."

"They think you're the best man. They think you're another Rockne. Oh, they don't think you're just like Rock. They think you can be just as successful and in your own way. Frank, can you be there?"

"I have to speak at dinner for one of our lads tomorrow night, but I'll be in Albany the day after. I'll be there early Wednesday morning. Eddie, I cannot tell you how thrilled I am. I simply cannot believe that Notre Dame wants me. Tell them I am most excited and most interested."

"You'll meet with Father Frank, but you realize that Father O'Donnell, who is president of Notre Dame, has the final okay. But not a word to the papers, Frank," said Dunigan.

"They won't hear a peep from me, Eddie. So long and thanks."

Leahy placed the receiver down on the cradle, turned to his wife standing only a few feet away, holding their small baby and looking apprehensive.

"Another bill collector, Frank?"

"No, Floss. That was the grandest phone call of my life. They want to give me Rock's job. Me! They want to give me, Frank Leahy, that job. Oh, Floss, I can't stand the thought of leaving all these great lads at Boston College, but I am going back to South Bend. Rock's job . . . me. Can you imagine that?"

Thus began the homecoming, the long return to alma mater, the spiritual fulfillment of one man's life. Whatever else he might be, Frank Leahy was charged now with upholding an ideal. Never again would he be the same person. The torch had been passed.

Francis William Leahy had been one of Rockne's favorite pupils, not because of his native ability but because of a depth of character that was constantly reflected in his application to the fundamentals of the game, and above all his inherent courage and will to win. He had come up the hard way as a boy on the Dakota plains. He grew up in a small town, Winner, South Dakota. His father, a farmer and freighter, who went into the produce business, was a soft-spoken, profoundly polite man who was yet tough enough to become an outstanding professional wrestler good enough to wrestle the famous world champion Farmer Burns, and realistic enough to teach his four sons to box because he had learned that the soft answer did not always turn away wrath.

Young Frank Leahy became an expert cowboy; he could ride a horse, rope steers, and at age sixteen he and a friend shepherded 150 horses through the Dakota Badlands. As a boxer he was good enough to box four tough rounds with one of the leading professional fighters, Ace Hudkins, the Nebraska Wildcat, and Frank was so impressive in that bout that several promoters offered him a career as a pro fighter.

He was a halfback at Winner High under Earl Walsh, a Rockne product who played alongside the immortal George Gipp in 1919–20. In Frank's fourth year at Winner High School, Leahy captained the football, basketball, and baseball teams in a single season.

Frank's older brother Gene had been an outstanding football man at Creighton University, but he wanted Frank to play football at a major college. Frank went to Notre Dame, loved everything about the place, checked in at the registrar's office, was assigned to a room in a dormitory, and then went in search of Coach Rockne's chief aide, Tommy Mills. Mills had been Gene Leahy's coach at Creighton and had talked with Gene about Frank, and when Mills got the job with Rockne, one of the players he wanted was Frank Leahy. He greeted Frank, and the coach and youngster talked things over.

Mills and Leahy were chatting away in the gym when they were interrupted by a stocky, square-jawed man with thinning hair.

Frank didn't have to be introduced to know who the man was. He gulped as Mills introduced him.

He gasped as he shook hands and managed to stutter, "Hello, Coach Rockne."

"Leahy, eh? You're the boy from South Dakota. Earl Walsh wrote me all about you. President of your class. Captain of football, baseball, basketball in your last year. Pretty good."

This was the type of brisk first-meeting chat that most newcomers received from Rockne. He must have sensed the bashfulness of this boy from the West, however, for instead of going on, he paused, and the tone of his conversation warmed. This marvelous ability to put socially backward youths at ease was a characteristic Rockne trait. Within a couple of minutes he was able to make a self-conscious lad feel like an old member of the Notre Dame family.

"Feel a bit lost here, do you, Frank? Well, we'll have you over that in a couple of days. Don't forget, there are a lot of fellows here in the same boat. Wait until Tommy here gets you out on that practice field. Everything will be okay."

All the while he was talking to Leahy, Frank realized that his body was being subjected to a thorough scrutiny by the coach. Before he left them, Rock spoke to Mills: "U-m-m-m, he's got a pretty solid pair of legs, Tommy. Good football legs."

None of the three suspected then that this shy young man from the western plains would one day be chosen by Rockne himself as the player most likely to succeed as a big-time coach and that the youngster would bear out that choice by returning to his alma mater and then turning out some of Notre Dame's greatest teams.

Frank was not quite big enough for a Notre Dame tackle back in 1928, although he did make the traveling squad. In 1929, however, he won a first-string post but severely injured an arm and became only a part-time player. He was all set for the 1930 campaign, had worked tirelessly all summer long. Then, on the last play of the final practice session for the opening game of the season against Southern Methodist, he suffered one of those horrible knee injuries that all but concluded his active football career.

All through the 1930 season, injured knee and all, Frank assumed the post of an "assistant coach," at Rockne's suggestion, and when the season was over, Rockne took him to the Mayo Clinic, the knee was operated on, and then when he was able to navigate around the campus without a crutch, Rockne helped him get a coaching post with Tommy Mills at Georgetown University.

Jim Crowley (center), one of the famed Four Horsemen, was appointed head coach at Fordham in 1932. Jim immediately named an all-Notre Dame staff to assist him. Crowley appointed chief aide Frank Leahy (left), as his line coach. Ed Hunsinger, Earl Walsh, and Glenn Carberry (extreme right) were named assistants. Within a year Fordham became a nationally ranked team.

Jimmy Crowley brought his strong Michigan State team to play Georgetown and was so impressed with Leahy's work on the Georgetown line that he offered Frank a job with him at State in 1932. Leahy, of course, jumped at the opportunity to work with one of the Four Horsemen.

That year, 1932, Crowley brought his powerful Spartan team to New York to play Fordham at the Polo Grounds, and State defeated the very strong Ram eleven, 19–13. Fordham officials were so impressed with the smooth, efficient, and powerful Michigan State team that they invited Crowley and his entire staff at State to take over the coaching posts at Fordham. That meant Leahy, Glenn Carberry, Earl Walsh, and Ed Hunsinger.

Under Jim Crowley at Fordham, Frank Leahy as line coach molded a unit for the Rams' line that was to be recognized as one of the finest in the nation. In Leahy's six-year tenure at Fordham the team won thirty-five games, lost eight, and tied seven. One of the units in the line became known as the "the Seven Blocks of Granite," and one of the stars of that unit was a rough, tough guard whose name was Vincent Thomas Lombardi. The Fordham eleven in 1937 was

undefeated and brought national recognition to Leahy. He began to be in demand at clinics, coaching schools, radio appearances, and banquets, and he never turned down an opportunity to talk football.

Now several coaching offers came to Frank Leahy, but he sorted out the offers, waited for the right opportunity. It came in 1939 from Boston College, and Frank quickly signed a two-year contract that called for $12,000 per year.

In his first year Coach Leahy took the Eagles to the Cotton Bowl, where they lost a heartbreaker to Clemson, 6–3. In 1940, Boston College was undefeated and was awarded the Lambert Trophy as "the finest team in the East." And Boston College was invited to the Sugar Bowl, where they met and defeated a powerful Tennessee eleven, 19–13, in one of the most exciting games of the season.

When all of the sportswriters cast their votes, the Boston Eagles were declared national champions in the final tally in 1940.

Boston College gave Frank Leahy a new five-year contract, and for the first time in his life, he felt secure for at least the next five years.

At 3:15 P.M. on the afternoon of Saturday, February 15, 1941, just five days after he had signed his Boston College contract and was set for the next five years, Frank Leahy was summoned to the Notre Dame campus to talk to Father O'Donnell, the president of Notre Dame. At the end of his meeting, Leahy who had already secured his release from Boston College, signed a contract to become head coach at Notre Dame.

The Cinderella story was now complete.

FRANK LEAHY ADDRESSES HIS FIRST NOTRE DAME TEAM

The new coach, smiling, shaking his head in greeting, looked out at the members of the Notre Dame football team, all seated in front of him, like in a proper classroom. The student body invited to hear the new coach grouped itself around the perimeter of the athletic hall, waiting to hear from the coach.

Frank Leahy didn't seem much older, much different than he had ten years earlier when he left Notre Dame and went off to become an outstanding football coach. There were those present who already called him "another Rockne."

The coach began to speak.

"Men," he said, "men of Notre Dame, for you today, as well as your coaches, this is a momentous occasion for all of us as we begin to write yet another chapter in that great volume of history of Our Lady's University. This is a great challenge, a great quest. We are searching for perfection in football, the same way we seek perfection in everything we do at Notre Dame. The football team is a symbol of what the entire university should be like. Perfection is the goal in Our Lady's holy name.

"It was not too long ago that Frank Leahy was a student here. I was never accused of being too swift on my feet, but when it became obvious that somebody was coming out on the field to replace me, I somehow found myself getting quicker and quicker. I have nothing against tackles. They are essential to the welfare of the nation. I used to be one myself. If it weren't for ex-tackles, food stores in this nation would be much poorer.

"One month ago, I received the greatest surprise of my entire life. For it was just about four weeks ago that the authorities at the University of Notre Dame saw fit to ask me to coach the football team at my alma mater. My meager vocabulary lacks the words to describe fittingly the monumental feeling of joy which permeated my entire body and soul. As I rode out here on the train to sign my new contract, some writers said that 'we had a rendezvous with destiny!' I do not subscribe to that. I feel like I am coming home. Here I am at the university consecrated to Our Blessed Mother. I am home . . . home at last."

Frank Leahy with the Notre Dame president, the Reverend Hugh O'Donnell, signs a contract as the new head coach at Notre Dame on February 15, 1941.

Elmer Layden (in street clothes) turns the head coaching reins over to Frank Leahy in 1941.

FRANK LEAHY IN HIS FIRST YEAR REVOLUTIONIZES THE NOTRE DAME OFFENSE

It was cold and the snow came tumbling down so hard on the campus at South Bend that Angelo Bertelli could hardly see five yards in front of him as he trudged to Coach Leahy's office. It was February 15, 1941, and spring practice was about six weeks away.

"I wonder what in hell coach wants," said Bertelli to no one in particular. "He sounded very serious. What did I do?" Angelo shrugged his shoulders, climbed the stairs, and pushed into Leahy's small office.

It looked as if Leahy had slept there for several weeks. There were empty milk bottles scattered around, sandwich wrappers over the desk, and all over the place there were charts and graphs of football plays. Bertelli slumped down into a chair.

"Ah, Angelo," said Leahy. "Let's get right to the point. Now, this concerns you more than anyone on the team, lad," said the coach. "You are just about the finest passer in the nation, bar none. But you are also about the slowest-running tailback I have seen since I played that position at Winner High. Now, Angelo, how would you like a game situation where all you had to do was concentrate on your passing? You would simply receive the ball from center, from a position directly behind the center. Matter of fact, you will be standing so close to your center, you actually will have one hand on his rump before you receive the ball. Then you would simply hand the ball off to the other backs and let them worry about the running."

Bertelli nodded his head. "Coach, you're talking about the T formation. Like the Chicago Bears use, right?"

"Exactly," said Leahy. "What you will do in the T formation, which is what I am installing this spring, is take the direct snap from center, drop back for seven or eight yards, and then pass the ball, hand the ball off to other backs, or run with the ball yourself. There's not as much deception involved, but it is better suited to the times and to many trends we are developing. There will be roars of disapproval from old Notre Dame grads, who will think it sacrilegious to do away with the Rockne system, but I fully intend to do it.

"With the center able to block for you, you will have more blocking, and with perfect timing, more faking is possible. It also enables us to use man-for-man blocking, and the wear and tear on personnel is lessened because faking and deception are stressed more than naked power. This is it, Angelo, Notre Dame's future."

Bertelli smiled. "Then I handle the ball on every play, right?"

"Every play, Angelo."

"How many plays do I have to memorize next month?"

"About eighty to a hundred," said Leahy. "But I do know that you'll be a cinch with this new offense. A cinch."

By the time the fall practice sessions began, all of the Irish coaches—Ed McKeever, Joe McArdle, John Druze, and Leahy—had examined every inch of the film the Chicago Bears had; discussed and practiced the T formation with each other, with every member of the team, and with the Bears' great quarterback Sid Luckman, who was a past master of the offense.

"No player I've ever had worked harder to improve than Angelo Bertelli," said Leahy.

Coach Leahy gives some last-minute instructions to his team before taking the field against Arizona in the opening game of the 1941 season.

Meanwhile McKeever was spending hour after hour working with Bertelli. Angelo was being primed for the quarterback spot, but he would have to beat out the veteran Dippy Evans.

Bertelli was from West Springfield, Massachussetts, and attended Cathedral High School there, where he played football, hockey, and baseball. He loved hockey, and as a youngster, he sharpened skates, cleaned the uniforms, and stayed late with the janitor of the Springfield professional team. The players liked Angelo and taught him the tricks of the game. In time he became one of the greatest high-school hockey players in the state. He was on the fourth football team in high school until the football coach, Billy Wise, saw him fire a pass with a simple flick of his wrist. Wise, who played for Holy Cross when they beat Harvard in 1925 and 1926, knew he had a natural forward-passing ace in Angelo.

Billy showed Angelo how to feint—how to look one way, throw another—and then started Angelo at halfback, and he responded by leading Cathedral to eight consecutive victories and an unbeaten season. And for his fine play Angelo was awarded a scholarship to Notre Dame.

At Notre Dame during the late summer Angelo worked out with the varsity right end, George Murphy, and the two players soon developed a passing combination that later in the season became the envy of every coach in the nation. It was like Rockne and Dorais of yesteryear.

September 27, 1941, was the day on which Frank Leahy made his debut as head coach of his alma mater, and against the University of Arizona Wildcats, led by Mike Casteel, Leahy's old colleague at Michigan State. Casteel had so inspired his team that they played Notre Dame practically even. At the half Notre Dame led by only 12–7.

There was one tactical achievement in that game that most football people tend to forget or ignore: Frank Leahy invented pass blocking for his quarterbacks. When Bertelli took the snap from center but never dropped back more than seven yards, his linemen would fall back to protect him in what the Notre Dame coaches described as "a pocket."

So in the second half, Bertelli got unbelievable protection in the pocket and filled the air with his passes. Angelo threw the ball fourteen times, completed eleven, and the Irish scored six touchdowns to romp over Arizona by a 38–7 margin.

When Leahy and his assistants reached their hotel rooms at the Oliver Hotel after the Arizona game, Frank was swamped with congratulations for his protection of Bertelli and was questioned about this new defensive posture by sportswriters and alumni. The idea soon was adapted by coaches around the country.

The following week, rain and a muddy field hampered the Irish backs against Indiana. But Dippy Evans slashed and slid his way through the big Hoosier line and tore the Indiana boys apart with his driving bucks into the line. For the afternoon's work,

Dippy came away with three touchdowns to lead the Irish to a 19–6 win.

Notre Dame stung Georgia Tech the following week as Leahy came up with a stunning, unique 4–3–1–2–1 defense against the razzle-dazzle Georgia offense, and the new defense worked like a charm, holding Tech scoreless as Bertelli again flooded the air with passes for a 20–0 win.

Carnegie Tech was easily beaten, 16–0; then the Fighting Illini were overrun as the Irish rolled on to a 49–14 victory.

Earl "Red" Blaik of Army had been coaching football much longer than Leahy. Though he earned his letter "A" in football, baseball, and basketball, Red had never played against the Irish. In 1918, his first year on the team, there was no game, and in 1919, the year that Walter Camp named Red on his All-American second-team, Red was ill with the flu and missed playing against George Gipp. As the football coach at Dartmouth his teams went through 21 games undefeated in 1937 and 1938, and he was recognized as one of the finest coaches in the nation. Army football under Blaik quickly regained its premier position in college football circles.

There were more than seventy-five thousand fans at Yankee Stadium in a deluge of rain that turned the field into a quagmire as Army faced Notre Dame in a battle that saw Bertelli and Dippy Evans at their best. But Army, led by Henry Mazur and a great tackle, Robin Olds, kept the Irish from scoring, and the game ended with neither team having much of an edge as time ran out. The final score was a 0–0 tie.

Hank Mazur had been one of Leahy's prize players at Boston College as a freshman and had accepted an appointment to West Point. Now as an Army halfback, it was Mazur's tremendous kicking that kept the Irish from scoring. Time after time, Mazur would boot the waterlogged ball fifty or sixty yards to keep the Irish at bay.

Undefeated Navy, the strongest team in the East, was a topheavy favorite when Notre Dame traveled to Baltimore in quest of its sixth victory of the season, before some sixty-two thousand fans. The two undefeated teams battled each other right down to the very last minute of play. This was easily the most thrilling Notre Dame-Navy clash in the fourteen years of their series. And the huge crowd saw Angelo Bertelli at his best. A substitute end, Jack Barry (now a judge in Chicago), was one of the heroes of the contest, which was fitting, for his father had been one of the great stars of the Knute Rockne era and an All-American end.

Notre Dame, with Bertelli and Dippy Evans sparking the offense, struck quickly and savagely and scored three touchdowns. But Navy came back to score twice and smashed down to the Irish 4-yard line but were stopped by a determined Irish line as the game ended with Notre Dame on top for its sixth victory in seven games.

Northwestern had one of the nation's greatest halfbacks in Bill DeCorrevont, and his great running kept the Wildcats in the game until the last minute. Bertelli flashed two bullet passes to Matt Bolger, who went over for a touchdown. Steve Juzwik added the extra point for a 7–0 lead. Northwestern scored as DeCorrevont took off for some nifty runs, but Juzwik blocked the extra-point try and the Irish went off the field with a 7–6 triumph.

Following the Northwestern game the Notre Dame squad appeared tired and listless as they began preparation for the final game of the season, against USC. Coach Leahy gave them a day off, but on Wednesday they appeared even more lifeless, and Leahy, quick to diagnose the situation canceled practice until Friday afternoon. Meanwhile, they could see a movie, take a ride, or do anything but play ball.

A giant pep rally was held on the South Bend campus the night before the USC game, and after the rally Dippy Evans, who had played some of his finest football, injured his knee horsing around while chasing Bill Reardon, a substitute guard. It seems that Reardon had planted a bucket of water above the ledge of Evans's door and then knocked on the door. Dippy opened the door and the bucket of water poured over his head. Naturally, he chased Reardon, but Dippy slipped and fell on his knee. It was cut and swollen, but Scrap Iron Young, Notre Dame's fine trainer, worked on the injured leg all night. The next day he fitted Dippy with a special brace, and Evans started against USC.

No mention of the injured knee was made to Leahy, but the fact remains that Evans played the greatest sixty minutes of his career as the Irish and Trojans battled. Each team scored three touchdowns, but Steve Juzwik's two extra-point conversions were the margin of victory, by 20–18. Juzwik, Bob Dove, Bernie Crimmons, Harry Wright, and Bertelli all came through with remarkable performances to give their young head coach his first undefeated season at Notre Dame.

It was Notre Dame's first unbeaten year since

Rockne's last team, in 1930. And there wasn't a reporter in the Irish dressing room after the game who wasn't mindful of the fact that Leahy had been associated with the 1930 squad.

'Weren't you sort of an unofficial assistant coach that last year, Frank?" asked a sportswriter for the *Chicago Tribune.*

"Coach Rockne was most gracious to me my senior year," said Leahy. "But I was not an assistant coach. Rock permitted me to observe members of the coaching staff at work, and it is true that some of the players did ask for my advice, which I was most proud to give them. But it would be pretentious of me to take much credit for the success of the 1930 team."

In three years as a head coach, two with Boston College, one at Notre Dame, Leahy had lost exactly two games and tied one. His sad face with the snap-brim hat decorated nearly every sports page in the country. And they were already telling anecdotes about him, as if he'd been a prominent coach for twenty years. His family, too, was getting large enough for the press services to group around the Christmas tree or to pose on their knees saying the rosary.

On the Tuesday after he had taken his first Notre Dame team to an unbeaten season, he read the headlines of a news series in the *Chicago Times* by sportswriter Ray Hunt: "The Story of Frank Leahy—He's Another Rockne."

Everybody in South Bend, Hunt explained, was comparing Leahy with their dead hero Rockne.

"They said there would never be another Rockne," said Hunt. "But when Leahy's Irish squad ran over Arizona, Indiana, Georgia Tech, and Illinois, they began to change their song. They forgave the 0–0 tie with Army, and the New Rockne chant became louder and louder as the Irish sank Navy and defeated Northwestern and USC.

"After the final game there were alumni in the dressing room singing and shouting, 'Our search for another Rockne has ended. We've got his prize pupil.' There are some differences, of course. Leahy has many of Rockne's mannerisms. He folds his arms during conversations much like Rock did. He's quick on repartee, too. And, like Rockne, he is a spellbinding speaker. His face sets occasionally like Rock's. And for want of a better word, he has a certain quality about him that can only be described as 'the Rockne touch.' Rock was a humorous man with a serious side. Leahy is a somber individual with a sense of humor beneath his gloom.

"A young man has come to replace the Old Master."

"OOH! THAT LAD CREIGHTON MILLER!"

Notre Dame fans and alumni across the nation, greatly enthused over the superb showing of the 1941 team, expected another championship season in 1942.

But they were soon disappointed as injuries to key players such as Dippy Evans, vital in the new offense, and Creighton Miller, who had bruised a bone in his foot and was expected to be out of action for six weeks or more, created havoc with the new system.

There were other injuries as the Irish entrained for Madison, Wisconsin, for a game on September 26 with one of the best teams Wisconsin had ever produced. Coached by one of Notre Dame's finest sons, Harry Stuhldreher, one of the immortal Four Horsemen, the Badgers created havoc with the new Irish offense to hold Notre Dame to a 7–7 tie.

Notre Dame's new offense at times showed great power, but four fumbles and all-around ragged play indicated to Leahy and his aides that the "T" was far from being a polished offensive maneuver, and in practice Leahy worked his players to a frazzle as they prepared for their first home game, this against an-

other powerhouse eleven, the Yellow Jackets of Georgia Tech.

But Bill Alexander's charges, still smarting from a 20–0 defeat by the Irish in 1941, took charge of the game and proceeded to administer a stunning 13–6 beating.

After the game Leahy drove home, parked the car, and told his wife, Flo, that he was ill and had to go to bed. He was so weak that Father John Cavanaugh, vice-president in charge of athletics, ordered him to forget football for a few weeks and to go the Mayo Clinic in Rochester, Minnesota, for complete bed rest.

Ed McKeever took charge of the team, quickly noting that the next game, against Stanford, would be a tough one, for the Indians were coached by another former Rockne great, Marchy Schwartz, and Marchy was out for a victory.

But McKeever, with telephonic orders from Leahy, whipped his team to a fighting frenzy and they easily defeated the strong Stanford eleven by a 27–0 score.

The following week the Irish, under McKeever's direction and Bertelli's ever-improving passing game, blasted a tough Iowa Pre-Flight team, 28–0. On October 24, at Champaign, Illinois was beaten, 21–14, in a game that saw the lead change three times.

All this happened while Leahy was in constant telephonic communications with McKeever. Nor had the team forgotten Leahy. After the victory over the Seahawks, George Murphy, a great Irish end and captain of the team, phoned Leahy and told him that the game ball with autographs of every player was on its way to the hospital.

Leahy was released from the Mayo Clinic on the Wednesday prior to the game with Navy and by the next day was out on the field, observing practice and getting last-minute details from McKeever.

The team entrained for the Navy game in Cleveland on Friday, and as time for the game approached on Saturday, the field was like a swamp of mud, rain, and sleet, everywhere. Despite the poorest field conditions in memory, the Irish put together a quick

touchdown and a field goal while holding Navy scoreless to come home to South Bend with a 9–0 win.

The following week, once again on the road, Notre Dame traveled to Yankee Stadium for the "big game" against a strong Army team. The game was a dreary one until the fourth period, when Bertelli passed for a short gain. Then Gerry Cowhig smashed through for a first down at Army's thirty-four yard line. Bertelli with a beautiful fake, handed off to Dick Creevy, who ducked through an opening in the line, slipped by a couple of Army tacklers, and raced across the goal line as Hank Mazur slammed him to the ground. But Mazur's tackle was too late and it was an Irish touchdown. Bertelli's kick was good, and Notre Dame took a 7–0 lead over Army.

Late in the period, Bobby Livingstone intercepted Carl Anderson's pass and ran the ball to the Irish twenty-yard line before a host of Army tacklers brought him down. On the next several plays, Corwin Clatt and Creighton Miller took turns pounding the Cadet line as they advanced to the Army forty-seven-yard

"Creighton Miller is the greatest back I've ever coached," said Leahy in 1970. An All-American in 1943, Miller was

named to the National Football Foundation Hall of Fame in 1976.

line. Then Tom Miller, Creighton's older brother, picked up seven yards. Another smash into the line by Tom Miller was stopped on the Army twenty-six.

Now there was less than one minute to play as Bertelli faded back to pass. His target was Creighton Miller, but Angelo's long pass was deflected by Army's Dale Hall and then once more by Hennessey of Army, but the ball magically fell right into the hands of George Murphy, who just stepped over the goal line, grinning like a Cheshire cat.

The kick for the extra point was blocked, and the game ended with Notre Dame in front of Army, 13–0.

This victory was a personal triumph for Frank Leahy. He had been roundly roasted by Irish fans and some sportswriters for abandoning the traditional Notre Dame shift for the "T," and some of his critics had said, "I told you so," after a tie and a defeat at the opening of the season. But if a Fighting Irish coach can defeat Army, then he knows he has some champions. Those who raised the roof about the adoption of the new system were a bit shortsighted. They were living in the past, and Leahy answered them all when he said, "Rockne himself was a great changer. He was always experimenting with his system, adding, changing, improving. If he were alive today, I doubt whether he'd be using the tactics that featured his 1929 and 1930 attacks. He'd be utilizing the newest and latest streamlined offense."

"Notre Dame football," said Leahy, "has always reflected the latest development, and it has introduced a few. The first indoor football game was played by an Irish team against Chicago in 1892; the first place-kick from scrimmage was made by a Notre Dame team."

November 14, 1942, saw a classic battle against an ancient rival as the Irish faced the Michigan Wolverines and more than fifty-four thousand frantic fans jammed every inch of Rockne Memorial Stadium at South Bend to see the battle between two foes who had not met on the gridiron since 1908, when Notre Dame, led by Captain "Red" Miller, lost to Michigan, 12–6.

Red Miller was on the sidelines to see his sons Tom and Creighton in action. So were the governors of Michigan and Indiana, and they witnessed one of the finest offensive exhibitions ever seen in the Midwest, by both elevens.

With the Miller brothers running wild, picking up gains of ten or fifteen yards on almost every play, the Irish charged downfield to the Michigan thirty-yard

line. Here Bertelli faked a pass to Creighton Miller, turned, and then pitched the ball to Bob Dove for a Notre Dame score. The kick was good, and it was 7–0. Michigan came right back, with Tom Kuzma and Don Robinson slicing the Irish line for huge gains; Robinson finally went over for the touchdown. The kick was good, and it was a 7–7 ball game.

Creighton Miller then took over the brunt of the offense and on successive carries drove the ball to midfield. Jim Mello, the Irish fullback, then cracked the Michigan line for fifteen yards, and on the next play Creighton Miller danced his way through the entire Wolverine line for thirty-five yards and a spectacular touchdown to give the Irish a 14–7 lead. But once again the Wolverines came back with a sparkling attack and another touchdown. The point was missed, and it was Notre Dame 14, Michigan 13.

On the old Statue of Liberty play, Bertelli faded back to pass and cocked his arm to throw the pass, but Creighton Miller spun around from his halfback post, took the ball out of Bertelli's outstretched hand, and raced fifty-four yards for another spectacular score and Notre Dame was out in front, 20–13.

But the Wolverines took over and quickly ran up nineteen unanswered point to win a seesaw struggle, 32–20, in one of the most exciting games of the year.

In the next two games, against Northwestern and Southern California, there was no doubt about the T formation coming into its own as the Irish battled a fine Northwestern team up and down the gridiron before coming away with a tremendous 27–20 win.

The Southern California game the following week was one of the most bitter in the long series between the teams as Bertelli and Creighton Miller sparked the offense to a 7–0 lead in the first period. Bertelli tossed a forty-eight-yard pass to Creighton Miller, who made a one-handed, over-the-shoulder catch and sprinted across for the score. In the second period, Angelo passed to Bob Livingstone who faked USC back Bob Musick out of position and rambled in for the second Irish score. The game ended with Notre Dame in front, 13–0, in one of the wildest, melee-filled college games of the year. When the gun sounded to end the battle, some ninety-four thousand fans poured onto the field at the Los Angeles Coliseum to continue battling each other.

On December 5, the Irish tangled with the Great Lakes Navy team composed of enlisted men and draftees, men who had played with every major college in the land. The Great Lakes team was actually an "All-Star" team, and the Sailors, who had not allowed a single point against them in their past six games, quickly took a 13–0 lead. Sparked by Minnesota All-American Bruce Smith, Great Lakes seemed unstoppable in the first half.

In the third period, Bertelli faked to Livingstone, then handed off to Cornie Clatt, who smashed inside tackle and with perfect blocking raced into the clear for a sensational eighty-two-yard dash and an Irish touchdown. Bertelli missed the extra point, and it was 13–6 Great Lakes.

After receiving a Great Lakes punt on the Notre Dame thirty-two-yard line, Bertelli handed the ball off to Creighton Miller, who cracked through the Sailors' line, reversed his field, and sped downfield for a spectacular sixty-eight-yard dash and an Irish touchdown. Johnny Creevey kicked the extra point, and the game ended in a 13–13 tie. Bertelli, Bob Dove, and Harry Wright were picked on a number of All-American teams as Notre Dame finished the season with a 7–2–2 record.

"If there ever was a lad whose memory pleases me the most," said Frank Leahy, "I would have to look back to that marvelous team of 1943 and select one player: Creighton Miller. Ooh! There was a young man of great impishness.

"Ah, that Creighton was high-spirited, and he had an unpredictable sense of humor. Once as a sophomore he bet his roommate that he could remove forty pennants from the wall without touching one of the tacks. He got most of the lower ones by throwing his sneakers at them. But the ones on top were more difficult. So he took a run up the wall and kicked the remaining pennants right off it. He won his bet, but the wall collapsed. That bit of mischief kept him out of practice for a few days.

"Creighton was a magnificent running back," said Leahy. "If he'd been born twenty-five years later he'd be worth at least $500,000 a year with an NFL team. He did incredible things for us in 1943, when we won the national championship and he was the main cog in the backfield."

In the opening game of the 1943 season, a tough Pitt team was easily defeated, 41–0, as Bertelli, Miller, and company ran the Panthers into the turf. A week later Georgia Tech, a power down South, was ambushed as Miller scored three times and Bertelli passed

and passed the Tech team dizzy as the Irish ran up a 55–13 final margin.

A week later, Creighton Miller and Angelo Bertelli wrecked mighty Michigan, 35–12, before a screaming crowd of more than eighty-six thousand fans at Ann Arbor.

On the first play from scrimmage, Miller took a hand-off from Bertelli, burst through tackle, reversed his field, and dashed sixty-six yards for a touchdown. Three minutes later, with the crowd still in a frenzy of excitement, Miller dashed fifty-eight yards for another score; however, the play was called back by an official. But Creighton was not to be denied that day; he was simply unstoppable. All told, he carried the ball ten times for 159 yards and scored two touchdowns in one of the greatest individual performances ever seen at Ann Arbor.

"As you might imagine," said Miller, "there were some great holes that I ran through—after all I had some great players up front, guys like Paul Limont and Johnny Yonaker at the ends, Jim White and Ziggy Czarobski at tackle, Captain Pat Filley and John Perko at guard, Herb Coleman at center, and in the backfield Jim Mello and Julie Rykovich were all outstanding. I remember that 1943 game so vividly," said Miller. "In the third period I kept looking up at the clock and there were about five minutes to play. I felt tired—real tired, and we were winning so easily, but I had been carrying the ball and running like hell and I was wishing the game was over. Never felt so tired in my life. We beat a very good team in Michigan," said Miller.

Just one week later, Miller, Bertelli, and Mello ran rings around Wisconsin, routing the Badgers by a 50–0 score. Then, like a well-oiled machine, the Irish trampled Illinois, 47–0, and shattered Navy, 33–6. And once again Irish fans across the nation were shouting hosannas for their young coach and his unbeaten team as they rolled into New York's Yankee Stadium for their annual bitter battle against Army.

After a brilliant six games, Angelo Bertelli left the team to enter the Marines, and suddenly eighteen-year-old Johnny Lujack found himself the starting quarterback in one of the biggest games of his life, before a crowd of more than seventy-five thousand hysterical fans.

THE KID FROM CONNELLSVILLE

Ever since his kid days, Johnny Lujack had been accustomed to winning. He grew up in the small town of Connellsville, Pennsylvania—population seventeen thousand. The fourth child in a family of six and the youngest of four boys, he was exposed to all kinds of sports activities and games from babyhood. His brothers—Val, Allie, and Stan—were good high-school athletes, and Allie made a big name for himself as an end at Georgetown University. John, who was named after his father, a boilermaker on the Pittsburgh and Lake Erie Railroad, had to follow a rugged path when he became the fourth Lujack to play for the local high school. But his brothers saw to it that John knew something about the major sports before he reported to the coach.

John was only thirteen years old and a skinny 130-pounder when he got his first taste of football at Cameron Junior High. He made the varsity team at Connellsville High as a sophomore in 1939. And it's doubtful if they will ever forget his sensational play. He was a ball of fire on the gridiron for three years and won letters in basketball and track. He didn't play high-school baseball, but his performance as an infielder was so startling with a local amateur team that the Pittsburgh Pirates scouted him and offered him a contract, which he promptly turned down—to go to college.

There was never any question about Johnny going to college.

"I was lucky," he recalled recently. "Dad was doing much better after all those years on the railroad, and I didn't feel it was necessary for me to get a job right away."

The scholarship offers poured in, and word got around of his dazzling football achievements, such as intercepting two passes against Mount Pleasant High and running each back for seventy yards and a touchdown. At one time fifty-five schools proffered him packages, and he had been offered an appointment to West Point if he wanted it.

Johnny didn't want to go to West Point. He didn't even look at any of the college offers. All he had ever wanted in his life was to go Notre Dame. It was his dream. He had avidly followed the exploits of the

An All-American in 1946 and 1947 and a Heisman Trophy winner in 1947, Johnny Lujack was voted the "greatest Notre Dame back in the past fifty years" by the nation's sportswriters in a 1965 poll.

Notre Dame's "board of strategy"—(left to right), John Lujack, Coach Leahy, and Captain Pat Filley—discuss last-minute tactics before the 1943 Army game.

Fighting Irish. He knew about Knute Rockne, Jesse Harper, the Four Horsemen, and immortal George Gipp, and Hunk Anderson, Jack Chevigny, Joe Savoldi, and Marchy Schwartz, and had seen the Knute Rockne motion picture until he knew every speaking part almost verbatim.

At his high-school graduation exercises, Johnny, the president of the graduating class as well as the school's premier athlete, was lauded by Congressman Buell Snyder, who startled and surprised the crowded spectators by announcing that he had appointed Johnny to West Point.

In a small town like Connellsville, it was a tremendous thing to be singled out for such a great honor, and it stamped him indelibly as one destined to make his mark in the world. And the people applauded and screamed for Johnny.

In the middle of that excitement, Lujack walked to center stage and said with humility, "I'm very happy and thankful for the honor you have bestowed on me. But my heart has always been at Notre Dame. I want to complete my education there and, if I can, play on the football team."

How Johnny Lujack fulfilled that ambition is one of the brightest chapters in the history of intercollegiate football. He became one of the superstars, a giant to take his place alongside the fabulous ones of the past: Red Grange, Jim Thorpe, Chris Cagle, Ernie Nevers, Sammy Baugh, Sid Luckman, Tom Harmon, Glenn Davis, Doc Blanchard.

There have been some magnificent football players at Notre Dame since Lou Salmon, Red Miller, Gus Dorais, and George Gipp, but none greater nor more versatile than the "kid from Connellsville, PA."

At South Bend, an Irish assistant coach, Bob Snyder, took one look at Lujack on the field and loved what he saw. Snyder spent extra hours working with John, teaching him the little intricacies—pinpoint passing, footwork, the faking motions in the backfield, so necessary for the success of the T-formation quarterback. John spent all summer between his freshman and sophomore years working at South Bend, practicing, practicing all the time. What impressed the Irish coaches aside from his offensive abilities was his great defensive ability. The first time out on Cartier Field, John tackled halfback Bill Early so hard in the open field that he lost four front teeth.

Notre Dame fans still remember the way he stepped into Angelo Bertelli's shoes for the big Army game in 1943.

And all the Connellsville kid did before the huge crowd was throw two touchdown passes, score another himself on a quarterback sneak, and call plays with all the skill and daring of Frank Leahy himself. Overnight Lujack propelled himself into the spotlight of college football by his spectacular play against Army as the Irish defeated the Cadets, 26–0. And overnight Lujack found himself the subject of cover stories in all the major magazines of the period.

The following week, against Northwestern, Lujack paced the Irish to their eighth consecutive victory with an easy 25–6 win. Then, on November 20, in a crucial game against the All-Star Iowa Pre-Flight team, vying with the Irish for the number one spot in college football, the Seahawks took an early 7–0 lead and held it for three periods despite the efforts of Lujack and halfback Creighton Miller, who ripped the Seahawks line for big gains all afternoon. The Seahawks scored again in the final period to go ahead, 13–7, but Miller and Jim Mello tore through and around them, and the Irish finally hit paydirt as Miller drove over to make the score 13–13. Fred Earley, called on to make that all-important kick, was equal to the task, and the Irish won a hard-fought battle, 14–13.

The victory over the All-Star Seahawks ran the Notre Dame string to nine straight and left no doubt in the minds of the experts that the Irish were headed for an undefeated season. But there was the final game, against a super Great Lakes Navy team on November 27.

Notre Dame scored early in the game as Miller and Lujack carried the brunt of the attack to the Great Lakes five-yard line, where Lujack cracked off tackle for the first score. Then the Great Lakes team charged out in the third period and put together a seventy-one-yard gain for a touchdown. But the Irish still led, 7–6. Halfback Dewey Proctor, who had carried the brunt of the Great Lakes attack, broke off-tackle and sprinted fifty-one yards for a touchdown. Steve Juzwik missed the extra point, and it was 12–7, Great Lakes at the half. There was no scoring in the third period. But late in the final quarter, Notre Dame put on a furious effort led by Creighton Miller and Jim Mello. In twenty plays it was Miller and Mello grinding out the yards as they marched slowly but surely to the Great Lakes goal line, and finally the Irish scored. Earley's kick for the extra point gave Notre Dame a 14–12 edge.

With sixty-six seconds to go in the game, Steve Lach, a former Duke star, passed to Pirkey for a gain. Then Lack passed to Anderson, who took the ball

When Coach Leahy decided to install the T formation in the Notre Dame offense in 1941, he called on Chicago Bears' ace quarterback Sid Luckman. Sid responded, spending hours teaching John Lujack the intricacies of the "T."

Coach Leahy's first Notre Dame team, in 1941, swept through to an undefeated season.

But it wasn't until years later, in 1972, that Miller and Coach Frank Leahy cemented a great friendship.

Creighton Miller, like his great predecessor George Gipp, was a reluctant hero who practiced when he felt like it, and his independent attitude irritated Leahy. Creighton's distaste for spring practice remains unparalleled in Notre Dame football.

"Football is a fall and winter sport," Miller said. "In the spring I like to play golf with Lujack and go over to St. Mary's College and visit with the girls. Coach got very annoyed with me and for a very long while I wasn't too popular with him."

Miller claims to this day that in four years at Notre Dame, he did not practice a single day during the spring practice sessions.

Upon graduation, Miller attended Yale University to take his law degree and to coach football there. He was drafted in the first round by the Giants of the

over his shoulder while running at full speed and fell across the goal line for a stunning 19–14 win over the Irish.

Joe Boland, a great Irish tackle in 1924, '25, and '26, was broadcasting the game over a radio network. He actually sobbed into his mike over the loss to Great Lakes. Yet the 9–1 campaign provided Leahy with his second national championship.

The following day came news from the wire services that the great Angelo Bertelli, who left the team in midseason for the Marines, had been named the winner of the Heisman Trophy. Bertelli was the first Notre Dame player to be thus acclaimed.

Creighton Miller won fourth place in the Heisman vote and was named to the All-America team as he scored thirteen touchdowns and ran for 911 yards. It was the second-best single-season rushing mark by an Irish back until 1976, when Al Hunter rushed for 1,058 yards.

NFL but decided to stay at Yale to finish his law courses and receive his degree.

Miller became the first employee of the Cleveland Browns as a chief scout and assistant and was instrumental in selecting Paul Brown as their first head coach. In 1956 Miller became the first legal counsel for the National Football League Players' Association and it was in his office in Cleveland that the Players' Association's first meeting was held.

An outstanding lawyer in Cleveland with such clients as George Steinbrenner, the Professional Bowlers' Association, and numerous others, Miller was inducted into the college football Hall of Fame in 1976 and is actively involved in the activities of the Notre Dame Monogram Club along with his great friend Johnny Lujack.

A TEXAN NAMED MCKEEVER

In the summer of 1938 Frank Leahy conducted a series of coaching clinics at various schools around the country. At a clinic at Texas Tech, Frank was particularly impressed with a series of lectures on backfield play given by a young assistant there, Ed McKeever. Frank asked Pete Cawthon, Texas Tech's head coach, to introduce him to McKeever, and Leahy and McKeever became immediate friends.

It turned out that McKeever had enrolled at Notre Dame as a freshman in 1929 but spent only one year at South Bend. He returned to his home in Texas because of an illness in his family. He went on to attend Texas Tech, where he became an outstanding halfback during a three-year span in which Tech played thirty-six games and lost only three.

McKeever invited Leahy to his home for dinner one evening after a clinic on backfield play that McKeever had given. During the evening Leahy said, "Tex, if I ever get a head coaching job, I'm going to call you." In 1939, when Leahy was appointed head coach at Boston College, he immediately selected McKeever as his backfield coach. When he was appointed to the Notre Dame post, Leahy summoned McKeever as his chief aide.

In 1944, when Frank Leahy entered the Navy, Ed McKeever took over the reins as head coach at Notre Dame. He also inherited a lot of headaches.

All-American Creighton Miller had graduated. Bertelli, Lujack, Rykovich, and the entire Notre Dame line had gone into various branches of the service, but Tex McKeever drilled his seventeen- and eighteen-year-old youngsters, juggled his lineup, and came up with a starting team led by Frankie Dancewicz at quarterback, Chick Maggioli and Bob Kelly at the halfback posts, and Elmer Angsman and Marty Wendell at fullback.

On the brighter side, Pat Filley, a two-year veteran and captain of the Irish eleven for the second straight year, was back at his right guard post, Fred Rovai was at left guard; George Sullivan and John Adams, all six-feet, seven inches of him, were the tackles; and Johnny Ray was at center. When McKeever led his Irish eleven onto the field at Pitt Stadium on September 30 for the season's opener, he expected to win, but hardly by the margin his team provided. Every man on the squad played their best game, and the Panthers were utterly routed by a 58–0 score. It was an awesome exhibition of sheer power, and the excited Irish fans were once again shouting, "national champs!"

The following week saw the Irish continue on their winning ways as they trounced Tulane, 26–0. Then the Irish traveled to Boston, where they defeated Dartmouth, 64–0—the sportswriters were calling McKeever "another Leahy."

The Badgers of Wisconsin fell by the wayside a week later, but only after giving McKeever and company a great fight. However, the superior strength of Notre Dame won out by a 28–13 score, and then the Fighting Illini battled the Irish throughout the game before losing a squeaker at Champaign, 13–7.

(Below) Coach Leahy and his chief assistants in 1942, Bob Snyder (left) and Ed McKeever (right).

(Bottom) Ed McKeever (fourth from left) was appointed head coach for 1944. He named five former Irish stars as his aides. Left to right, Adam Walsh, Hugh Devore, Jake Kline, McKeever, Clem Crowe, and Walt Ziemba.

Then a mighty Navy team, bolstered by a horde of all-stars who were taking the Navy Pre-Flight courses, was just too much for Notre Dame and wore down the Irish regulars by a 32–13 score. It was the first Navy victory over the Irish since their 3–0 victory in 1936.

On November 11, Army, with one of their truly great teams, led by quarterback Doug Kenna, Doc Blanchard, Glenn Davis, and Max Minor, all All-Americans, simply ran over, around and through Notre Dame and inflicted the worst defeat in Irish history by a whopping 59–0 score at Yankee Stadium.

The Cadets had dedicated this important game to a man who was seated on the sidelines in a wheelchair at midfield. He was Colonel Red Reeder, who had wrapped himself in a white blanket to hide the fact that he had recently lost his left leg in the Normandy invasion on D-Day.

Reeder, a former Army star and assistant football coach, had been the commanding officer of the 12th Infantry, 4th Division, the second unit to hit Normandy Beach on D-Day. In the landing Red was hit by a shell and knocked unconscious but was rescued by several of his men. Red was flown to this game from Walter Reed Hospital, Washington, in General George Marshall's personal plane.

There is little doubt that Blanchard, Davis, Kenna, Dale Hall, and company were the best college football team in the land in 1944. Not since 1938 had Army scored a touchdown against the Irish, but this day in 1944 they were, in the words of their coach, "Red" Blaik, "the greatest Army team of all time."

Before the game McKeever delivered a pep talk to the Irish squad. He told them a sad story about his poor, sick father who was lying in bed and whose very life depended on the outcome of the game.

The first practice of the 1944 season, and the new coach, Ed McKeever, hands the ball to Captain Pat Filley as the Irish assistant coaches (kneeling) and players look on.

"Go out and win this for my pop," he concluded.

In the last quarter of the game, a weary, disgusted Notre Dame back looked at the scoreboard, ducked his head into the huddle, and said, "Guys, I'm not certain if the score reads in the forties or the fifties, but I'm positive of one thing: McKeever's old man is sure dead."

Just one week later, on November 18, the Irish,

fully recovered from the Army avalanche, drubbed Northwestern, 21–0, and in successive following weeks defeated Georgia Tech, 21–0 and Great Lakes, 28–7.

Excluding the Army and Navy defeats, Ed McKeever had worked miracles with the 1944 squad, and he so impressed the officials at Cornell with the job he accomplished at Notre Dame that they gave him the head coaching post at Cornell.

HUGH DEVORE NAMED HEAD COACH (1945)

In 1945, the final year of World War II, Hugh Devore was named head football coach to succeed the departing Ed McKeever.

The youngest of nine children, Hugh was born in Newark, New Jersey, was an all-around athlete at St. Benedict's Prep there, won three letters at Notre

Dame under Coach Hunk Anderson, and co-captained the 1933 Irish eleven that won but three games and lost five. But they still tell of the game against Pitt in 1931 when Hugh took out three Pitt linemen with one savage block that paved the way to an Irish touchdown as the Irish won, 25–12. Devore caught

Left: High Devore was captain and a star end in 1932. Right: Thirty-one years later, Devore as the new Irish head coach

with the team captain, Bob Lehmann, and the Irish mascot, Lucky.

a pass and scored a touchdown against Army in 1932 as the Irish took a 21–0 victory over the Cadets. Bruised and battered and taped from head to foot, Hugh played through sixty minutes in the spectacular 13–12 Irish win over Army in 1933.

Devore graduated in 1934 and began coaching under Elmer Layden at Notre Dame that fall. From 1935 through 1937 under Jim Crowley, Devore scouted for Fordham, and his reports helped fashion Fordham's three straight scoreless ties against Pitt. From 1938 through 1941 Devore coached with moderate success at Providence College. In 1942 he went to Holy Cross. And then in 1945 he became the head coach at his alma mater.

Quarterback Frankie Dancewicz captained the 1945 squad, which featured a number of potential stars, including two quarterback substitutes, George Ratterman and Frank Tripucka. Bill Fischer was two years away from All-America recognition at guard; Johnny Mastrangelo, an outstanding guard, was an All-American in 1945 and 1946; Bill Walsh, at center, and Pete Berezney, a big tackle, were potential stars. In the backfield Devore also had Phil Colella and Terry Brennan as his halfbacks and Frank Ruggerio and John Panelli at fullback.

On September 29, the Fighting Illini eleven opened the season against the Irish before a South Bend crowd

of more than forty-one thousand, and they saw one of the best games of the year between two evenly matched teams. Notre Dame managed to score the game's only touchdown and came away with an opening victory for Coach Devore, 7–0.

The following week the Irish traveled to Georgia Tech and handed the Bulldogs a savage 40–7 trimming. Dartmouth, Pittsburgh, and Iowa were thrashed by resounding scores, and once again the experts were

In the 1945 game against Navy, Hugh Devore, head coach of the Irish, shouts instructions to his team.

hailing Notre Dame as one of the leading teams in the land. Then on November 3, at Cleveland, before an overflow crowd of more than eighty-two thousand, the Middies played the Irish to a 6–6 tie. The game was one of the most brutal contests the Irish ever played. Irish fullback Frank Ruggerio needed thirteen stitches in his jaw in addition to losing a few teeth. Bud Angsman had eleven teeth knocked out by Navy tacklers. John Panelli was out with a shoulder separation, and guard Vin Scott was hospitalized with a concussion. Not a man emerged from the Navy game completely unscathed, and meeting Army the following week was a horrendous prospect.

Army's marvelous backfield, featuring Arnie Tucker, Glenn Davis, and Doc Blanchard, and aided by experienced players in every position, swept through, over, and around Notre Dame's battered warriors and simply ran the Irish into the turf at Yankee Stadium by a 48–0 score. Davis scored three touchdowns, Blanchard scored twice, and Dick Walterhouse converted six extra points.

"We did our best," said Irish quarterback Frankie Dancewicz after the game, "but we were simply overmatched. In all my years of playing football I've never encountered a team so powerful, so versatile as this year's Army team. They were unbeatable."

FRANK LEAHY RETURNS: THIRTY-EIGHT GAMES WITHOUT DEFEAT

Lieutenant Frank Leahy was discharged from the Navy on November 15, 1945. He returned to the Notre Dame campus to sign a new ten-year contract and to look over some of the material that would be available to him in 1946. Most of the players were complete strangers to him, since the colleges had been playing freshmen while he had been in service.

Professional teams had offered Leahy fabulous contracts. There was one for a long period that amounted to nearly $500,000, but Leahy's heart was on the campus at South Bend, and he proceeded at once to get down to work. He reoccupied his old office, reassembled his coaching staff, and began the manhunt for new players.

The postwar market for college football players created an unusual situation. Literally thousands of fine young athletes were now being discharged from the services, and they were returning to colleges as tough, war-hardened young men and were eager for more action on the nations' gridirons.

Most of the Notre Dame men who had been called from classrooms to the armed forces flocked back to South Bend as soon as they were discharged. Although a few players had kept active by playing service football, many of the war veterans found football a tough row to hoe after slogging in the infantry or being confined to a ship or the cockpit of a plane.

Leahy wisely scheduled a tough three-month spring training period, and gradually the squad rounded into condition. The Leahy drive became legendary; his scrimmages were exhausting and unending. At one point in 1946, the campus was awash because of a cloudburst. But football practice continued unabated

and ended with an extra five laps around the field.

"You never know," said Frank, "what kind of weather we could have on any Saturday."

The years from 1946 through 1949 were to bring to Notre Dame and to Frank Leahy the most glorious era ever known in college football. During this period the Irish football team put together a string of thirty-eight games without a single defeat and won national championships in 1946 and 1947, were runners-up to Michigan in 1948, and were national champions again in 1949.

For the opening game of the 1946 season, against Illinois, Frank Leahy set his lineup with the following men:

At quarterback Johnny Lujack had returned to school after his service in the Navy and would develop into the most celebrated quarterback in Irish history. At the halfback posts Leahy had Emil "Red" Sitko and Terry Brennan. Sitko, a tough, chunky ball carrier, was most valuable because of his explosive start. On quick opening plays Emil could burst through the line for five, ten, or fifteen yards. After fifteen to twenty-five yards, nobody could stop Sitko.

Terry Brennan was the kind of back who "got the job done." He would get the five, six, or seven tough yards when it was needed. He ran the opening kickoff back for ninety-seven yards against Army in 1947, and he was a threat every time he carried the ball. On the bench Leahy had Bob Livingstone, a flashy, gifted player, a letter winner in 1942, Bill Gompers, and Coy McGee. At fullback Jim Mello and John Panelli were outstanding ball carriers.

Notre Dame had great depth in the line. There

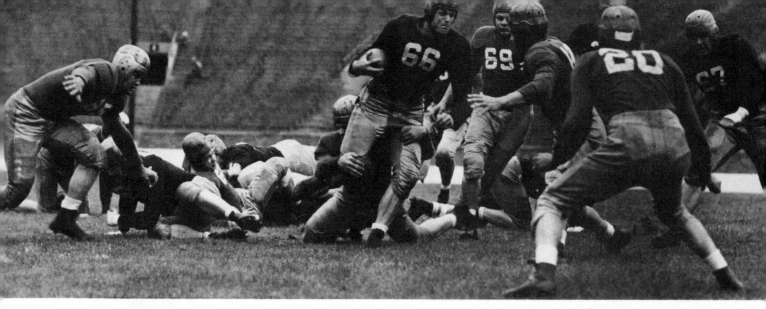

(Top) In the 1946 annual spring game between the varsity and former varsity members, No. 66, Floyd Simmons, varsity back, is about to be stopped by a host of "old-timers," including No. 69, Frank Szymanski of the 1943–44 team, and No. 65, Cornie Clatt, a fullback on the 1946–47 team (far left).

(Above, left) Coach Frank Leahy, back at Notre Dame in 1946 after two years in the Navy, and with this All-Star lineup once again guides the Irish to the national championship.

(Above, right) The Irish backfield in 1946 (left to right): Emil Sitko, Jim Mello, Johnny Lujack, and Bob Livingstone.

was Jim Martin, a big, blond crew-cut ex-Marine who won a presidential citation for going ashore at Tinian, then a Japanese-held island where thousands of enemy soldiers were encamped, to get vital military information before U.S. forces invaded the island. Martin was the type who could play any position on the line and do the job. At the other end, Jack Zilly could catch any ball thrown near him. At tackle the Irish had George Connor and Ziggy Czarobski. And they were as different in temperament as they were

in playing style. Connor was a muscular "Adonis" at six-three and 230 pounds. At one time Connor was seriously considered for the leading role in one of the Tarzan remakes in Hollywood. He was a natural leader and almost impossible to block. Czarobski was a man of humor and whimsy, with a vast appetite for food and life. He was the classic extrovert: All season long he lobbied for a date with a movie starlet, Liz Scott, and at the end of the season, when Notre Dame played USC, Ziggy was invited to Liz's home

(Top) Leon Hart, an end, played on four undefeated Irish teams, 1946 to 1949. In 1949 Hart received the Heisman Trophy.

(Above) Jim Mello, an outstanding Irish fullback on two national championship teams, 1943 and 1946, has spent the past twenty-seven years working with handicapped youngsters and adults at the Mansfield Training School in Connecticut.

in Hollywood for a party. He brought along Lujack, Creighton Miller, and several members of the team. Ziggy had a tendency to gain weight in huge globs, and Leahy warned him that he'd lose his chance if he didn't report in good shape. So Ziggy got a construction job during the summer and got up regularly at 5:00 A.M. to do roadwork. By September he was down to a suitable weight, 213 pounds. A year later Ziggy was an All-America selection.

At the guard posts, Leahy had John Mastrangelo and Bill Fischer. Fischer hailed from Laurium, Michigan, which was George Gipp's hometown, and would go on to become an All-American and earn recognition as the finest interior lineman in college football. At center George Strohmeyer (middle name, Ferdinand) was the kind of guy who would hand you your teeth if you mentioned his middle name. Another center was Bill Walsh, who'd already won two varsity letters.

Illinois had one of the strongest teams in the Big Ten in 1946, had started their season by soundly beating a strong Pittsburgh team, and were primed for the Irish on September 28 at Champaign.

After a scoreless first quarter, Sitko dashed off-tackle, burst into the clear, and kept going for a spectacular eighty-three-yard run. But Red was downed on the Illini two-yard line. On the next play Bob Livingstone cracked through for a touchdown. After an exchange of punts, Jim Mello scored Notre Dame's second touchdown on an off-tackle drive, and Earley kicked the extra point to give the Irish a 13–0 lead. Terry Brennan scored on a short plunge, the kick was good, and now it was 20–0 in the third period. Cornie Clatt scored another touchdown, Earley converted, and Notre Dame had a commanding 26–6 victory over Illinois.

Jim Mello, who was stationed at the Great Lakes Naval Station during the war, played football under the legendary Paul Brown there, and when Jim returned to South Bend in 1946 he played his finest football.

One week later, against Pitt, he led the Irish attack again in a brilliant display of offensive football as he scored twice on long runs. Jim had help from Terry Brennan, who also scored two touchdowns. Lujack's pinpoint passing was brilliant, and he riddled Pitt's defenses seemingly at will for an easy 33–0 rout of the Panthers. Next on the list of victims was an old foe, Purdue. The Boilermakers were easy victims as Lujack, Mello, and Brennan ran wild to roll up a 49–6 win.

The Irish caravan rolled on the following week to a smashing win over Iowa, 41–6. This time it was Red Sitko who sparked the Notre Dame offense as he dashed for two touchdowns in an all-around display that had the huge crowd applauding his every move.

At Cleveland, Navy put up a stout defense for the first quarter, but the Irish backfield pounded the Navy line for long gains and four touchdowns in a 28–0 rout.

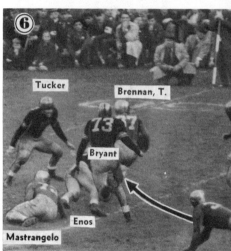

In 1946 Army, with a record of twenty-five consecutive victories, was headed for the national championship. If they could defeat Notre Dame, it would be clear sailing for the Cadets. But the Irish had championship aspirations as well, and a five-game winning streak. Here in these remarkable stop-action photos is one of the big plays of the game.

(Top, left) It's the fourth quarter. The score is 0–0 as Lujack fakes a shovel pass to halfback Bill Gompers. But Lujack spins and hands the ball to Terry Brennan.

(Top, center) Terry cuts to his left as George Connor drives in to block two Army men, giving Terry a big hole.

(Top, right) Terry has just hit the hole and drives into the Army line as Lujack and Gompers continue to fake as if they have the ball.

(Above, left) Terry is through the line

(Above, center) And is out in the clear, perhaps for a touchdown.

(Above, right) Suddenly Army's All-American Arnie Tucker comes from nowhere and sets himself to stop Terry.

(Right) Brennan cannot get away from Tucker and is brought down after about ten yards.

Now the nation's top sportswriters were predicting that the Army-Notre Dame game would be a classic battle, and even though the Army still had the incredible "Touchdown Twins," Blanchard and Davis, Notre Dame had Lujack, Mello, Sitko, and Terry Brennan.

Army, though, was the big favorite, for the Cadets had put together a string of twenty-five consecutive victories, and a crowd of more than seventy-four thousand jammed every inch of Yankee Stadium for

the contest. The emotional stress promoted by the game made the "big town" vibrate as sportswriters angled their stories to suggest a Hatfield-McCoy feud between the two rival schools, and the public cried for more of the same.

One hundred sportswriters and wire-service reporters jammed the press box, and there were reporters from Australia, Sweden, and Great Britain.

Frank Leahy, the worrying warrior, had no illusions about snapping the Cadets' victory skein, and a sign he plastered on the wall of the Notre Dame locker room was ample evidence of this. In bold-face figures it was brutal: "59–0 and 48–0" (the scores of the Army wins in 1944 and 1945).

The West Pointers were no longer four-deep in every position, as they had been in the boom days of 1944. Graduation had thinned their ranks, and now only the first-stringers were veterans of the all-conquering campaigns of the fabulous Black Knights from West Point. Co-captains Doc Blanchard, "Mr. Inside," and Glenn Davis, "Mr. Outside," still were the most spectacular one-two punch in college football. But Doc was bothered now by bad knees. Davis still was the flashiest broken-field runner of them all, and if he could get out in the open field, it was touchdown, Army.

Coach Red Blaik still was blessed with one of the finest quarterbacks in West Point history in Y. (for Young) Arnold Tucker, who had established himself as an outstanding passer and runner, an all-around star the equal of any college player in the game.

There was little doubt that the Cadets of 1944 and '45 were among the finest football teams in collegiate history, and in 1946, with a line that for the most part was intact after three seasons as a unit, they seemed just as formidable.

But the Irish had an All-Star lineup of their own and were primed for a tremendous battle. They were smarting under the indignity of the two crushing defeats in 1944 and '45. They were gunning for Army.

Quarterback John Lujack was the key man in the Notre Dame "T." He was a flawless tactician who could run, pass, and kick, and on defense he was one of the best blockers and tacklers on the team. In harness with the rest of the starting backfield—Jim Mello, Emil Sitko, and Terry Brennan—Lujack was the only indispensable element in the Irish attack.

When pressed for a guess about the outcome, Leahy predicted an Army win, 28–14, but quarterback Lujack had a slightly different idea. "I never walked out on a football field with a Notre Dame team expecting to lose," he said.

Sportswriter Terry Shore, writing about the game in his syndicated column, wrote: "In the biggest play of the entire football game, Doc Blanchard, all 205 pounds, 'Mr. Football' of 1945 and '46, tore around his right end, sped twenty yards down the sidelines, and seemed headed for a certain touchdown. He lumbered like a high-speed tank and in a brilliant burst past the Irish secondary, he had pierced the entire Irish defense—except for the safetyman, Lu-

jack. Doc swerved toward the south sideline and gauged the yardage between him and the point of contact with John. At the final instant, Doc pivoted and then drove on, but Lujack wouldn't be fooled. He drove into Blanchard, wrapped both arms around Doc, and brought him to the turf in a bone-crushing tackle that shook both players. Lujack was the only man on the Irish squad in a position to stop the play. The battle of the century, or battle of all time ended just where it started: Army 0, Notre Dame 0."

When the Irish squad returned to their dressing room, Leahy locked the door and started to talk to his team.

"Men, you played your hearts out today, but you were not quite good enough. Remember one thing now: The test of a great champion is how he reacts to adversity on the days when it is bound to come."

The players silently began to undress and head for the showers.

Leahy's twelve-year-old son found a football and began passing it back and forth to a player. They were young, and time had not stopped for them.

Terry Shore, a sportswriter for the New York *Daily Mirror* said, "Coach, the tie score will look good after the season is over." But Leahy didn't offer a reply. He just smiled sadly and said he did not feel very happy about it at the moment.

A week after the Army game, on November 16, the Notre Dame players got their act together and thrashed the Northwestern Wildcats in the rain and snow by a 27–0 score. The fifty-six thousand hometown fans there saw the Irish notch their sixth victory and began to realize they were watching a team of destiny.

In New Orleans the following week, Tulane was easily defeated, 41–0, by a Notre Dame eleven led by big Jim Mello who sparkled and scored two touchdowns. Ernie Zalejski scored twice, and Terry Brennan and Coy McGee also scored.

Frank Leahy was ill and Moose Krause, who had been assisting him, took charge of the team for the final game of the 1946 season, against Southern California. It was the twentieth anniversary of the first meeting between the two rivals, and USC had done very well. The series stood at ten wins for Notre Dame, six for USC, and one tie. And it didn't look as if USC would win for quite a while, as the Irish were loaded with talent for years to come.

The dramatics started early as Coy McGee ran the opening kickoff back in a sensational eighty-yard dash for a touchdown, but the play was called back as the crowd still was filing into Rockne Memorial Stadium at South Bend. One play later it was McGee once more, running like a scared deer for seventy-seven yards and the first Irish score. Shortly thereafter, George Ratterman, the brilliant but erratic number two quarterback, directed a passing attack that covered seventy yards, and then he lofted a beautiful twenty-two-yard pass to Leon Hart for a touchdown. This time the kick was good, and it was 13–0 Notre Dame at the half. USC scored in the third period to make the score close, 13–6. Minutes later Coy McGee led a sixty-yard march and then plunged over for another Irish score. In the final quarter Gerry Cowhig smashed through tackle, cut back, and dashed into the end zone for the final tally to make the score 26–6.

Leahy phoned Moose Krause after the game. "I figured Leahy would be happy that we won," said Moose. "Instead his first words were, 'I gave you the starting lineup, Moose. Who in hell is this Coy McGee you stuck in my lineup?' "

The 1946 season was history.

Johnny Lujack, George Connor, John Mastrangelo, and George Strohmeyer were picked on the All-America teams. And when the final votes were tabulated, Notre Dame was selected by consensus over Army as the national champions. The voters undoubtedly were influenced by the fact that Notre Dame's only close game was with Army; but the Cadets, in their final game, had only squeaked by Navy, 21–18, in a contest that ended with the Midshipmen on Army's three-yard line.

NOTRE DAME'S GREATEST TEAM

The 1946 season was over, but another season had just begun. On December 30, Notre Dame and Army jointly announced a temporary severance of football relations after a final game at South Bend in 1947, because it "will be good for both schools and for intercollegiate athletics as a whole."

The announcement was full of goodwill and friendship. In essence it said that the Notre Dame-Army game had grown too big and produced too many problems and that a breathing period would be salutary.

Discussing a preview of the 1947 season, a week before the first game against Pitt, Coach Leahy said, "To an uncommon degree this season will be a replay of the last one. If little important talent has been drained off by graduation and the professionals, equally little has been added. The flowback from the armed forces is now down to a trickle, and civilian freshmen once more are barred, except in the Southern, Southeastern, and Border conferences.

"Army, the wartime terror, is the notable exception to the postwar rule, the one major squad to lose drastically by graduation. Navy is raring to get even with us for last year's disappointment but has one of the toughest schedules.

"Notre Dame is a prize example of what you can expect. We lost six fine players, but quickly we filled the gaps with others who may be even better. We've added smartness and balance. This season we'll have Lujack, Connor, Strohmeyer, Bill Fischer, Sitko, Brennan, Hart, McGee, and Jim Martin. That's darn good."

Notre Dame opened the 1947 season with Johnny Lujack at quarterback, Terry Brennan and Emil Sitko as the halfbacks, and John Panelli at fullback. Jim Martin and Leon Hart were the ends, Captain George Connor and Ziggy Czarobski the tackles, Bill Fischer and Marty Wendell were at the guard posts, and Bill Walsh was at center.

On October 4 at Pittsburgh, the Panthers obviously had polished their play against Illinois the previous week and were sharp and well prepared—and they kept the Irish offense bottled up for the first six minutes of play.

Then Terry Brennan uncorked a thirty-four-yard pass to Jim Martin, who made a spectacular catch for a first down on the Pitt fourteen-yard line. Two plays later Terry slammed over for the first touchdown. The kick was good, and it was 7–0 Notre Dame.

Frank Tripucka, in for Lujack at quarterback, fumbled a pass from center, Pitt recovered the ball, and then DiPasqua of Pitt slammed over from the ten-yard line. The kick was missed, and the score was 7–6.

That was as close as Pittsburgh came the rest of the game, for a fired-up Lujack completed pass after pass and scored three times as the Irish, despite six fumbles, romped over the sturdy Pitt eleven, 40–6.

Purdue, the next opponent, had lost an earlier game to Wisconsin and were not given the slightest chance to beat Notre Dame, but they provided stiff opposition and actually outplayed the Irish during the first half. However, Notre Dame scored on two pass plays and a field goal by Steve Oracko and took a 16–7 halftime lead. In the second half Lujack and Tripucka went to work and filled the air with passes to beat the Boilermakers, 22–7.

In the third game of the season and the first home game for the Irish, Nebraska brought a tough, beefy, aggressive line to South Bend. It was the first game between the Cornhuskers and the Irish since 1925, when Nebraska beat one of Knute Rockne's fine teams by a 17–0 score, and the Irish were bent on revenge.

With John Lujack masterminding the "T" in a beautiful offensive display, Notre Dame passed Nebraska dizzy, but it was the magnificent open-field running of speedsters Coy McGee and Emil Sitko that had the big home crowd of more than fifty-six thousand standing and screaming with excitement as the Irish tore up and down the field for an easy 31–0 victory.

Iowa was next on the schedule and fought their hearts out, but they simply were not quite good enough as Terry Brennan scored twice and Larry Coutre scored a third touchdown to give the Irish a decisive 21–0 victory before a hometown crowd of more than fifty-six thousand.

Next, Navy was scuttled by the brilliant passing attack of Lujack and Tripucka. Two aerials accounted for the first Irish touchdowns, and then Lujack broke away for a brilliant seventy-two-yard run that had the huge crowd roaring; but John fumbled on the next play and Navy recovered to prevent another score. Bob Livingstone scored in the third period on a forty-two-yard romp, and the final score was Notre Dame 27, Navy 0.

And on November 8 at South Bend, a game that Coach Leahy and his staff had planned and pointed to for a year: sweet revenge against Army, who had rolled up humiliating scores against the Irish in 1944 and 1945.

Frank Leahy met Red Blaik the day before the 1947 game at a small luncheon for Army-Notre Dame officials. "Earl, I think you are going to be very happy with the results after this game," said Leahy. Blaik snapped, "I'll tell you one thing," said Red, "we're going to give you one hell of a fight."

And they did—for the first two minutes of the game.

The first kickoff by Army's Jack Mackmull went out of bounds. The second kickoff was pulled in by Terry Brennan on his three-yard line, and behind superb blocking, Terry picked his way down the west sidelines, using his blockers shrewdly, until he broke

Coach Leahy (center) huddles with his "brain trust" in preparation for the opening game of the 1947 season, against Pitt. Left to right, quarterback Johnny Lujack; No. 81, Captain George Connor; No. 38, Jim Martin; and No. 82, Leon Hart.

Terry Brennan fumbles the ball after a long gain against Nebraska in 1947. No. 37 on the ground is Nebraska guard Frank Wilkins. No. 82 is end Leon Hart.

clear at midfield and raced ninety-seven yards for a touchdown. Fred Earley kicked the extra point, and it was 7–0 before the game was three minutes old.

Army punted after gaining a first down and then Brennan, Sitko, and Mike Swistowicz marched upfield. In just thirteen plays the Irish covered eighty yards, and Lujack passed to Leon Hart for the second Irish score.

(Above) Terry Brennan, No. 32, is shown on the Army seven-yard line after picking up some fifteen yards. He was tackled on the Army three-yard line. He scores on the next play in the game against Army in 1947. No. 81, George Connor; No. 67, Army's Ray Drury; No. 33, Elwyn (Rip) Rowan of Army; No. 63, Joe Henry of Army.

(Above, right) Irish halfback Emil Sitko leaps high into the air to intercept a pass intended for Bill West (right), Army halfback. No. 32, Johnny Lujack, holds his hands out to

Sitko for a possible lateral pass in the game against Army in 1946.

(Right, top) Leon Hart, Notre Dame's All-America end (82), is about to be stopped by two Army players after an end-around play in 1946 game at Yankee Stadium.

(Right, bottom) The 1947 national championship team won nine straight games. It was the second straight undefeated season for the Irish eleven.

The march was a masterpiece of quarterbacking by Johnny Lujack, who mixed his plays brilliantly and surprised the Cadets with the variety of the Irish offense. At the half Notre Dame led 13–0.

Army held in the third period until Bob Livingstone capped a forty-nine-yard march by driving in for a touchdown from the six-yard line. Earley once more kicked the extra point to give the Irish a 20–0 lead.

Army's attack began to roll late in the third quarter when Rip Rowan, Bobby Stuart, and Arnie Galiffa combined for some fine running plays as the Cadets advanced to the Irish six-yard line. Then in the final period, Rowan plunged over from the six for Army's only score.

Notre Dame took over as Coutre and Swistowicz ripped Army's line to shreds; Coutre tallied Notre Dame's final touchdown as he drove in from the twelve-yard line to give the Irish a brilliant 27–7 win.

Frank Leahy was a professional pessimist to whom every day was a "bad day." But in preparing his team for Northwestern the following week, Leahy reminded his team that the Wildcats had a history of lying in the woods for Notre Dame. Northwestern had surprised the Irish in 1935, just one week after Notre

Dame's great win over Ohio State, and had beaten them 14–7. In 1942 the Wildcats had given Leahy a bad scare as the Irish squeaked out a thriller, 27–20. Therefore, thought Leahy, an uninspiring game by the Irish could mean a beating.

And it almost happened. The Irish defense was lackadaisical, but fortunately the offense came through with a plucky performance and just managed to beat off the stubborn Wildcats, 26–19.

Notre Dame now was thinking ahead to the end of the season and its stature in college football, for it was one of the three teams scrambling for the lead in the wire service polls for the national championship. The other two teams were Southern California and Michigan, and Michigan seemed to have the edge.

Leahy went out to the West Coast to scout USC, and Moose Krause led the Irish against Tulane in a rout. The Irish scored five touchdowns in the first quarter. Brennan and Sitko scored twice in the game, and other scores were made by Bill Gompers, Cornie Clatt, Panelli, Livingstone, and Jim Brennan (Terry's brother) as the Irish, using nearly every member of the squad, romped, 59–6.

On December 6 the Irish attack—vicious, thump-

ing, and varied—simply was too good for Southern California in a game that would decide the national championship. But for the first half of the game it was a battle, and the Irish left the field leading by the slim margin of 10–7.

The second half saw Notre Dame pull away, with Sitko blazing seventy-six yards and Bob Livingstone dashing for ninety-two yards, both men scoring, and then Panelli scored, and it was all over for USC. The Irish ran up a 38–7 victory.

Five members of the 1947 squad made the All-American teams: guard Bill Fischer, tackles George Connor and Ziggy Czarobski, the sophomore end Leon Hart, and John Lujack. Lujack also won the coveted Heisman award. . . . And Notre Dame was ranked No. 1 in the nation ahead of the mighty Michigan Wolverines.

Outside the Notre Dame locker room after the game, Bill Stern was finishing his postgame broadcast when he spotted Red Grange, the incredible former all-time Illinois great, walking toward Leahy's office. Stern started to question Grange.

"You know why Notre Dame is the best college team in the nation?" said Grange. "It's because Frank Leahy is the greatest college coach who ever lived. He's greater than Rockne. Now, I'm not knocking Rock. But Leahy is the very best. He's a total perfectionist. Consequently, his players don't make too many mistakes.

"They complain about Leahy," said Grange. "They say he teaches dirty football, but that's bull. . . . The reason they complain is that Leahy is superior and he wins. They stay clear of Notre Dame for one reason. They don't want to get beat. Red Blaik wants to get off the schedule, for one reason. He knows if he plays Notre Dame he's going to look bad. Frank Leahy's success is the result of long, long hours of work. They also say that Leahy is a sour person, and he can be when he's preoccupied with football. But when he's got nothing else on his mind he's one of the nicest guys I've ever met."

From the 1947 championship team Notre Dame lost its great quarterback Johnny Lujack, who certainly belongs to Notre Dame's list of gridiron immortals. As a passer, runner, and offensive and defensive star, John was a poised player whose individual efforts plucked victory from apparent defeat on a number of occasions. They also lost the All-American tackles, Captain George Connor, and one of the most beloved of all Notre Dame players in Ziggy Czarobski. But there still was a large group of experienced and proven players around whom Coach Leahy once again set to work to build the 1948 varsity. Foremost among the returnees were fullback John Panelli, halfbacks Terry Brennan and Red Sitko, quarterback Frank Tripucka, ends Jim Martin and Leon Hart, guards Marty Wendell and Captain Bill Fischer, and center Bill Walsh.

And the 1948 eleven proceeded to establish new records: The team broke all Irish marks for ground gaining with 3,194 yards. It also set new Notre Dame records for winning sequence and undefeated sequence. It surpassed by one game the twenty games in succession won by the teams of 1929, '30, and '31, and also by the teams of 1919, '20, and '21. All these teams were coached by Rockne except the 1931 eleven, which was coached by Hunk Anderson.

Luke Carroll, a leading sportswriter for the *New York Herald Tribune*, wrote about Notre Dame's opening game of the 1948 season against Purdue: "Notre Dame began another season with a victory, but they probably used up a full season's quota of luck in outpointing a furiously fighting Purdue eleven 28–27."

Notre Dame utilized every method known to man to score against Purdue and resorted to plays that weren't even anticipated in the rule book. But they were able to keep their undefeated record clean mainly because fullback John Panelli zigzagged his way to a touchdown after a blocked kick; because Al Zmijewski intercepted a Purdue pass and ran it over from the nine-yard line; and because Steve Oracko, having missed three extra points after touchdown, was able to kick a twenty-five-yard field goal with about three minutes left to play.

Purdue made it close to the very end of the game and scored a touchdown on the final play, but Notre Dame still managed to hang on to a one-point lead as the contest ended.

Coach Leahy dug into his bag of tricks and came up with one of the most startling plays ever seen. Frank Tripucka and Bob Williams, both quarterbacks, stood behind the center, and each quarterback whirled simultaneously, faking handoffs to everybody in the backfield. It was a play that had Purdue guessing, but only one of the double-quarterback spins made a long gain, and the odd formation soon was discarded.

Next on the list of opponents was Pittsburgh. This time the Panthers were easy prey as Tripucka, Williams, and four other Irish backs scored to give Notre Dame an easy 40–0 triumph. The win was Notre

Husky Emil Sitko, a brilliant Irish halfback, drives for fifteen yards against Navy with two tacklers hanging on to him in the 1948 battle against the Middies.

Coach Leahy and his 1948 captain, Bill Fischer.

Dame's twentieth victory without defeat since the final game of the 1945 campaign.

In the seventeenth renewal of the gridiron rivalry between Notre Dame and Michigan State, the Spartans, under Coach "Biggie" Munn, started the game on October 5 at South Bend by charging right down the field to score a touchdown as Lynn Chadnois, a great halfback, sparked their offense. Notre Dame, not to be denied, scored after runs by Sitko, Panelli, and Mike Swistowicz. The kick for the extra point was missed, and State led, 7–6. Then it was Sitko and Bill Gay carrying the ball again and again for substantial gains to State's fifteen-yard line. Then Tripucka tossed a pass to Swistowicz, who dashed fifteen yards for the second Irish score. In the final period Terry Brennan scored and it was all Notre Dame as the Irish outpassed and outran the rugged Spartans for a 26–7 victory.

In Davenport, Iowa, the following week, the Irish scored forty-six seconds after the game began as Panelli took a lateral from Tripucka and sprinted thirty-five yards for a TD. Iowa came back to tie the score at 6–6. But then it was Notre Dame's game as Panelli, Bill Gay, and Larry Coutre piled up touchdowns in each period to give the Irish a 27–12 victory.

Although the team moved easily through Nebraska, 44–13, bowled over the hapless Navy eleven, 41–7, and crushed Indiana, 42–6, it seemed to lack the polish and machinelike precision of the 1946 and '47 teams. This was not due to the loss of such players as Lujack, Connor, and Czarobski; rather, it was

Leahy's practice to use as many of the reserves as he possibly could, to hold down the scores against the weaker teams, and also to develop his sophomores while he had the chance. When Sitko, Brennan, McGee, and Panelli were forced out with injuries, Leahy came up with such fine players as Larry Coutre, Billy Gay, and Jack Landry behind a great line led by Martin, Wendell, and Leon Hart.

It was bitter cold, windy, and a threat of snow was in the air at South Bend on November 13 as two of the nation's finest elevens, Notre Dame and Northwestern, battled each other in a furiously exciting clash that had a crowd of over fifty-nine thousand spectators standing throughout most of the game. Nothing was held back, and both teams used every trick in their bag. Play was so furious that every block and tackle could be heard all over the vast stadium.

Northwestern, with one of its finest teams, took the opening kickoff and proceeded to march to the Irish nine-yard line. Here Notre Dame stiffened, took over, and then smashed and hacked its way down the field, and John Panelli pounded across for the first Irish touchdown.

The Wildcats struck back in the third period as Art Murakowski, one of the great backs of Northwestern football, broke off-tackle and sped ninety yards for a Wildcat score. Bill Farrar kicked the extra point, and Northwestern was in front by a 7–6 score. The teams battled through three periods to a standstill.

Then with the pressure on and the game hinging on every play, the Fighting Irish bounded back with a vengeance. With the ball on their thirty-yard line, Billy Gay and Jack Landry took turns blasting the Northwestern line for five yards, eight yards, ten yards at a time, and then finally, with three minutes left in the game, Gay dove over for the touchdown that gave the Irish a hard-fought victory by the slim margin of a touchdown. Notre Dame 12, Northwestern 7.

The University of Washington fell victim as the Irish simply ran over the hapless Huskies and scored twenty-five points in the first period. Leon Hart, the great All-American end, scored two touchdowns and Panelli, Terry Brennan, Bill Wightkin, and Bill Gay also scored as Steve Oracko converted four kicks as the Irish romped, 46–0.

The 1948 team now had won nine straight games, and some sportswriters recalled that prior to the season Coach Leahy had cautioned his players: "We may lose one, perhaps two, and then maybe get a tie along the way. We've got to get Frank Tripucka to move better than he has shown. He can pass and kick, but he can't run with the ball."

Now only Southern California remained, and the Trojans had never beaten a Frank Leahy team.

But this Southern California team was out for victory, and playing inspired football, they took a 14–7 lead over Notre Dame with less than one quarter remaining in the game—and the national championship in the balance.

Billy Gay had played a remarkable game all afternoon for the Irish, and now he approached an official and asked, "Ref, how much time do we have for the game?"

Referee Jim Cain replied, "Just two and a half minutes, son."

"That's time enough for us," said Gay as he moved back into position in the backfield.

Southern California's Charley Peterson kicked the ball to Notre Dame's one-yard line and Gay plucked the ball out of the air and started moving up his right sideline. Irish blockers were expertly whacking Trojan players out of Gay's path, and Billy sped eighty-six yards to the Southern California thirteen-yard line.

And now there were only ninety seconds left to play.

Quarterback Bob Williams, subbing for the injured Tripucka, slipped through the line for three yards. A pass—Williams to Gay— failed. Panelli crashed the line for two yards and then Red Sitko, playing one of his greatest games for the Irish, cracked over for the touchdown that brought the score to 14–13 in favor of Southern California.

With thirty-four seconds left to play, Steve Oracko calmly stepped back, brushed the grass from his right foot, stepped forward, and booted over the extra point that gave Notre Dame a 14–14 tie.

The tie with Southern California, however, cost Notre Dame a third consecutive national championship. Michigan was moved to the top position, while Notre Dame moved into second place in the national ranking.

Bill Fischer, Leon Hart, Marty Wendell, and Emil Sitko were named to numerous All-American teams as Notre Dame closed out its sixty-second football season with a marvelous 9–0–1 record.

"COACH LAYDEN, MEET NOTRE DAME'S QUARTERBACK IN TEN YEARS"

"Back in 1938 my brother Hal Williams worked in the Notre Dame publicity office with Charlie Callahan," said Bob Williams, "and when the team traveled to Baltimore to play against Navy, my big brother Hal brought me over to Coach Elmer Layden and said, 'Coach Layden, meet Notre Dame's quarterback in ten years. This is my kid brother Bobby.'

"Hal later on became a foreign correspondent for the *Baltimore Sun*," said Bob Williams recently, "and later became Sunday editor for the paper. He's now retired. But I guess he was an accurate forecaster."

Eleven years after being introduced to Coach Layden, Bob Williams was a junior quarterback at Notre Dame, with two years spent as an understudy to the Irish's first-string quarterback, Frank Tripucka.

Coach Leahy had kept Williams under cover in 1948, but not steadily; he had the experienced, first-rate Tripucka, who had played on the 1946 and 1947 national championship teams.

As Tripucka's understudy, Bob got little chance to display his many talents. He seldom ran the team until the Irish had a commanding lead, and then Leahy usually ordered him not to use any passes or

(Top, left) "Nobody received more personal attention from Coach Leahy than the quarterback," said All-American Bob Williams. "Every individual move was studied and practiced and practiced . . . for hours on end until you were ready to drop," he said. "But I have to admit, when game time rolled around, we were ready." "I had to practice the center snap with my center, Jerry Groom [No. 50], for hours at a time. And if I dropped the ball, it was five laps around the track," said Williams (No. 9 in photo).

(Top, right) Coach Leahy studies the passing form of quarterback Williams and corrects and critizes every move in practice.

(Above, left) A quarterback's footwork, like a boxer's, has to be quick and nimble. This rope-skipping exercise, ten to fifteen minutes daily, is a must for all backs.

(Above, right) Quarterbacks under Coach Leahy had to handle the ball like a magician. In the photo Bob Williams is shown faking a hand-off to Bill Barrett with his right hand . . . but actually hands off to No. 30, Jack Landry. No. 37 is the blocker on this play.

certainly not to attempt any unorthodox plays.

Bob did play in two games in 1948, without restrictions, however. In the Southern California game, Leahy gave Bob full charge of the team when Tripucka was carried off the field, hurt so badly that he would not reenter the game at all during the second half.

In a previous section we have described that game in detail. But in the final minutes it was Bob Williams's strategy that led to the Irish's final score.

But with Frank Tripucka, Terry Brennan, Ralph McGehee, Captain Bill Fischer, Marty Wendell, Bill Walsh, and John Panelli graduated, Coach Leahy would have to be a magician to continue Notre Dame's unbeaten string, which now had reached twenty-eight consecutive games.

But Leahy, even though predicting dire things were in store for Notre Dame, said, "At least I've got a great quarterback in Bob Williams. Not too much else, though."

No one expected Notre Dame to field a championship team in 1949, including Coach Leahy, nor did the experts expect much from the starting quarterback, Williams.

The nation's sportswriters did not expect an unknown rookie to outshine their preseason choice of All-America quarterback, the great Army star Arnie Galiffa. Even Notre Dame fans were totally unprepared for Williams's performance; their attention centered on Leon Hart, Emil Sitko, Larry Coutre, and Co-captain Jim Martin.

But against Michigan State on November 5, 1949, in the sixth game of the season for the Irish, Bob delivered the first of a string of surprises that led to his unanimous nomination as an All-American. In the five games prior to the Michigan State contest Williams performed admirably at quarterback but attracted little individual attention. But in the State game he gave one of the most extraordinary performances of the year.

He completed thirteen of sixteen passes, two of them for touchdowns. He sprinted forty yards for another touchdown and skillfully directed the Irish

Coach Leahy (center) and four stars of the undefeated 1949 national championship Irish team. Kneeling: Emil Sitko (left) and Co-captain Leon Hart. Back Row: Bob Williams (left) and Co-captain Jim Martin.

attack against a foe who was supposed to give Notre Dame her first defeat in four years.

Tossing fourth-down passes with the poise of a veteran, the "kid from Baltimore" thoroughly jumbled everyone's calculations on the Irish strength.

Earlier in the '49 season Williams had practiced his talents admirably. Bob first victimized Indiana with his fourth-down-pass routine as his play and Emil Sitko's three touchdowns and brilliant all-around exhibition easily defeated Indiana, 49–6. Bob then threw a touchdown pass in the 27–7 Irish win over Washington and then directed the 35–12 defeat of Purdue.

Tulane followers traveled from New Orleans to South Bend to see their national championship hopes rise by a Green Wave defeat of the Irish. But a much-abashed group of rebels trekked back home with a 46–7 loss. In the game Williams completed nine of eleven passes, two of them for touchdowns.

Only a week before the Michigan State game, Williams realized one of his life's ambitions: He played for Notre Dame in his hometown Baltimore's Memorial Stadium. His appearance was brief, but his passes to Ernie Zalejski, Sitko, and Larry Coutre were masterful. Zalejski was brilliant as he ran for three touchdowns as the Irish shut out Navy, 40–0.

In later games, Williams continued to amaze the press in victories over North Carolina, 42–6; Iowa, 28–7; and Southern California, 32–0.

Today, football squads travel swiftly in chartered jet planes and without any distractions, but in 1949 the trip to Dallas for the SMU game was made by train, and the Notre Dame squad, after nine consecutive victories over the nation's greatest elevens, was in a holiday mood. All the coaches and their wives were along; several special cars carrying parents of the players as well as alumni and press were attached to the special Notre Dame train. At every stop there were autograph collectors, admiring young females, and young high-school players wearing their school jackets and looking forward to the day when they could also be gridiron stars at Notre Dame. It was all like a great pre-holiday party.

And with the Southern California game in the history books, Notre Dame arrived at Dallas ready to tackle Southern Methodist University in a game that would rival in excitement any that the Irish had ever played.

The Mustangs had already lost three games, and their great star, Doak Walker, the Heisman Trophy winner the preceding year, had been injured and would not play. The SMU team still had a fine halfback in Kyle Rote, but the Irish did not expect much of a game in their final outing of the season.

Commenting on the game, Frank Leahy said, "During the first half, even though we scored and had a 14–0 lead, I felt we were fighting for our lives. I knew how General Custer must have felt at Little Big Horn. They just kept coming at us like they wanted to win and . . . were going to win.

"And that Kyle Rote became almost a superman in the second half. He gained at will, scored two great touchdowns, and was responsible for a third. The score was tied at 20–20 and for the first time all season long we had only a few minutes to prove we really were a championship team."

Now quarterback Williams gathered his team for that one drive that would count. Emil Sitko, Fran Spaniel, Leon Hart (who played fullback when a couple of yards were badly needed), and Bill Barrett took turns driving holes through the SMU line. Finally the Irish reached the six-yard line, and Barrett sped around left end for the Irish go-ahead touchdown. Notre Dame 27, SMU 20.

Back came that whirling dervish Kyle Rote.

He was a one-man team, carrying the ball on every play and gaining ground. He picked up ten yards on a sprint, then another fifteen yards on a shovel pass, then another dash up the middle, and now Rote danced through the line and was out in the clear, seemingly headed for a score. Then suddenly he was crushed to the ground on a tackle from behind on the Irish twenty-six-yard line.

And the big Dallas crowd was going crazy.

Fred Benners passed to Rote, and Kyle ran to the five-yard line. Then Rote tried a jump pass, that looked good . . . but all of a sudden the Irish center, Jerry Groom, intercepted it, and the game ended on that play.

Yet Frank Leahy, after his great immediate joy over the victory and his fourth national championship, knew the future was bleak.

Sportswriters were comparing Frank to the greatest coaches who ever lived. A few said that he was the greatest, better than Rockne, better than Warner or Stagg. "The Master Coach," they were now calling him.

"I WANTED TO QUIT IN 1949," SAID LEAHY

When Knute Rockne plummeted to his death in 1931, football critics said:

"Notre Dame will never see his like as a coach."

Well, they were right in one sense and wrong in another. For inspirational fervor, for pulse-quickening personality, for character-building, for super salesmanship, and for his strategic grasp of football, Rockne never had an equal.

None of Rockne's successors at Notre Dame could approach the Norwegian genius as a coach, until Frank Leahy, his favorite pupil, assumed leadership of the Irish grid forces in 1941.

And now in 1949, in his seventh season at South Bend, Leahy was recognized as the greatest teacher of football fundamentals and developer of team cohesion the game had known, with the possible exception of Red Blaik.

Lacking Rockne's lambent personality, Leahy personified precision in football coaching. Rock's teams were known for their subtle timing and savage blocking; but, keeping pace with the growth of the game, Leahy had gone beyond Rockne in developing a synchronized offense. Leahy's players blocked and tackled with more ferocity and even greater skill. And

the Leahy "T" attack was more flexible than Rockne's shift.

Rockne was the magnetic extrovert, winning friends even as he won games, and sugarcoating the bitter pills he forced rivals to swallow. Leahy, on the other hand, was the intense introvert, admired rather than loved by his players. And somehow the routs that Leahy's teams inflicted on his opponents left an acrimonious aftermath that was not apparent under Rockne's "leave 'em feeling happy" stewardship. And that's where the problems began.

There were those in important posts at the university who were undermining him; they were The anti-football priests at Notre Dame who cringed whenever Notre Dame's football success was mentioned in the press and who fretted endlessly when the school's fame was measured in yards gained instead of brilliant scholars graduated. And they managed to bring enough pressure against Leahy and his football program by 1950 to reduce the number of football scholarships from thirty-two to eighteen. The reduction almost wrecked the incomparable, Notre Dame football program.

Stunned by this incredible action, Frank begged

for a suitable explanation but received none. And the pressures on him began to increase.

"I was being blamed for the fact that Army discontinued the series with Notre Dame," said Leahy. "I was being blamed for the fact that several Big Ten schools either dropped us or wouldn't schedule us. They said that I was unpopular with every coach in the country, which certainly wasn't true.

"And several times I went to Father John Cavanaugh and asked him about the overall situation. I also told him that if he agreed I was responsible for the schedule changes, I was prepared to resign.

"I told Father John that I might leave after the Championship 1949 season," said Leahy. "The Los Angeles Rams had made inquiries and had made a great offer and I was sorely tempted. But I considered it an honor to be head coach at Notre Dame. To me it was a sacred trust. How could I give it up to join the professionals? It seemed indecent.

"I wanted to quit in 1949," said Leahy.

But after he talked with his captain, Jerry Groom, and told Groom that he wanted to leave Notre Dame, Jerry said:

"Coach, remember what you said . . . what you solemnly promised my parents when I enrolled? . . . You said you would be my football coach for four years. Well, I have another year to go, coach."

That talk with Jerry Groom convinced Frank Leahy to stay at Notre Dame.

The anti-Leahy attacks continued until just after the 1950 season, when Father John Cavanaugh issued a public statement making him perhaps the first college president ever to be forced to explain how proud his school was of an undefeated championship team.

"Leahy is blamed for wrecking the Notre Dame schedule by developing teams that win most of their games," he said. "He was brought here to win and to achieve excellence. If he didn't win they would be asking to fire him. His is, indeed, an unsolvable problem. At Notre Dame we have no apologies about wanting winners. We want our students to win debates, in the classroom, on the baseball diamond, and in the more important battles of life. The football team is a great example of how perfection may be attained. We shall always want Notre Dame men to play to win as long as there is a Notre Dame.

"Frank Leahy is the greatest man in American Athletics today," said Father Cavanaugh.

Concessions were made and the number of football scholarships began to rise again, but never again to the pre-retrenchment level of the 1940s.

The doom that Frank Leahy had predicted became a reality in 1950, and for the first time since 1940, the Irish was not ranked in the top ten teams of the nation, for they had lost the heart of their 1949 championship eleven. All-Americans Leon Hart, Jim Martin, and Emil Sitko, as well as Gus Cifelli, Larry Coutre, Walt Grothaus, and Frank Spaniel had graduated and when the Irish barely eked out a 14–7 win over North Carolina in the season's opener, Leahy did not feel any happier over the outcome.

John Carmichael, sports columnist for the *Chicago News*, lunched with Leahy two days before the next game, against Purdue.

"John," said Leahy as they sat in a hotel dining room overlooking Lake Michigan, "you are about to

"Even though this team, with Bob Williams, Captain Jerry Groom, and Jim Mutscheller, lost four games in 1950, it had as much heart as any team I ever coached," said Frank Leahy.

witness one of the great debacles in college football. Purdue is going to shellac us."

And for once Leahy was right. The game wasn't even close.

An eighteen-year-old Purdue quarterback, Dale Samuels, passed for three touchdowns; two more Purdue scores were called back by the officials, but the Boilermakers ran up a 21–0 lead.

Notre Dame scored twice in the final period. But the final score was 28–14, and Notre Dame's five-year unbeaten streak of thirty-nine games was over. The Irish had not been beaten since losing to Great Lakes on December 1, 1945, and only a tie 0–0 with Army and a 14–14 tie with Southern California had come between an all-victorious streak. It was only the fourth loss Leahy had suffered in his eight-year coaching career at Notre Dame.

There were tears in Irish eyes at South Bend after the game. By the end of the season the tears would be a flood. And it would grow worse.

After beating Tulane, Notre Dame lost to bitter rivals Indiana and Michigan State, tied Iowa in a 14–14 thriller, and defeated Navy and Pitt. The season ended with a two-point loss to Southern California, 9–7. Thus ended a season that saw the Irish post a 4–4–1 year, the first non-winning season Notre Dame had seen in seventeen years.

"I suffered much self-doubt that year," said Frank Leahy, "much self-doubt."

So after the humiliation of the 1950 season, Frank Leahy began to rebuild the Irish.

In the opening game of the 1951 season, Notre Dame trampled Indiana 48–6 as fullback Neil Worden showed the hometown fans a "new Irish look" by scoring four touchdowns, all in the second period. Johnny Lattner, Bill Barrett, and Del Gander also scored, and Minnie Mavraides kicked six extra points as the Irish amply demonstrated their devastating new look.

The following week Johnny Petitbon, a speedy 190-pounder, took the opening kickoff in a game against the University of Detroit and sped eighty-five yards for a touchdown. A few plays later Petitbon scored again with a brilliant eighty-yard run. Five minutes later, Petitbon took a lateral pass from quarterback John Mazur and sped 61 yards for his third touchdown of the period as an aroused Irish squad romped over Detroit, 40–6.

Playing the best teams in America during the rest of 1951, the Irish finished with a 7–2–1 record. There was a 20–20 tie with a surprising Iowa team. The one glaring loss, to Michigan State by 35–0 on television, was the biggest margin any team would ever make against a Leahy-coached squad. The other loss was 27–20 to SMU, who brought their great passing star, Fred Benners, to South Bend. Benners completed thirteen passes in the first twenty-five he threw and was responsible for all four of the SMU scores.

The gridiron world was put on notice that Notre Dame was back on top of the college football world when the Irish concluded the 1951 season with an exciting come-from-behind victory over a strong Trojan squad led by All-American Frank Gifford and Pat Cannamela, a spirited, driving back.

Notre Dame, with a 6–2–1 record then, took the field in an unaccustomed position: underdog. The Trojans, with a 7–2–0 record, were favored, and Gifford, USC's great halfback, was the reason.

The game started out rough, with both teams hitting hard and often. In the second period, Irish guard Tom Seaman and USC tackle Bob Van Doren stood toe to toe for a full minute and slugged it out punch for punch until the officials could stop the fight and send both men out of the game.

In the second period Gifford tossed a bullet pass that traveled thirty-five yards to Co-captain Dean Schneider for a first down on the Irish forty-four-yard line. Then Gifford took over. On successive plays he moved to the twenty-yard stripe. Then, with USC fullback Pat Duff clearing the way, Gifford sped across the goal line for a USC score. Giff missed the conversion and it was USC 6, Notre Dame 0.

Then the Irish went to work, and eighteen-year-old quarterback Ralph Guglielmi took personal charge of the Irish offense. He passed to halfback John Petitbon for ten yards. Then another pass, to Chet Ostrowski, was good for thirty-five yards and a first down on the USC fifteen-yard line. Now USC geared up to stop Guglielmi's passing, but Ralph promptly faked a pass and handed off to Johnny Lattner, who sped across the goal line for a touchdown, and it was tied at 6–6.

USC quickly intercepted a wobbly pass by Guglielmi and took the ball to the Irish thirty-four-yard line. Dick Nunis moved the ball to the thirty, then Gifford sped ten more yards. Dean Schneider passed to Jim Sears, and it was good for a first down on the five-yard line. Sears drove in for the score. Gifford missed the conversion, but it was USC 12, Notre Dame 6.

Near the end of the third quarter, Guglielmi started

a ground attack, with Lattner and Neal Worden driving through the USC line with a vengeance as they covered seventy-three yards to tie the score. Bob Joseph missed his second conversion try, and it was a 12–12 game.

In the final period, Guglielmi, Worden, Petitbon, and Lattner combined for another tally. Joseph kicked the extra point, and it was 19–12 as the game and the season ended on a very high note for Notre Dame.

Television had entered the college football scene late in 1950, and the Dumont TV network televised a number of Irish games that initial year. The 1951 Notre Dame-Michigan State game drew the largest viewing audience up to that time, with stations from Boston to Omaha tuning in to the games. Notre Dame, Michigan, Ohio State, Army, Navy, and Penn were leaders in the TV movement because they could televise their games and still draw capacity crowds. The Irish, because of their demonstrated national appeal, were in on the ground floor of television; but the new medium was hurting 95 percent of the smaller colleges, who were now demanding controls that would limit the games televised and give them a proportionate share of the expected huge financial returns.

In 1949 Ed "Moose" Krause, one of the most popular of all Notre Dame stars, an All-American in football and basketball, was named athletic director. It was a job that demanded all of his efforts in the organization and administration of some twenty-three sports in the Irish athletic program and that left little time for other Notre Dame duties.

By this time the TV situation had reached a critical stage and was turned over to Father Theodore Hesburgh, who traveled to the meetings and conventions of the National Collegiate Athletic Association (NCAA) and joined with other leading colleges in the development of a controlled TV program that satisfied most members of the NCAA and that would last until well into the 1980s.

In 1952 Father Hesburgh was named president of Notre Dame, while Father Edmund Joyce became the administrative vice-president and chairman of the athletic board.

Since then Father Hesburgh's career has reached far beyond the campus at South Bend. Consistently ranked among the most influential Americans in both education and religion, he has served six U.S. presidents in varied capacities and has been deeply involved in key social and moral issues of the day.

Under the leadership of Fathers Hesburgh and Joyce, Notre Dame has grown in public esteem and academic distinction from a student body of five thousand in 1952 to more than ninety-five hundred today, while the operating budget has soared from $9 million to more than $176 million.

A leading authority and spokesman on athletics, Father Joyce as well as Father Hesburgh received the Distinguished American Award from the National Football Foundation and the Football Hall of Fame. Father Joyce also is a founder of the College Football Association.

As Moose Krause settled in and took over all the duties of athletic director, Frank Leahy finally was free of all the complicated duties necessary to handle the athletic director's job, and he could do what he always preferred doing—concentrate on the job of coaching his boys, then go home to the family, perhaps even play a bit of poker with friends on a Saturday night during the off season.

The move to curtail Leahy's duties as athletic director was mainly for his health, but it had come a bit late. The normal pressures of coaching had been magnified by the stinging personal criticism and the concerted efforts to have him fired. He beat all those efforts, just as Jesse Harper and Rockne had beaten them in an earlier time, because there always were people with huge stadiums anxious to parlay big gate receipts with a chance to "knock off the top team."

But Frank Leahy was older in 1952, and the several trips to the hospital were beginning to take their toll. He no longer had the vitality to work eighteen to twenty hours each day, then catnap on a cot in his

Reverend Theodore Hesburgh, president of Notre Dame (right), and Reverend Edmund Joyce (left) both retired in 1987.

office and be ready to go at 5:30 A.M. for the daily meetings with his coaches. His friends were beginning to notice his weariness and begged him to slow up.

But the champ still had a punch, and in 1952 he would make his opponents toe the mark. He would beat the big teams, and the complaints would begin once more.

In early 1952 Francis Wallace wrote: "I picked Notre Dame to finish fourth nationally. I thought Maryland had the best club, then Michigan State, Georgia Tech, and Oklahoma were next, in that order."

Talking about the 1952 season, Frank Leahy said:

"Father Hesburgh was one of the first men to congratulate me on the 1952 season, which I thought was probably the finest achievement of my entire life. It could have been one of Notre Dame's worst years.

A total disaster. The schedule was finally tough enough to satisfy the worst of my enemies. It was the best job of pure coaching that I ever did, and it helped me forget my worries that were left over from the terror of the 1950 season and about my own possible incapabilities. The material was just a year away from what I thought was greatness. We had all the necessary ingredients—experienced players at nearly every position, speed, strength, determination, and quality people.

"But the schedule, with Pennsylvania to be followed in order by Texas, Pittsburgh, Purdue, North Carolina, Navy, Oklahoma, Michigan State, Iowa, and the University of Southern California was truly one of the most difficult ever undertaken by a Notre Dame team.

"Yet somehow we survived the ordeal."

JOHNNY LATTNER

John Lattner was imbued with the Notre Dame spirit from the moment he set foot on the campus as a green freshman in 1949: "I came down that driveway and I saw that golden dome with the statue of our Blessed Mother all lighted up, and it was one of the biggest thrills of my life. I got kind of choked up and I was awful glad that I came here to school," recalled Lattner.

"The Notre Dame indoctrination, particularly of the football players, is as relentless as the Marine Corps' boot training," said Lattner. "The first night, they showed the freshmen the movie *Knute Rockne: All-American* with Pat O'Brien, and with Ronald Reagan portraying Notre Dame's first All-American, George Gipp. I left the theater kind of all choked up," said John. "I was ready to kill anybody who said a word against Notre Dame."

A gangling, sensitive boy until he was about ten or eleven, Lattner lived most of his young life in a German-Irish neighborhood on Chicago's West Side. "I was sort of a sissy as a kid," said John. "But my pa wouldn't break up a fight if he saw me in it. He wanted me to learn how to handle myself." John soon found himself playing football with the kids in the area. His mother recalled, "John wanted to grow bigger and stronger like his idol, Superman. So he went on a cod-liver oil binge and once drank seventeen pints of the stuff in a single week."

At Oak Park's Fenwick High School, John won All-State honors as an end in 1948. The following year, elected captain, John was shifted to halfback, where he became the bread-and-butter player and averaged eighteen yards per carry. He made All-State again, the first player in Illinois history to make All-State two years in a row at two different positions. John also led Fenwick to the city championship game, which was watched by sixty-seven thousand fans. After the football season he found time to captain the basketball team and lead it in scoring during his four years and to win two track letters, for the 100- and 220-yard dash; his all-around prowess attracted a record number of colleges who offered the moon to Lattner. But he went to Notre Dame.

One day as a member of the Notre Dame freshman squad—called the "Hamburger Squad"—Johnny brought down a varsity star with a tooth-rattling tackle. Coach Leahy took time out to compliment John right on the field. This morale booster was all Lattner needed, and the following season of 1951 John made the Irish varsity and started his first game, against Indiana.

In the third period of that game, Notre Dame moved to the Hoosiers' five-yard line, and Leahy motioned to Lattner to go into the game. Quarterback John Mazur put his arm around John in the huddle and said, "Johnny, this one is for your sick dad." On the play Lattner bulled into the end zone, carrying three Indiana tacklers over the line.

A serious student with an eighty-one average, an accounting major, John was a terror on the field.

Quarterback John Lattner (No. 14), after a long gain against Purdue in the 1953 game, is about to be downed by a host of Boilermaker tacklers.

Coach Leahy said of him: "He's the best all-around player since John Lujack in 1947."

In the two-platoon era, when offensive experts never risked their fakes and feints by playing defense, Lattner was one of college football's rarities, a throwback to the turtleneck sweater age of sixty-minute iron men.

In three years as Notre Dame's regular halfback, John averaged better than forty minutes a game, carried the ball 350 times from scrimmage, and gained thirty-four yards less than a mile. He scored 120 points and intercepted thirteen passes.

Winner of the Maxwell Trophy in 1952, Lattner became the only player in history to take the award twice. John also won the coveted Heisman Award and trophies from the Washington, Detroit, and Cleveland touchdown clubs for being the nation's top collegiate football player.

There were many great moments and many great thrills in his marvelous career. "But," said Johnny, "I guess the biggest thrill of all was when I was nine years old. It was on a Sunday morning and I drove

Dad's truck for the first time—right through the local butcher's window."

"That John Lattner, ooh! What a ball carrier he became," said Leahy. "In the opening game of 1952 against Pennsylvania, it was Lattner and Tom Carey and Ralph Guglielmi who marched the ball down the field for a touchdown, and Mavraides kicked the extra point.

"But Penn was fighting just as hard as we were, came back in the final period when Bud Adams passed to Eddie Bell for a score, and they tied the game at 7–7 as time ran out."

At the University of Texas a week later, the game was dedicated to Jack Chevigny, who starred for the Irish in 1926, 1927, and 1928. Chevigny later was named head coach at Texas, and in 1934 his Texas eleven beat Notre Dame 7–6 in one of the biggest upsets of the year. Chevigny was one of the nation's heroic young Marine lieutenants in World War II, and he died leading his company to battle against the Japanese at Iwo Jima.

Halfbacks Joe Heap, Johnny Lattner, and Dan

Johnny Lujack (with ball) assists Coach Leahy with his quarterbacks Tom Carey, No. 2, and Ralph Guglielmi, prior to the opening game of the 1952 season.

Wayne Edmonds, the first black Notre Dame varsity player.

Shannon led the Irish to a 14–3 victory over the Longhorns after Texas had jumped off to a 3–0 lead at halftime. But the fire and drive and speed of the Irish backs were too much for the Texans on this day. A week later a strong Pittsburgh team aided by a missed extra point and a safety upset the Irish 22–19.

Purdue, North Carolina, and Navy were beaten in successive weeks.

"I know that Our Lady was riding on our shoulders in our bitter battle against a rough, tough Purdue eleven," said Leahy. "The Boilermakers fumbled the ball eight times—the first eight times they had the ball—but the best we could do was a 26–14 win."

North Carolina came to South Bend and played it tough against the Irish, and it was a 7–7 game until one minute to the end of the half. Then the Irish went to work. Notre Dame's end Art Hunter, who was to be an All-American the following year, snagged a bullet pass from quarterback Guglielmi and dashed over for a touchdown. Bob Arrix kicked the extra point and the Irish led 14–7. In the final period, substitute fullback Tom McHugh slashed his way for two scores, and Irish halfback Joe Heap sped eighty-four yards for the final tally to give Notre Dame a 34–14 win.

Then it was a sparkling, hard-fought battle against Navy, with Irish fullback Neil Worden scoring twice to give Notre Dame a 17–6 victory.

The following week saw the Sooners of Oklahoma visit South Bend for the first game ever between these two titans. Oklahoma had one of their great teams and was rated number one in the nation.

"Their backs, Bill Vessels, Ed Crowder, Buddie Leake, and Buck McPhail, literally tore up our line pretty much all day," said Leahy, "but our lads Guglielmi, Joe Heap, Neil Worden, and Lattner played their hearts out.

"John Lattner was the key to our game. He intercepted a pass that looked like a sure touchdown and then ran it back twenty-seven yards that set up our second touchdown, which tied the score at 14–14. Late in the game when we were ahead, Lattner recovered an Oklahoma fumble that prevented a touchdown, and we were able to squeeze out a 27–21 victory.

"We lost two games and tied another," said Leahy, "and I must talk now about our great defensive linebacker, Dan Shannon. He was superb all year and particularly so against USC in the final game of the year, which we won 9–0. Dan was in USC's backfield more often than their own players.

"I coached very hard in 1952, far too hard. I found myself incapable of taking any time off," said Leahy. "And I was a regular visitor to the doctors. I was being treated for nervous exhaustion and was ordered by my doctors to relax in the off-season. But I found I simply could not. I knew that the 1953 team would be my greatest, and I was eager to begin assembling all the people. I couldn't wait for practice to begin."

1953: FRANK LEAHY'S GREATEST TEAM

The year 1953 was notable for the fact that the liberal substitution rule that had led to the introduction of platoon football was done away with, and the calendar was turned back to the days of sixty-minute players—who played on offense and defense for the entire game.

Doing away with the platoon system came as a stunning shock to all the coaches, and there was a terrific outcry by many of them, who predicted that the change would make for inferior football and would subject players to a greater physical burden, with a consequent increase in injuries. It was a trying year for most coaches in making the readjustment, since few college players had ever been trained in both offense and defense.

The Rules Committee also cut spring practice to twenty days, and legislated against the "sucker shift" designed to pull opposing players offside. It was a ploy specifically directed against Leahy and a few other coaches.

In the opening game of the season, on September 26 at Oklahoma, the Irish faced a team that had not lost a home contest in twenty-four games, and the Sooners were fired up to avenge the 1952 beating at South Bend.

Quarterback Johnny Lattner fumbled the opening kickoff on the two-yard line, recovered the ball, and then drove to the Notre Dame twenty-three-yard stripe. Neil Worden fumbled the ball, Oklahoma recovered, and then scored their first touchdown to lead, 7–0.

Four plays later, Guglielmi passed to Joe Heap who dashed into the end zone to score Notre Dame's first touchdown. Minnie Mavraides kicked the extra point, and it was 7–7. Oklahoma moved into the lead at 14–7 on a brilliant sixty-two-yard pass from Bud Leake to Carl Allison. But just four plays later Neil Worden scored and it was 14–14.

With the score tied at 14–14, Guglielmi made up a special pass pattern for Joe Heap "because our regular pass patterns were being covered by Oklahoma," said Ralph. "I had just intercepted an Oklahoma pass on their forty-one-yard line, and I thought they would be vulnerable to a first-down pass. I told Heap, 'get out there to the left and zigzag and try to get out in the open. And I'll find you with the ball, somehow.' "

On the play Guglielmi ran to his left, then threw diagonally to his right, to Heap, who was an easy target in the Oklahoma secondary, and Joe scampered across the goal line for the touchdown.

"I knew if the play failed," said Guglielmi, "I'd be back on the bench, maybe for the entire season. That's why I have such great respect for Heap," Ralph said.

Later in the third period, Guglielmi took the ball from his center, faded back to his right, back . . . back and then saw Joe Heap all alone. Ralph arched a thirty-six-yard pass to Heap, all alone in the end zone, and it was 21–14 Notre Dame. Several plays later, after a series of plays, Neil Worden, a workhorse all afternoon, banged across from the ten-yard line for another Irish score. Oklahoma scored near the end of the game, but it was too little and too late to make a difference as the Irish took a well-played battle, 28–21.

The following week, with his lineup intact, Leahy started Lattner, Guglielmi, Joe Heap, and Neil Worden in the backfield. The line consisted of Dan Shannon, Frank Varrichione, Ray Lemak, Jim Scrader, Minnie Mavraides, Art Hunter, and Captain Don Penza. It was a team that sports experts said could have easily beaten most of the professional teams in the NFL.

Purdue was easily defeated as the fired-up Irish rolled up thirty-seven points in forty-one minutes and romped to an easy 37–7 victory. Pittsburgh gave the Irish a battle, but Notre Dame had too much for the Panthers, who fell by the wayside before the battering-ram shots of Lattner, Worden, and Heap and Guglielmi's passing, and it was Notre Dame 23, Pitt 14.

Georgia Tech, unbeaten in thirty-one games, visited the campus at South Bend for the first game between the two schools since 1945. They were the defending Southeast Conference champs, had one of their top teams, and were ranked number one, nationally.

Notre Dame took the opening kickoff and showed tremendous speed and power, and in ten plays Neil Worden thundered across the goal line for the first Irish score. Tech got the ball but fumbled; the Irish recovered and started to march once again. With

Behind brilliant blocking, Neil Worden (No. 48), Irish fullback, bursts through this huge hole and dashes for fifty-five yards against Georgia Tech in 1953. Tech players Sam Hensley (No. 48) and Frank Brooks (No. 26) are blocked by Irish defensive linemen to make the play work.

Lattner, Worden, and Heap driving, and with Guglielmi's pinpoint passes, Notre Dame marched to the Yellow Jackets' seven-yard line. Here they fumbled the ball as the half ended further scoring.

"During the first quarter of the Georgia Tech game, I suddenly felt as if I couldn't breathe," said Leahy. "I sat down on the bench and tried to calm myself, then found that I had a sharp pain around my heart. At the half I wanted to ask one of our coaches to help me to our locker room, but I didn't want anybody in the stands to know I was ill. I managed somehow to make it on my own. I sat down in the coaches' room, off the players' big room, took out a pencil and a flash card to make some notes on what to tell our lads. I dropped the pencil, picked it up. Then I dropped the card and pencil. I heard Bill Earley, one of my coaches say, 'You don't look good, coach. What's the matter?' That's when I blacked out.

"Next thing I recall, I saw John McAllister, our equipment man. Mac was crying. I'd worked for Mac when I was an undergraduate twenty-three years before. Somebody handed me a paper cup of whiskey and I got it down. And now the pain got so bad and I was so weak I thought I was passing away, and I told Father Joyce. The others left the room and Father gave me the last rites of the Church."

Captain Don Penza went in to check on Leahy's condition, and finding his coach receiving emergency treatment and the last rites, he returned to the field crying. He told the players about Leahy's condition, and most of the players soon were sobbing.

"But Georgia Tech scored a touchdown because we were so confused we didn't know what we were doing on the field," said Johnny Lattner. "Then we got mad because Tech tied us, 7–7, and we started to move the ball."

In the third period, Heap returned a kickoff thirty-eight yards. The drive was climaxed by a Guglielmi pass to Heap for another Irish score. Mavraides' extra point made the score 14–7.

Notre Dame got a break in the fourth period when Jim Carlen, Tech's quarterback, fumbled the pass from his center with the ball on their thirteen-yard line. The ball scooted into the end zone, and an alert Art Hunter dove on the ball for an Irish score to make it 21–7.

Tech came back with a superb fifty-three-yard pass for a touchdown in the last period to bring the score to 21–14, but Joe Heap and Lattner combined to bring the ball down to the Tech one-yard line, and Lattner scored the final touchdown for a 27–14 victory. As he crossed the Tech goal line, the entire Notre Dame student body sang "Happy Birthday" to Lattner. It was John's twenty-first birthday.

"Several hours later," said Frank Leahy, "when I woke up, I was in the hospital. I'd found out that we won, and that made me feel a whole lot better. I knew then I'd never coach another season. The doctors only made it official when they told me any more coaching would bring on another attack of acute pancreatitis, and that might prove fatal. All jobs have tensions. But coaching football eats out a man's insides. And at Notre Dame, the pressure is worst. Not from within the school. My bosses were always telling me not to worry if we lost a couple of games. But Notre Dame's millions of fans expect us to win. Our football tradition was built on victory under Knute Rockne, the greatest coach who ever lived. I felt myself I should try to maintain that tradition. Anyhow, I hate to lose. Always did."

Frank Leahy was out of the hospital by Wednesday, four days after the Georgia Tech game, but his coaching was to be only supervisory. Joe McArdle would direct the team, with assistance from Bill Earley, Bob McBride, and Johnny Lujack. Terry Brennan, coach of the freshman squad, handled other coaching chores.

Under the direction of McArdle, the Irish rolled over the next several opponents: Navy was routed, 38–7; Penn was beaten, 28–20; and North Carolina was trounced, 34–14.

In 1953, Iowa had one of their finest teams, and on November 21 they had Notre Dame reeling and on the ropes and led the Irish 7–0 on a cold and blustery afternoon at South Bend.

Just before the end of the first half, with the ball on the Iowa twelve-yard line and Notre Dame desperately in need of a time-out, Leahy signaled his tackle Frank Varrichione to fake an injury to get a time-out call. (Leahy had been informed earlier by an official that he had used up all his official time-outs.) This was a standard semi-legal ploy that most of the coaches had used at one time or another; now Notre Dame needed that ploy.

At a signal from the bench, Varrichione moved into the huddle, then let out a terrible scream, clutched his back, and fell to the turf. The referee immediately blew his whistle, and Varrichione was led off the field.

During the time-out Guglielmi had been given a play to call, and as soon as time was in, he calmly took the pass from center, faded back and threw a beautiful, flat, angling pass to Irish end Dan Shannon, who made a marvelous one-handed catch in the end zone, and it was 7–7 as the half ended.

Late in the fourth quarter, Iowa's Frank Gilliam caught a pass on the Irish four-yard line and dashed across the goal line for the Hawkeyes' second touchdown. The kick for the extra point was good, and Iowa had a 14–7 lead. Now a hometown crowd of more than fifty-six thousand spectators shouted themselves hoarse for an Irish tally.

Iowa led 14–7 with just a few minutes remaining in the game and Notre Dame's nine-game winning streak and hopes for an undefeated season seemed to be coming to an inglorious end.

Only three minutes remained to play when gutty Ralph Guglielmi took charge. Three times he found halfback Johnny Lattner with quick, short flip passes, and Lattner picked up five, nine, and fourteen yards on the plays as the Irish pounded away at Iowa and toward the goal line.

Now only six seconds remained.

Once more Guglielmi took the pass from center Jim Schrader and faded back . . . back . . . back. Suddenly Ralph spotted Dan Shannon in the end zone, whirled in his tracks, and once more shot the ball to Shannon, who smothered the ball with one hand and fell across the goal line for a touchdown. Sophomore Don Schaefer kicked the extra point, and Notre Dame had come from behind to tie Iowa 14–14 in one of the most incredible college football games ever played.

When Shannon caught the touchdown pass, Frank Leahy, on the sidelines, jumped into the air, took his hat off, and started to do his interpretation of an Irish jig as Notre Dame partisans almost tore the stadium apart in their enthusiasm.

And up in the press box the writers were making a

big story of Varrichione's fake injury ploy, and by morning sports pages across the country were assaulting Leahy's character and coaching attitudes.

One week later, a crowd of more than ninety-seven thousand spectators jammed the Coliseum in Los Angeles for the annual Notre Dame-Southern California battle, and shortly after the opening kickoff it looked as if Coach Jesse Hill and his inspired Trojans were going to win their biggest game of the year. They marched sixty-two yards to the Notre Dame fifteen-yard stripe before they were halted by a stubborn Irish defense. Notre Dame took over but USC's defense held and the Irish gave up the ball.

The play went back to USC, and the Trojans moved it to the Irish forty-yard line, and then Aramis Dandoy punted on fourth down. The kick—a low, line-drive effort—went straight into the waiting arms of Joe Heap, who demonstrated the finest display of open-field running as he turned, twisted, dodged, and broke away from every Trojan tackler for a spectacular ninety-seven-yard run and a touchdown. Guglielmi missed the extra-point try and the score was 6–0.

USC rooters were stunned by the sudden turn of events.

On the next series of plays the Irish once again took the ball and ripped and slashed away at the Trojan line to march seventy-one yards in nine plays as Lattner cracked in for another Irish score. This time Guglielmi made the extra point.

USC scored after Des Koch, playing his last game for the Trojans, dashed forty-three yards to the Irish five-yard line, then caught a pass on the five-yard stripe and went in for a touchdown to make the score 13–7.

Irish pride, stung by USC's effort, struck back quickly. Neil Worden dashed fifty-five yards right through the USC line and then carried the ball over from the five-yard line. Guglielmi kicked the extra point and now it was 20–7.

In the third quarter Lattner, having one of the greatest days any Irish player ever had, sparked another tally as he and Guglielmi combined in play after play. They ran and passed USC dizzy, and Lattner finally scored. Not it was 27–7. USC came

back with a quick touchdown, but Lattner and company marched right down the field for another Irish score. It was Lattner's third touchdown of the day. And now it was 34–14. Pat Bisceglia recovered a Trojan fumble in the end zone for still another Irish touchdown.

In the final quarter Lattner rammed through for his fourth score. Mercifully the gun sounded two minutes later and put an end to the carnage.

The huge USC crowd sat stunned in the stands as the Irish rooters sang and danced through the vast stadium as the game ended. It was one of the worst beatings USC had ever received; a 48–14 drubbing.

One week later, Southern Methodist was trounced 40–14 as Neil Worden slashed his way to three touchdowns in his final appearance for the Blue and Gold. Lattner scored twice, and Frank Varrichione recovered a fumble in the end zone for another score.

As the game ended, the entire Irish squad raced over to the sidelines, hoisted Coach Frank Leahy on to their shoulders, and marched him over to the west stands, where he waved and blew kisses to his wife, Florence.

It was to be Leahy's last appearance on a Notre Dame field as head coach.

John Lattner was named to the All-America team for the second straight time and received the Heisman Trophy. Art Hunter and Captain Don Penza also were named to the All-America squad.

One of the Irish coaches told a story near the end of 1953 about Johnny Lattner's value to the team.

It seems that Florence Leahy, the coach's wife, was chasing one of the Leahy children to administer some sort of punishment. She fell on the stairs. And then she called Leahy.

"Frank," she said, "I'm sorry to call you off the practice field, but I'm in the hospital. I broke my left leg running after one of your kids."

There was shocked silence on the other end of the line.

"Frank," she continued.

"Yes, Floss . . . yes, I heard you.

"Frank," she said, "better me than John Lattner, huh?"

CHAPTER 6

TERRY BRENNAN IS SO YOUNG TO BE HEAD COACH

On January 31, 1954, Frank Leahy resigned as Notre Dame's head football coach. His doctors had given him an option: "Give up coaching or die." And so Leahy resigned.

There were various noises of protest from sportswriters and broadcasters around the nation, but the loudest noises were the sighs of relief from coaches on the Notre Dame schedule.

And on a chill Friday in January 1954, Father Theodore Hesburgh, president of Notre Dame, summoned the freshman coach, Terry Brennan, to his study. It was 10:00 P.M. when Father Hesburgh told the twenty-five-year-old Brennan that Frank Leahy had resigned and that if he thought he had enough experience to handle the head coaching job at Notre Dame, it was his. Terry Brennan accepted the challenge.

When she heard the news, a charming woman in Milwaukee turned to her husband and asked: "Why did they select Terry? He's so young." The woman was Terry Brennan's mother, Mrs. Katherine Brennan, and the same question was on many other lips across the nation.

The best possible answer came from Terry himself. "In this job," he said, "I'll age fast."

The day after Brennan was named to succeed Leahy, Terry was introduced to the press at a luncheon at the Morris Inn, the lovely hotel that stands just outside the main gate of the campus on the edge of the university's eighteen-hole golf course.

Sportswriters, photographers, and newsreel cameramen had come from all over the nation to meet the young man who was taking over the biggest job in college football. They had come, too, to say good-bye to the retiring Leahy, whose record at Notre Dame, which included six unbeaten teams in eleven years, was one of the best ever made by a major college coach. It was a day laced with excitement and occasional dashes of sentiment.

In the midst of the emotional good-byes to Leahy and warm greetings to Brennan, a reporter asked, "Aren't you nervous, Terry, becoming coach of Notre Dame at twenty-five?"

"I don't know," he said. "I'll be twenty-six in a few months."

It took more than a streak of Irish luck and an undiluted Irish ancestry for Brennan to win the head coach's job at Notre Dame. What made him the top choice in a field that conceivably might have included nearly every coach in the nation?

First and foremost, Terry was a Notre Dame man, a remarkable embodiment of the qualities of high scholarship, strong character, and outstanding athletic

Frank Leahy (left) chats with Terry Brennan at a luncheon given in their honor. Brennan was appointed Notre Dame's head coach to succeed Leahy on February 19, 1954. Brennan's appointment had been announced a day earlier.

prowess that the college likes to stress. As an undergraduate, 1945–49, Terry maintained a classroom average of eighty-five. He majored in philosophy, an unlikely major for a football star, and had just missed graduating *cum laude*. He was a member of the Student Council, and as an eighteen-year-old was elected president of his class. Joe Doyle, the highly respected former sports editor of the *South Bend Tribune*, was in a few classes with Terry and says he stood out not so much because he was a football player but because he had a mind of his own and always spoke up in class clearly and objectively.

Terry wasn't one of Notre Dame's greatest halfbacks in a postwar period of many star backs, but he was a really fine player. Younger and smaller (five feet, eleven inches, 170 pounds) than most, he started thirty of thirty-eight games in his four years on the varsity, and in two of those, 1946 and 1947, he scored more points and ran with the ball more times than anyone else on the team. Three of the teams he played on were undefeated. Coach Leahy, commenting on the frequent use of Brennan in 1948, said: "When it was third down and four to go, I don't know of a better back to get those yards than Terence."

When Father Hesburgh announced Brennan's appointment he made no reference to his youth, but he cited some of the things Terry had accomplished since he left Notre Dame in 1949.

"After graduating Notre Dame," said Hesburgh, "Terry enrolled in law school, first at Loyola, then at DePaul, where he received his law degree in June 1953. Terry went to law school mornings, taught two forty-minute classes in accounting at Mount Carmel High School, and coached the football team in the afternoon; he studied his law cases at night and his game movies. In three of those four years, he continued that dizzy schedule," said Father Hesburgh. "His Mount Carmel teams won successive city championships, something no other school had ever done.

"Terry was only twenty years old—barely older than some of his players—when he was named head coach at Mount Carmel High. Yet there was little question of his authority."

"In the final analysis," Terry said, "people judge you on whether you know what you're doing."

Once when his high-school team was in training before a big game, his players insisted on roughhousing by wrestling each other until one o'clock in the morning. Terry, afraid somebody would get hurt, warned them to stop.

"I guess they didn't believe me," he said. So one morning, at one o'clock, he abruptly called for forty minutes of calisthenics under the stars. He never encountered that problem again, nor ever had to discipline a player.

Born in Milwaukee on June 11, 1928, one of six children, Terry always had to fight against being overshadowed by older men. First it was his dad, a fine football player at Notre Dame and Marquette. Then it was his brothers (Terry is the youngest of four Brennan boys.) Brother Jim was a star halfback at Notre Dame in 1944–'46 and '47.

As a football player Terry is best remembered for his ninety-seven-yard touchdown dash against Army in 1947 on the very first play of the game.

It was in the classroom, however, that he took his most significant steps toward becoming Notre Dame's head coach. When Notre Dame was challenged by a famed educator, Dr. Robert Hutchins, a foe of big-time football, to produce just one football player who could discuss Aristotle's "Ethics" on a radio panel, Brennan was selected. His articulate, clear headed performance impressed Rev. John Cavanaugh, then president of Notre Dame, and Father Hesburgh, then one of Terry's religious teachers.

Growing up in Milwaukee, the Brennan boys started an athletic complex in their backyard. "I don't know how my mother put up with it all," Terry said. "We had a pole-vaulting setup there and we used to throw the shot, too. Then we had a three-hurdle track in the driveway. We'd race out of the garage and then on down the drive. And of course we played basketball and football there."

Terry became a pole vaulter in high school, and by the time he reached Notre Dame he was vaulting twelve feet, six inches without much effort.

After he was named head coach in January 1954, a reporter said to him, "I've finally found a similarity between you and Rockne. You were both pole vaulters." Terry got a big laugh out of it and would repeat the story at banquets.

In the days before his illness in 1953, Frank Leahy was delighted with the work of his freshman coach, Terry Brennan, and when Leahy became ill, Brennan helped Joe McArdle and Bill Earley with some of the varsity chores. When Leahy decided to retire in early 1954, Brennan was the only candidate the Notre Dame officials considered.

On the Friday that Terry was given the job—with strict orders over the weekend to keep the story secret—he burst into the home he was renting and yelled to his wife, "Hold on to your hat, Kel—I'm it!" On Monday, when the first wave of reporters arrived with several policemen, a neighbor next door rushed over and asked, "Kel, is anything wrong?"

Discussing his approach to the job, Terry told a reporter that his team would not be a carbon copy of previous Notre Dame teams but that he would not make change for the sake of change.

"Remember Frank Leahy's record," he told the reporter. "It took some good original ideas to win all those great games over the years. I'm not going to throw any of them away."

The first major move Terry Brennan made in his new job was to retain Leahy's aides. Johnny Druze, who had been with Frank since his coaching days at Boston College, was his first assistant. Terry also retained Bill Earley and named Bill Fischer, George Dickson, and Francis Johnston as assistant coaches.

When the Notre Dame players reported for practice in the fall of 1954, Brennan realized that he was in the most difficult spot in his young life for a young man with his limited coaching experience. He was following a genius who was even now being compared to the incomparable Knute Rockne.

Brennan was taking over a team that was unbeaten in ten games in 1953, a team that Coach Frank Leahy called "The greatest team Notre Dame ever had." There would be constant comparisons and criticisms, some by the Old Master himself, who did not make life any easier. Brennan was taking over a team that had lost six All-Americans, including one of Notre Dame's greatest backs, Johnny Lattner. Also lost were Neil Worden, Captain Don Penza, Art Hunter, Minnie Mavraides, Jim Schrader, Art Nowack, Paul Robst, Bob Martin, Dick Washington, and Rockne Morrissey.

Terry was heartened with the return of ends Dan Shannon and Paul Matz, who were co-captains; tackle Wayne Edmonds, the first black to be recruited; tackles Sam Palumbo and Frank Varrichione; guards Ray Lemak and Pat Bisceglia; a fine center in Dick Szymanski; and several great backfield starters, including Tom Carey, Joe Heap, Don Schaefer, Dick Keller, Dick Fitzgerald, Paul Reynolds, and one of Notre Dame's great quarterbacks, Ralph Guglielmi. There was also the Louisville, Kentucky, freshman that Leahy had predicted would be, "one of Notre Dame's greatest stars," Paul Hornung.

On September 25, the Irish opened their 1954 season before more than fifty-seven thousand hometown fans at South Bend, with former coach Frank Leahy one of the spectators and with reporters,

cameramen, and TV crews from all over the nation on hand to record the event.

Terry Brennan made his debut as head coach a success by defeating the Texas Longhorns, 21–0.

Texas threatened as the game opened and reached the Irish seven-yard line before they were halted and Notre Dame took over. It was their only threat of the day.

Quarterback Ralph Guglielmi led a spirited, well-coordinated Irish attack as he personally accounted for two touchdowns, passing for a third, and then intercepting two Texas passes at crucial spots.

Guglielmi's interception of a pass on his own nineteen-yard line and a fifty-two-yard runback set up the first Notre Dame score in the second period. Dan Shannon then went over the goal line on a nineteen-yard pass play from Guglielmi. Ralph also smashed over for a score in the third period, and then in that same period bucked across for his second touchdown, from the five-yard line.

And now there were visions of another undefeated season.

But the following week Purdue's great star Len Dawson passed for four touchdowns as they defeated Notre Dame 27–14. But the Irish rebounded the

Dick Szymanski, a six-three, 230-pound linebacker, played under Coach Leahy from 1951 to 1953 and in 1954 was one of the stars of Coach Terry Brennan's first team. Syzmanski was later a pro football player and general manager of the Baltimore Colts.

following week with a smashing win over a highly rated Pittsburgh team, 33–0.

Michigan State, led by Duffy Daughterty was one of the leading teams in the nation. With a Rose Bowl victory over UCLA the preceding January, the Spartans had a record of three straight wins over Frank Leahy-coached teams, and now they were counting on win number four. But Terry Brennan's eleven, playing before a hometown audience of some fifty-seven thousand roaring fans, played their hearts out to upset the Spartans in an amazing come-from-behind display to win, 20–19. The game ended as State scored and then tried to tie the Irish with the extra point after the touchdown, but Pat Bisceglia deflected the kick and Notre Dame had their biggest win of the season. It was a stunning win for Brennan and the Irish over a State team that had been ranked number three in the nation in 1953.

On October 30, just one week after the win over Michigan State, Notre Dame, now ranked among the leaders in the nation's football fraternity, defeated a strong, stubborn, tough Navy team by a 6–0 score. The game was played in Baltimore and witnessed by sixty thousand. The Navy team, coached by Eddie Erdelatz, went on to a national ranking and won the Sugar Bowl game at the end of the season. "Terry Brennan has a truly outstanding team," said Erdelatz, "and that quarterback Guglielmi is a great one."

There were days, however, when the Irish coaching staff worried about this much-lauded successor to Lujack, Bertelli, and Bob Williams. Twice since enrolling at Notre Dame, Ralph Guglielmi had been serious about quitting. And he wasn't too sure he wanted to go to Notre Dame in the first place.

Guglielmi had been a three-sport star at Grandview Heights High School in the suburbs of Columbus, Ohio. He wasn't the top prospect in the state; other quarterbacks rated higher. Notre Dame coaches were more interested in Don Bucci of Youngstown, who had a better record than Guglielmi.

Though Ralph, the only child of Marino and Rose Guglielmi, wanted to attend Notre Dame when he was younger, nearby Ohio State really excited and attracted him during his senior year. The deciding factor may have been a personal visit by Coach Leahy during one of his off-season speaking and scouting tours in early 1951. But even after Leahy's visit, Ralph still was unconvinced.

"Naturally, I was thrilled by Coach Leahy's personal visit to me. I don't think many kids ever experienced that kind of thrill. But I had every intention of attending Ohio State [where his mother was a housemother for a fraternity] until one night in early June," Ralph recalled.

"I don't know whether it was a dream or just my subconscious desire coming forth. When I went to bed that particular night, I was dead set on Ohio. In the morning, I was just as convinced that I should attend Notre Dame. And two days later I was in South Bend and registering for my freshman classes."

But Ralph's wasn't a happily-ever-after story. There were other incidents that almost made him leave Notre Dame.

The first incident followed his marvelous showing in the 1951 Southern California game. With three years of eligibility remaining, Ralph again became the target of Ohio State partisans. One Ohio executive is supposed to have offered "everything but the moon" if Ralph would switch schools. It was supposed to include a medical school scholarship, a car, some cash, and a job for Ralph's father.

The next time Ralph packed his bags to leave Notre Dame was official. The day after the 1953 undefeated season, Ralph, who had been called "the most improved player" on the team, and his roommate, Joe Heap, were caught carousing off campus limits after

Ralph Guglielmi, Notre Dame quarterback from 1951 to 1954, led the Irish to four outstanding seasons.

the midnight curfew. Both were suspended for the remainder of the semester.

Ralph was bitter at the suspension.

"But later after thinking it over, I realized that the school was sincere in not making a football player something special."

If Ralph's indecision regarding the strict code of student behavior suggested a lack of maturity on his part, then his operation of the complicated "split-T" offense for Coach Terry Brennan corrected such an impression. Guglielmi handled the quarterback chores with a boldness and conviction that amazed Notre Dame's opponents.

In 1951 and 1952, under Frank Leahy, when Irish quarterbacks played only on offense, Ralph would enter a game with enough bench instructions to call an entire series of plays.

In 1953, under Leahy, the quarterback had to stay in the game on defense, and the Irish coaches discovered Ralph was more ingenious when left on his own.

Much of Guglielmi's defensive ability and all his offensive skill he credited to his idol Johnny Lujack, who was his backfield coach in his sophomore and junior years.

"Johnny helped me in almost every phase of the game," Ralph explained. "There are dozens and dozens of mistakes a quarterback can make, many of which go unnoticed, except by the coaches."

Comparison of teacher and pupil are tough to make.

Lujack's best years were with the championship 1946 and 1947 teams. At his peak, Johnny was three years older than Guglielmi.

Guglielmi showed that he had fully matured in the 1954 season under Coach Terry Brennan, and Ralph's quarterback play during the year ranked him alongside Bertelli, Lujack, and Bob Williams.

Ralph's superb all-around play in the Michigan State battle of 1954, one of the most exciting games in Notre Dame history, was followed by his pinpoint passing and excellent signal calling in the Navy game and proved to one and all that Guglielmi had arrived.

During the next several weeks, Ralph's inspired play at quarterback sparked crushing victories over a number of top teams in the nation: On November 6, there was a 42–7 win over Penn; this was followed by a romp over a strong North Carolina eleven, 42–13; and then the Irish crushed Iowa, 34–18. This was basically the same Iowa team that had humbled Leahy squads in three of four previous challenges.

Under Terry Brennan, the Irish juggernaut rolled on unimpeded much as it had done under Leahy. Notre Dame had won all but the Purdue game on the 1954 schedule.

So on the bone-chilling afternoon of November 27 at South Bend, Coach Jess Hill brought his USC Trojans in for their annual battle. This was the twenty-sixth meeting between the two teams, and USC had been every bit as impressive as Notre Dame that season. The Trojans had won eight and lost two close games, and they were primed for the Irish.

After the first fifty-four minutes of the game, Notre Dame fans were rubbing their eyes in disbelief, and the bookmakers were checking the airline schedules for flights to Mexico.

The score was 17–14 Southern California, and a crowd of over fifty-six thousand shocked South Bend fans sat, silent hearts on their sleeves, for the biggest upset of the season.

Notre Dame had possession of the ball on their twenty-eight-yard line. It was third down and three yards to go. Trojan fans were already celebrating their smashing victory, screaming and dancing in anticipation.

Calmly, quarterback Guglielmi called the play: "Okay, guys, let's go with the big one." He nudged halfback Jim Morse. "Now, get this one, Jim." Morse nodded. "Throw it. I'll get it."

Back in formation, Guglielmi called the play, took the pass from center Dick Szymanski, faded back to his left, dodged a tackler, and then flipped a short bullet pass to Morse, who brought the Irish fans to their feet, screaming with delight as he dodged and sped seventy-two yards through the entire USC team for a last-minute touchdown. Then to add insult to injury, Notre Dame scored on a two-point safety to make the final score Notre Dame 23, USC 17.

After the game the Trojans boarded the team plane for California to prepare for Ohio State in the Rose Bowl. Notre Dame had a date with Southern Methodist in Texas.

The Notre Dame-SMU game was a battle to the very last minute, with both teams throwing caution to the winds in an effort to win.

Jim Morse returned the opening kickoff forty-one yards as the Irish blocked beautifully. Then on successive pass plays—Guglielmi to Morse and to Joe Heap—Notre Dame moved to the SMU four-yard line, and Heap bulled over to give Notre Dame a 6–0 lead. The kick for the extra point was missed. The Mustangs picked up the tempo and then lost the

"Joe Heap could run, pass, kick, receive passes, and run back kickoffs better than anyone I ever coached," said Frank Leahy. Heap played at Notre Dame from 1951 to 1954.

eighty-nine yards and another Irish touchdown. Schaefer's extra-point kick was good, and Notre Dame now had a comfortable margin 26–14 as the game ended.

The glorious victories over Southern California and SMU ended an excellent first year for young Terry Brennan, who led the Irish to a remarkable 9–1–0 season and fourth place in the national rating of all college football teams.

Ralph Guglielmi took fourth place in the vote for the coveted Heisman Award, but he was the first choice on everybody's All-America teams. Frank Varrichione and Dan Shannon were also All-America selections, and a hard-running, flashy sophomore, Paul Hornung, although playing only 130 minutes during the season, showed much promise. He was the third-string quarterback behind Guglielmi and Tom Carey, but when Hornung was sent in to play, the entire team seemed to respond. In the seventh game of the season, against North Carolina, Hornung intercepted a pass and dashed seventy yards for a score. In that game Paul completed five straight passes, and ran for thirty-eight yards on a reverse as the Irish ran up a 42–13 win. And it was just the beginning of a remarkable career that was to place Hornung among the all-time All-Stars.

Terry Brennan's 1954 squad had had two years of Frank Leahy's coaching, and the bulk of the Leahy staff still was with Brennan during 1954. But in 1955 only end coach John Druze was retained by Brennan. Officials and experts on the Notre Dame scene warned Terry about letting the experienced coaches go; but it is customary for a new head coach to bring in his own men, and Terry did just that.

Bill Fischer, Bill Walsh, and Jack Landry, former teammates of Brennan's on the 1946–'47 national championship teams, were brought in to assist Terry. All of the new coaches had had some professional experience and were expected to impart valuable pro techniques. It was all accepted as very forward-looking.

ball on downs. But Heap fumbled; SMU recovered, and the Mustangs' John Roach dashed in for a touchdown. Ed Barnet's extra point was good and it was SMU 7, Notre Dame 6.

But Guglielmi hit on a couple of long pass plays and then scored from the SMU six-yard line to make it 13–7 Notre Dame after the point after touchdown.

SMU could not advance the ball as the second period began following the kickoff, and Bob Scannell, Notre Dame's fine end, blocked Johnny Roach's punt, scooped up the ball on the twenty-five-yard line, and outraced several SMU tacklers to score for Notre Dame. In the third period Heap, closing out a brilliant career, took a handoff from Guglielmi, eluded two SMU tacklers, broke through the line, and sped

"I WAS DISGUSTED AT NOTRE DAME," SAID PAUL HORNUNG

The 1955 Irish backfield, with Jim Morse, Don Schaefer, Paul Reynolds, Aubrey Lewis, and Paul Hornung, looked formidable. Hornung was moved from halfback to quarterback because the split-T formation could readily adapt to his all-around versatility. The Irish line was the big question mark. Captain

Ray Lemak, a three-year star at his tackle position, played his heart out all year long on one leg. His right knee was badly battered, but Ray was in the game until the last whistle sounded. Pat Bisceglia, a sturdy guard, also played with a battered knee. So did Gene Kapish, a fine end. Jim Mense was the only

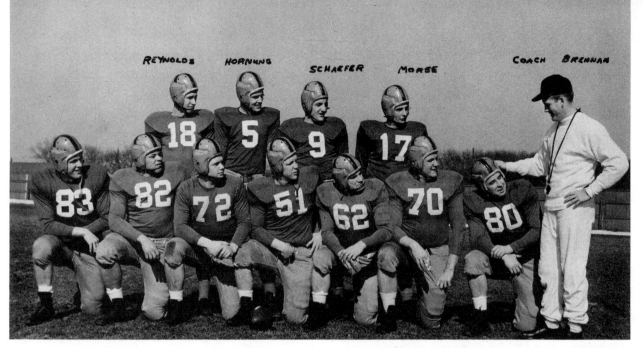

REYNOLDS   HORNUNG   SCHAEFER   MORSE   COACH BRENNAN

Terry Brennan's second season as head coach in 1955, was a most successful one, for the Irish won eight and lost two games. Paul Hornung, halfback; Don Schaefer, fullback; and guard Pat Bisceglia were named to the All-America team.

capable center; if he were injured, the entire line would suffer.

It was here in the line that Brennan and his new coaches had to concentrate, and they did a remarkable job by utilizing the reserves held over from the Frank Leahy era.

But it was the remarkable showing by Paul Hornung that brought smiles to Brennan and his coaches as Paul was simply brilliant throughout the spring and fall practice sessions. He could do everything on a football field. He could pass and hit his target at fifty yards. He could kick like a demon, and although he was not the fastest man on the team, he was nearly unstoppable once out in the open.

"Notre Dame didn't come after me quite as strongly as some of the other schools," said Paul Hornung. "They never even scouted me. The first I knew that they were interested in me was when they wrote Coach Miller, my coach at Flaget High School in Louisville, and asked him to send films of my pal Sherrill Sipes and me in action. (Notre Dame Athletic Director Moose Krause said Sipes and I were the only kids up to that time ever offered full-time scholarships on the basis of films alone.) Next thing I knew we were invited to South Bend for the Southern California game. After the game we met Frank Leahy, the head coach. But that's all there was to it; no commitments, no offers made.

"A month or so later, and after I had offers from Georgia Tech, Indiana, Kentucky, and a dozen other schools, Notre Dame started to move in. One day I got a call from Bob McBride, Leahy's chief assistant. McBride was coming in to see me.

"When I met McBride I was greatly impressed. I had heard all about his play with the 1941, 1945, and the great 1946 national championship teams and his great World War II record, and it was a thrill just to meet Bob. Bob told me that Sherrill and I both had the grades to get into Notre Dame and that both of us would get a four-year scholarship—tuition, room and board, and books. And if we wanted to go on to graduate school, we could become assistant coaches. Then he invited us up to Notre Dame.

"It was early in the spring when Sherrill and I drove up to South Bend, and it was cold and damp. We stood in the middle of the campus. It looked bare. All the guys were in class and everything seemed gray and desolate.

"I looked at Sherrill, and Sherrill looked at me, and I said, 'Let's not go here.'

"And Sherrill said, 'Right. Let's get out, fast.'

"Before we could leave, McBride took us to see Coach Leahy.

"Here was one of the world's great salesmen. He could sell ice cubes to Eskimos in winter. He was sitting behind his desk, wearing those rumpled clothes. His face looked worried and concerned. Then he advanced on us, shook our hands, broke into a wide smile, and put his arms around Sherrill and me.

" 'Lads,' he said, 'you would both look awfully good wearing the blue and gold of Notre Dame. And Our Lady needs you here.'

"That did the trick. We got the feeling that we simple, country kids were talking to a saint; not a mere football coach, not a man—but something a little above.

"Then Coach Leahy looked right into my eyes and said, 'Paul, not only will you get a first-rate education here, but I think I can make you the greatest football player in the country.'

"There was silence for about ten seconds. Then Sherrill said, 'Where do we sign?'

"Leahy smiled. 'We don't sign here, lads. We just shake hands.'

"We shook hands and left the campus feeling like we had just left a corner of heaven.

"Sherrill and I drove home to Louisville, packed

Paul Hornung was an All-American in 1955 and 1956 and the Heisman Trophy winner in 1956. He developed into one of the all-time pro stars during Green Bay's championship seasons under Vince Lombardi.

our bags, and a few days later we enrolled at Notre Dame.

"We had been at Notre Dame for about two months, and had become discouraged and unhappy. Sipes and I never got to play any games with the freshman team, we were just part of the hamburger squad—that's the group of guys who scrimmaged the varsity and they made hamburger out of us. We got the hell kicked out of us every day," said Hornung.

"That was bad enough, but Sherrill and I were having problems with our grades and other things. The football players each had a varsity man assigned to him, sort of a tutor and adviser. Johnny Lattner was assigned to me. Johnny was a halfback, a Heisman Award winner, and an All-American, and John was there if I needed help. But I never felt it was right to go to him with our troubles.

"Then I hurt my elbow and Sipes hurt his knee and one day after we got mashed up, we sat down and wrote a letter to the coach at the University of Miami about transferring. But we never mailed the letter.

"Then a couple of days later I got a tremendous boost to my confidence when we played in the Old-Timers' Game.

"The Old-Timers at Notre Dame, most of them All-Americans and professional players, square off in an annual game against the varsity team at the end of spring practice.

"I finally got into the game in the third quarter and I had my best game at Notre Dame. I passed five times in a row, all completions; ran for thirty-eight yards. Three of my passes were good for touchdowns, and with a couple of minutes to play, I passed to an end, Bob Scannell, for another score. All told I had a hand in twenty of our points as we beat the Old-Timers, 49–26.

"The next day, the sports editor of the *Louisville Courier* started his story of the game this way: 'The famed Golden Dome of Notre Dame's campus had a young rival today—a golden-haired football player named Paul Hornung, who had everybody taking note of his sensational play.'

"That was the start of everybody talking about me, calling me 'Golden Boy.' "

Southern Methodist, defeated by the Irish in a bitter struggle in the final game of the 1954 season, played Notre Dame in the opening game of the 1955 campaign, this time at South Bend.

The game, played September 24, should have been

another war, but the Irish took things in stride and came away with an easy 17–0 shutout. Indiana had beaten the Irish in 1950 and were set with another strong team, but Notre Dame, with Hornung and Morse sparking the offense, romped over the Hoosiers by a 19–0 score the following week.

The Miami Hurricanes, rated as one of the nation's new powers in collegiate football, were the favorites as they met Notre Dame in the Orange Bowl for the first clash between the two teams. But Terry Brennan's team shut down the strong Miami offense and defeated the Hurricanes 14–0 in the first night game the Irish had ever played. It was the third straight shutout victory for Notre Dame.

Terry Brennan now had won eleven consecutive games and twelve of the thirteen he had coached thus far at Notre Dame. It was a record that compared with those of the finest Notre Dame coaches: Harper, Rockne, and Frank Leahy.

The bubble burst, however, on October 15, when Michigan State, rated just behind Oklahoma in the national ratings and eager to avenge the previous year's one-point loss at South Bend, quickly jumped off to a 7–0 first-quarter lead. But quarterback Paul Hornung engineered a spectacular fifty-yard pass to Jim Morse. Paul was actually in the grasp of a State tackler when he let fly with the ball, and Morse caught it on the five-yard line and drove over for the score. Hornung kicked the extra point and it was a 7–7 ball game.

But State's quarterback, Earl Morrall, and Gerry Planutis scored touchdowns to give State a 21–7 win.

One week later, in an abrupt about-face, Notre Dame roared back to smash out a 22–7 triumph over Purdue, then followed with an impressive win over a tough Navy team, 21–7, who battled the Irish to the final whistle. Next it was on to Philadelphia and a stunning 46–14 romp over Penn. North Carolina battled Notre Dame tooth and nail, but a last-minute effort by Hornung gave the Irish a 27–7 victory.

Iowa had a reputation as Notre Dame's Jonah, and the Hawkeyes appeared on the road to an early score, but their star back, Bill Happel, fumbled on the Iowa forty-four-yard line, and the Irish recovered the ball. Hornung set to work and tossed two passes good for a first down on the Iowa ten. On the next play Dean Studer scored and it was 7–0 as Hornung added the extra point.

The Hawkeyes tied the game in the third period on a plunge by Fred Harris from the Irish five-yard line. Jim Freeman kicked the extra point and Iowa had tied the game, 7–7.

In the fourth quarter, the Hawkeyes took the lead after Don Dobrino passed to Jerry Reichow and then kicked the extra point for a 14–7 edge.

But then Hornung took things into his own hands by speeding thirty-eight yards to midfield. On the next play, Paul was chased by a swarm of Iowa tacklers but got off a spectacular fifty-yard heave to Jim Morse all alone on the goal line, and Jim fell across the line for the touchdown. Hornung converted, and the score was 14–14.

"There were only four minutes to play when we got the ball," recalled Hornung, "and we started to move. I drove into the line for five yards, but we failed to gain on the next two plays. Now it was third and eleven and I tossed a thirty-five-yard pass to Morse, and we were now in position to try a field goal with but two minutes left in the game.

"I was very excited when we lined up for the field-goal try," said Hornung. "I had never been so tense and nervous before. I remember exactly what was on my mind just before I tried the kick. I was thinking of that game my senior year in high school when we played Chattanooga Central, when I tried a field goal with the score 7–7 and missed. Just before the kick against Iowa, standing there all alone with the crowd shrieking, I kept repeating to myself, 'Let's not have another Chattanooga game. . . . Let's not have another Chattanooga game.'

"Jim Morse held the ball on the Iowa eighteen, which made it a twenty-eight-yarder. Jim got the pass from center, placed the ball perfectly, the line held, I kicked, and it went through the center of the crossbars.

"Right after the kick, the game ended and my teammates and some fans picked me up, hoisted me onto their shoulders, and carried me off the field. It was a wonderful feeling.

"The next week, on the Coast against Southern Cal, I had another big game, but we lost. And when you lose, I don't care how big a game you personally have, you just don't feel elated.

"Southern California opened up with a touchdown. Then I ran eight yards for a score to even it up. Then they picked up two more touchdowns and now had a big lead.

"I hit Morse on a big pass play—a sixty-yarder that set up a touchdown and put us behind by one point, 21–20.

"But USC then exploded for three closing touchdowns. Their great back Jon Arnett went sixty-four yards for one, and ninety-five thousand fans went home satisfied with the win. At least the USC fans did.

"I had quite a game statistically. I gained 259 yards, passing and ninety-five running, and that total of 354 yards was the most accumulated by any college player in 1955.

"Shortly after the season ended, Jim Morse and I were having dinner together at South Bend and we talked about how great it was to win eight games out of ten. And, jokingly, I said to him, 'Wouldn't it be funny if we were 2–8 in 1956?' "

The 8–2 season earned Notre Dame ninth place in the national ranking. Paul Hornung, Don Schaefer, and guard Pat Bisceglia were All-America selections.

With a 17–3 record in his two years at Notre Dame, Terry Brennan was nationally accepted as the coach who would continue to keep the Irish on a high plane during the next several years. He was named coach of the year by the Washington, D.C., Touchdown Club, one of the nation's most prestigious organizations in football, and was selected to coach the East team in the annual East-West Game the next year.

But 1956 was to be another kind of season for Notre Dame, and for Terry Brennan it was a time for testing.

TERRY BRENNAN'S YEAR OF TRAVAIL

The 1956 edition of the annual Notre Dame *Dope Book*, which previewed the coming season for Irish supporters, carried an article by Coach Terry Brennan that stated: "This is the youngest and most inexperienced team ever to represent Notre Dame. Six of our seven linemen, regulars on the 1954 team, had graduated. The same situation is present in 1956. But a year ago," said Terry, "there were a number of reserve players with game experience who could jump in and do a creditable job for us. . . . To the credit of these men and to the coaches, we did come up with a line that performed fairly well . . . most of the time. But this year hardly any reserve strength is returning."

In addition to the lack of experienced players, there were a significant number of changes in Brennan's coaching staff.

Johnny Druze, who had arrived at Notre Dame with Frank Leahy in 1941, abruptly left to take over the head coaching post at Marquette. He was replaced by Jack Zilly, an end on the 1946 national championship team. Jim Finks, a former Pittsburgh Steeler quarterback, retired as a player and joined Brennan's brain trust as the backfield coach.

"We opened the '56 season against Southern Methodist," said Paul Hornung, "and we were fourteen-point favorites to beat them, but we took a beating, 19–13. It was the first opening-day loss for Notre Dame since 1934. We almost caught them, but time ran out.

"We were behind 13–0 when I passed fifty-five yards to Jim Morse for a touchdown, and then I kicked the extra point. Then with ten minutes left to play, on our forty-three-yard line, I got away for fifty-seven yards and another score. The kick was blocked. Two minutes later, they scored again for a 19–13 lead. We got moving again with everybody contributing and were down to their seven-yard line as time ran out. One more play . . . ten more seconds . . . and we would have tied them.

"The next week we beat Indiana, 20–6. I got lucky and completed fifteen passes for 121 yards and rushed for eighty-one yards. Aubrey Lewis ran for our third touchdown.

"And that was our last win until my last home game at South Bend.

"Purdue beat us, 28–14. I tossed two passes good for scores and ran a kickoff back for fifty yards. But Purdue intercepted one of my passes, and that set up the winning touchdown.

"Against Michigan State it was a rough and tough game, and even though they had an outstanding, nationally ranked team, we played them to a 7–7 tie at halftime. But in the second half they walloped us 47–14 and I got my first injury as a college player when I tackled State's speedy halfback Dennis Mendyk as he broke out into the open and was headed for another touchdown. I got him on a shoestring tackle but banged up my left hand.

"The next week we played the number one team in the nation, Oklahoma, and it was a disaster. I carried the ball a couple of times for small gains, but they were too big and smart and too experienced for us and we got beat, 40–0.

"Then in succession Navy beat us 33–7, and the next week it was Pittsburgh and another drubbing.

"I started the Pitt game at fullback and got away for a fifty-six-yard touchdown, then intercepted a pass and ran it back for another fifty-five yards, but they overwhelmed us, 26–13.

"My last home game was against North Carolina, and I wanted it to be special. It was a good day for me as I scored two quick touchdowns for a 14–0 lead. Then with their great halfback Ed Sutton running the ball, they came back to tie the score. I scored a third touchdown and we finally just did beat them, 21–14. And for the second time in my college career, at game's end my teammates and friends carried me off the field.

"I still have a piece of the goalpost from that game.

"My thumb was pretty bad and I didn't play much against Iowa and they beat us, 48–8. My final college game was to be on the Coast against Southern California, and naturally I got into a real hassle.

"I had come back to our dormitory one night and Jules Tucker, a local businessman who was a 'father confessor,' helper, and good friend to all Notre Dame players, was waiting for me. 'Paul,' he said, 'Coach Leahy wants you to be on his television show.'

"The Leahy show was a national TV show and he was going to present the All-America team on the program.

"I told Jules it sounded okay, but I would have to get permission from Coach Brennan.

"Coach Brennan said, 'First of all, Paul, you know the rules: Nobody goes on any television show right before a game while we're on a trip.' Brennan went on, 'It was a rule that Leahy put in himself when he was here. Secondly,' Terry continued, 'Leahy's show goes on all over the country at eleven P.M. in the East and Midwest. We're not having a good year, and I think we'd get a lot of criticism having one of our players seem to be out late just before a big game.'

"So I sent Coach Leahy a wire that I couldn't make it because of the rules. And he got peeved and sounded off about Notre Dame's team 'lacking the spirit of former Notre Dame teams.'

"There were all kinds of reverberations about the episode, and it got to the point where Coach Brennan was warned by a high Notre Dame official not to reply to Leahy's comments 'or he could be in danger of losing his job . . . immediately.'

"That got us all fired up for the USC game. They were heavily favored and we gave them a rough time. My thumbs were injured and Bob Williams started the game and played most of it at quarterback and did a helluva job. I played halfback for a few plays and did manage to run back a kickoff ninety-five yards for one score. Williams was outstanding. He passed for one score and added another with a jaunt off-tackle, but we got beat, 28–20. And after the game Coach Leahy said, 'It was Notre Dame's best game of the year.'

"On the morning of December sixth, I was still in my dorm when I got a call from Tom Harmon. Tom had been one of Michigan's great halfbacks and was now a television sports commentator in California.

" 'Congratulations, Paul,' he said.

" 'For what?' " I was curious.

" 'For winning the Heisman Trophy.'

"I nearly fell off my chair. I really couldn't believe it. That call from Tom Harmon was the greatest thrill of my life, being named the outstanding college football player of the country."

The experts were having a field day analyzing the worst record in Notre Dame history, one that saw the Irish win only two games while losing eight, a team that scored 130 points to their opponents' 289.

When Notre Dame collapsed in 1956, the first reaction everywhere was one of stunned amazement. Then, as minds cleared, there came perplexed questions. Had the incredible 2–8 season been some sort of accident, some strange trick of fortune?

Or did something willful lie behind it?

Was there some new secret policy of de-emphasis?

Some critics even suggested there were those in the administration who were calling for the eventual elimination of the game that made Notre Dame one of the most famous institutions in the world.

"Winning and losing football games runs in cycles," said All-American Creighton Miller, the great Irish star of the 1940s and now an attorney in Cleveland. "Terry Brennan is a fine coach, but he was handicapped by a lack of scholarships . . . scholarships for football players going back a couple of years, and it caught up with him. If the lean years are evaluated properly," said Miller, "I'm sure the school

Bronko Nagurski ranks as one of the all-time great college and pro stars. Bronko, Jr., a six-two, 225-pound tackle, was one of the finest Irish stars, 1956–59.

Bob Williams was an outstanding quarterback for the Irish from 1955 to 1958. These days he is better known in the Pittsburgh region as Dr. Bob Williams, one of the more prominent physicians in the area.

will regain prominence. In 1957 it will be difficult, but in 1958, there'll be some very good material and a good team. By 1959, Notre Dame will again be a power."

Father Hesburgh, Athletic Director Moose Krause, and Brennan denied there was de-emphasis. And Brennan was given a vote of confidence and a new contract and two new assistant coaches to add to his staff for 1957.

Heisman winner Paul Hornung was gone and so was Captain Jim Morse, but Terry Brennan and his coaches had been grooming Bob Williams and George Izo as backup quarterbacks, and both men were impressive during the fall practice sessions. Terry also had a number of outstanding players returning—a tackle, an end, a center, and a couple of guards who would create havoc with the nation's leading teams in 1957 and '58.

Bronko Nagurski, Jr., at six foot, two inches and 225 pounds, whose dad, Bronko, Sr., still is remembered as one of the greatest college and professional stars in the history of football, was an All-State tackle in high school and would prove to be one of Notre Dame's finest linemen; Monty Stickles, big, fast, and rangy at end, would become another All-Star; and Bob Scholtz at center, Al Ecuyer at guard, and Chuck Puntillo and Dick Prendergast would give the Irish one of the finest front lines in college football.

In Bob Williams at quarterback, Dick Lynch and Aubrey Lewis at halfback, and Nick Pietrosante at fullback, Notre Dame had a backfield that had ability, quality, and character and would give Irish opponents sleepless nights during the next three seasons.

In the opening game of the season, Notre Dame traveled to Purdue, and within three minutes after the opening kickoff, the Irish had marched down the field for a touchdown as Lynch passed to Lewis for thirty-seven yards. Then Williams faked a pass and handed the ball to Lynch, who sped across for a score. Late in the game Williams tossed a fifty-nine-yard pass to Bob Wetoska to the Purdue nine-yard line, and Frank Reynolds smashed over for another Irish score. Final score: Notre Dame 12, Purdue 0.

Indiana was easily defeated as Williams, Lynch, Lewis, and Pietrosante ran wild—over and through the Hoosiers for a 26–0 victory.

1957: NOTRE DAME VOTED "COMEBACK TEAM OF THE YEAR"

"Old Notre Dame not only wins over all, old Notre Dame wins after all!"

That famous opening line, written by the late Charlie Dunkley, longtime Associated Press sportswriter, could have been repeated on October 12, 1957, when the Irish surged from behind to whip favored Army, 23–21, before ninety-five thousand spectators at Municipal Stadium, Philadelphia.

The victory, the third successive win of the season for Coach Terry Brennan, in a renewal of the once-traditional series temporarily suspended after 1947, ranks with the greatest of the great Fighting Irish moments on the gridiron. The victory ranks with their fourth-quarter rally to beat a previously unbeaten Army team, 13–12, in 1933, after the Cadets had taken a 12–0 lead on a Notre Dame team that had suffered five defeats that season.

It ranks with the Notre Dame whirlwind finish that defeated Ohio State, 18–13, in 1935 after the Buckeyes had taken a 13–0 edge.

The win over Army ushered a new Irish hero onto the list of men who have made Notre Dame great in football: Monty Anthony Stickles, a 220-pound sophomore end from Poughkeepsie, New York.

All Stickles did was place-kick a field goal thirty-nine yards squarely between the crossbars to give Notre Dame the victory when a surging Army Mule was fighting to hold an edge that had dwindled—in ten minutes—from 21–7 to 21–20.

It was the first successful field goal by the versatile Stickles. Prior to the winning field goal, Monty had missed on three of four attempts in previous Irish games.

The defeat was a bitter one for the Corps of Cadets, who had cheered wildly when Army appeared to have the game well in hand and on the verge of turning the thirty-fifth game of the intersectional rivalry into an Army rout. There was an added sting to the Army defeat when Monty revealed after the game that he would have attended West Point but had been rejected because of poor eyesight.

A twelve-letter winner at Poughkeepsie High School, Monty played center and became the first basketball player in Dutchess County to score a thousand points

(he scored 1,172). It was his basketball play that attracted most of the college scouts, and he received more than forty scholarship offers. "But my greatest thrill in high-school ball," said Monty, "was scoring three touchdowns in a conference championship game to come from behind and to beat Newburgh High for the title."

"I was overwhelmed by all the scholarship offers," said Stickles, "but I was determined not to become a football bum. I wanted a solid education."

When Monty received notice that he had won a scholarship to Notre Dame in June 1956, the first thing he did was buy a small suitcase. The traveling bag remained in his closet until late August, when it was time to report for football practice at South Bend.

Then Monty crammed enough clothes into it to last for two weeks and took off. In his Poughkeepsie home he left a trunk fully packed.

Monty would not allow his high-school success to overshadow reality. He knew that the transition from high school to college football always was difficult, and at Notre Dame ofttimes impossible for the high-school hero.

"I had to find out if I was good enough to make the Notre Dame squad," said Monty. "Two weeks after practice started, I knew I had a chance, so I called up Mom and asked her to send the trunk along because I was going to be here for a while."

The phone call did not surprise Mrs. Stickles. She chose Notre Dame after West Point rejected Monty. She then wrote a letter to Notre Dame, and the school dispatched Jim Finks, a former NFL star to go to Poughkeepsie to check out Monty Stickles. Finks spoke with townspeople and with Monty's high-school coach and then wired Notre Dame to grab Monty—fast. Terry Brennan followed with a scholarship offer, and Monty quickly grabbed the opportunity.

(Right, top) Fullback Nick Pietrosante (No. 39) dashes for twenty-two yards against Oklahoma in 1957. Irish blockers include Monty Stickles (No. 50) and Bronko Nagurski (No. 70).

(Right, bottom) Iowa halfback Kenny Pleon (No. 11) is about to be stopped by Irish tacklers Chuck Lima (No. 48), Bronko Nagurski (No. 70), and Frank Kuchta (No. 75) in 1957.

As Notre Dame moved through practice sessions for Army, Monty, the third-team end, was moved up to the second team because of an injury to Bob Wetoska. Monty had hoped to play against Army, for all his relatives and friends had traveled to Philadelphia for the big game. But he had no idea he would see much action.

After the opening kickoff, the Cadets quickly jumped into a 7–0 lead when speedy Bob Anderson, Army's yearling (sophomore) sensation, raced eighty-one yards to score on the Black Knights' second play from scrimmage.

Notre Dame tied the score when Nick Pietrosante, the Irish fullback, slammed across from the one-yard line and Don White kicked the extra point.

The second period was scoreless as both teams battered each other up and down the field. In the third period, Army began to move as Dave Bourland, the Cadets' quarterback, picked up twenty-eight yards, and seven plays later, Army's sensational All-American Pete Dawkins smashed over from the six-yard line. Don Hilliard added the extra point and Army led 14–7.

Later in the period, with Dawkins and Anderson carrying the ball, Army advanced to the Irish five-yard line, and Anderson carried the ball over for another Army score. Harry Walters kicked the extra point, and it was 21–7. Now Notre Dame looked hopelessly outclassed.

But Bob Williams—a great quarterback this day—sparked an Irish drive by taking Army's kickoff and returning the ball thirty-five yards. Then Nick Pietrosante, who had already gained 139 yards, took the ball from his center and headed around his own right end, then suddenly veered to his left and raced sixty-five yards to score. Stickles added the extra point. Suddenly the score was 21–14, and the jam-packed crowd was in an uproar as Notre Dame received the ball on their forty-two-yard line with twelve seconds left in the third period. Then in seven consecutive running plays Notre Dame's fine halfback Dick Lynch crashed through for the third Irish touchdown, making the score Army 21, Notre Dame 20.

Now Stickles had to kick the extra point—the tie-making point—and he missed.

"Looking back at missing those kicks—three out of four," said Stickles, "I think I was too eager and kicked the ball too soon. I didn't give my holder a chance to put the ball down in the correct spot."

Notre Dame kicked off and Army tried a short pass over the middle of the line. The ball was deflected by Irish guard Frank Geremia right into the eager arms of Pietrosante, who brought it to the Army twenty-six-yard line. Three plays later Notre Dame was on the twenty-two-yard line.

Time and opportunity were now running out.

On the sidelines Terry Brennan nervously paced up and down, but knowing that Stickles could kick for distance, ordered the place-kick.

Quarterback Bob Williams took the pass from center and touched the ball down on the twenty-nine-yard line.

Now Stickles took his time.

"I knew I'd never tried a field goal before, but I told myself this was a heckuva time to think of that. Then I just drove into the ball. I almost fell on my face when the referee signaled a field goal."

Notre Dame was the winner, 23–21.

And Notre Dame's coach, Terry Brennan, who ran the opening kickoff ninety-seven yards in the last previous Army–Notre Dame game, in 1947, calls the 1957 victory "a marvelous team effort. And the greatest victory in my four years of coaching at Notre Dame."

Two weeks later, on October 26, in South Bend, Notre Dame just managed to eke out a 13–7 win over the rugged Pitt Panthers.

Navy, fired up and determined, faced Notre Dame on November 2. Undefeated, they were tougher and faster than Army and pounded out an impressive 20–6 victory over the Irish, who were sluggish in the cold, the rain, and the mud. The following week, the highly touted Michigan State Spartans, on their way to the number one position in the national ratings, slammed into the Irish from the opening kickoff and proceeded to a 34–6 victory.

Oklahoma, with visions of another national championship and riding the crest of an incredible four-year winning streak of forty-seven games, were three-touchdown favorites. But the Irish reached back for that "old Notre Dame spirit" and played as if the national title were at stake. Sparked by the superb play of Bob Williams and Dick Lynch and the driving power of Nick Pietrosante, Notre Dame scored with two minutes left in the game. Williams passed to Lynch, then to Lewis. And Pietrosante, like a raging bull, smashed time and time at the Sooners' line. Then just as time ran out, Williams passed to Lynch, who burst in for the winning score.

The 7–0 upset of the powerful Sooners was proclaimed the biggest victory of the year for the Irish and sent the Sooners reeling in shock.

The 1958 Irish eleven ended the season with a 6–4–0 record. Co-captain Al Ecuyer, Monty Stickles, and Nick Pietrosante were named to the All-America team.

It was a page right out of the old Rockne story.

The following week, a listless, tired Irish team was easily defeated by Iowa, 21–13. Then, in another of those inexplicable turn-arounds, showing a complete reversal of form, Notre Dame easily ran roughshod over Southern California, 40–12, and ran wild over Southern Methodist, 54–21, in the season's finale.

From "disappointment of the year" in 1956, Notre Dame became the "comeback team of the year" in 1957. Terry Brennan became the first college coach in football history to be selected "coach of the week" twice in one season by the Associated Press.

The 7–3–0 season in 1956 earned Brennan an extension of his contract, and Notre Dame prepared once again to assume the place in the sun they had occupied for so long as 1958 came into being.

TERRY BRENNAN IS FIRED

Prospects for the 1958 season were the most promising in years as twenty-five veteran lettermen, including such stars as quarterbacks Bob Williams and George Izo, fullback Nick Pietrosante, and linemen Monty Stickles, Al Ecuyer, Bronko Nagurski, and Bob Scholtz were back in excellent physical condition and ready to compete.

The young coach was no longer so young, but he had survived several grainy campaigns and felt this was his year. He had added two assistant coaches to his staff in the persons of Bernie Crimmons and Hank Stram. Crimmins had served five years as an assistant to Frank Leahy. Stram had been the backfield coach

at Purdue and at Southern Methodist. Stramm had played football at Purdue, had coached there, and had scouted and kept copious notes on Purdue and Indiana players that in 1958 that would come in very handy for the Irish. Indiana was the first opponent on the schedule and the Irish easily defeated the Hoosiers as halfback Bill "Red" Mack, making his debut on the Irish varsity, sparked the team to an early 7–0 lead and they romped to an 18–0 win.

Red Mack again led the Irish attack the following week against Southern methodist as Notre Dame defeated the Mustangs 14–6. And then it was Army and the Irish at South Bend in a game that would be the last between the two rivals until 1965.

For this dramatic game Notre Dame united all of its celebrities: Jesse Harper, Elmer Layden, Frank Leahy, and leading Army officers and former stars were on hand at South Bend for the big game.

But the Cadets, with one of their greatest stars, Pete Dawkins, taking full charge of the Army offense, was too fast and too aggressive for the Irish this day. Jack Morrison scored the Cadets' first touchdown in the first period and Army held on to that lead until well into the last quarter, when Stickles tackled Army's quarterback, Joe Caldwell, behind the goal line for two points. Dawkins swept his right end for Army's second touchdown, and the game ended with the final score Army 14, Notre Dame 2.

Sometimes a single play can determine the course of an entire season of play—or a career. Had Notre Dame defeated Army, as it might have, the Irish squad would have gained the confidence it sorely needed and might even have generated the momentum necessary to win a few close games . . . games that were lost by a field goal or a single touchdown.

Monty Stickles kicked three field goals for all nine points as Notre Dame defeated Duke in a bitter battle by a 9–7 score, and a week later the Irish lost one of those heartbreakers to bitter rival Purdue, 29–22. In an about-face, the Irish completely submerged a young, aggressive Navy team by a 40–20 score. Then on November 8, the Irish traveled to Pittsburgh and absorbed a bitter 29–26 loss to a Pitt team that gave no quarter. Near the end of the game, George Izo almost pulled victory out of the five: He tossed a beautiful pass to Red Mack, a forty-seven-yard effort. Red was all alone and in the clear but lost his balance and fell out of bounds as the game ended.

The Tarheels of North Carolina, arrogant and strutting a six-game winning streak, came into South Bend eager to avenge five successive previous losses to Notre Dame. But Izo, Mack, and Stickles were too much for North Carolina and they were beaten by the Irish for the sixth straight time by a 34–24 score.

Iowa's Big Ten champions, one of the nation's leading football powers (they finished number two, behind LSU, in 1958) with two straight victories over Terry Brennan's Irish squad, hosted a football party for the Irish on November 22 at Iowa City, but the Hawkeyes were anything but polite as they thrashed Notre Dame in a well-played battle. The Hawkeyes jumped out to an early 13–7 margin at the half. The Irish scored their lone touchdown of the first half as quarterback George Izo lofted a fifty-nine-yard aerial to Monty Stickles, and the Irish All-American outraced three Hawkeye tacklers into the end zone for a TD.

In the third period, halfback Bob Scarpitto slanted off-tackle for thirty-eight yards for the second Irish score after another Izo pass to make the game much closer than the 19–14 score indicated. In the final period Iowa opened up and scored two touchdowns for a 31–14 lead. As the game ended, Izo, playing one of his finest games, bulled his way across the goal line for the final Irish score. But it was Iowa's game, 31–21.

One week later Notre Dame traveled to Los Angeles for their final game of the 1958 season against their perennial rivals the Trojans of Southern California.

Notre Dame was trailing 13–12 in the third period when Frank Reynolds returned a USC kick thirty yards to the Trojans' thirty-seven-yard line. The Irish backs pounded USC's line and advanced the ball to the twenty-one-yard line. Then Bob Williams faded back . . . back trying to spot an open receiver, found Bob Wetoska on the ten-yard line, and fired a bulletlike pass to Bob, who dragged and carried three USC tacklers across the goal line for a touchdown. On the extra-points try, Williams passed successfully for a two-point conversion and the Irish took the victory by a 20–13 score.

And that win just did make it a winning season for Notre Dame and Terry Brennan: a 6–4 season.

And now the rumble in Chicago papers and the wire services carried daily stories about the imminent firing of Terry Brennan. Then the rumble became a roar, and the stories all across the nation on a cold, bleak period during Christmas Week told the story on front pages across the land.

"Notre Dame fires Coach Terry Brennan . . . during Christmas Week."

A day after Terry was fired, it was announced that Joe Kuharich, a former Notre Dame player under Elmer Layden, had signed a four-year contract as Notre Dame's new head coach.

No firing of a football coach ever shook down such a thunder of criticism as the dismissal of thirty-year-old Terence Patrick Brennan by the University of Notre Dame. Seldom if ever has any single decision in sports history received such a horrible going-over. Critics included nationally prominent writers and editors who were graduates of Notre Dame. The general press was no harsher in its criticism than some of the Catholic press.

Monty Stickles is pouncing on a Purdue fumble to recover for the Irish in the game against Purdue in 1958.

As Pitt eked out a stunning 29–26 victory in 1958, Monty Stickles (left) and Bob Scholtz await the final whistle in the rain and mud.

The sports editors, particularly, blasted Notre Dame's action as wrong, unnecessary, shortsighted, and incomprehensible. They said the public image of the school had been damaged . . . a damage that could not be easily repaired.

Notre Dame, they declared, had made unequivocally clear its position on football: It would abide nothing less than a series of teams consistently high in the weekly polls, with frequent national championships. That was what the school's "win 'em all" traditionalists had become accustomed to in the coaching dynasties of Knute Rockne, the architect, and Frank Leahy, the reaffirmer, and nothing less would do.

The dismissal of Brennan was recommended by the faculty board in control of athletics, of which Father Edmund Joyce, executive vice-president of the university, was chairman. Although the official vote was unanimous, there was dissent for a time by at least one member of the board, Father Charles Sheedy, dean of the School of Arts and Letters. Edward (Moose) Krause, director of athletics, attended the board meeting but had no vote.

In his official defense of the firing, Father Hesburgh spoke of his desire for excellence. He also implied that Brennan's teams lacked Notre Dame's traditional training and spirit. But he did not explain what constitutes the norms of training or spirit, either in his own judgment or his advisers'.

Arthur Daley, sports editor of *The New York Times*, wrote:

"No college in the country, in all probability, has as many devoted followers as has Notre Dame. Here is The People's Choice in a most sentimental form, all of it packed in the glow of pure idealism. Yet this was the school that sacked Terry Brennan. The entire business is so completely out of character that it leaves observers bewildered and gasping."

Popular Boston sports editor Bill Cunningham wrote:

"Editorial reaction across the country has been marked by a striking unanimity. Again and again the firing of Terry Brennan has been interpreted as an official statement of policy: 'Win or else.' Terry Brennan's teams won 32 games and lost 18 during his five seasons. That's a winning percentage of .640. I just hope the Dodgers would do as well."

In a statement, Father Joyce said: "In all of the excitement stirred by the release of Terry Brennan, one simple fact was generally overlooked. Instead of abandoning the principles which have given us a soundly conceived athletic program within an academic framework, it is precisely because we refuse to compromise our educational integrity that outstanding coaching leadership is so imperative. In Coach Joe Kuharich, an able, experienced, and devoted Notre Dame man, we confidently expect such leadership in the future."

CHAPTER 7

LOCAL BOY MAKES GOOD: JOE KUHARICH (1959—62)

As a grade-school kid, Joe Kuharich hung around the Notre Dame football field from the moment that school let out until the practice sessions were finished for the day. One day Knute Rockne took Joe by the hand and led him into a practice session, a circumstance looked upon by some observers as an omen.

Joe played on the sandlots of South Bend when his pals had no ball. The kids would wrap some rags together and use it as a football. His brother said Joe always organized the games even though he was younger and smaller than the others. "He was small but scrappy, probably the most aggressive kid I ever coached," said high-school coach Forest Wood of Riley High School.

Scrapiron Young, Notre Dame's outstanding trainer under Rockne and Layden, saw Kuharich in several high-school games and was so taken with Joe's fighting spirit that he recommended him to Coach Elmer Layden, who gave Joe and several other South Bend boys football scholarships.

Kuharich became a regular guard as a sophomore and throughout his playing career grew in stature, not merely as a player but also because of his obvious knowledge of the game. "He had an uncanny ability to diagnose an opposing offense," said Coach Hunk Anderson, "and he could intelligently detail this information on to his teammates. He was tough and aggressive, and even though he never weighed more than 155 pounds, he could and did take on opponents who outweighed him by as much as fifty pounds and take them out of the play.

"Joe lived, ate, and slept football," said Anderson, "and seemed to spend every waking minute thinking and talking about strategy. And he constantly surprised his teammates with his mastery of his classroom subjects, too. He had his master's degree before he left Notre Dame."

Upon graduation, Kuharich coached the Irish freshmen team, then played professional football with the Chicago Cardinals. He spent four years in the Navy, then played with the Pittsburgh Steelers and became their line coach. There were four years as head coach at San Francisco University. His last team at San Francisco was undefeated, with a 9–0 record. That record brought him back to the pro ranks as head coach of the Chicago Cardinals. In 1955, he was named the pro coach of the year with the Washington Redskins, and in December 1958 he signed a four-year contract with Notre Dame.

On September 27, 1959, the Irish, under Coach Joe Kuharich, opened the season at South Bend against a rough and ready North Carolina eleven. North Carolina had never beaten Notre Dame in the ten games played between the two schools. Their outstanding coach for many years, amiable Jim Tatum, had died, and the Tarheels had pledged a Notre Dame victory to Tatum's memory.

But Notre Dame, playing without the services of an outstanding quarterback, and with only twelve lettermen returning, displayed a hard-hitting, fast-moving attack that ran up a 20–0 lead over North Carolina in the first half and then played solid defensive football in the second half to whip the rugged Tarheels, who were held scoreless until the last thirty seconds of the game. Final score: Notre Dame 28, North Carolina 8.

Hunk Anderson, enthusiastic as a young sophomore, rushed over to congratulate Joe Kuharich on the team's first victory. Pounding Joe on the back, Hunk said, "Joe, I liked the way these kids hit. Reminded me of our days. Keep it up."

One week later, Purdue outclassed the Irish with a 28–7 win, but then California was defeated 28–6 in a game that saw quarterback George Izo sparkle with several long passes to his favorite target, Monty Stickles.

Michigan State, with an outstanding team, proved too big and too fast for the courageous Irish and shut them out, 19–0. Linebackers Myron Pottios and Jim Crotty, two of the best defensive players on the squad, were both injured and would be on the sidelines for the remaining games of the season.

The Northwestern Wildcats played like wildcats under their new coach, Ara Parseghian, and defeated the Irish 30–24 in a wild and woolly passing game, with Northwestern besting the Irish in one of the roughest games of the season.

Navy had a new head coach, Wayne Hardin, and his Middie team played Notre Dame to a thrilling 22–22 tie until Monty Stickles booted a field goal with thirty-two seconds to play to give the Irish a magnificent last-minute victory. It was one of the most exciting games ever played at South Bend, and Irish fans went wild with joy as Stickles' kick went between the crossbar for the winning margin.

Georgia Tech helped the Irish celebrate the fiftieth anniversary of "The Notre Dame Victory March" at South Bend on November 7, and the Irish, inspired by the stirring music and the air of nostalgia over the campus, managed to hold Tech to 7–7 at halftime. But in the second half the Yellow Jackets scored another touchdown to give them a 14–10 edge, just enough to win. It was the first Tech win over Notre Dame since 1942.

A trip to Pittsburgh in the rain and mud brought the Irish another defeat, by a score of 28–13.

With Iowa and Southern California remaining on the schedule, Joe Kuharich's team had won only three games and had lost five.

In the Pittsburgh airport after the game, the grim Irish captain, Ken Adamson, said to a reporter: "We'll beat Iowa and Southern California and finish even, with a 5–5 record."

Iowa took a quick opening lead as they scored a touchdown, but the Irish rallied behind George Izo's

(Right, top) Three generations of Irish football history are represented in this photo as the Irish prepare for the Navy game in 1959: Jesse Harper (left) was the Irish head coach, 1913–17; Don White (center) is the Irish quarterback; Joe Kuharich (right) is the head coach.

(Right, center) Coach Joe Kuharich's first Notre Dame team, in 1959, won five and lost five.

(Right, bottom) There were but three minutes left to play, and the score was tied: Notre Dame 19, Iowa 19. The Irish had just scored a touchdown. Then Monty Stickles calmly booted the extra point (note ball in flight) to give the Irish a thrilling 20–19 squeaker in this 1959 battle.

fine quarterbacking. Izo had missed several games because of a severe knee injury, but against Iowa he was at his very best as he connected with a number of passes to end Monty Stickles. The Hawkeyes had a 19–13 lead in the last period when Izo unlimbered his great arm and tossed a beauty of a pass to Irish halfback, George Sefcik, who dashed twenty-five yards to tie the score at 19–19.

Now over fifty-eight thousand tense and rabid Iowa spectators were up and howling as Stickles prepared to kick the all-important extra point. The pro-Iowa crowd screamed in agony while Irish fans roared in delight as Monty's kick was good, and Notre Dame had upset the Hawkeyes, 20–19.

So Joe Kuharich approached the end of his first season as head coach of the Fighting Irish with less than even a mediocre season's record. He needed a victory over USC to bat .500. Notre Dame and her proud sons are not pleased with coaches who win only 50 percent of their games. They are not pleased with coaches who win only 75 percent of their games. When you walk along the paths of Rockne and Leahy, nothing less than 100 percent is expected . . . demanded.

The dismal season certainly wasn't caused by a lack of labor or concentration on the part of Coach Kuharich. The week prior to the USC game, the coach had been scheduled to speak before the annual Notre Dame banquet for 250 coaches in Chicago. With the Trojan game just around the corner, Joe felt he couldn't take the time and sent his regrets . . . thus incurring the wrath of Chicago's mayor, Richard Daley. But Joe may have lost more than that. When he decided that he couldn't make the engagement, Joe suggested Duffy Daugherty of Michigan State as a replacement. And to the delight of Daugherty, he found himself surrounded by a host of outstanding high school coaches, who would think of Michigan State when they recommended a school for a star player.

Southern California traveled to South Bend, where they hadn't won a game in twenty years, for the "big game" with the Irish. Coach Don Clark's Trojans had had a marvelous season, winning eight games and losing only to UCLA. They were Rose Bowl–bound and meant to go . . . if they could beat the Irish.

November 28 . . . South Bend . . . The weather was so cold and snowy that both teams were forced to practice indoors. The weather was cold. But the Trojans were colder.

The game was but three minutes old when sophomore Gerry Gray, a six-foot, two-inch, 195-pound fullback, smashed through the Trojan line and seemed headed for a score. He rambled thirty-eight yards, was hit by a Southern California tackler, and fumbled the ball. Fortunately, the ball squirted out of bounds and it was Notre Dame's ball on the ten-yard stripe. On the next play Gray bowled over two Trojan tacklers and scored the Irish touchdown. Stickles' kick made it 7–0.

There was no further scoring until the third quarter. Then Gray, who had been gaining steadily against the Trojans all afternoon, scored again, climaxing a fifty-five-yard drive.

Angie Coia of Southern California received the kickoff, fumbled in the end zone, and was trapped for another two points for Notre Dame. Who tackled Coia? It was Gerry Gray, having the finest day a Notre Dame back had had all season long.

Southern California finally scored in the last two

Monty Stickles (No. 80), the Irish All-America end, takes a hand-off from quarterback George Izo (No. 3) as George Williams (No. 76) opens a huge hole in the Southern California line and Monty picks up thirty-five yards in 1959.

minutes of the game to leave the score at 16–6.

Coach Don Clark of Southern California said that Notre Dame was the strongest team USC had met all season long, including Rose Bowl-bound Washington.

Coach Joe Kuharich said, "Now that the season's over, we're just beginning to learn. Next year will be a question mark. We'll have five seniors, and twenty-one juniors to carry the team."

Sportswriters and experts covering the USC-Notre Dame game came away convinced that the Irish would be contenders for the national championship in 1960—and that Joe Kuharich had done a very good job in his first year.

EIGHT STRAIGHT LOSSES!

Football fans of today will find it hard to believe that the 1960 Notre Dame team, with outstanding players such as Nick Buoniconti, Red Mack, Myron Pottios, Mike Lind, Norb Roy, and Daryle Lamonica could possibly lose eight straight games, but that's exactly what happened.

In 1960 the Irish opened once again without a quarterback seasoned by one or two years of varsity play. It was a talent they sorely needed but never found that year.

Nick Buoniconti, guard, and co-captain of the 1961 Irish team, was named to the All-America team in 1961 and was a standout performer for the championship Miami Dolphins for several years.

Rockne had developed a long line of quarterbacks, starting with Joe Brandy in the 1919 season; Harry Stuhldreher, 1922–24, then the great Frank Carideo, 1928–30. Frank Leahy had Angelo Bertelli, Johnny Lujack, Bob Williams, Ralph Gugliemi, and Paul Hornung, All-Stars all.

In 1960, Kuharich found himself without an outstanding quarterback as George Izo and his understudy Don White both had graduated. It was a situation that confounded Joe all season long and resulted in the poorest year in Irish football history.

Notre Dame opened the season with rookie George Haffner as the quarterback, and George did a superb job leading the team to a surprising 21–17 victory over California.

In the second game of the year Purdue ran through, over, and around the Irish for a resounding 51–19 win. Then the debacle continued as Notre Dame lost successive games to North Carolina, Michigan State, Northwestern, Navy, Pitt, Miami, and Iowa before winning the season's finale against USC.

After the season ended, Notre Dame gave Joe Kuharich a vote of confidence, the same vote of confidence it had given Terry Brennan after Terry's first bad year. And to make it more emphatic that Kuharich was not operating under a win-or-else dictum, Notre Dame extended his contract for two more years.

Oklahoma, a perennial national contender during the past ten years, opened the season at South Bend to kick off the 1961 season, and the crowd of more than fifty-five thousand spectators were riveted to their seats as the fireworks began.

Angelo Dabiero, a solid, three-year veteran, broke away for a sensational fifty-five-yard sprint through the entire Sooner team and scored Notre Dame's first touchdown of the fledgling season. Mike Lind and Dabiero combined on successive plays to carry the ball to the Sooners' twenty-two-yard line. Then Lind, a rugged, hard-hitting fullback, smashed through for

The starting lineup for the 1961 team.

another Irish touchdown. In the third period, with the score 13–6 in favor of Notre Dame, Dabiero and Lind carried the ball to the Oklahoma five-yard line, and then it was Lind through the line for a third touchdown. Final score: Notre Dame 19, Oklahoma 6.

Purdue had humiliated Notre Dame in 1960 with a 51–19 beating, and in 1961 the Boilermakers wanted to extend their win streak over the Irish and proceeded to score the first time they got the ball, advancing seventy-nine yards to a touchdown. The game was just two minutes old, and the Boilermakers had a 7–0 advantage. But Notre Dame came back with a vengeance. Led by Daryle Lamonica at quarterback and Gerry Gray, the Irish advanced steadily upfield, and Gray smashed through the Purdue line for a twenty-five-yard touchdown sprint. The kick was good and it was a 7–7 tie. Then Purdue scored twice within ten minutes to lead, 17–7. Then Skippy Ohl of Purdue added three more points to the Boilermakers' total by kicking a magnificent forty-five-yard field goal to give Purdue a 20–7 lead.

Lamonica tossed two short passes then heaved a thirty-yard pass to Jim Kelly, who plowed over for Notre Dame's second touchdown. Now the score was Purdue 20, Notre Dame 13 as the first half ended.

In the third period, once again it was Lamonica and Gray gaining ground steadily through the air and on the ground. Then Lamonica tossed a short pass to Kelly, who dashed in from the five-yard line for another Irish score.

Now it became a spine-tingler of a game as the clock ran down and both teams battled up and down the field. Notre Dame tried for a two-point conversion as Lamonica passed to Kelly, but the ball just slipped through Jim's hands and the score remained Purdue 20, Notre Dame 19—and time was running out for the Irish.

There were two minutes to play as two sophomores, Paul Costa and Jim Snowden, now in the backfield for the Irish, began to move the ball upfield. Slowly but surely they picked up small gains of three, four, six yards, just enough for a couple of first downs. Then Costa broke into the open for twenty-nine big yards and Notre Dame prepared to try for the game-winning field goal.

Lamonica held the ball on the twenty-two-yard line and as the Purdue crowd of more than fifty-one thousand held their breath, Joe Perkowski stepped into the Irish Hall of Fame with a beautiful twenty-nine-yard kick for the three points. As the ball flashed between the crossbars, the referee blew the whistle signifying the game was over, and the Irish had a magnificent, well-played, 22–20 victory.

Then it was a great win over Southern California as Lamonica scored two touchdowns on short bursts through the Trojan line and then passed 19 yards to Kelly for another. Joe Perkowski kicked another field goal, this time a forty-nine-yard boot, and the Irish had the game well in hand, shutting out the Trojans, 30–0. And Joe Kuharich's Notre Damers had a winning streak of four straight games.

Michigan State ended Irish hopes of a longer winning streak with a 17–7 victory, after Notre Dame had held State scoreless for three periods. Then Coach Ara Parseghian brought his Northwestern Wildcats to South Bend, and they outlasted the Irish to win, 12–10.

Navy then traveled to South Bend, quickly jumped into a 10–3 lead at halftime, and finally defeated the Irish, 13–10. It was Notre Dame's third straight loss.

The following week the Irish engaged a strong Pitt team. First one side would take the lead, then the other. Both teams played hard, aggressive football until an Irish reserve, seldom-used Charley O'Hara, slashed and dashed his way forty-nine yards for a touchdown late in the fourth quarter. The score by O'Hara gave Notre Dame the edge over Pitt, 26–13, and the Irish finally won, 26–20, in a contest not decided until the final minutes of play.

On November 18, Syracuse University brought a determined team to South Bend for the first game ever between the two teams. Some twenty-six years later, Syracuse fans who saw the game still argue about the result. It was a game that defied description and ended in a near riot.

Syracuse was ahead of Notre Dame, 15–14, and the clock showed there was no more time left in the game. The game was over . . . almost.

But George Sefcik knelt to hold the ball for an attempt at a forty-five-yard field goal. Just as Sefcik was placing the ball he was bumped by Walt Sweeney, a Syracuse end. The ball rolled to a stop on the turf, but the head linesman had noticed the infraction and dropped his flag as the time showed 0:00. Game over?

However, the rules state a game cannot end if a penalty was committed on the last play. Syracuse was penalized fifteen yards, and Perkowski was given another try for a field goal, from the thirty-one yard line, and made the kick good—after the game had officially ended. It was an incredible, come-from-behind, "believe it or not" victory. Final score: Notre Dame 17, Syracuse 15.

At Iowa the following week, Notre Dame played as if they were anxious for the season to end, and the Hawkeyes easily defeated the Irish, 42–21, with an avalanche of touchdowns.

At Duke for the final game of the season, Dabiero sped fifty-four yards through the entire Duke eleven to score the first touchdown as the game opened; then Mike Lind plunged over from the six-yard line. But that was the total of Notre Dame's scoring effort as the Blue Devils rolled to a 37–13 triumph to close out another lackluster 5–5–0 season for the Irish.

In Joe Kuharich's three years as head coach, Notre Dame had lost eighteen games while winning but twelve. It was the poorest three-year record in Notre Dame history, and the anguished howls of alumni were heard from coast to coast for a new football coach.

In his South Bend column, Joe Doyle, a popular and widely read sports editor, wrote:

It is hard to believe the same football team played the various parts of the schedule. One moment the Notre Dame team of 1961 seemed to be an eager, hustling squad that believed it could beat any opponent. At other times it was indifferent, lethargic and unable to cope with anything out of the ordinary on offense, or defense. It looked like a skilled team at times; and at other times like an also-ran. Some capable players played their final game in the worst three year losing streak in Notre Dame history. Any forecast for the future would seem to be very bleak. Some of those players who will be seniors next year are good ball players and some have been found lacking. One player will be chosen Captain. He will have a very tough time in 1962.

Joe Kuharich's problems in 1962 were immediately apparent to those familiar with Notre Dame football. The Irish had lost their two top ends, four outstanding tackles, three varsity guards, two veteran halfbacks, and place-kicker *par excellence* in Joe Perkowski, all by graduation. To add to Kuharich's problems, hard-running fullback Mike Lind, captain of the 1962 squad and a three-year veteran, was injured early in the year and saw very little action.

Kuharich did manage to recruit a number of outstanding players, including Nick Etten, a husky six-foot, two-inch, 225-pound tackle, son of former Yankee first baseman Nick Etten; Ed Rutkowski and Denny Phillips, rated as two of the finest backs in high-school football, from the Hershey, Pennsylvania, area; a top prospect in Bill Pfeiffer, a quarterback; and another young quarterback, John Huarte, also looked very good.

But Daryle Lamonica, with two solid years of varsity experience, started at the quarterback spot as the Irish faced the perennially tough Oklahoma Sooners in Oklahoma in the opening game of the season. Ed Rutkowski, the young sophomore flash from Hershey, starting his first game for the Irish, scored Notre Dame's first touchdown with a burst through the Sooners' line from the ten-yard stripe. Oklahoma matched the Irish with a touchdown of their own, and it remained a 7–7 deadlock until late in the third period, when Bill Ahern scored for Notre Dame to make it 13–7. The Sooners battled to the final whistle but were stopped short of the goal line. Halfback Frank Minik's savage tackle of an Oklahoma back saved the game for Notre Dame, for the tackle, on the eight-yard line, was so hard that the Oklahoma back fumbled, and at that moment the game was over.

Then Notre Dame was completely outplayed in four straight contests. First they lost to the hard-running Purdue Boilermakers by a 24–6 score. Then it was on to Wisconsin and a battle with the Badgers, who were to go on to one of their finest seasons. They easily defeated Notre Dame, 17–8. The following week Michigan State and their great All-America back George Saimes crushed the Irish, 31–7. Saimes scored three touchdowns as State piled up its seventh straight win over Notre Dame.

Next, Ara Parseghian and his Northwestern team stormed to a crushing 35–6 win over the Irish as the Wildcats went on to an undefeated season.

All of a sudden Daryle Lamonica found a "golden touch" to his forward passing and began to throw on target. And Notre Dame came alive and defeated a strong Navy eleven at Philadelphia by a 20–12 score. Navy was in the lead in the third period when Lamonica tossed a forty-five-yard pass to Denny Phillips for a touchdown. Several plays later, Lamonica took the ball on a quarterback sneak and scored another touchdown as the Irish came from behind to sink Navy.

A week later against a strong Pitt eleven, Lamonica pitched four touchdown passes, three of them to end Jim Kelly, as the Irish played near-perfect football before a South Bend crowd of more than fifty-two thousand spectators and slugged Pitt by a 43–22 score.

Now it was Joe Farrell's turn to star in the game against North Carolina, and the husky Farrell pounded away at the Tarheels to score two touchdowns. Lamonica also scored, and now the Irish were alive and moving with a 21–7 victory, their third in a row.

The Iowa Hawkeyes stormed into South Bend on November 24, intent on adding the Irish to their winning streak. Iowa had won seven out of their last eight games against the Irish and were counting on another win. But this day and this time they were out of luck, for Lamonica engineered three successive touchdown plays in the last period to give Notre Dame a convincing 35–12 victory. It was the fourth straight win for the Irish, and everyone was now convinced that Kuharich had found the winning combination and that 1962 would be "the year of the Irish."

Lamonica had won all five of the games he had been at quarterback that season, while Notre Dame had scored 132 points to their opponents' sixty. The night before the final game of the season, against Southern California at Los Angeles, Lamonica predicted a three-touchdown Irish win. This time Daryle was wrong. It was a long afternoon for Lamonica. A very long afternoon. He completed only seven of twenty-four passes as the Trojans had too many guns for the Irish and easily defeated them, 25–0.

Back at South Bend, a heavy quiet descended upon the campus. There were long and somber faces all over.

Joe Kuharich's four-year record of 17–23–0 was the poorest in Notre Dame's history, and the rumors of his imminent departure were everywhere, from *Life* magazine to the sports pages of every major newspaper in the nation. Nobody felt worse about the situation than Joe, but he seemed helpless to do anything to improve his team.

HUGH DEVORE NAMED HEAD COACH (1963)

Just two weeks before practice began, on March 13, Kuharich, convinced that he would be fired, announced that he would be leaving Notre Dame and returning to pro football as supervisor of NFL officials.

On the same day, there was an announcement from Notre Dame that the Old Reliable, Hugh Devore, who had pinch-hit for Leahy in 1945, had been appointed "interim coach."

Devore, an outstanding end on the 1931–33 teams under Hunk Anderson, had graduated in 1934 and served with Elmer Layden as an assistant coach, then moved over to Fordham with Jim Crowley. He was head coach at several schools, then was named head coach at Notre Dame in 1945 when Frank Leahy went into the Navy. In 1948 Devore went to New York University, where the Violets had gone from one of the powerhouse teams of the East, with a 49–15–4 record in a seven-year period under Chick Meehan, into a period of decline.

NYU gave up football in 1942 and '43, resumed after a fashion, and played strictly class B football.

Devore did an outstanding job for three years with all sorts of official restrictions placed upon his recruiters, and for three years he walked the plank of small-time football in the biggest city in America.

He went to Green Bay as an assistant coach for one season, then back to Dayton University for three years. In 1956 Devore was appointed head coach of the Philadelphia Eagles, and in 1958 it was back home to Notre Dame under Terry Brennan and then under Kuharich. Then in 1963 Hugh Devore was the head coach.

Devore said, "I don't know why they picked me to be Notre Dame's head coach, but I'm going to make it the best football season I've ever had."

And with just one minute to go in the opening game of the season, on September 28, at South Bend, Notre Dame led Wisconsin. But the Badgers, in a last-minute desperation drive, pulled the game out of the fire with a touchdown and a two-point conversion and defeated the Irish, 14–9. Against Purdue the following week Notre Dame had a 6–0 lead in the final period, but Purdue scored and kicked the extra point to win, 7–6.

Southern California traveled to South Bend for their annual battle with their Irish rivals, and as usual, USC and Notre Dame waged a bitter and exciting struggle. The Trojans, with such All-America stars as quarterback Pete Beathard, end Hal Bedsole, and the sensational Mike Garrett, scored first, but Notre Dame came right back and surprised the Trojans with a tremendous running attack led by sophomore halfback Bill Wolski and tied the score.

The hometown crowd erupted. This was Notre Dame fighting back as Notre Dame always had come back. The Trojans scored again, but Notre Dame exploded with Wolski and Frank Budka, who was in the game at quarterback. Budka did a marvelous job of faking as if he were going to pass, then taking off and running the ball. And Notre Dame scored again to tie the count at 14–14.

In the second half it appeared that Southern California's poise and experience—they had twenty-six lettermen suited up for the game—would be too much for the game Irish eleven. But Budka and Wolski punched at the big Trojan line time and time again for five and six yards, steadily moving on their way to another score.

Now Notre Dame moved down to USC's fifteen-yard line and more than fifty-nine thousand hysterical Irish fans were up and screaming for a score, one that would win for Notre Dame.

Now Hugh Devore sent in sophomore Ken Ivan—they called him Ivan the Terrible, Ivan calmly booted home a magnificent thirty-three-yard field goal, and Notre Dame had defeated one of the nation's great teams by a 17–14 score.

The momentum of the upset victory over USC carried over to the following week, when the Irish once again traveled over a tough road, this time against UCLA, and produced another surprise as they simply outfought the Bruins to win by a 27–12 margin.

Thus within two weeks, Notre Dame had successively defeated two California teams—two of the nation's strongest teams—and were ready to tackle a third California eleven, Stanford University. The Irish moved quickly against Stanford, quickly scored two touchdowns, and it looked like an easy win. A third Irish score was missed when a Notre Dame back intercepted an Indian pass and with a clear field ahead fumbled the ball deep in Stanford territory.

And the game suddenly turned away from Notre Dame after that one misplay.

The Indians began to utilize a sound running game mixed with an occasional pass, quickly scored four times, and walked off the field with a 24–14 win.

The Stanford loss, on national television, was a heavy blow to Irish pride, and from then on Notre Dame's expected comeback that season ran into a dead end.

The next week, against Navy, Roger Staubach simply was too good and too sharp, with pinpoint passes that floated over Irish hands but right to Navy receivers for five touchdowns and an easy 35–14 win. Then it was Pittsburgh and another defeat, 27–7.

Michigan State's great All-American Sherm Lewis exploded for eighty-four yards and a last-period touchdown after Notre Dame had hung on to a 7–6 lead for three periods, and the Spartans pulled out a hard-fought victory, 12–7. It was a bitter pill for the Irish after outplaying a much stronger State eleven.

The game with Iowa was canceled due to the assassination of President John F. Kennedy, an honorary alumnus, whose father, Ambassador Joseph Kennedy, had been a member of the Notre Dame Board of Trustees.

The final game of the season, against Syracuse at Yankee Stadium, provided the New York team with sweet revenge as they scored a touchdown with less than four minutes left in the game to win by a 14–7 score. Once again, as in a number of other Irish games that year, Notre Dame led Syracuse until the final minutes, only to lose to the heavier guns of their opponents.

And once again, after Devore's dismal 2–7–0 season, the search began for a new head coach.

CHAPTER 8

THE ERA OF ARA PARSEGHIAN
(1964—74)

Michael Parseghian was born in Moosh, Armenia, now part of Turkey. A sturdy, well-built youngster, Mike moved to Smyrna, Turkey, enrolled at the Border Mission School, and quickly learned English, French, Italian, Greek, Turkish, and Arabic. When still a teenager he moved to Athens, got a job, and to escape Turkish atrocities in the Balkans, came to the United States. He arrived in December 1916, was drafted in 1917, and was sent to France as a liaison man between French and American officers. Back in Paris on leave, he met and fell in love with pretty Amelie Bonneau, married her, and arranged to bring her to the United States after the war. He did, a year after he returned to Akron and landed a job with the First National Bank.

On May 21, 1923, a son, Ara, was born to the young couple. Ara was named after an Armenian king of about the ninth century B.C. who became something of a legend in Armenia's struggle to be free.

Through most of their youth, Parseghian and his brother Mike—two years older—were cultivated as carefully as possible.

"Ara was the quietest boy in the family," said his mother. "I never once thought that he would ever be an athlete."

Their father impressed upon the boys the profound advantages of an understanding of music, art, and dancing, and the boys went along until one day Ara jogged down to the nearby Akron YMCA to play basketball.

As soon as he was able to put on a pair of long pants, Ara would sneak off to play football with the older kids, and the only way Mom could get him home was to come after him with a sawed-off broomstick she used for the family wash. As an eighth-grader, Ara was everybody's nomination for "toughest kid in school." "The Board of Education was having a great deal of trouble with vandals who were breaking windows in the schools," said older brother Mike, now a Toledo businessman. "So they just hired Ara to patrol the grounds. The checks came directly from the Board of Education. Ara was mighty proud of that."

At South Akron High School, Ara is remembered as a kind of Jack Armstrong with Wheaties. "He worked like the devil for his varsity S," a classmate recalled.

Coach Frank Wargo remembers one game against Steubenville High School, an Ohio team made up of mostly miners' sons. "Ara was tough. But Steubenville had a fullback, a tough one. On the first play from scrimmage," said Coach Wargo, "the two boys met head on, and you could hear the helmets crash all over the field. Both boys went down. After a few seconds Ara jumped up. They carried the other kid off the field."

"I didn't know what sport I liked best at the time," said Ara, "basketball or baseball."

Only one sport was ruled out for the Parseghian boys:

"Mom was afraid we'd get hurt playing football and so that was completely off-limits," Ara said. Mike never did play football, but in his junior year in high school, Ara went out for the South Akron High team and promptly won a varsity post as a guard. However, when Momma found out that Ara was playing football, there were any number of scoldings and arguments. Finally Ara did get his mother's permission, but she never would go to see him play.

Graduating from South Akron High, Ara enrolled at Akron University, quit school to join the Navy, and won a starting position on the Great Lakes Naval Station football team. After the war he enrolled at

Miami, Ohio, where he played football and won Little All-America recognition.

The Cleveland Browns drafted Ara in 1947 with six semester hours to go before graduation, and he left school to play with the Browns. "I was twenty-four years old then and didn't have too many years left for pro ball. And the money looked very good to me and I wanted to give the pro game a whirl."

Ara played one full season with the Browns in a backfield that included such stars as quarterback Otto Graham, fullback Marion Motley, and Edgar Jones. But a hip injury ended Ara's pro football career after that one season.

His association with Coach Paul Brown of the Cleveland team left a profound and lasting impression on Parseghian. Superficially, Ara appeared to be Brown's complete opposite—intense, volatile, emotional—while Brown was cool, aloof, and self-disciplined. "But Brown was a very intense person," said Ara. "More so than you'd ever believe. I say a lot of things Paul said because he said them while I was playing for him. But there's no one who controlled the psychological aspect of football better than Brown did."

Woody Hayes, then head coach at Miami of Ohio, selected Ara as an assistant, and Ara guided the freshman team through a perfect four-game season. When Hayes left in 1951 to take over as head coach at Ohio State, Ara succeeded him at Miami. He was an immediate winner there, carving out a 39—6—1 record in five years and then was selected to take over a Northwestern University football team whose fortunes had sunk to an all-time low.

At Northwestern, Parseghian struggled against all odds and turned the team into real Wildcats. Although his second season at Northwestern was a dismal one, Ara's solid coaching ability and personality turned the Northwestern program into a respectable one that challenged the top teams in the Big Ten, and Northwestern won their share of games. In 1963, for example, he beat his old mentor, Woody Hayes and Ohio State, in one of the big upsets of the year, 17—8.

Such victories, plus four straight wins over Notre Dame during Joe Kuharich's reign, gave Parseghian an inside track when he applied for the Notre Dame post left vacant by the departure of Joe Kuharich.

Father Joyce met with Parseghian and in a few days called Ara to inform him the job was his.

Parseghian brought three of his Northwestern aides to Notre Dame, men he had coached or played with

at Miami: defensive backfield coach Paul Shoults, offensive line coach Dick Urich, and offensive backfield coach Tom Pagna. Five Notre Dame men completed the staff: John Ray, Dave Hurd, Joe Yonto, George Sefcik, and John Murphy.

"At first, Ara did not show too much elation about the decision to take the Notre Dame job," said his chief aide, Tom Pagna. "It wasn't until we were on campus for a week or so, solidly, that he got caught up with the Notre Dame spirit. One night in January," said Pagna, "we were having staff meetings quite late at night, trying to familiarize ourselves with the players and the school. We heard this great commotion outside our window. I got up to look. I couldn't believe what I saw. I called to the rest of the coaches and to Ara.

"There in front of the Rockne Memorial Building were hundreds of students, all carrying torches. They were singing the famous 'Notre Dame Victory March' and chanting, 'Ara . . . Ara . . . Ara.' Ara turned to us with tears in his eyes. Maybe at that moment he recalled the inscription in his high-school yearbook where a close friend predicted, 'Someday, you will be the head coach at Notre Dame.'

"He turned back to the singing students for another moment, then smiled. We knew that he was ready."

Ara was introduced between halves of a basketball game on the campus, and the students gave him a ten-minute standing ovation.

At the start of the 1964 season, Parseghian whipped out a letter written by a former Notre Dame player, Don Hogan, who had been seriously injured in an auto accident and never again would be able to play football. Rockne couldn't have done it any better. Voice quivering with emotion, Ara read the letter to his spellbound players: "Being a Notre Dame football player automatically puts you in the national spotlight, more so than players from any other school. Don't let those fans down. Be honest with yourself. Give that second and third effort. Bring Notre Dame football back where it belongs—on top."

Ara discarded Notre Dame's old uniforms and pads ("too heavy," Ara said) and replaced them with new lightweight gold pants, blue jerseys, and helmets whose color was keyed exactly to the Golden Dome itself. Out went the old split-T formation offense, with its quarterback keepers, replaced by the pro-style slot-T and the dazzling stacked-I formation, in which three backs line up in a straight line behind the center, then shift to one side or the other.

The day he arrived at Notre Dame, John Huarte,

Coach Ara Parseghian, in his first year as head coach in 1964, looks unhappy as he battles the snow and his team struggles with the Pittsburgh Panthers. The game was won in the final minute by Notre Dame, 17–15.

John Huarte's Heisman Trophy-winning all-around play at quarterback in 1964 led the Irish to the national championship.

like most incoming freshmen, had a queasy feeling in the pit of his stomach. Sure, he had been a star quarterback back in Santa Ana, California, at a small high school named Mater Dei, but that was a three-day bus ride from South Bend and Notre Dame.

Huarte was quiet, lonely, and insecure. Notre Dame was one of those magical places he had read about. "I looked up at the Golden Dome, then the Rockne Memorial Stadium and was in awe," he recalled.

It was if he did not belong in this hallowed place where Knute Rockne, George Gipp, the Four Horsemen, Bertelli, Lujack, Lattner, and Bob Williams had walked. And the feeling would not go away.

When he walked into the Notre Dame locker room that very first day to pick up his football gear, the equipment manager ordered him out. Huarte's name wasn't on the list of scholarship players.

It turned out to be a clerical error.

"I thought I'd come for nothing," Huarte said.

He played a little, but even when he was a junior in 1963, the coaches were still calling him, "Hey, you."

"They didn't even know my name," he said. "They had eighty to a hundred guys to work with, and they only knew the first thirty or forty."

"And the longer I stayed around the field the worse I felt, because I didn't even get into the scrimmages."

If ever a player seemed destined for anonymity, it was John Huarte. Until the 1964 season, few had ever seen him play.

A few of the coaches didn't even know how to pronounce his name (it is Hew-art).

That is why it still is hard for some to believe, twenty-three years later, that a guy the coaches knew as "Hey, you," as a junior could come out of nowhere to win the Heisman Trophy a year later. Surely it had to be another clerical error.

But now the trophy sits on the piano in his office in Tempe, where he owns a chain of several tile-supply outlets. But the Hiesman Award looks just as shiny as it did twenty-three years ago, when he received college football's most coveted prize from New York's Downtown Athletic Club.

Huarte's senior season was memorable in college football.

He probably still checks the Heisman every now and then just to make sure it really is his name engraved on it.

He was the fifth-string quarterback as a junior and had played a total of forty-five minutes in three years. Then he got some breaks.

One afternoon, during spring training in 1964,

Parseghian walked over to where Huarte had been passing the ball to a couple of players. That day his passing was excellent, and he had thrown to his ends with superb, pinpoint passes of forty and fifty yards.

Parseghian pulled Huarte to one side: "John, I've been watching you and I like what I see. You're my quarterback for the season. I don't care if you throw six interceptions in our first game. You are Notre Dame's quarterback. Now, you're gonna have to live with me for ten weeks this fall. I'm counting on you. Notre Dame is counting on you."

"We were looking for a quarterback, a kid with the innate skills," said Assistant Coach Tom Pagna. "A kid with a good arm, and Johnny Huarte had a great arm. He had quick hands and feet, but he was not the aggressive natural leader a quarterback should be. Perhaps it had something to do with his failures of the two proceding seasons, when he was seldom used. He had to have confidence in himself before he could have the confidence of his teammates. And when Ara told him 'You're my quarterback,' that started his confidence flowing and his improvement. We worked him hour after hour, day after day handling the ball— feinting, faking, hiding the ball on every play. He became a truly great ballhandler and faker; and a leader, an intellectual type who performed, who was followed because of what he had done and what he could do."

Ara next visited with Jack Snow, the six-foot, two-inch, 220-pound end he had singled out as Huarte's number one passing target. Between them Huarte and Snow were to break all of Notre Dame's previous passing records.

"Coach gave each of us a chance to show what we could do," said Jack Snow. "He'd be right in there with us, doing our exercises, snapping the ball from center, showing us how to block and run. He told us we were good, made us really believe in ourselves, gave us confidence in our individual abilities."

On September 26, Notre Dame's 1964 team traveled to Madison, Wisconsin, to take on the Wisconsin Badgers.

"On the way to Madison," said Tom Pagna, "I prayed that Huarte's injured shoulder that was separated during spring practice would be ready for this big game." So did Ara. And Notre Dame.

But Huarte, moving with the grace of a ballet dancer and with no indication of a previous injury, handled the ball beautifully on the slippery field. He hit Jack Snow with two pinpoint passes right on target for long gains. Then Ken Ivan kicked a beauty of a thirty-one-yard field goal to give Notre Dame a 3–0 lead. A few plays later Huarte dodged a couple of Badger tacklers, spotted Snow all alone about thirty yards downfield, and zipped a beautiful pass to Jack, who caught the ball over his shoulder and continued all the way in for an Irish touchdown. The play covered sixty-one yards. On the sidelines, Parseghian and his coaches were beside themselves. In the second half, Huarte was sensational as he connected with pass after pass, completing fifteen of twenty-six passes for a total of 270 yards, a new Irish record. One pass play featured a forty-two-yard touchdown pass to Snow. And Ara Parseghian had won his first Notre Dame victory over a rival, by 31–7.

Next, Purdue traveled to South Bend, confident they would take the Irish. After all, they had defeated Notre Dame quite easily, with five wins in the last six games between the two schools. As the game opened the Boilermakers, led by their sophomore star Bob Griese, drove seventy-five yards for a score, mostly by passes to Bob Hedrick, a South Bend native. But Huarte promptly passed the Irish to Purdue's three-yard mark, where Ivan's field goal was blocked.

Purdue took over and failed to gain. On fourth down Griese's kick was partially blocked by the Irish, and the ball was recovered by Notre Dame at midfield. Huarte once again led the Irish to a touchdown, and now it was 14–7 Notre Dame.

In the third period, Griese's kick was blocked by Kevin Hardy, a six-foot, five-inch, 250-pound tackle. The ball caromed into Alan Page's arms, and Page, another six-foot, five-inch husky, picked up the loose ball and drove fifty-seven yards for an Irish score. Final score: Notre Dame 34, Purdue 15.

A group of more than 750 Notre Dame students made the trip to Denver the following week for the first Notre Dame game against the Air Force Academy. On the very first play of the game, Johnny Huarte barely missed on a ninety-four-yard pass play to Snow. But Huarte came right back with a forty-five-yard bomb to Nick Eddy, and the sophomore halfback raced in for the first touchdown of the game. Huarte's deft ball handling had the Air Force players guessing. He was like a magician as he faked to one Irish back and then handed off to Eddy who, playing his finest game, once again scored. The final score was an easy 34–7 victory as the Notre Dame defense limited Air Force to a total of thirty-seven yards rushing.

UCLA, with solid wins over Pitt, Penn State, and Stanford, traveled to South Bend the following week, and once again it was Johnny Huarte and his great arm beating the Bruins, 24–0. Captain Jim Carroll and his huge linemen, Kevin Hardy, Alan Page, Tom Regner, and Dom Gmitter, were in the UCLA backfield most of the game, and it was their bone-crackling tackles and subsequent fumbles by the UCLA backs that led to three Notre Dame touchdowns.

And now the chant went up in South Bend, "We're number one . . . we're number one. . . ."

They were not too far off base, for a poll of sportswriters voted Ohio State, number one, Notre Dame number two in the national ranking of college teams as of this date in the season.

Stanford rolled into South Bend. Their star was the leading running back in the nation in the person of Ray Handley, but the Irish wrecking crew of Hardy, Page, and company so manhandled Handley and his teammates that Stanford did not make a first down until well into the third period. Meanwhile, Huarte, once again the deft magician, completed twenty-one passes for more than three hundred yards, a new single-game school record. Jack Snow, the great Irish end, caught eight of Huarte's passes, while Bill Wolski smashed across for three touchdowns as the Irish victory train rolled to a smashing 28–6 victory.

Then the Notre Dame caravan moved on to Philadelphia and a battle with Roger Staubach and Navy. Roger moved his Middies to the Irish eight-yard line as the game began but got no farther as the tremendous Irish line shut down Navy without a single point. Huarte tossed a screen pass to Nick Eddy, and the fleet-footed speedster dashed seventy-four yards for the first of half a dozen touchdowns as Notre Dame buried Navy, 40–0.

Against a strong Pittsburgh team, the Irish, moving on the ground as the game began, marched eighty yards up the field as Joe Farrell and halfbacks Bill Wolski and Nick Eddy tore the Panther line to shreds, and it was 7–0 Notre Dame before most of the spectators were in their seats.

On the next series of plays, Huarte, noting that the Pitt defense was moving up close to stop the Irish running game, took the pass from center, faked to one of his halfbacks, wheeled, and completed a ninety-one-yard scoring play to Eddy for the second Irish score for the longest pass in Notre Dame history until it was eclipsed by a Blair Kiel to Joe Howard play against Georgia Tech in 1981.

But fumbles by Wolski and Denny Conway paved the way for a Pitt touchdown, and then the Panthers ran the ball for a two-point conversion. Now the score was 14–8, and things were going sour for the Irish.

Wolski and Jim Carroll were injured and Pitt, taking advantage of the injuries and a sudden Irish letdown, began to move the ball upfield. A Pitt fumble and Notre Dame had the ball. Now Joe Farrell, a big fullback, took charge for the Irish and repeatedly slashed the Pitt line for huge gains. With forty seconds to go in the half, Joe Azzaro, a sophomore from Pittsburgh but playing for the Irish, booted a thirty-yard field goal to give Notre Dame a little breathing room, and the score was 17–8 at the half.

As the second half started, Pitt surged up the field and battered the Irish line with an eighty-yard advance and a score. And suddenly Notre Dame was fighting for its life as Pitt, gamely challenging the unbeaten Irish, had tasted blood and wanted more. The score was now Notre Dame 17, Pitt 15.

Pitt was down to the Irish sixteen-yard line, and it was fourth down and one yard to go as the big play of the game began.

Pitt massed its attack and drove in for the one yard they needed to keep going. But Captain Jim Carroll, back in the game for this crucial play, rallied his troops and the Irish held.

When the play was declared dead, Pitt had failed to gain the yard they needed. It was Notre Dame's ball and they held on as time ran out. And it was another Irish win, 17–15.

And the big game was coming up.

Hated Michigan State had beaten the Irish eight straight years.

Paper streamers festooned the trees on the Notre Dame campus. Strings of firecrackers chattered like machine guns. Signs were everywhere.

"Hate State!"

"Sons of Erin, Unite!"

"Rub State Noses in the Irish Sod!"

The Irish campus was alive as it had never been before and probably never will be again. There were rallies, parades, marches, and there were "Hate State" buttons and banners all over the place.

This was the year and this was the week to beat State.

Athletic Director Moose Krause surveyed the sellout crowd of 59,265 and said with a sigh, "We could have sold 250,000 tickets for this game."

He could have sold a million—to all the members of the "subway alumni," the vast group of Americans who had never attended Notre Dame but who had fallen in love with the Irish football team and had adopted them as their very own. They were in every big city in America, and for them there was only one college football team in the land: Notre Dame.

Down beneath the stands, wearing his lucky brown pants and a blue sweater with NOTRE DAME lettered across the front, Coach Parseghian stood in the middle of the noisy locker room. "Everybody stay where you are!" he yelled. Then, pounding his fist into his palm, he began to talk.

"Boys (bang), you read the papers (bang). The predictors (bang, bang) say Michigan State is going to beat the tar out of us. But we (bang) are a better team than they are. We're going out there (bang) and prove it (bang)."

Then along with the rest of the Fighting Irish, Parseghian sank to his knees and bowed his head.

"Hail Mary, full of grace . . ."

Sportswriters had billed it "the game of the year."

It was that—for Notre Dame and for the thirty-five million fans watching the game on television, the millions more clustered around radios in bars and stores and barber shops. And what they got in terms of game excitement was beyond their wildest dreams.

In the next two hours, Notre Dame systematically took a tough Michigan State team apart at the seams.

State won the toss and received the kickoff but failed to gain ground against the hopped-up Irish defense. And now it was Notre Dame's ball on their own thirty-six yard line.

Now Parseghian was the magician as he called for a trick play he had been saving for State. He used a double-wing offense that looked like a pass play to State. As the Spartans wheeled in to cover for a pass, Huarte flipped the ball to Nick Eddy, who took off around right end and with the speed of a missile went sixty-four yards through the State defense, which was completely baffled by the play.

The Spartans, still groggy at the suddenness of the Irish attack, could not gain any ground, and the Irish took over once more.

This time it was Joe Farrell cracking the middle of the line for fifteen yards, then five more and then ten more. On the fourth such play, Joe faked a plunge through the line (he didn't have the ball), sprinted downfield and took a long pass from Huarte to the State eight-yard line. Then it was Huarte faking to Farrell and passing to Snow for another Irish score.

State had the ball now, but failed to gain ground as the Irish defense was just too tough this day. Notre Dame took the ball on downs.

Once again the powerhouse Irish backs began to

rip and tear at the Spartans and moved slowly but steadily downfield. A pass from Huarte to Snow picked up nineteen yards. Another Huarte pass, to fullback Bob Merkle, gained twenty-one. Then Huarte turned Nick Eddy loose, and the 195-pound halfback smashed in for another score. Huarte passed to Snow for the two-point conversion, and it was Notre Dame 21, Michigan State 0 at halftime.

As the third period began, a desperate Spartan team ripped off a fifty-one-yard pass that cut the gap to 21–7.

But Huarte came right back. This time, when he found his receivers covered, John simply outran State defenders and dashed in for another touchdown on a twenty-one-yard jaunt.

Now Ara put in the subs, who ran through State for another score, and it was 34–7. It was a spectacular display of football by Notre Dame, and before a nationwide TV audience.

Then it was another battle against Iowa, the following week at South Bend. Iowa always had fought the Irish to a standstill, and though they were 3–5 for the season thus far, the Hawkeyes had toppled top-ranked Ohio State from its undefeated spot and were ready to topple the Irish.

The temperature was thirteen degrees above zero at South Bend on the day of the game, and the snow and ice were bound to affect both teams. It was definitely no day for a slick ball handler like Huarte, no day for his gaudy passes. But the experts were all wrong.

Huarte once again proved that he was the greatest college quarterback in football by tossing a magnificent sixty-six-yard pass to Jack Snow, and the Irish had a touchdown. Wolski and Nick Eddy also contributed touchdowns, and the Irish walked away with an easy 28–0 victory, clinching their claim to the number-one ranking in the nation.

All Ara Parseghian thus far accomplished in this, his first season at Notre Dame, was to take a team with a 2–7 record in 1963 and bring it to a 9–0 record. Now Notre Dame fans were using the same adjectives to describe Parseghian as they had described Knute Rockne and Frank Leahy in the past. Sports experts called Ara's work at Notre Dame "one of the finest coaching efforts of all time."

Now all that stood in the way of the Irish and the national championship was a game against the University of Southern California, a team that had haunted many Notre Dame coaches in the past.

Notre Dame now had the chance to finish the most

amazing comeback in college football history and to conclude the most dramatic sports story of all time. The Irish were hungry to win the national championship for the first time in fifteen years and go down in the annals as the Pheonix that had risen from ashes to glory. The coaching staff was meeting, meeting, talking, planning, planning, scheming. "First thing," said Tom Pagna, "was to get the staff to believe in each other; then the squad to believe in the staff and to believe in themselves. They developed a camaraderie. In practice sessions, the offense cheered the defense, and the reverse. One could get the feeling, feel the change. It began with maybe we could win, and it became *we are going to win.*

And always there was Don Hogan on the sidelines, at the training table, in the locker room; for here was a player, a fine halfback in 1962 who spoke with authority. Don was the spark plug of the '62 team, a player who could get those extra three, four, or five yards when needed most. He could have been an All-Star on any other team in the nation. He had been severely injured after the '62 season in an automobile accident, returning from Christmas Mass. He had been hoping, praying that he could come back and play in 1963. When his doctors finally admitted that he could never again wear the Blue and the Gold uniform he so loved, he had written a letter to the team: "I'll be out there every day watching you. If a practice seems too long or you get tired along about the fourth quarter, just think for one second that a guy named Hogan would give anything in the world to trade places with you; and if he could, he would never give up. Give it that second effort to *bring Notre Dame football back where it belongs. On Top.* And when you do give it the effort, someone in the crowd will get the message and that someone will be mighty proud of you."

Right from the opening kickoff the Irish magic was in working order as Irish linebacker Ken Maglicic tackled Trojan ball carrier Rod Sherman so hard that Sherman fumbled and Notre Dame recovered the ball.

Jack Snow was being guarded by two Trojan defensive backs, so Huarte faked to Snow and passed to Nick Eddy. Then Huarte passed to Phil Sheridan. Both passes were for solid gains, and the Irish had the ball on the USC eight-yard line. Two attempts by Joe Kantor and Eddy failed to move the ball, so Ken Ivan was brought in and booted a twenty-five-yard field goal.

Then Notre Dame took over after USC's drive stalled, and Huarte alternated four successive passes to Snow and Phil Sheridan, and then John found Snow all alone in the end zone; he tossed a short pass to Snow, and it was 10–0 Notre Dame.

Huarte than proceeded to show how good he really was. He moved the Irish seventy-two yards on pass plays to Snow and Sheridan; when the Trojans massed to stop Snow, Huarte shifted to a running attack, and Wolski slugged the ball in for a touchdown. Now the score was 17–0, and it looked as easy as pie.

The third quarter found the tide of battle shifting to USC as Mike Garrett, their 9.8-second speedster for the hundred-yard dash, ran the kickoff back to the USC thirty-four-yard line. Now Craig Fertig, USC's fine quarterback, began to move his team. Fertig moved sixty-six yards in ten plays and then Garrett crashed through for a touchdown.

Suddenly it was a football game once again.

Now Huarte rallied his teammates and the Irish drove upfield with a smashing running attack that ate up yardage and time. Bill Wolski, Nick Eddy, and Joe Kantor took turns hammering at the USC line, and finally Kantor drove in for a touchdown—but an Irish player was holding, and the referee ruled that the touchdown play did not count.

That single infraction cost Notre Dame dearly.

Down by ten points, USC took the ball over on downs and hacked away at the Notre Dame line for good yardage. Then Fertig connected with two short passes, followed by a savage burst through the line for another gain. Then it was Fertig passing to Hill and, the Trojans scored a touchdown. Now it was 17–13 Notre Dame.

And there still were five minutes to play in the game.

Notre Dame had the ball, but suddenly the big Irish machine that had punched the USC line apart stalled, and USC took over on their own forty-yard line.

Now there were two minutes left to play.

A pass, Fertig to Hill, and USC had the ball on Notre Dame's forty-five-yard line. Once again, Fertig passed to Sherman, now on the three-yard line, and Rod danced in for the touchdown that gave USC a 20–17 lead over Notre Dame.

And before Notre Dame could start play after the kickoff, the game ended.

For the Cinderella team the clock had struck twelve.

As the game ended, only their training and discipline moved the stunned Notre Dame team to run off the field. Once they reached the dark, chill tunnel that led to their locker room under the stadium, most of the players slowed down to a shuffle. They reached the locker room where only an hour before, in high spirits with their comfortable and convincing lead, they had listened to their coach's plea and had cheered him. Now they were dazed, stonily silent.

Only a few gold helmets were slammed on the concrete floor. Only one or two players kicked or punched at locker doors. Even the clatter of their cleats seemed muted. They were not bitter. They were badly hurt. None would talk about what had happened, even though time after time, judgments by game officials had completely frustrated Notre Dame's attempts to score and put the game away for good.

Ara Parseghian came in at the end of the sorrowful procession, pouncing like a panther suddenly let off

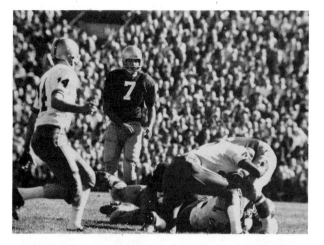

(Right, top) Irish quarterback John Huarte (7) has just handed off the ball to halfback Jim DiLullo (43) who is downed by Purdue players after a short gain in a 1964 game.

(Right, center) On the sidelines, Coach Parseghian is unhappy with the progress of the play as No. 31, Irish back Joe Kantor, misses a key block.

Irish back Tony Carey (No. 1) vainly tries to knock down the pass from USC quarterback Craig Fertig to halfback Rod Sherman (No. 12). The pass was good for a USC score and a 20–17 Trojan win over the Irish in 1964.

leash, head down, his dark eyes flashing his fury and disbelief. He ordered the team into the center room, and the four varnished doors were slammed shut.

In his hoarse, outraged voice, he shouted his affection for them and how proud he was of them. He told them they were still the best football team in the country. As their leader he knew what they thought about the several penalty calls. But he had determined not to comment on that part of the game, and he told the players to keep their mouths tightly shut. They would, he said, have to suffer this defeat like Notre Dame men—in silence.

Then he told them that they could let it all out right here and now. Behind closed doors the players wept together—some sobbing hysterically, others moaning like men in great pain. It was over in a few minutes. The doors swung open and the players moved toward their lockers along the corridors outside the room.

They left their coach slumped on one corner of an equipment trunk to ponder those last bizarre thirty minutes of Notre Dame football.

It was a full thirty minutes before anyone dared to get near him, to offer some words of cheer.

Several weeks later, at the Annual Football Hall of Fame dinner at the Waldorf-Astoria Hotel in New York, Father Joyce, Coach Parseghian, and Captain Jim Carroll accepted the MacArthur Bowl: "For consistence in championship performance, winning its first nine games against major college teams from East to West, Notre Dame has been adjudged the outstanding team in the nation."

Quarterback John Huarte won the coveted Heisman Trophy.

Huarte, Jim Carroll, and Jim Snow were unanimously named to the All-America team, and defensive back Tony Carey also was named to it.

Coach Ara Parseghian was named co-coach of the year, along with Coach Frank Broyles of the unbeaten Arkansas team.

A TOUGH ACT TO FOLLOW

"In 1965 we lost one of the great passing combinations in Notre Dame history in Johnny Huarte and Jack Snow," said Assistant Coach Tom Pagna, "and we could not replace their skills at those positions. We did have a good running and blocking group, and we were solid defensively. The thirst of the year before was not lacking, and the leadership of Captain Phil Sheridan, a top-notch end, was excellent. It could have been another championship season, but we just couldn't pass well enough."

Coach Parseghian had four quarterback candidates: Tom Schoen, John Pergine, Dan Koenings, and Bill Zloch. Schoen was the quickest but was an erratic passer. Pergine was the biggest, had a strong arm, but was inaccurate. Koenings was the best passer but didn't have the agility, and so Bill Zloch was the choice for the quarterback post.

Zloch was a fine high-school quarterback. He was hurt as a freshman at Notre Dame and was moved to a split-end post. He was six-feet, four inches and 215 pounds and was quick as a big cat. By his own admission Bill was not a good passer. But he was smart, understood the offense, could direct the team, and was deft at faking and feinting with the ball. The team knew this and responded to his leadership, and

he turned out to be a fine quarterback at Notre Dame.

In the opening game, against the University of California, at Berkeley, Nick Eddy, Larry Conjar, and Bill Wolski had a field day and rushed for a total of 381 yards and a smashing 48–6 victory over California. Nick Rassas, the Irish middle safetyman, returned three punts for 115 yards and intercepted two passes. (Rassas came to Notre Dame without a scholarship because he wanted to follow his father, who had been a fine end for Elmer Layden in 1938–40.)

Now the selectors around the country made Notre Dame the number-one team on the basis of their easy conquest of a fairly good California team, and they awaited the clash between the Irish and Purdue, rated number six in the nation.

The game was to be a test between Notre Dame's marvelous runners and a Purdue passing attack with the great Bob Griese, the Purdue quarterback who had one of the nation's leading receivers in Bob Hedrick.

It was one of those classic games they still talk about, with the lead changing often. Griese had one of the finest days of an incredible career. He completed nineteen of twenty-two passes for 283 yards, with three touchdown passes, including one for the winning touchdown, as the Boilermakers came from behind to eke out a heart-stopping 25–21 victory over the Irish.

"We can't expect to win any scoring duels with our type of offense this year," said Parseghian. "That was the most fantastic passing performance I've ever seen. We tried everything, tried to rush Griese, to zone off receivers, but when the passer is throwing strikes, nothing works."

"Our next game would be a tough one," said Tom Pagna. It was Ara's first game against his former team, Northwestern, coached by his former assistant Alex Agase, and after only six plays Phil Clark of Northwestern intercepted a Bill Zloch pass and sped fifty yards to a touchdown to make it 7–0 Northwestern.

Then Nick Rassas intercepted a pass and dashed ninety-two yards to tie the score. A few minutes later, Nick returned a punt seventy-two yards for another score. Then Tom Schoen at quarterback directed a sixty-nine-yard drive for still another touchdown. Schoen looked like the quarterback of the future as he completed pass after pass to lead the Irish to an easy victory. Final score: Notre Dame 38, Northwestern 7.

Ara Parseghian and Paul Dietzel had been great friends and teammates at Miami and had remained buddies, but now in 1965 Dietzel was head coach at Army, and Army and Notre Dame were set to meet in a head-on collision at night in New York.

The Notre Dame-Army game at Shea Stadium was the first between the two teams in New York since 1946, and when it was announced and scheduled for New York, the game was an instant sellout. But the game proved tame in comparison with previous Army-Notre Dame battles. Army had no offense at all, and the Irish were content to spurt to a 17–0 victory.

On the day of the Southern California game at South Bend, just before the officials called for Captain Phil Sheridan and USC Captain Mike Garrett for the toss of the coin and before Parseghian grouped the players near the sidelines for a last word, Tony Carey walked to the center of the players' circle. Tony carried the heartbreak of falling down as the Trojans scored the winning touchdown in 1964, and there was only one way he knew to rid himself of that grief. "Look, guys," he stammered. "I've been living with this thing for one whole year. No one's ever blamed me, but I've lived just to pay these guys back."

He didn't have to say another word. His supporters came to his rescue. "We'll get 'em, Tony." "Make

'em pay for '64." "Let's do it with class, though," Jim Lynch reminded. "Clean, tough, and hard."

USC's star, halfback Mike Garrett, who would win the Heisman Award that season, was stopped on the opening kickoff and would be held in check all afternoon by a fighting mad Irish eleven that could do no wrong.

Larry Conjar, the junior fullback, was unstoppable and rammed his way to four touchdowns as he played his finest game in an Irish uniform. Nick Eddy, married just a week prior to the game, also played a superb game; so did Bill Wolski and Bill Zloch as the Irish ran roughshod over USC, 28–7.

Now Notre Dame had moved up to number four in the ratings and the following week drubbed Navy, 29–3.

Next in line was Pittsburgh, and Notre Dame simply was too good for the Panthers. Bill Wolski scored five touchdowns and Ken Ivan kicked nine extra points as the Irish shattered Pitt by a 69–13 score. The passing of Bill Zloch was near perfect as he hit with six out of seven passes for 184 yards. The Irish backs Conjar, Wolski, Nick Eddy, and quarterback Bill Zloch looked so good that sportswriters were talking about the "New Four Horsemen."

North Carolina had defeated a tough Ohio State eleven and had just beaten a strong Clemson team. But after a dull, scoreless first half, Notre Dame rallied to roll up a 17–0 triumph as Nick Eddy continued his brilliant play.

Having won seven games while losing but one, Notre Dame was in a position to finish the season with another great year. But two of the toughest opponents were waiting just around the bend: Michigan State, with an undefeated team and loaded with talented ball players, and the Miami Hurricanes were just as good.

Michigan State, Rose Bowl-bound and with two tremendous linemen, Bob Lucas, who weighed 268 pounds, and Don Smith, at 286 pounds, were in the Irish backfield most of the afternoon and forced quarterback Bill Zloch to hurry his passes before he could find his key receivers. Thus the Irish passing game was throttled, and when Notre Dame tried to run the ball, those huge Spartan tackles were there to shore up the line and stop the play.

Notre Dame scored first when Ken Ivan kicked a thirty-two yard field goal, and the Irish led until midway into the third quarter. Then Zloch tried a pass, but it was intercepted by State, who took over the ball on the Irish nineteen-yard line. The Spartans' fine quarterback Steve Juday, threw a touchdown pass, and State was in front by a 6–3 score.

State came up with a first down on the Irish thirty-yard line late in the game, and then Clint Jones broke away and scored State's second touchdown and the Spartans had the victory by a 12–3 margin.

Bill Zloch shouldered all the responsibility for the loss. He felt he had failed everything that was Notre Dame. His body was a mass of bruises, but that didn't concern him. He was the last to leave the locker room, and Ara went over to him.

"Aw, coach," he said, sobbing, "I let the team down. I let all the guys down."

Ara had been Bill's greatest defender all season. He accepted the fact that Bill wasn't a great passer. Bill didn't claim to be, but he was the best the Irish had, and he had helped the team when they needed him.

"You didn't let us down, Bill," Ara said. "Ordinary players would have cracked out there today under all that tremendous pressure and abuse. And you didn't give up. I'm proud of you. We wouldn't have seven wins right now without you. Don't you forget that."

"Playing in the final game of the season in the heat of Miami Stadium didn't help our offense. The best scoring attempts were field-goal attempts. Miami nearly scored on a try of some fifty-two yards, but the ball hit the crossbar and bounded out without a score. Ken Ivan missed on three different occasions, and the game ended 0–0. It was the only time in eleven years at Notre Dame that we didn't track up a score," said Tom Pagna.

After the game, Parseghian praised his team:

"I'm proud of you guys, just so damn proud of the way you hung in here tonight and all year. Don't any of you hang your heads. You don't need an alibi. There's no need to. You're Notre Dame men. You gave your best and you must concede something to a worthy opponent. They played their best against us, too."

Two weeks later the team was honored at the annual banquet at Notre Dame, and the farewells were sad for the several graduating seniors. Included was Nick Rassas, who addressed his teammates:

"Recently I have been privileged to be selected as an All-American," he told the audience. "I have also signed a pro football contract for more money than I ever thought possible. But let me say here and now, I'd give it all up right this minute to play one more year for Notre Dame. My dreams have all came true and I'm saddened that they are over."

"After graduation," said Rassas, "I played pro ball for a couple of years, then took my M.B.A. Fortunately, I realized that life with the pros would last but a few years, and so I finished my graduate courses and took a job with the First National Bank in Chicago. I've been there thirteen years and am a vice-president today."

That night after the football banquet, the 1966 season began for Coach Ara Parseghian and his coaches. They had to find an outstanding passer somewhere, someplace.

Tom Schoen would be back in 1966.

Sophomores Coley O'Brien and Terry Hanratty looked good with the freshman squad. And sophomore receivers Curt Henaghan and Jim Seymour were the most talented of the ends.

"We already worried about our games against Michigan State and Purdue," said Assistant Coach Tom Pagna. "State was rated number one in the nation, while Purdue, with its incredible passing star Bob Griese, would be back to haunt us again, and they were rated number eight. We were rated number six."

"After a year-long passing drought," said Pagna, "our first concern was to come up with a quarterback who could pass the ball. And throughout 1965, Ara had his sights set on two outstanding freshmen, Coley O'Brien and Terry Hanratty."

"After watching the two quarterbacks in action, Ara began to glow in staff meetings," said Pagna.

Terry Hanratty's route to South Bend from Butler, Pennsylvania, was a circuitous one. He thought about going to Penn State—until he persuaded himself he could not meet the entrance requirements and therefore did not apply. His parents had separated about the time he was ready for college, and his grades were not all they might have been. But there was never any question about Terry's athletic ability. Older brother Pete, at the time a graduate student at Georgetown, was a high-school track star, and the Hanratty home was really a gym with chairs and a TV set.

"Our living room was like a boxing ring," recalled his sister Peggy. "Our backyard was a baseball diamond. I was always stumbling over makeshift bases."

Yet Mrs. Edward Hanratty abhorred violence—including football. She refused to sign Terry's Midget League application when he was ten (he got a neighbor to sign instead). Then he quarterbacked his team to the championship, but she had never seen him play until she tuned in to the nationwide telecast of the Notre Dame-Purdue game in 1966. Then she almost expired from fear that he would "fall on his face in front of all those people."

Not that Mrs. Hanratty wasn't a sports fan: She named Terry after her favorite baseball player, Terry Moore of the St. Louis Cardinals, and she'd played on the tennis team at Slippery Rock Teachers College. Terry came on early and strong. He won two letters at Butler High in basketball. He pitched a no-hitter the first time he took the mound for his high-school baseball team. He broke his brother's school high-jump record on his first try. But the fellow who really raised Terry's competitive hackles was a quarterback from just down the road, in Beaver Falls, Pennsylvania, a fellow named Joe Willie Namath.

So Terry's biggest thrill in high school was beating Joe Namath's high school, Beaver Falls, 41–21, scoring a touchdown on an eighty-two-yard quarterback sneak.

The film of that high-school game, forwarded to Notre Dame by a scout, probably was the one Ara Parseghian was idly viewing when he suddenly started to yell. "Number eleven? Who's that number eleven? We've got to get him." They did. Number eleven was Terry Hanratty.

At the Shrine of the Little Flower High School in Royal Oak, Michigan, about five miles north of Detroit, the football coach, Al Fracassa, announced in 1966 that he had retired football jersey number forty-two, the blue and gold jersey worn by "the greatest athlete I've seen in ten years of coaching." Number forty-two had been worn by Jim Seymour, a gangling "big kid" who was Shrine's version of Frank Merriwell.

The son of a well-to-do oil company executive, Jim had a more than ordinarily comfortable childhood: big luxurious house, backyard swimming pool, a guitar to play folk songs on, later the use of the family Pontiac (but not the Cadillac) to drive girlfriends to the "hops" that Shrine staged on autumn Friday nights after the football games.

In basketball, Jim was merely great. In track, he was almost invincible: After the third meet of his sophomore year, he was never beaten in the high or low hurdles. In football, however, Jim Seymour was pure gold. He was six feet, three inches and 175 pounds as a sophomore, and by the time he was a junior, Shrine had one of the finest teams in the state. As a senior Jim caught thirty-one passes for 560 yards, picked up another 164 yards as a halfback and averaged 44.2 yards per punt. College offers came in

from all over the nation. Jim said, "How could I go anyplace but Notre Dame? All the nuns at Little Flower High School were praying that I would go there. Of course, when I talked the situation over with Coach Parseghian and saw the Gold Dome and the Rockne Memorial Stadium, that clinched where I would be during the next four years."

All during the week of September 18 as Notre Dame prepared to settle a score with Purdue, Ara Parseghian was careful to speak softly when in the vicinity of Terry Hanratty.

"I want to be very casual, relaxed," Ara explained. "I don't want to get him nervous like me."

It was not easy, because Parseghian is a chatty, excitable man. As he talked about his players he had the popeyed look of a man holding his breath.

And in the final days before the September 24 date against Purdue, Parseghian had a series of "super-closed" practice sessions behind locked gates. In those final sessions, Ara could not believe the way Hanratty was throwing the football. What was more, he could not believe the way sophomore James Patrick Seymour was catching Terry's passes.

End Jim Seymour, three-time All-American, 1966–68, and his quarterback, Terry Hanratty, set all kinds of passing records for the Irish during that period.

Hanratty and Seymour now presented Parseghian with the chance to reestablish the kind of offense he had in 1964 when John Huarte was throwing to Jack Snow.

There was a snag, though: Hanratty and Seymour had never played a game for Notre Dame even as freshmen, because the Irish do not play a freshman schedule. That meant that in the match-up of quarterbacks with Purdue, it would be the rookie Hanratty against All-American Bob Griese, a brilliant, experienced performer who had started twenty-two straight games and had never once looked anything less than terrifying. The job he did on Notre Dame in 1965 was remembered with pain around South Bend.

It was doubtful, therefore, that the Notre Dame defense would be anywhere but up for the game. "The coaches did not have to say a thing to get us ready for Griese," said tackle Pete Duranko. The next big job was to keep Hanratty calm, and of course there was no way to do that—a big opening game at home, national television, pressure, pressure, pressure.

Finally, there was that night before—the concession Notre Dame makes to hysterics, the pep rally. Since Parseghian came to launch what was advertised on lapel pins as "THE NEW ARA IN NOTRE DAME FOOTBALL," Notre Dame pep rallies became happenings. Ara cleared his throat and six thousand students screamed their heads off. Human pyramids were built and collapsed spectacularly as the last man up ripped open his shirt to reveal a huge green tattoo on his chest: "IRISH." The students screamed, "Ara . . . Ara . . . Ara," and when Ara got up to talk, they cheered every fragmentary sentence.

So during all this was Hanratty terrorized? No, Terry was not. He was calm. He slept well. He had no trouble swallowing. His coaches found they could even kid him, and they did.

Privately, the Notre Dame coaches were confident that the poise of Hanratty and Seymour was genuine, and after the team breakfast Saturday, fullback Larry Conjar told a friend that he was amazed. "Here I am, a senior. I can hardly get a mouthful of food down. I can't sleep, not a wink. I'm nervous as a cat, and old Terry's calm as anything and eating more than anybody else. And have you seen Seymour? What a pair they are going to be for the next three years."

Nevertheless, the plan devised by Parseghian was to give Purdue the ball first, establish the Irish defense, and allow Terry a chance to get used to the ringing crowd noise. Then, after a couple of running plays, he would be free to throw the ball at his pleasure.

"I would just love to see them try to cover Seymour one-on-one," said Ara. "One-on-one he'll beat somebody and get us on the scoreboard in a hurry."

As the game began, Terry did not complete a pass until Notre Dame's second possession. Then he wound up, and while being hit from the side completed a marvelous forty-two-yard pass to Seymour. Jim made the catch among three Purdue defenders, and it was to begin a pattern maddening to Purdue and absolutely intoxicating to the 59,075 people snuggled into Knute Rockne Memorial Stadium.

Seymour was now 6 feet, 4½ inches, 210 pounds, and fast. On straight fly patterns and on one-on-one coverage in the first half against Purdue, he consistently beat his man and caught passes. Purdue Coach Jack Mollenkopf admitted later, "We didn't realize how good Jim was. When we started to give him the coverage he deserved, we opened up more places for their attack."

But even the double coverage and jamming did not stop Seymour, and whenever he was allowed a nickel's worth of air space, *voilà!*: Hanratty found him with a bullet pass.

As the game opened Hanratty tried a couple of running plays, and then he faked a pass to Seymour and threw to Rocky Bleier.

Rocky was hit very hard and fumbled the ball. LeRoy Keyes, a Purdue speedster, plucked the ball just off the ground and sped ninety-five yards for a touchdown.

The Irish came right back.

Nick Eddy took the Purdue kickoff, and behind some of the most superb team blocking by Bob Gladieux, Don Gmitter, Conjar, Seymour, and Rocky Bleier, who all but flattened Purdue's first wave of defenders, Nick threaded his way ninety-seven yards for a touchdown that tied the score at 7–7.

A few minutes later, Seymour beat five-foot, eleven-inch Bob Corby on a pass that would have been a touchdown, but the pass was slightly underthrown. Then Hanratty threw the ball to Seymour almost seventy yards and the Irish had a first down on the Purdue thirty-yard line. On the next play, it was Hanratty to Seymour for the touchdown.

"That pass was no accident," said Parseghian. "They have done that too often in practice."

Three minutes later, Hanratty to Seymour on a thirty-nine-yard pattern, and Jim went in for Notre

Dame's third touchdown. Now the score was 20–7, Notre Dame in front.

Griese had a difficult day as Parseghian had ordered four men to drop back and float with the receivers. As a result, Bob's primary receivers were almost always covered, sometimes by four and ofttimes by as many as six Irish defenders.

"Flush him out," was the order put out by Defensive Coach Johnny Ray of Notre Dame, and fourteen times Griese had to run with the ball, his receivers covered and his pocket crushed down by Captain Jim Lynch, ends Tom Rhoads and Alan Page, and tackles Pete Duranko and Kevin Hardy. It was a tribute, however, to Griese's brilliance that he still gained more ground than he lost rushing, and to the sharpness of his passing that after Notre Dame went ahead 20–7, Bob mustered Purdue once more on a brilliant seventy-five-yard drive that cut the score to 20–14 and revived Purdue's hopes—for the moment.

There were but eleven minutes to play, and Hanratty started his attack once more. He drove the Irish fifty-six yards to the Purdue forty-four-yard line, eating up precious time. Finally, after Purdue took over on downs and fumbled, Notre Dame recovered and Hanratty drove downfield once again. This time he pitched to Seymour, who drove across from the seven-yard line. Now it was Notre Dame 26, Purdue 14.

His final pass reception was Seymour's thirteenth of the day, giving him 276 yards gained in all. *No receiver in Notre Dame history*—not Knute Rockne, Jack Snow, Jim Kelly, Leon Hart, Monty Stickles, or Jim Mutscheller—ever had such a day.

Hanratty finished with sixteen completions in twenty-four tries for 304 yards. He was the last man out of the locker room. When he finally emerged, Johnny Ray grabbed him by a bare shoulder and said, "Hey, Terry, aren't you glad I helped you get a scholarship here?"

"Yes, sir, coach, you bet," said Terry.

"You bet I am."

In the Northwestern game the following week, Nick Eddy, now one of the most dangerous runners in the nation, provided the only score for the Irish in the first half of the game. They did, however, pound the Wildcats for four touchdowns in the third and fourth periods to defeat the Wildcats easily, 35–7. It was a triumphant homecoming for Ara Parseghian.

Army was third on the schedule, but the Cadets, undefeated until the Notre Dame game, never had a chance. The Irish scored the first time Hanratty got the ball, and then scored again less than 120 seconds

later, when Seymour blew right past the Cadets' secondary and gathered in a perfect forty-yard pass for a touchdown. The final score was 35–0—"a military disaster," as one noted sportswriter put it—the worst drubbing Notre Dame had ever handed Army in a thirty-eight-game series that went back to 1913.

North Carolina was the next victim, and the Tar Heels could almost say that they stopped Terry and Jim . . . almost. Hanratty completed only five passes, and only one of them went to Seymour. But it was a gorgeous fifty-six-yard strike that Jim picked out of the air with one hand and without breaking a strike crossed over the goal line in four giant strides. Final score: Notre Dame 32, North Carolina 0.

With thirty-mile-per-hour wind gusts at Norman, Oklahoma, it was obvious that no passing attack would decide the Oklahoma-Notre Dame game. Only a wildcatter would gamble on a pass against unbeaten Oklahoma. But Hanratty gambled in the wind and rain and made it look easy. Terry passed to Seymour for a forty-seven-yard touchdown play; another Hanratty pass to Seymour set up a field goal, and then Terry simply passed and passed and passed, completing eleven of seventeen passes for 139 yards and the Sooners were beaten, 38–0, the worst Oklahoma defeat in twenty-one years.

"Good Lord, they're only babies," Coach Parseghian insisted—as if he could hardly believe it all himself. And now the sportswriters were calling Hanratty and Seymour the "Dynamic Duo," the "Teen Terrors," and the "Super Sophs." Fervent Notre Dame subway alumni were handing out stickers proclaiming "Green Power," and normally hardheaded football experts like Don Klosterman of the Baltimore Colts and Gil Brandt of the Dallas Cowboys were calling Hanratty and Seymour "the best passing and receiving combination at Notre Dame in the past twenty-five years"—quite an endorsement, since that list included such as John Lujack, Frank Tripucka, Ralph Guglielmi, Paul Hornung, George Izo, and John Huarte. Klosterman said, "These two kids could make any pro team in the country."

Notre Dame had little trouble hanging on to their number-one rating during the next three weeks. Navy was trimmed, 31–7; Pitt was trounced, 40–0; and Duke was annihilated by a 64–0 air bombardment as Hanratty and Seymour ran wild. Now the stage was set for the most talked-about college match-up, perhaps of all time—Notre Dame, ranked number one, and Michigan State, ranked number two.

"The Notre Dame campus was absolutely chaotic

the entire week," recalled Tom Pagna. "The students held rallies, dorm meetings, and parades every night. Even though it was a road game, the campus was covered with spectators and reporters hoping to see anything that would take them behind the scenes of this big battle."

Spartan Stadium at East Lansing was a madhouse. People were seated in every aisle, and some even managed to filter onto the field. The police were powerless. The usual splendor of college football games was missing. No one cared about the bands, the marching, the cheerleaders. They just wanted to see this game—this battle to the death.

Notre Dame was not in the best physical condition for this battle against State. Coley O'Brien, the number-two quarterback, was ill. Coley had been missing his pass plays in practice and had lost his snap. During a physical examination the doctors reported that Coley had diabetes. O'Brien tried his best to cope, but for the time being he did not have the endurance. Irish running back Nick Eddy had injured and reinjured a shoulder and would not play.

As the game began, neither team could mount an effective drive in the first quarter as the flow of the game shifted up and down the field. During a series of plays, Hanratty rolled out to pass, but a Michigan State tackler had him cornered. He tried to run, but Bubba Smith, the Spartans' gigantic end, smashed Terry to the ground and fell all over him. That finished Hanratty for the season with a shoulder separation.

State scored twice in the second quarter on a touchdown and field goal and led the Irish, 10–0.

Then Coley O'Brien came into the game and played the game of his young life. He took over at quarterback for the Irish and in four plays moved the team fifty-four yards and passed to Bob Gladieux for thirty-four additional yards and the first Irish score, and now it was 10–7 Michigan State.

After the Notre Dame touchdown, O'Brien came to the sidelines and Hanratty grabbed and hugged him, sore shoulder and all. "You were great, baby, just great!" he shouted.

O'Brien was drained from his efforts on the field in the first half. Dr. Engel tried to balance his blood sugar in a corner of the locker room as Parseghian yelled words of encouragement to his players.

At halftime Notre Dame went into the dressing room behind 10–7 but came out inspired by Parseghian's pep talk, and they were smoking. Coley O'Brien, rested and fired up, took the Irish from their twenty-

yard line to State's thirty with three marvelous passes. Then Rocky Bleier, Larry Conjar, and Dave Haley smashed at State's massive line three times and moved the ball to the ten-yard stripe. Now the Irish fans were screaming.

Joe Azzaro came onto the field as the fourth period began, picked up a couple of stones that were lying on the turf, measured off his steps, and calmly kicked a field goal to tie the score at 10–10.

As the game wound down, a punting duel began with first Michigan State sending booming kicks to the Irish, and then, when Notre Dame failed to make headway, the Irish kicker, Kevin Hardy, would drill a long kick back to State. Azzaro tried a field goal from the forty-one-yard line, but it was wide.

There was more punting. . . .

And now with less than two minutes left to play, both coaches played it safe. On the last series of plays, with time running out, the Irish tried to move on the ground. There were no pass plays, no tricky ball handling, for the championship was riding on every move.

The last play of the game resulted when Smith broke through and tackled O'Brien on the Irish thirty-five-yard line, for a seven-yard loss. Now with one more play O'Brien, rather than try for a field goal, on orders from Parseghian just took the ball and drove into the line, and the game ended with Spartan fans booing the Irish.

Most of the experts chastised the Irish for "playing it safe" on the final play. They contended that Ara should have tried for a field goal. "He should have tried to win," said a noted sportswriter. "After all, it was for the national championship."

That one play, "playing for a tie," would leave a mark on Notre Dame football and Parseghian.

Notre Dame's final game of the season, against Southern California, would now decide the national championship, as the Associated Press vote had the Irish number one, while the United Press tally showed Michigan State number one and Notre Dame number two.

Notre Dame would have to win convincingly over Southern California, and with Hanratty, Bleier, Gladieux, and George Goeddeke, all starting players, out with injuries, the Irish still were being challenged by the Trojans, who were Rose Bowl-bound and aching once more to knock the Irish from a championship position, much as they did in 1964.

Tom Schoen, Notre Dame's third-string quarterback, timed a pass from the Trojan quarterback, Toby

Page, intercepted it and raced forty-seven yards for a score. The next time the Irish got the ball they drove eighty yards in eighteen plays for another score, and it was 17–0 at the half.

When the offense took the field for the second half, assistant coach of John Ray of Notre Dame hollered, "My God, you guys, we just got to get another score."

The Irish not only picked up another score, they also picked up thirty-four more points in the air and on the ground and trampled the hapless Trojans, 51–0.

The pollsters agreed: Notre Dame was number one in both the AP and UP final ratings. Notre Dame did have to share the MacArthur Bowl with Michigan State, but there were no complaints except from the University of Alabama, which also had gone undefeated.

Although he would never publicly declare it, the 1966 Notre Dame team undoubtedly was the finest Parseghian ever had.

Ten players—Nick Eddy, Captain Jim Lynch, Tom Regner, Alan Page, Pete Duranko, Paul Seiler, Kevin Hardy, Jim Seymour, Tom Schoen, Larry Conjar, and George Goeddeke—were named to the All-America team, more than from any other Notre Dame team in history.

"None of us on the coaching staff had the slightest notion anything was troubling Coach Parseghian as we got ready for the 1967 season," recalled Assistant Coach Tom Pagna. "But there was something wrong.

"Ara had worked his way up in life, at Miami and Northwestern, earning little money at each of the schools. But after a couple of years at Notre Dame and then the national championship, the monetary rewards and the resulting recognition changed a lot of things. He was now a national celebrity, was in demand for banquets, meetings, clinics, endorsements, appearances on radio and television, and the nation's press beat a path to his doorstep.

"But that was not the problem affecting Parseghian.

"One day after practice," said Pagna, "I asked about Karan's health. Karan was the Parseghians' firstborn. Then there was Kris and Mike. I had noticed Karan was having mobility problems and I sensed that it was MS and I mentioned it to Ara and he was shocked that I had brought it up. It was plain he was greatly troubled.

"At any rate, Ara talked to his coaches about his pain over Karan's illness.

" 'I think you guys have a right to know this,' he said one morning. 'I've been spending a good deal of time the past few months doing work for the Multiple Sclerosis Foundation. Katie and I have just found out that Karan has developed the disease.'

"That was the burden that Parseghian had to bear in 1967 and thereafter, one that only a few people knew about."

And as the season began there was added pressure on Ara to win 'em all again. Notre Dame students and fans wanted to win another championship. So did Ara and the coaches.

There were a number of outstanding players returning from the 1966 national championship squad: Terry Hanratty, Coley O'Brien, Rocky Bleier, Kevin Hardy, Jim Seymour, place-kicker Joe Azzaro, and enough monogram winners to give the Irish another great season . . . and with luck, another championship.

"But unfortunately," said Tom Pagna, "our players didn't have quite the ability or enthusiasm they had in 1966."

In 1966 Hanratty had become a national celebrity. He had completed 53 percent of his passes, thrown for eight touchdowns, and had gotten his picture on the cover of *Time* magazine along with his receiver Jim Seymour.

But 1967 was a bit different.

At the season's start, enemy coaches had changed their basic concepts of pass defense to stop Terry, and wherever Seymour ran on the field, he was covered by two or three of his opponents. The result: four interceptions against Purdue, five against USC, and both games resulted in defeat for Notre Dame, the only two defeats of Terry Hanratty's three-year varsity career there.

In the opening game of the season, California traveled to South Bend, and Hanratty, Seymour, and company handed the Golden Bears a neat 41–8 trimming. All Terry did was complete fifteen of thirty passes for 205 yards to chalk up the Irish's eleventh consecutive victory.

The following week Purdue had some bad news for the Irish as they replaced marvelous quarterback Bob Griese, who had gone on to play pro ball with the Miami Dolphins, with another great young quarterback with an arm as proficient as Griese's. His name was Mike Phipps, and all Mike did was throw fourteen completed passes for two touchdowns. Hanratty, too, was amazing against Purdue. He connected twenty-nine times of sixty-three attempts and accounted for 366 yards and one touchdown. But it simply wasn't enough this day as Purdue eked out a 28–21 victory to snap the Notre Dame eleven-game winning streak. Those four interceptions beat the Irish.

The next week Hanratty led Notre Dame to a 56–6 rout of the rugged Iowa Hawkeyes. Terry connected with nine of ten passes and directed the team to a 35–0 halftime lead. Then Parseghian rested Terry and allowed the subs to play the second half.

Southern California came to South Bend still smarting from the 51–0 setback of the previous season—they were steaming for revenge, and they got it. Hanratty had his poorest day as a passer, completing but ten of twenty-three passes. And those five interceptions sealed Notre Dame's doom this day.

USC just happened to have one of the greatest running backs in history in the person of O. J. Simpson, who took the ball on almost every play and went through the Irish line as if it were made of papier-mâché. USC went on to upset the Irish by a 24–7 score.

Like many good passing combinations, Hanratty

Bob (Rocky) Bleier, a standout performer on three Irish teams, 1965–67, and captain of the 1967 team. Wounded and severely injured during the Vietnam war, Rocky recovered and rejoined the Pittsburgh Steelers, where he helped inspire them to several Super Bowl championships.

and Seymour had become too confident with one another. The quarterback had developed a false sense of security and felt he could get the ball to Jim, and that Jim could get the ball, no matter how. But he wouldn't always get the ball.

Terry sat in his room back at school one afternoon and sulked.

"I was pretty well disgusted with myself," he recalled.

The problem, as Parseghian saw it, was a "psychological block." Terry had gained so much confidence in Seymour that he was forcing the ball when he should have looked for alternate receivers."

Terry's search for a solution to his passing problems led him to seek outside advice. He especially looked up to Johnny Unitas after reading a book based on Unitas' life story.

"I wrote John a letter," said Terry, "and told him about my problems and asked his advice. I told him how much I admired and respected him. I never really expected an answer. He must get thousands of letters from kids, asking all kinds of crazy questions.

"But he wrote back—a very nice two-page letter. He thanked me for my comments about him and set down a few rules I should keep in mind. The principal point he made was to hold on to the ball as long as possible, and know exactly what I was doing before I threw the ball. He really didn't say anything more than what my coaches had already told me.

"I got Johnny's letter on the Saturday morning of the Michigan State game, and I never had any more interceptions."

And Notre Dame never lost a game after that for the rest of the season.

The Irish found a running game with Captain Rocky Bleier, who was an inspirational leader all season long. Later Rocky would become an inspiration for the entire nation with his heroic and valiant service in Vietnam and then his excellent play with the Pittsburgh Steelers.

Bleier, Bob Gladieux, and Jaffe Zimmerman provided the spark of the running attack as Illinois was beaten 47–7. Michigan State was beaten, 24–12; Navy fell by a 43–14 score; Pitt bit the dust, 38–0; and Georgia Tech succumbed, 36–3, for Notre Dame's five-hundredth victory. Then the Miami Hurricanes battled the Irish tooth and nail in a furious night contest in Orange Bowl Stadium in Miami before bowing by 24–22.

Thus the Irish finished the season on a glorious note, regaining a national rating, in fifth place behind

USC, Tennessee, Oklahoma, and Indiana.

"We were all drained after the Miami game," said Tom Pagna, "and as we entered the locker room to celebrate, there came Captain Rocky Bleier. He had been operated on for a severe knee injury earlier in the season, but played a couple of games with great personal courage. As Rocky hobbled into the locker room on crutches his teammates cheered him. 'Rocky! Rocky!' they shouted. Ara walked over to him and placed the game ball in his hands. As we went to congratulate him, the tears were flowing from all of us."

Knute Rockne had the Four Horsemen, George Gipp, and the Seven Mules, and they caused him many sleepless nights with their pranks and wisecracks while he was at Notre Dame.

One of Parseghian's Fighting Irish groups was a trio called the Three Owls. Their real names were Terry Hanratty, Ron Dushney, and Bob Gladieux.

The Owls weren't too troublesome. They didn't start fights, but they just didn't happen to think they had to attend classes on a regular basis.

Dushney was a real clown and kept the players relaxed with his antics. One day Ara watched him commit error after error on a goal-line series of plays and he hollered at Ron, "Dushney, you know what you need? You need a swift kick." Ron looked over at Ara and said, "Coach, you're exactly right." So Ara smiled, told him to bend over, and kicked him. Then Ara called the same play, and Ron ran it in for a score. Ara then said, "See, Dush, all you needed was a bit of encouragement."

Bob Gladieux was an outstanding high-school star in several sports and yet in practice would almost always foul up a play. One day Ara exploded. "Damn it, Bob, don't you ever look at your play book?"

Later Gladieux confided to Assistant Coach Pagna, "Every time I get near the coach I freeze up. "I had to laugh," said Pagna. "I knew what he meant. It happened to a lot of us as players."

Hanratty, third member of the Three Owls, was dubbed the Rat, and his teammates played one practical joke after another on him, but Terry enjoyed the ribbing just as much as his teammates.

THE EMERGENCE OF JOE THEISMANN

Oklahoma, smarting after six consecutive losses to Notre Dame, visited South Bend in 1968 to open the season, and they were thirsting for revenge. The Sooners were highly rated in 1968 but were no match for the Three Owls, and the rest of the Fighting Irish as Hanratty, Gladieux, and Dushney ran the Sooners ragged. Hanratty completed eighteen out of twenty-seven passes for 202 yards and two touchdowns. Gladieux caught six passes and was outstanding, while Dushney consistently rolled up impressive yardage as he returned two kickoffs for spectacular runs. It was an impressive 45–21 win over Oklahoma, strong contenders for national honors, and the Irish fans already were screaming, "We're number one . . . we're number one."

Notre Dame's defense was rated over the offense in 1968, but Purdue charged over and around and through the Irish defense as their quarterback star, Mike Phipps, and running back LeRoy Keyes simply could not be contained. Phipps picked the defense apart as he clicked on sixteen passes and two touchdowns, Keyes scored two touchdowns, and Purdue left town with a 37–22 victory.

"We managed to score at will against Iowa," said Assistant Coach Tom Pagna, "and ran up a total of fifty-one points to defeat Iowa easily even though our pass defense was sloppy in allowing Iowa to score twenty-eight points."

Two Big Ten opponents went down to defeat in succession as Notre Dame easily defeated Northwestern, 27–7, and then trampled the Illinois eleven, 58–8. There was a tremendous surge of confidence as the defensive team showed they could close down the enemy's passing game. In the Illinois game Terry Hanratty moved ahead of the immortal George Gipp as Notre Dame's all-time total-offense leader.

Then the team traveled to East Lansing for the all-important battle against Michigan State, and as usual the "big game" was filled with all sorts of intriguing talk and situations and controversy that lasted for many months after the game.

Duffy Daugherty, State's outstanding coach, told the media in a press conference before the battle that if Notre Dame won the coin toss and elected to receive, State would try an onside kick. Parseghian did not know whether to believe him or not. At any rate, Notre Dame did receive the kick. It was onside as Duffy had said, and thanks to a good bounce,

Michigan State recovered the ball and took advantage of the golden opportunity, moving the ball forty-two yards in six plays for a touchdown. Notre Dame never did recover from that first score but still were in the game, trying to come from behind. There were two minutes left to play in the game and the Spartans had a 21–17 lead. But the Irish had a marvelous opportunity to score and win. Notre Dame had the ball on State's three-yard line, third down. Two previous running plays had failed to gain ground, and Parseghian sent in a pass play, Hanratty to Seymour. Jim was in position to catch the ball easily but was knocked to the ground by a State player. The interference was obvious, but the official responsible for calling the infraction had been knocked to the ground. He did not see the play. None of the other officials saw the play, and amid all of the controversy, Hanratty attempted to run the ball in but was stopped. State took the ball, and time ran out for Notre Dame.

Parseghian was enraged after the game was over.

Back in his office he looked at the game film over and over and each time would scream out loud, "You mean to tell me that wasn't interference? "You're damn right. I'm going to write the Big Ten office. I'll show them how they cost us the game." Then in a cooler moment he let the entire affair drop.

The Irish gave vent to their anger the following week as they let it all out and ransacked Navy by a 45–14 score, and the world seemed blue and gold for Ara and the Irish until the practice drills started for the Pitt game the following Saturday.

It happened during a Wednesday scrimmage, a rare one for the Irish. Hanratty took the ball and was supposed to fake to his fullback and then pitch the ball to Gladieux in a wide sweep play. On the play, Terry took the ball, slipped, and then saw the defense close in and tried to run. He headed for the sidelines and was hit hard. He twisted his leg as he fell, and his knee snapped. The injury was serious enough to require surgery, and Hanratty's superb three-year career at Notre Dame was over.

The injury to Terry Hanratty meant the beginning of a new one for anther record-breaker-to-be in the person of Joe Theismann.

"From what we had seen on his high-school film," said Tom Pagna, "Joe was an outstanding runner but not too good a passer. But when he reported as a freshman, we discovered a couple of things about Theismann not obvious on film. Joe could throw much better than we thought, and he had great football sense.

"For a quarterback, Joe was small," said Pagna. "He was just six feet tall and weighed no more than 160 pounds, but he was sinewy and tough.

"With but thirty minutes of varsity experience, Joe started against Pitt. We kept the offense on the ground until we had a 7–0 lead," said Pagna, "then we let Joe throw the ball. And he did a wonderful job. Rolling, ducking side to side, Joe completed passes for twenty and twenty-nine yards, threw two touchdown passes to Coley O'Brien. The final score was Notre Dame 56, Pitt 7."

Theismann's performance was reminiscent of the time when All-America quarterback Angelo Bertelli entered the Marines during World War II and was replaced by an eighteen-year-old sophomore who was to rewrite Notre Dame football history: Johnny Lujack.

Georgia Tech traveled to South Bend determined to revenge the 36–3 defeat of the year before, but Theismann, handling his position in a masterful fashion, guided the Irish to a 34–6 victory over the "Rambling Wrecks." Then there was a two-week layoff before the Irish flew to Los Angeles for the annual battle with USC.

In 1970, quarterback Joe Theismann set an all-time Notre Dame record by completing 155 passes during the year.

USC was rated the nation's number-two football team, and Coach John McKay, still smarting from the 1966 defeat inflicted by a horde of Fighting Irish who had devastated the Trojans with a shocking 51–0 beating, was bent on sweet revenge. McKay knew that a win over Notre Dame would give him undisputed position as the number-one team in the nation over Ohio State, and he had primed his team for weeks. USC was undefeated, having won nine straight games, and with their great running back O. J. Simpson having an incredible season, McKay figured he had all the cards. And on paper he did.

But Parseghian, utilizing a six-man front line with two linebackers in tight, held the mighty O. J. powerless throughout the entire game. Simpson could gain only fifty-five yards all day long.

Theismann opened the game with a sharp pass to Jim Seymour. But USC's Sandy Durko intercepted and raced twenty-one yards for a Trojan score, and within forty seconds USC had a 7–0 lead. But the Irish struck back. Theismann threw several short passes and in eighteen plays moved the ball eighty-six yards. Then one of the remaining Three Owls, Ron Dushney, crashed in from the five-yard line, Scott Hempel converted and now the score was tied at 7–7.

As the first quarter ended, Ron Gladieux, another Owl, took a Theismann pitchout and raced fifty-seven yards for a touchdown. Hempel's kick gave the Irish a 14–7 advantage.

Then the crafty Theismann provided some magic of his own. He flipped a short lateral pass to Coley O'Brien, who dashed to his right and shot a pass back to Theismann, who had slipped into the end zone, for another score. Hempel again put the ball between the uprights for the extra point, and it was 21–7 Notre Dame.

USC's Simpson finally broke through for a touchdown in the third period to make the score 21–14. In the final period, a Theismann pass was intercepted, and USC's quarterback Steve Sogge passed to Sam Dickerson, and the Trojans tied Notre Dame, 21–21. The game ended shortly after that play.

"Deep down in my heart," said Joe Theismann, "I think we should have won that game. We had them on the run."

"I'm disappointed," said O. J. . . . . "I wanted to go out a winner."

Notre Dame ended the season with seven wins, two losses, and a tie. The Associated Press pollsters ranked the Irish number five in the national ratings.

Going into the 1969 season, the Three Owls,

backfield stars Terry Hanratty, Ron Dushney, and Bob Gladieux, had graduated. All-American Jim Seymour and his teammates on the front line Tim Mounty, Tom McKinley, George Kunz, and Jim Winegardner also had graduated. Halfback Coley O'Brien, who occasionally flashed with the brilliance of a great star, also had departed, leaving the Notre Dame squad weakened beyond description.

Thus in 1969 Ara Parseghian started the season against Northwestern with a quarterback, Joe Theismann, who had half a year's varsity experience, and a backfield composed of Ed Ziegler and Denny Allen at halfback and Bill Barz at fullback, all with limited experience.

When he arrived at Notre Dame as a freshman "walk-on" Mike Oriard was an enthusiastic kid who weighed just 191 pounds. But when told he was rather light for a center, he worked on his size year-round, lifting weights, running wind sprints, and eating wheat germ. By his senior year in 1969, Mike was the regular center and had built himself up to a strapping, muscular six feet, three inches and 225 pounds and was elected a co-captain along with linebacker Bob Olson. Mike majored in English literature and upon graduation received a Rhodes scholarship. He played professional ball with the Kansas City Chiefs, received his doctorate, and today is a professor of English literature at the University of Oregon.

A Northwestern interception in the first quarter and a field goal and the Wildcats suddenly had a 10–0 lead over the Irish, who seemed to be playing in a deep trance in this first game of the season.

Parseghian suddenly changed his offense; he did little or no passing and concentrated on a running game against the big, slow Northwestern line. The strategy paid off and Notre Dame hammered away, scoring five touchdowns for a 35–10 victory.

"Our backfield was probably the slowest, but guttiest," said Assistant Coach Tom Pagna. "None of the guys were exceptionally big, but they worked like beavers. But we were not noted for our speed this year."

The following week, All-American quarterback Mike Phipps once again provided Purdue with the punch, completing twelve passes for 213 yards as Purdue once again defeated Notre Dame, 28–14.

In 1964 Johnny Huarte had Jack Snow to throw to; Terry Hanratty and Jim Seymour became a record-breaking passing duo for the Irish in 1967 and '68; and now in 1969 Joe Theismann began to assault that record, passing to Tom Gatewood.

Against Michigan State, Theismann's feinting, fading back, always-on-the-move style worked like magic as he passed ten times to Gatewood for 155 yards; three of Joe's passes to Gatewood were good for touchdowns, and Notre Dame was back on the winning track with a 42–28 victory. The following week, the Irish traveled to New York's Yankee Stadium and a battle with their longtime foe, Army. The game was a walkaway as Theismann, Gatewood, and company roughed up the Cadets, 45–0. USC came to South Bend the following week, and once again it was a bitter struggle. The Trojans had lost their great star O. J. Simpson, but in his place they had another ace in Clarence Davis, a speedster.

The score was tied 14–14 when Scott Hempel, Notre Dame's great kicker, tried a forty-eight-yard field-goal attempt. The wind was behind Hempel as he made a great effort. The ball sailed straight as an arrow right to the crossbar . . . then it hit the bar and bounced back, short of the mark by six inches. The game ended in a 14–14 tie.

"Gentlemen," said Coach Parseghian to the press after the game, "this was a helluva football game and no place for the timid. Both teams were very well prepared, and they performed extremely well. This was a great college football game."

Notre Dame won its next five games with ease.

In New Orleans in a night game, the Irish easily trampled over Tulane, 37–0; playing host to Navy, they passed the Middies dizzy with a 47–0 trimming. The following week Pitt was savaged 49–7, and then Georgia Tech was beaten in a night contest, 38–20.

There was one game left on the schedule, against Air Force, and during the preparation for the game an announcement was made by university officials regarding participation in a bowl game at the end of the season. The university had accepted an invitation to the Cotton Bowl—if the team could win the final game.

Air Force waged a gallant battle, but they were bombarded from the air by Theismann, and Notre Dame eked out a 13–6 victory and were bowl-bound for the first time since 1925, when Knute Rockne accepted an invitation to the Rose Bowl and Notre Dame defeated Stanford.

Notre Dame's opponent in the Cotton Bowl was the number-one-ranked Texas Longhorns. As the game began, Notre Dame jumped out in front with a twenty-six-yard field goal by Scott Hempel. Then a beautiful play: Tom Gatewood, instead of racing out for a pass, hesitated at the line, blocked his man out, then hesitated another second and raced downfield. The defensive backs, sucked in by Gatewood's blocking tactics, allowed Gatewood to go downfield completely in the open, and then Theismann tossed a great pass to Gatewood, who took the ball over his shoulder and raced in for a touchdown on a fifty-four-yard play.

But Texas came back and drove downfield on eighteen consecutive plays and scored the go-ahead touchdown for a 14–10 lead with ten minutes to play in the game.

Then Theismann went to work. Calling his own number on two straight plays, Joe advanced the ball twenty-five yards; then he uncorked a lovely straight-as-an-arrow pass to Jim Yoder for a touchdown that gave the Irish a 17–14 edge with seven minutes to play.

Then Texas put together one of the most thrilling drives in college football as they went seventy-six yards in just under five minutes. There were close first-down calls each time Texas advanced the ball; each time the play had to be measured before the officials awarded the Longhorns another first down. There were penalties and a number of close plays, with Texas receiving the advantage on each call the referee made. Texas scored on a quick down-and-out pass play. The ball was thrown low, nearly touching the ground, but Jim Spetrer of Texas snagged the ball before it hit the ground, and he reached the Irish two-yard line for a first down. The Longhorns then took the ball in for the go-ahead touchdown for a 21–17 edge.

There was one minute to play, and Theismann utilized every feint, every kind of pass in his repertoire and moved the Irish to the Texas thirty-eight yard line. Then a Theismann pass was intercepted on the Longhorns' nine-yard line, and time ran out for Notre Dame.

"The bowl game was a fine experience for the players and the university," said Tom Pagna. "Our hotel rooms and the food were first rate. It was like a paid vacation, and the university gained over $200,000 for its minority student scholarship fund. We hoped it would be the start of a great tradition."

"Looking at our personnel in 1970, I had to say that we had some of the most unusual individuals on that squad," said Tom Pagna.

"Tom Gatewood was a 6-foot, 2½-inch halfback who weighed 210 pounds and he was quick as a big cat. An outstanding student with a 3.5 average, Tom was a delight to work with. He wasn't just right for a halfback," said Tom, "so Ara and I decided after watching him leap high into the air and catch passes that we were going to use him at an end position. And all he did was to be named to the All-America team for two straight seasons."

In his senior year, 1971, Gatewood, along with teammate Walt Patulski, a tremendous 6-foot, 6-inch, 260-pound end, were elected co-captains and were among the most popular men on the campus. Upon graduation Tom took a position with the Mutual Broadcasting Company.

Street-smart Larry DiNardo, offensive captain in 1970 and one of the finest guards to ever play that position for Notre Dame, was raised in New York, in an Old World tradition where the very word of his parents was law, with no questions asked. When Larry was named co-captain in 1970 in his senior year, his unending enthusiasm, magnificent play, and leadership inspired his teammates to a superb 9–1–0 campaign, and a postseason game against Texas in the Cotton Bowl.

Ed Gulyas was one of a handful of walk-ons and a fellow who contributed greatly to the team during the 1970–73 era. He did not lack the ability, but he just couldn't get too enthused at practice until he was told that he could be a starter if only he would concentrate and take the game seriously. And once he tasted success, he really bore down.

At the start of the 1970 season, Notre Dame figured to be so good that it would be invited to virtually any bowl game it desired. And that's just the way the season turned out.

In the opening game of the season, Northwestern was easily defeated, 35–14. Then Purdue traveled to South Bend. Always a fearsome opponent, Purdue had beaten the Irish in nine of their previous twelve games and were eager to savor another victory. This time, however, Joe Theismann, rapidly developing into one of the finest Irish quarterbacks, threw three passes to Tom Gatewood for touchdowns, and the Irish got sweet revenge with a blistering 48–0 beating of the Boilermakers.

The Parseghian household was open house after each home game, and this night the celebration lasted until the wee hours as friends, alumni, university officials, and invited guests jammed the home until 5:00 A.M.

The following week, Michigan State.

Notre Dame had not won over State since 1949, a twenty-one-year drought, and the Spartans were openly crowing over those statistics. This time, however, Notre Dame trimmed a surprised State team 29–0, with a hard-driving running attack mixed with a devastating passing game. The Irish were not to be denied this day.

At South Bend, Army brought in a contingent of some twenty-five hundred cadets, but they were not enough to overcome a sparkling air and ground attack by Theismann and company, and the Black Knights were beaten by a whopping 51–10 score.

Dan Devine, head coach at Missouri, had prepared his Tigers for an upset win over the rampaging Irish, but Notre Dame was unbeatable this day and took a hard-fought battle by a 24–7 edge.

Navy was blown out by a devastating passing attack by Theismann to the tune of 56–7. Then Pitt was defeated, 46–14, to give Notre Dame its seventh straight victory of the year and the number-one rating in the nation.

In the Pittsburgh game, Joe Theismann became Notre Dame's all-time total offense leader with a career record of 5,432 yards.

Georgia Tech decided they could shut down the running game that Notre Dame had utilized so successfully all season long, so they set up an eight-man line up front throughout the first half of the game. The strategy worked well for Tech, and the score was 0–0 at the half.

Then in the locker room Parseghian devised a play to counter this unusual defensive move. Trailing, 7–3, with nine minutes left in the game, Ara decided it was time to try his strategy. His idea was to send two backs and two ends out as receivers—to flood their three-deep secondary with his four men. The play worked to perfection. Theismann completed a forty-six-yard play to halfback Ed Gulyas on the Tech thirty-six-yard line. Six plays later, Dan Allan slugged the ball over for an Irish touchdown and a 10–7 victory.

"To have a successful season," said Parseghian, "a team must win the type of game we won over Georgia Tech. I was particularly proud of our club, the way we continued to come back. They drove eighty-two yards in the final quarter. That's the sign of a great team. This was the third time this year we've had to come from behind to win, and we've done it each time."

The following week Louisiana State, with one of their best teams, battled Notre Dame through three quarters with neither team able to develop a scoring punch. There were less than three minutes to play

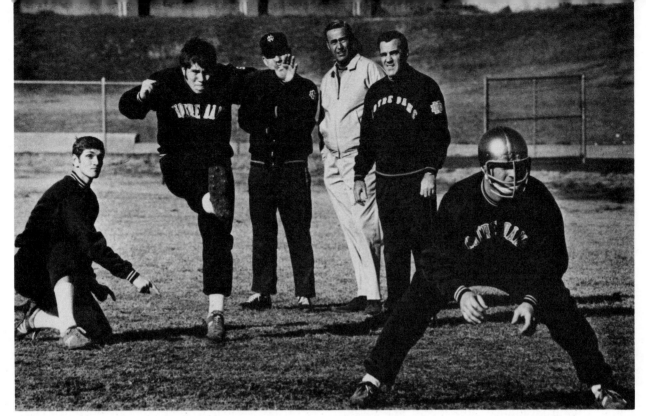

Just minutes before the LSU game in 1970, Scott Hempel takes several warm-up kicks under the watchful eyes of Coach Parseghian. Quarterback Joe Theismann (left) holds the ball for Scott. In the game, Hempel kicked a twenty-four-yard field goal to win the contest for Notre Dame, 3–0.

in the bitter struggle when Irish back Jim Yoder was forced to punt from the Notre Dame forty-five-yard line. Jim's effort was worthy of nomination to the Notre Dame Hall of Fame as he booted the ball fifty-four yards—an extraordinary kick as the ball went out of bounds on the *one-yard line*!

With their backs to the wall and time running out, the Fighting Tigers were in a desperate position. A wrong move and the Irish were in scoring position. Three running plays by State moved the ball to the seven-yard line, and then they kicked to Notre Dame. Irish safetyman Clarence Ellis returned the kick to the LSU thirty-six-yard line. And Theismann went to work. Joe passed twice to Gatewood, and now the ball was on the seven-yard line.

There was time for just one play.

Scott Hempel came into the game, looked around at the ground, picked up a couple of pebbles, smoothed the grass, then quickly kicked the ball over the crossbar for a twenty-four-yard field goal to give the Irish their hardest-fought victory of the season, 3–0. It was the ninth straight win for the Irish.

Notre Dame teams coached by Ara Parseghian were getting used to a lofty position in the annual football ratings. The Irish had been nationally ranked among the first ten teams of the nation ever since Parseghian had taken over as head coach in 1964. Now, on their way to battle against Southern California, the Irish,

ranked number four, felt secure and confident of victory. Thus far, however, John McKay's teams had cost Notre Dame one national title. Now they provided the means for earning another.

"Notre Dame is strong, where we're weak," said Coach McKay. "Right up the middle. Notre Dame isn't as good as everyone says . . . they're better."

"It shapes up as a very dreary afternoon for the Trojans," said sportswriter Jeff Prugh of the *Los Angeles Times*.

It was a dreary afternoon—but not for the Trojans.

The twenty-eighth of November dawned dull and overcast, and by game time the sky was as black as a pawnbroker's heart, and it began to rain and then pour.

But as the game began, it didn't seem to bother the Irish. They took the kickoff and in twelve plays drove eighty yards for the first score. Theismann connected with passes to Gatewood, and then Gulyas drove in for the tally.

However, the complexion of the game suddenly changed as quarterback Jim Jones guided the Trojans to three touchdowns for a 21–7 first-quarter lead. But midway through the second quarter Theismann connected on three consecutive passes for another Irish touchdown, and now the score was 21–14.

A Trojan field goal made it USC 24, Notre Dame 14 at the half.

Coach Parseghian and two of his All-Americans, Joe Theismann (left) and tackle Mike McCoy.

The rain continued to come down, making it almost impossible to pass the ball. In the second half Darryll Dewan fumbled on the Irish seventeen-yard line and USC scored. One minute later, Theismann was hit by three burly USC tacklers, fumbled the ball, and the Trojans recovered for another score. Now it was 38–14.

But Theismann was not through. Joe was now passing on nearly every play and completed most of them. There was a forty-six-yard toss to Larry Parker for an Irish score. Then Joe scrambled twenty-two yards for another touchdown, and Notre Dame was within range at 38–28.

However, that was all the scoring for the day, and once again the Trojans prevailed. And once again Parseghian was devastated by a loss to Southern California.

The loss cost Notre Dame the national championship.

In the Cotton Bowl game against the favored Texas Longhorns, Texas scored in the first few minutes of the game when quarterback Ed Phillips broke through the Irish line and dashed sixty-three yards but could not move any farther. So they promptly kicked a field goal and led the Irish, 3–0.

That, however, was just about the entire offense Texas was able to generate for the rest of the game. They fumbled the ball nine times, and the Irish recovered five of them.

Just after Texas scored the field goal, Theismann threw a twenty-six-yard pass to Gatewood, who dashed in for the score. However, he injured his leg and was out of the game. Notre Dame then recovered a Texas fumble on the thirteen-yard line, and Theismann scored once more. In the second period Theismann again ran the ball in, this time from the fifteen-yard line, for another Irish touchdown.

Jim Bulger, a substitute quarterback, threw a long pass to Clarence Ellis good for thirty-seven yards. Then Scott Hempel kicked a thirty-six-yard field goal to make the score 24–11 with twenty-four seconds to play in the half.

The second half was a defensive battle as Theismann, who had injured his hand in the third period, played cautiously. Gatewood was out, and Notre Dame played a controlled defensive game. The thirty-game winning streak the Longhorns had compiled during a three-year period was halted by a smart, aggressive Notre Dame squad that simply outplayed the tough Texans all the way for a decisive 24–11 victory.

Notre Dame's record for 1970 was 10–1–0 and only Nebraska had a slight edge over the Irish. At least that's what the Associated Press experts said, and they voted Nebraska the number-one team and national champions. Notre Dame was voted number two in the national ratings.

Joe Theismann, Tom Gatewood, Clarence Ellis, and Larry DiNardo were named to the All-America team, and Coach Parseghian and his colleagues settled down for a few weeks' rest before charging into another season.

SOME NEW CHALLENGES

"The face of all college campuses was changing in the late 1960s and early '70s," said Tom Pagna. "The world and its values were being rearranged. The war in Vietnam led to campus demonstrations, draft evasion, peace marches, women's liberation, marijuana; these were the topics affecting all our lives, and college football was not quite that important."

Student involvement in the football program had

become a problem. Snake dances, pep meetings, and torch rallies were now played down, and the players for the first time began to resent the tough training restrictions imposed on the team and the individual players.

"Our staff meetings in the early '70s were more like courses and discussions in social work as we had to deal more with problems of discipline, conditioning, and attitude," said Pagna. "We had to walk a very tight line to handle such problems with the Vietnam war raging and some of our players being called up to serve in the armed forces.

"And with all that," he continued, "we had to turn out a competitive team in 1971, one that would carry on the spirit and tradition of Notre Dame football. It was no easy task."

Let's look at the returning stars: sixteen of twenty-two starters returned from last season's Cotton Bowl winners, including Tom Gatewood, 210 pounds of the finest wide receiver in the nation, who caught seventy-nine passes for 1,166 yards in 1970; Ed Gulyas, who ran for 558 yards in 1970; Walt Patulski, now six feet, six inches and 260 pounds, left end on a defensive line that averaged 260 pounds; Clarence Ellis, an All-America deep back, who started out by feeling he did not belong on a Notre Dame first team. Ellis now was better than ever and a bit more confident.

"The Cotton Bowl, that was a start," Patulski said. "People are saying things like, 'Joe Theismann, somehow, someway, managed to win all those games for us.' This year we don't have Joe. But we'll do it without him."

"Toughest decision that we had to make all season long," said Pagna, "was the problem of our quarterback. We did not have an experienced 'take-charge guy,' as we had usually had in previous years. We had four diverse, inexperienced candidates.

"First there was Jim Bulger, tall, rawboned, almost Namath-like, with a great arm but only limited experience. But when he threw the ball," said Pagna, "you needed a surgeon to remove the ball from the receiver's chest. Then there was Pat Steenberge, who played about forty minutes last year as Theismann's backup. His throwing was just adequate, but his background of working with Theismann makes him stand out. Bill Etter, the Notre Dame heavyweight boxing champion, was just fair, and then there was Cliff Brown—no experience but a great arm.

"We opened the season with Steenberge," said Pagna, "but the other fellows all got a chance to play, and they all performed well. Of course, it was no contest. We beat Northwestern by 50–7."

Purdue was the next Irish opponent. The teams slipped and struggled in the rain on a bitter-cold day. Purdue contained the Notre Dame attack all afternoon and led the Irish 7–0 with three minutes left to play. But somehow, as Purdue tried a third-down punt, the kick was blocked and Fred Snowden fell on the ball behind the goal line, and the score was 7–6 in favor of Purdue.

Parseghian decided to attempt a two-point conversion.

Steenberge was supposed to roll out to his right for a run, but at the last moment he would fake a pitch, then wheel to his right and throw a pass to Mike Creaney at left end. The play worked like a dream, and Creaney hugged the ball to his bosom as he fell across the goal line for the two points—and Notre Dame had snatched an 8–7 victory right out of Purdue's hands.

Bill Etter started against Michigan State in place of Pat Steenberge, who had injured his leg in the Purdue game, and played an outstanding game. He completed ten of sixteen passes, and that was more than enough to beat the Spartans by a 14–2 score.

Etter suffered an agonizing knee injury near the end of the State game that ended his career, and then it was up to Cliff Brown to run the team against the Miami Hurricanes. Cliff had an outstanding arm and was a fine athlete. He became the first black quarterback at Notre Dame, and he did a marvelous job as he guided the team to victories against a raging Miami Hurricane squad, 17–0, and then went on to lead the Irish to a win over a rugged North Carolina team, 16–0.

At this moment, Cliff Brown was in the throes of the most beautiful and most harrowing period in his young life. Cliff was the "big man" on the team. The first black Notre Dame quarterback. He wasn't used to dealing with the press. They thought him abrasive. And ofttimes, as he came off the field after a series of plays, some fans booed him—not because he played poorly, but because he was the *black* Notre Dame quarterback, and there were those who did not like this situation at all.

Ara was touchy about the situation as it related to his quarterback, and it bothered him all year long.

Then the Trojans stormed into South Bend on October 23 and completely outplayed the Irish. Ed Garrison, USC's 180-pound end, caught five passes, scored two touchdowns, and set up a third score as he outmaneuvered the Notre Dame defense all afternoon and USC romped off with the "upset of the season," a stunning 28–14 victory. The loss to USC was the first of the season for Notre Dame after five straight victories.

The next three weeks saw the Irish in a complete reversal of form. There were successive wins: First, Navy was defeated, 21–0. Pitt was demoralized by a shattering 56–7. And then Tulane was beaten, 21–7. The three wins gave Notre Dame an 8–1–0 season and an invitation to play a postseason game in the Gator Bowl in Florida.

Coach Parseghian called a special team meeting to discuss whether the players wished to accept the Gator Bowl bid. During the meeting, Ara described the arrangements for the trip and then asked the players to vote on whether they wanted to play. After Ara and the other coaches left the meeting, the players became involved in a heated discussion about the arrangements for the game, and a bitter controversy broke out among those who wanted the game and those opposed. Finally the players voted not to play in the game. The dissension caused by heated arguments that broke out led to much bitterness, and the resulting disharmony led to a poorly played finale, against LSU.

The poor spirit of the players and several key injuries suffered in the Tulane game resulted in a 28–8 defeat by the Fighting Tigers, led by their great star Bert Jones. As a result of the loss, Notre Dame wound up the year with an 8–2–0 record.

"The events of the year affected Parseghian deeply," said Tom Pagna. "There were a number of personal problems that Ara did not discuss with us, and added to that was the reaction of some of the players who resented the tough regime and discipline all season long, and they made themselves heard. The atmosphere at home and on the field contributed to the most important decision Ara would make in 1974. It was a decision that would change all our lives, forever."

"Tom Clements was an outstanding performer from his earliest freshman days," said Tom Pagna. "He had a great arm, was a fine runner, when he had to move out of the pocket. He was a leader, like Theismann, yet had a quiet confidence about him, unlike Theismann. Clements truly had ice water in his veins, never lost his composure, and was anything but showy. He took criticism well, but if it didn't

make sense he would ask for an explanation. Tom may have been quiet, but because of the respect his teammates had for him, he was an outstanding leader and fine quarterback for us."

The 1972 season started with outstanding victories. First, Northwestern was beaten 37–0. Purdue was shellacked by a 35–14 score. Michigan State was shut out, 16–0. And Pitt was trampled, 42–16. With four victories in a row over good, solid teams, it looked as if the Irish were on their way to another national title.

And then there was Missouri.

The Missouri Tigers, now coached by Al Onofrio, had lost two games, including a humiliating 62–0 loss to Nebraska on October 14, just one week prior to the Notre Dame game.

Ara pleaded with his team not to take Missouri lightly. He knew that the Tigers had a solid quarterback in John Cherry who could pass and run. He also knew that a major college team smarting from a beating like they had absorbed from Nebraska would be out to prove their worth in the next game. And the next game was with Notre Dame at South Bend.

The Tigers, out for Irish scalps, played their hearts out and took a 24–14 lead, increasing it to 30–14 with ten minutes left to play in the game. The Tigers got a big assist from an official as Cherry handed the ball to his fullback on the Notre Dame one-yard line. He bobbled the ball but continued into the end zone without the ball. Notre Dame players had fallen on the ball on the one-yard line. But an official did not see the fumble and it was ruled a Missouri score.

Notre Dame protested vigorously but to no avail, and the touchdown prevailed.

Notre Dame, now fighting mad, put together a tremendous drive in the final ten minutes as Tom Clements was all over the field, throwing passes and taking the ball himself on several plays as the Irish scored two touchdowns to bring the score to 30–26, but time ran out for the Irish and Missouri took the game in what was called the biggest upset of the season.

The Irish players were downcast and dispirited after the loss to Missouri, but Ara rallied the team, and the players responded with outstanding performances against the next three opponents. Texas Christian was beaten, 21–0; Navy was trounced, 42–23; Air Force was bombed by Clements and company and defeated, 21–7; and Miami was beaten in Orange Bowl Stadium, 20–17.

Then the final and dramatic, regular-season game, against USC.

Coach John McKay had assembled some of the most athletically talented players ever on one football team: Ed Garrison, a world-class sprinter; Mike Rae, a baseball and football star; Lynn Swann, good enough to have beaten a fellow player in the long jump at an Olympics tryout; and Tony Davis, one of the fastest, shiftiest backs in college football. In the opening moment of the game, Davis took the kickoff and slipped, dodged, and twisted his way in the clear and was away for a ninety-seven-yard touchdown run. But the Irish, led by Tom Clements, came roaring back to the USC thirty-five-yard line, and then Bob Thomas kicked a forty-five-yard field goal and the score was 6–3.

Rae passed to USC's great end Swann, who dove for the ball and missed. An official ruled that there was interference by Notre Dame on the play, and the ball was USC's on the Irish one-yard line. On the first play Tony Davis took a hand-off from his quarterback, Mike Rae, and rammed his way across the Irish goal line. Rae's kick for the extra point was good, and the Trojans had a 13–3 lead.

With twenty-five seconds still left in the first quarter, halfback Eric Penick fumbled a hand-off and Dale Mitchell recovered for USC on the Irish nine-yard line. On the next play Davis slanted off-tackle and rammed in for his third touchdown, and now it was 19–3 USC.

The score remained 19–3 during most of the second quarter, but just before the half ended, Tom Clements called time and raced to the sidelines to talk things over with Parseghian. He came back into a huddle with his teammates, then whispered a terse few words: "Number sixty-two on one—let's do it."

Suddenly the team seemed to come to life as Clements picked up the tempo. He called the signal "sixty-two . . . hip." The ball was snapped to him on the "hip," and he quickly faded back and passed to Mike Creaney, and the big, six-foot, four-inch tight end snared the ball on his fingertips and raced to the USC thirty-five-yard line before he was brought down. Another pass, to Gary Diminick, was good for ten yards; then another bullet toss, to Willie Townsend, and the speedy Irish star raced in for a touchdown. The kick for the extra point made it 19–10 with USC still out in front of the Irish.

Notre Dame's defense held USC and the Irish took over the ball and Clements again went to work. He passed to Creaney once more for thirty-five yards and then another to Diminick, and the speedy halfback raced in from the USC twenty-five-yard line for another Irish score. The kick for the extra point was good, and now it was a nail-biting thriller, with the Trojans leading Notre Dame, 19–17.

Notre Dame kicked off and Tony Davis received for USC and sped seventy-five yards for his fourth touchdown of the day. Now the Trojans were out in front by a 25–17 score.

Once again Clements went to work. Calmly he took charge and directed his troops upfield. Art Best, a workhorse all afternoon, drove through USC for ten yards. Then the six-two Best picked up four yards and then five more as he slugged his way for extra yards. Then Clements faded back and tossed a long, arching pass to Creaney for thirty-five yards and an Irish touchdown, and now the zigzag battle became a scorcher with USC holding a 25–23 lead.

But USC, with Davis playing his greatest game, scored a fifth touchdown, and as the Irish defense wilted, the Trojans picked up two more scores and were victorious, 45–23.

In the Notre Dame dressing room a disconsolate Parseghian sat alone, silent and brooding.

"Cheer up, coach," said sportswriter Terry Shore. "There's still the Orange Bowl, and there's always next year. This is only one game."

"That's not it," said Ara. "Don't you realize that I've got to look at Anthony Davis for two more years?"

Any thought of the 1973 season had to be delayed because of the impending battle with Nebraska in the Orange Bowl.

Coach Bob Devaney of Nebraska had announced that this would be his last season with the Cornhuskers, and they were prepped for the game against their rivals from South Bend. They wanted this game for their coach and their great running back Johnny Rodgers, the new Heisman Award winner. Rodgers also was in his final game for the Cornhuskers. Nebraska had last defeated Notre Dame in 1922, and although the teams had met thirteen times, the Irish had won eight, including two games in a row in 1947 and 1948. And now Nebraska was out for revenge.

It was the Johnny Rodgers show in the Orange Bowl. All John did was score three touchdowns and pass for a fourth as the Cornhuskers simply ran through, around, and over the Irish squad for a shattering 40–6 defeat. And Notre Dame finished with an 8–3–0 season.

A CHAMPIONSHIP SEASON

By the time 1973 rolled around, Ara Parseghian had become one of the nation's most recognizable personalities. In constant demand as a speaker at banquets, clinics, and sports functions, Ara found it impossible to walk into any airport without being recognized.

There was one occasion that was unique.

Ara flew to New York for a speech during a cab strike. He was in a terrible hurry, and fortunately a friendly Irish fan noticed the ND insignia on his briefcase and decided to help. He grabbed Ara, led him out to a cabbie, and in a few moments got a driver to stop.

"I've got Notre Dame's coach here, and he's trying to get downtown in a hurry," the fan explained to the cabbie.

The driver consented and the fan hopped into the cab with Ara and the driver sped away. During the course of the ride the fan, proud of his accomplishment and now regarding himself as a lifelong friend of Ara's, leaned over and tapped the cabbie on the arm.

"See, buddy, now you can tell your family tonight that you drove Joe Kuharich around New York."

There was a new look and a new spirit on the Notre Dame campus. Female students had been admitted for the first time to this all-male school, and they brought with them a bright, fresh spirit and outlook to Notre Dame and to football. The exciting pep rallies, the marching band, and new lovely, acrobatic women cheerleaders added a new dimension to the games, and the stirring "fight songs" were once more a vital part of the games.

"For the longtime Fighting Irish fans it was a throwback to the 'good old days' when football was a way of life and Notre Dame teams were number one," said Tom Pagna.

"In 1973 our team typified this new desire . . . this new enthusiasm for football, and it was fun again to see the spirited young men fight their hearts out for a position on the squad," he continued. "And we broke precedent by naming tri-captains: There was an offensive captain, Frank Pomarico, a defensive captain, Mike Townsend; and a team captain, Dave Casper."

Early in the season, the closely knit family of Dr. Henry Clements of McKees Rocks, Pennsylvania, was struck by tragedy. Thirteen-year-old Alice Clements, his sister, was hit by an automobile. She died of injuries just before Tom was to take the field in the opening game of the season, against Northwestern. Tom was not informed of the tragedy until well after the game was over.

The Wildcats had to bear the brunt of one of the speediest Notre Dame backfields, with Eric Penick, Art Best, Wayne Bullock, and Clements. Penick and Best were timed at under ten seconds for the hundred-yard-dash, and the way they ran around and through the Wildcats brought sheer joy to Parseghian and his coaches. Clements was like a Prussian field marshal as he ran the team with verve and style, and his passes were "right on the money" as Notre Dame punished the Wildcats to the tune of 44–0.

"After the game Clements was told of his sister's tragedy, and George Kelley and I represented the coaching staff at the funeral," said Pagna. "It was a very sad occasion for all of us."

The following week Art Best scored on a sixty-five-yard dash early in the game against Purdue as the Boilermakers took a 20–7 drubbing on their home field.

Michigan State, always a tough opponent, intercepted a Clements pass in the fourth quarter and drove in from the fifteen-yard line to bring the score to 14–10, but the defense, led by Tri-captain Mike Townsend at tackle and his sidekicks Gerry DiNardo, Dave Casper, Steve Sylvester, Steve Neece, and Pete Demmerle, held the Spartans in check with some magnificent line play, and the game ended with the Irish maintaining their precious four-point lead, 14–10.

Rice's coach, Al Conover, had prepared an unusual bit of strategy for their game against Notre Dame: He invited eighty priests to be on the sidelines as his guests, hoping their prayers would bring victory for the Rice squad. They didn't help as Notre Dame, with Tom Clements at his very best, lead the Irish to their fourth win of the season, 28–0.

The following week Army broke out quickly and kicked a field goal to lead Notre Dame, 3–0, but suddenly the Irish came alive and raced to nine touchdowns and a 62–3 triumph. Ara did all he could to hold the score down, but at one point freshman Tim Simon took an Army punt and raced downfield for seventy-two yards and a touchdown. Ara was upset, but how could you scold a freshman for doing exactly what he was trained to do? It was impossible to stop the Irish machine that day.

USC roared into South Bend the next week for the annual battle against the Irish. They had soundly defeated Notre Dame in the past four games, and the Irish were ready and primed for the Trojans. This year the campus was once again aroused over a football game, and there were pep meetings and parades, with the band playing the "Victory March." Some enterprising students reproduced pictures of great Trojan halfback Tony Davis doing his end-zone touchdown dance. Those photos were in every room, every dorm, so that it was impossible to escape a Davis photo on the campus.

Southern California blazed into South Bend riding the crest of a twenty-three-game streak without defeat, and Davis and company intended to bring home a Notre Dame scalp and number twenty-four.

"We were ready for USC," said Tom Pagna. "There was no team that I've ever been with that was more prepped up for a game than this team. There was no way that Southern California could beat us."

The first time USC got the ball, quarterback Pat Haden threw a screen pass to Lynn Swann. But Luther Bradley, Irish linebacker, big and strong at six feet, three inches and 225 pounds, hit Swann with a tackle that could be heard all over the stadium. Swann fumbled the ball, and Notre Dame recovered and scored a touchdown. At the end of the first half it was 13–7 Notre Dame.

The biggest play of the game came shortly after the start of the second half. Penick took a handoff, dashed around left end, broke into the clear, and sped eighty-five yards for a touchdown. It was the kind of play that required perfect blocking from the Irish: Frank Pomarico, Gerry DiNardo, Casper, and every other man cut down the opposition on an "almost perfect play" as Notre Dame jumped into a 23–14 lead, which they maintained to the end of the game.

Tony Davis was held to a total gain of only fifty-yards, and he did not get one pass reception.

Navy was easily beaten, 44–7, and then Pitt, with an outstanding back in Tony Dorsett and some outstanding new players recruited by their new coach, John Majors, was primed to defeat the Irish. But they were easy victims to a great passing and running game and the Irish easily defeated the Panthers, 31–10.

Air Force flew into South Bend the next week for a major game seen on national television, but despite the use of most of the substitutes, Notre Dame trounced the Falcons, 48–15.

That left just one game to be played during the regular season—against the Miami Hurricanes in Miami.

A victory over Miami would give Notre Dame a perfect 10–0–0 record for the season, one that no Notre Dame team had registered since Frank Leahy's 1949 squad won the national championship with a 10–0–0 record.

Miami was tough and wanted desperately to win. They had beaten Texas and nearly had defeated top-rated Oklahoma before dropping a 24–19 game to the Sooners. But this night Notre Dame simply was too fast and too smart and easily defeated the Hurricanes, 44–0. Clements, Penick, and Best were outstanding, and Tri-captains Frank Pomarico, Mike Townsend, and Dave Casper played like the outstanding players they were.

At the end of the regular season, undefeated Alabama was ranked number one, Oklahoma was ranked number two, and undefeated Notre Dame was ranked number three. The Sugar Bowl Committee invited Alabama and Notre Dame to meet in the Sugar Bowl for the national championship, and both schools consented.

On their own, Notre Dame players voted to stay on campus during the Christmas holidays and to practice for the big game.

A record-breaking crowd of more than eighty-five thousand spectators were treated to a pulsating struggle that lasted until the final moment of the game as Notre Dame won a thriller, 24–23.

The game opened with Notre Dame holding Alabama in a superb defensive effort that checked the Crimson Tide without a single yard gained in the first quarter. Then Tom Clements proceeded to fill the air with passes. He threw for nineteen yards to Casper, twenty-six more to Casper, and fourteen yards to Pete Demmerle. Then Wayne Bullock capped a sixty-four-yard drive by smashing in for a touchdown, and Notre Dame had a 6–0 lead.

Alabama came back in the second period to drive the length of the field for a score as Randy Billingsley dashed in from the six-yard line. Bill Davis put Alabama in the lead, 7–6, with the extra-point conversion.

On the kickoff, speedy Al Hunter caught the ball on his seven-yard line, tucked it to his chest, and

Irish quarterback Tom Clements tosses a few warm-up passes prior to the 1973 Sugar Bowl game between Alabama and Notre Dame.

sped downfield ninety-three yards, aided by perfect blocking, to score a touchdown. The Irish tried for a two-point pass play and were successful as Clements tossed to Demmerle. Notre Dame was in front, 14–10, as the half ended.

At the start of the second half, Alabama moved ninety-three yards and then Wilbur Jackson dove across the Irish goal line, the extra point was good, and the score was now Alabama 17, Notre Dame 14.

Irish linebacker Drew Mahalic recovered an Alabama fumble in midair and raced to the Alabama twelve-yard line. On the next play, Eric Penick raced

in. Bob Thomas's kick made the score 21–17 in favor of Notre Dame.

Alabama's Dick Todd handed off to Bob Stock, then raced to the sidelines and Stock lofted a return pass to Todd, who smashed in for an Alabama tally. 'Bama missed the kick and hung on to a slim two-point lead.

Notre Dame came back quickly and decisively as Clements directed the strategy to perfection. He passed to Hunter, then to Dave Casper, a thirty-yard toss that brought the ball to the Crimson Tide fifteen-yard line.

The crowd, now up and screaming, realized there were just four minutes left to play as Parseghian sent in Bob Thomas for a field-goal attempt.

There was almost complete silence as Thomas quickly picked up a couple of stones, smoothed the grass in front of the ball, then promptly stepped back, drove forward, and booted home the field goal that gave Notre Dame a 24–23 lead and the national championship in the most thrilling bowl game in collegiate football history.

In a scene as chaotic as anyone ever had seen in a college dressing room, a jubilant group of Irish players and coaches whooped it up after the game.

Ara spoke to his team: "They voted us two things," he said. "One is the Sugar Bowl Trophy," and the team cheered and cheered. "Two," he yelled, "is the MacArthur Bowl, symbolic of the national championship."

With that announcement, bedlam reigned for the next hour as the national champions doused their coaches with Pepsi instead of champagne.

The wonderful thing about the 1973 squad was that Notre Dame figured to be just as good in 1974. The returning players and the new and outstanding freshmen coming in made the Irish favorites to repeat as national champions.

TEN YEARS FOR ARA

Ara Parseghian had been the head coach at Notre Dame for ten years—ten of the most exciting, harrowing, frustrating, yet most brilliant years of a coaching career that saw him lift the previous mediocre record of the Irish and acquire two national championships. They were also strong contenders to the championship in three other seasons. Under Ara, Notre Dame teams had won eighty-five games while

losing fifteen, with four ties. Only the immortal Knute Rockne and Frank Leahy had stayed at Notre Dame for longer periods. Rockne coached at Notre Dame from 1918 to 1930. His teams won 105 games and lost twelve, with five ties. Leahy was head coach from 1941 to 1943 and from 1946 to 1953. His teams won eighty-seven times, lost eleven games, and tied nine.

But the ten years of constant battle had taken their toll on Ara and on the lives of the members of his family, for his life was no longer his own. He was constantly on the move, with appearances on television, radio, speaking engagements, clinics, benefit appearances for MS, and then the actual coaching, which kept him on an eighteen-hour-a-day schedule from early February until the end of the year.

"And by 1974," said Tom Pagna, "Ara was less dynamic, less energetic, and quite morose at times. And he no longer clowned around at staff meetings. It was all business."

In interviews he explained that doctors had been warning him to take things easier because of high blood pressure. It could get bad enough to kill him. He revealed that he was taking six pills daily: two for his high blood pressure, two tranquilizers, and two sleeping pills.

As practice began for the 1974 season, something happened to Ara and his Irish legions on their hoped-for way to their second consecutive national title. Ara and his coaches began to question each other about their luck.

"Whatever happened to the 'luck of the Irish'?" they cried. And for good reason.

Six varsity members of the team ran afoul of university regulations and were suspended for a full year. They included some of the team's top talent: Ross Browner, outstanding end; Luther Bradley, safety; and Al Hunter, halfback.

Browner and Bradley started as freshman in 1973 and were called "super" players by their coach. Additionally, Willie Fry, another suspended player, had been a first-rate substitute end.

Four other varsity players were injured early: Eric Penick, an outstanding running back, fractured an ankle and was out for two months. Steve Quehl, an outstanding tight-end candidate, was in an automobile accident and was lost for the year. Tim Simon, slated to be the top punt returner, had an eye nearly poked out in a strange backyard accident. And Bob Zanot, another back, suffered a serious knee injury in the first practice session of the fall.

That brought the total loss of personnel before the first game to ten players, all of them of varsity caliber. Nine of the other players were vital performers.

On the surface Notre Dame still appeared to have an outstanding team as the season began at night with Georgia Tech, a team that had battled the Irish on every occasion. This time Notre Dame easily won out by a convincing 31–7 score.

Perhaps things were not as bad as they seemed?

Then, just prior to the Northwestern game, Ed Smothers, a dear friend of Ara's and an honorary coach, died suddenly of a heart attack. Smothers and his wife had acted as "surrogate parents" for the Notre Dame black players and helped Ara make the few blacks comfortable at Notre Dame.

Northwestern was easily defeated by a 49–3 score. But the Irish played as if they were mechanical men. There was no spark, no dash to their game, and Ara screamed and yelled at the players during the halftime intermission. The second half saw better execution and better team spirit.

Next, Purdue came into South Bend, and this day they suited up a rather mediocre team, by Purdue standards. But they were spirited and full of fight and piled up a 24–0 lead before Notre Dame woke up. The Irish never could get their offense untracked and lost to an inferior Purdue team by 31–20.

"Since mistakes cost us the Purdue game," said Assistant Coach Tom Pagna, "Ara planned a conservative game against Michigan State, and that strategy got us a hard-fought 19–14 win.

"We got by Rice, 10–3, playing spiritless ball.

"Our attack consisted of Tom Clements passing to end Pete Demmerle and then Wayne Bullock running hell out of the ball," said Pagna, "but that was enough to win."

In two consecutive games at South Bend, Army was trounced, 48–0, as the Irish, for the first time that year, played up to their championship form. Then the following week Miami was easily beaten, 38–7. The Irish traveled to Philadelphia for a battle against a strong Navy eleven on November 2. Under the direction of former Navy halfback George Welsh, the Middies were strong, tough, and fast.

"Offensively against Navy," said Pagna, "we moved the ball all over the field, but the Navy punter, John Stufflebem, kept us bottled up in our own territory with marvelous kicks of forty-eight and fifty-five yards, regularly."

With just ten minutes left in the game, Tom Clements tossed a short pass to Demmerle, who smashed across from the six-yard line. The kick was good, and Notre Dame had a 7–6 edge over Navy.

Randy Harrison then snatched a desperate Navy pass in the final minute and scrambled forty-five yards for another score as the Irish took a 14–6, tremendously hard-fought battle.

In the dressing room after the game, a weary, haggard Parseghian told the press, "It's a win, that's all that counts."

But the pressure of the Navy game and the many other problems that season encouraged Ara to evaluate his personal situation. When he returned to South Bend after the game, he called a family council of war. With his wife, Katie, and his brother Mike at his side, he talked about his situation and feelings all through the night. When the family meeting adjourned for some sleep, Ara had made up his mind. He would resign from his job as head coach after the season.

His decision firmly made, Ara kept it a secret. Not even his coaches knew about the decision to leave his job.

Trailing 10–7 in another nail-biting game against Pitt, Ara told his team at halftime, "You are causing my hair to turn gray. I told them they were going to make me a replacement for TV's Kojack."

With eight minutes to play in the game, Notre Dame took over the ball on their own forty-five-yard line. In twelve plays Clements either passed—for a fifteen-yard gain—or moved the team on the ground some forty yards. Then on a fake hand-off, Tom ran in for the touchdown that gave the Irish the game, 14–10.

"This is not the first time Notre Dame had fallen behind this year," said Ara, "but we scored in the fourth quarter to win. I am very proud of the team and the way they came back to beat a really good football team."

In the game against Air Force, which was the last home game of the season for the Irish, the varsity ran up a 24–0 lead and then Ara sent in the reserves, who scored two more touchdowns to give the Irish a 38–0 win. Tom Parise, filling in for the injured Wayne Bullock, was outstanding as he carried the ball ten times for 108 yards.

In the final game of the regular season, against Southern California on November 30 in the Los Angeles Coliseum, it was obvious that Notre Dame and Southern California had chosen well. This forty-eight-year-old rivalry between the two schools had clearly established the Irish as the dominant partner. But since John McKay's first year in 1960, things had

evened out a bit. That year the series stood, Notre Dame twenty-one wins, USC nine, and two ties. In the next thirteen years USC won six, Notre Dame had won five, and there were two ties.

And on this day in November they could hardly have been better matched. The Trojans were favored by four points, but the Irish were rated number one defensively.

The game began in a too-familiar pattern as the Irish caught USC off-guard with some run-action passes and pulled out in front as Tom Clements completed nine of twelve passes and Notre Dame scored twenty-four points to take a 24–6 lead at halftime.

It looked like an easy win for the irish.

But then came seventeen minutes of hell for Notre Dame, for in those seventeen minutes the eighty-four thousand spectators at the game and millions who were watching on television saw the most incredible turnaround in collegiate football. In those seventeen minutes, the Trojans scored forty-nine points, almost at will.

Tony Davis, USC's great star, opened the second half and electrified the crowd with an unbelievable 102-yard touchdown sprint through the entire Irish squad. Several plays later, Davis again scored. Then it was quarterback Pat Haden and then Haden twice more on quick, short passes. Then Haden again passing to Ed Phillips for a score, and then Phillips scored on an interception, and it was USC 55, Notre Dame 24.

After the game, Irish linebacker Greg Collins sat in the locker room staring at the tips of his shoes. Suddenly he looked up and asked, "Say, what was the final score, anyway?"

Parseghian had little to say.

On Saturday, December 14, Ara, his wife, Katie, and Father Joyce attended a party in Elkhart, Indiana, when suddenly a newscast reported the story that Parseghian had resigned.

Twenty-four hours later Dan Devine, former head coach of the Green Bay Packers, was publicly named to succeed Parseghian.

CHAPTER 9

DAN DEVINE:
AND ONE FOR THE ROAD

Ara Parseghian hadn't left the field at the Orange Bowl after Notre Dame had defeated Alabama, 13–11, on January 1, 1975, and already two youths were running through the end zone trying to catch the TV camera's eye, holding up a banner that read:

"Ara was Fine, but Dan's Devine."

The king is dead, they were saying, long live the king.

It seemed a shame that Parseghian, retiring after eleven years as Notre Dame's head football coach, wasn't even allowed to make his final bow and get off the stage before the first fanfare was being played for his successor.

But Parseghian's players were not going to let him go that lightly.

"Don't kid yourself," said senior tackle Steve Sylvester. "This was Parseghian's night. One sign doesn't change that."

"There are a lot of seniors on the team," said guard Gerry DiNardo. "In a certain perspective, all of us are seniors, because it's the last time any of us will be playing for Parseghian."

In his final game as a college coach, Parseghian wrote a brilliant last chapter to his Notre Dame career, taking over a team that had been humiliated in the last game of the regular season by Southern California and directing the Irish to a victory over ten-point-favorite Alabama, the only 1974 undefeated team in a major bowl game.

Notre Dame held the Crimson Tide to sixty-two yards net rushing, scoring both of its touchdowns following Alabama mistakes—a fumble on an attempted punt return, and an offside that produced a first down on a field-goal attempt. There were a number of strange plays when the ball wobbled like some unseen force had steered it off its course.

Was Ara getting aid from the Notre Dame legends?

"If I thought I was getting that kind of help," he said, grinning, "I wouldn't have worried like I did."

Ara said he didn't make any extended pregame speeches about his departure. "I didn't want to over-burden them."

In the last few minutes before Notre Dame came onto the field, Parseghian talked mostly about the regular-season-ending defeat at Southern California. He told the players not to play the game for him but for themselves—and for the tradition of Notre Dame. Afterward there were tears, some of them Parseghian's.

Fullback Wayne Bullock scored Notre Dame's first touchdown on a four-yard smash through the 'Bama line. Dan Reeve added the extra point.

Notre Dame drove sixty-eight yards for its second score, with Mark McLane going over after taking a shovel pass from Tom Clements.

Alabama made it 13–3 at halftime as Dan Ridgeway kicked a twenty-one yard field goal. The Crimson Tide did not score again until 3:13 remained in the game, when Richard Todd threw a fourteen-yard pass to Russ Schamun, who dashed forty-eight yards for the touchdown.

"If I had been able to take a few months off after the Orange Bowl," said Ara, "I might have gone back to Notre Dame. But it doesn't work that way. I needed a few months off. But that won't fit in with the recruiting. A prospect wants to see the head coach's office."

It was a festive group of men in the locker room after the game. Ara entered with tears of joy in his eyes. He gathered his players and coaches around him and spoke:

"I've never had a victory in my career with a group of guys so dedicated," he said. "You showed all those who were down in the mouth about us. Father

Toohey," he shouted, "come on over and say the prayer! We've got a lot to be thankful for!"

So ended his 243rd game and twenty-fourth season as a head coach, eleven at Notre Dame. And at fifty years of age, young in years but tired, worn out, and just a little gray, he was leaving one of the great coaching careers in football.

Ara slowly showered, dressed even more hesitantly, and shook hands once more with all around him. On his way out of the Orange Bowl locker room, he stood for a moment to look at the players' lockers, now deserted. Slowly he turned from the scene, wiped a tear from his eye, and headed for the team bus that would carry him away from the scene of his memories.

OUT OF THE FRYING PAN

Since 1894, when Notre Dame hired its first head football coach, twenty-three men have held that title. Only a handful of names come to mind: Harper, Rockne, Layden, Leahy, and Parseghian. Others are remembered but in a much less heroic light: Devore, Brennan, Kuharich. Most of the pre-Harper-Rockne-era coaches have been forgotten altogether . . . try to name one. Even the coach with the best winning percentage in the history of the university, John L. Marks, with an incredible 13–0–2 record in 1911 and 1912 for a 1.000 average, has faded into obscurity.

Of the successful coaches since Harper, only two managed to leave with their health and spirit intact. Elmer Layden was one, Ara Parseghian the other. Anyone who has ever met Ara would bet on that, for along with television appearances and writing assignments, Ara spends his time operating a successful insurance agency in South Bend.

Coach Parseghian's reign was not an easy one to follow. In eleven seasons he won ninety-five, lost seventeen, and tied four for an .848 average. Only Knute Rockne and Leahy posted better percentages in the modern history of Irish football. But it was Parseghian's intimidating record that Coach Devine confronted when he arrived in South Bend.

Coach Devine came to the Golden Dome from the Green Bay Packers where, in his second season, in 1972, he led the Pack to a 10–4–0 record and the National Football Conference Central Division championship, Green Bay's first divisional title in five years. However, his total four-year stint with the Packers was somewhat less than dazzling, 25–28–4, and the situation at Green Bay had become ugly. There were even vague threats to Devine and his family after the Packers lost more games than they won, and so Dan was delighted to come to South Bend.

"Out of the frying pan into the fire," said an oracle.

During three years at Arizona State University, Devine posted a 27–3–1 record. In his last season, 1957, Dan guided ASU to their first unbeaten season, and for the first time in their history, the Sun Devils were nationally ranked.

Devine's 10–0–0 record that year attracted the attention of the University of Missouri, and in 1958, as head coach at Missouri, Devine posted a rather shaky 5–4–1 season.

The 1959 season was a slightly better one as Dan chalked up a 6–5–0 record and Missouri won a bid to the Orange Bowl, where the Tigers were defeated by the highly ranked Georgia Bulldogs, 14–0. Devine led the Tigers to an undefeated season in 1960 and fifth place in the national ratings; it was the first national ranking for a Missouri team in the long history of the varsity football program there.

Until its 1961 Tigers defeated Navy in the 1961 Orange Bowl, Missouri had never won a bowl game. Under Devine, Missouri won in the Bluebonnet Bowl in 1962; the Sugar Bowl in 1966; and in 1969, in the Gator Bowl, the Tigers defeated a powerhouse Alabama team, 35–10.

A "black Irishman" of medium size, Dan Devine has the face of a choirboy and a voice to match: Strangers are always astonished to learn that in 1975 he was forty-six years old and the father of seven. His manner is pleasant but not effervescent, and in casual conversation he has a disarming undercurrent of humor. His friends tell you that he is not a fiery type but still is nobody's patsy; not a high-pressure recruiter, but an effective one; not an original thinker, but a coach whose diversified tactics keep opponents guessing.

At a breezy press conference at South Bend, Devine discussed his problems at Green Bay and then went on to talk about his approach to the Notre Dame post.

"I'm delighted to be here at Notre Dame," he said,

"and basically I'm going to give Notre Dame fans the same kind of aggressive football they had under Ara Parseghian.

"I've been using the same type of offense that Ara has. I always run the quarterback and use the sprint-out pass. Our offensive philosophies are somewhat similar. I'm not a drop-back-passer type of coach.

"We're going to be a very young, inexperienced team," said Devine, "but eventually we'll put it all together."

Devine's record at Arizona State and Missouri gave him the third-highest winning percentage among college coaches at the time. All four of his Missouri teams finished among the top twenty, and his 1960 eleven were undefeated in eleven games.

But despite his outstanding record, Dan Devine began his tenure in the eye of a storm. The 1975 Irish were torn with more division than any college team Devine had ever coached.

A number of players recruited by Ara Parseghian were bitterly disappointed when he resigned. They threatened to transfer to other schools. They resented Devine and found it difficult to adjust to his quiet, moody ways after the enthusiastic, preppy dash of an Ara Parseghian.

Ed Bauer, a co-captain in 1975, recalled the resentment that year, especially among the seniors. "I had a lot of respect for Coach Devine, but let's face it, he took a completely different approach to the game, and any number of players, particularly the seniors, plainly resented him.

But Devine rode out the storm and began the fall practice with some superb good luck. Five varsity players suspended in 1974 for various violations of the dorm regulations had been reinstated and were eligible to play in 1975. They included: Ross Browner, the 6-foot, 3½-inch, 220-pound All-Star end; Willie Fry, another All-Star end; Luther Bradley, a slashing defensive back who was 6 feet, 2 inches and weighed 210 pounds, and two fast-stepping halfbacks, Al Hunter and Don Knott.

However, early-season drills failed to produce a leading quarterback candidate to replace Tom Clements, an All-America selectee. Rick Slager and Frank

Head coach Dan Devine leads his Irish eleven onto the field for the first practice of the 1980 season.

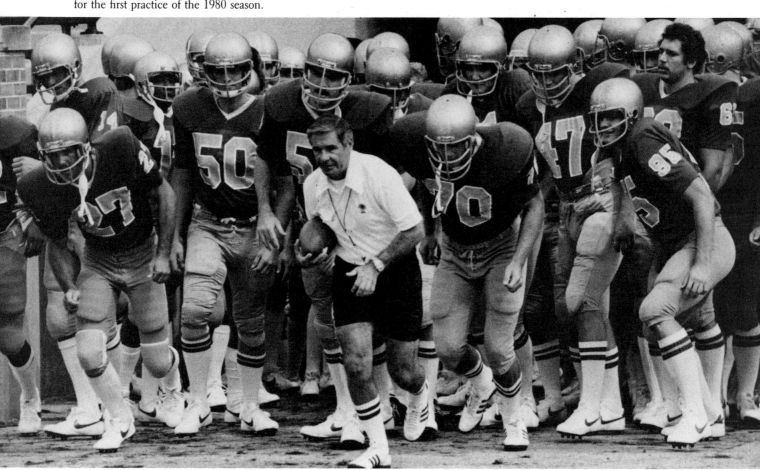

Allocco had been injured. That left freshmen candidates Joe Montana and Gary Forystek.

The Devine Era at Notre Dame dawned on a Monday night in September at Foxboro, Massachusetts, on a playground abandoned by the New England Patriots.

In its first football game under Dan Devine's guidance, Notre Dame ground down Boston College, 17–3, before more spectators than the Patriots ever saw at home, over sixty-one thousand frenetic fans. But it remained to be seen whether Devine was a Notre Dame coach in the lofty tradition of Rockne, Leahy, and Parseghian, or heir to the frayed mantle of Hunk Anderson, Elmer Layden, Hugh Devore, and Terry Brennan.

New England visits by Notre Dame are rare. This was, in fact, the first visit of a Notre Dame football team there, and no Boston College team had ever appeared on national television before this night.

Impartial football authorities such as Jimmy (the Greek) Snyder and Seymour Cohen predicted an easy Notre Dame victory. But when Boston College kicked off to start the game and held the Notre Dame offense to short gains on the first three series of downs, the screaming Eagles' crowd had visions of the biggest upset victory in BC football history as fullback Keith Barnette and halfback Glen Capriola quickly advanced the ball to the Irish thirty-five-yard line. But here Notre Dame's line held, and the Irish took over the ball on downs.

Notre Dame then started to move, and aided by a forty-five-yard dash by halfback Mark McLane, the Irish moved to the BC eighteen-yard-line; then Dan Reeve booted a twenty-five yard field goal for a 3–0 Irish lead.

There were but eleven seconds remaining in the second period when Fred Steinfort, the Eagles' talented kicker, booted a tremendous forty-five-yard field-goal effort, and the score was tied at 3–3 as the half ended.

Soon after the second half began, Notre Dame had fourth down and inches to go, and they went for the first down and got it on a quarterback sneak.

Then quarterback Rick Slager steadied his troops and the Irish came together and started to move upfield. Cool in the face of a determined pass rush, Rick threw completions for eighteen yards, then twelve, then twelve more, before turning the swift, slick Al Hunter loose for a touchdown.

Starting the final quarter, Slager mixed his passes and runs in a judicious blend that produced the final seven points. They looked like a fine Notre Dame team in the second half as the Irish simply piled up yardage and held an aggressive BC team scoreless to give Dan Devine his first win as Notre Dame's head coach, 17–3.

After the game, a worn-out Devine told a jampacked roomful of reporters, "Pressure? I never would have taken this job if I thought I was going to die in my very first game. . . . But I'll be honest: Boston College's fine play had me dying several times during this game."

In a strange quirk of scheduling, Notre Dame traveled to Purdue five days later and defeated the Boilermakers, 17–0. "This time I was really dead on my feet," said Devine. "Purdue is always rough."

Northwestern stormed into South Bend the next week, determined to avenge a series of humiliating defeats by the Irish during the past fourteen years; not since 1962 had the Wildcats taken the measure of the Irish, but this year they were cocksure they were going to win. They did score quickly in the first period. It was Northwestern's first touchdown against the Irish since 1971, but Notre Dame came back to tie the score at 7–7. During the Irish drive, quarterback Rick Slager was injured and the promising freshman sensation, Joe Montana, entered the game.

Willie Fry, a 6-foot, 3½-inch Irish end, smashed through and blocked a Wildcat punt. Four plays later, Jim Browner dashed in for Notre Dame's second score. Montana passed to Ted Burgmeier, who broke into the clear for fifty yards before he was downed. Then Montana passed to Mark McLane, who cracked the Wildcat line and scored from the fourteen-yard stripe. At halftime the score was 21–7 Notre Dame.

Joe Montana opened up in the second half with another touchdown pass, then Dan Reeve booted a forty-four-yard field goal as the Irish ran up a 31–7 margin, the final score. Freshman fullback Jerome Heavens gained 106 yards in fifteen carries and was most impressive throughout the game. On October 4 at South Bend, the Irish put on a strange performance for a team that had entered the game unbeaten and ranked eighth in the nation and even stranger when you consider that with four minutes left to play, the Irish looked like they would pull the game out. Notre Dame had just tied the score 3–3 on a thirty-five-yard field goal by Dan Reeve and then had the Spartans in trouble at the State twenty-nine-yard line.

Then in a split second, Tyrone Wilson, the Spartan fullback, shot through the Irish line, veered to his left, and raced seventy-six delirious yards without being touched, and it was Michigan State 10, Notre Dame 3 as the game ended.

"I feel as badly about losing this game as any in my entire life," said Devine. "This is one we had and then blew it."

The following week the Irish trailed North Carolina by fourteen points going into the last quarter, but magnificent passing by Montana gave the Irish a 14–14 tie with two minutes left in the game. Then Montana tossed another pass, this time to Ted Burgmeier, who burned up the turf as he sped some fifty yards, and Notre Dame had scored the go-ahead touchdown to win, 21–14. It was a heart-stopper for Devine and the Irish.

Air Force had lost five games and tied one before meeting the Irish, but you would never know it as they thoroughly outplayed Notre Dame and led the Irish 30–10 after three quarters. Then, as time was beginning to wind down, Notre Dame scored three touchdowns in five and a half minutes, aided by a sensational fifty-five yard dash by the equally sensational Jerome Heavens, and the score was 30–30 with Notre Dame set to try for the extra point. Dan Reeve did this job for the Irish, who had a heart-stopping, last-minute, 31–30 victory.

In the City of Angels, the script was much the same.

USC's coach, John McKay, was unhappy with the performance of his team after the Trojans had beaten Oregon 17–3 for their seventh win of the season. "This is the poorest passing team I've ever seen," said McKay.

It sounded very much like one of Knute Rockne's diversionary tactics, even though the Trojans were now ranked number three in the nation.

And all over the Notre Dame campus were familiar signs: "Revenge Over USC" . . . "Ring Ricky's bell" (for Ricky Bell, USC's superb back) . . . "Here Lies USC's Offense" . . . Thousands of students roamed the streets of South Bend chanting, "Never again! Never again!"

But on that chilly Saturday afternoon of October 25 at South Bend, Bell ran . . . and ran . . . and ran as USC won a hard-fought battle, 24–17, after Notre Dame had taken a 14–7 halftime lead. And it was Ricky Bell who picked up 165 yards and led the Trojans to victory.

Dan Devine regrouped his weary Irish battlers for the next two contests, against Navy and Georgia Tech, and Notre Dame won both games. Navy was beaten, 31–10, and Georgia Tech absorbed a 24–3 thumping as the Irish prepared to battle a Pittsburgh team that had one of the nation's great backs in Tony Dorsett.

Dorsett on this particular day was unstoppable as he ran the Irish defense into the ground. All Tony did was run for three hundred yards and score two touchdowns as the Panthers kayoed any hopes that Notre Dame might have of a bowl bid as they ran over and through the Irish by a 34–20 score.

At Miami, Florida, the Hurricanes played the Irish even but only for the first quarter, as both teams scored on field goals and it was 3–3. In the second period Notre Dame scored on touchdowns—by Jerome Heavens, and by Ken MacAfee on a pass from Rick Slager. Then the Irish scored once more, on a safety, when Browner tackled a Miami back behind the goal line for two points and a thorough defeat of the Hurricanes by a 32–9 count.

Thus ended Dan Devine's first season, at Notre Dame as head coach with an 8–3–0 record.

But on the campus at Notre Dame and across the land, the first grumbling about the new coach's record began to be heard. And in South Bend, Chicago, New York, and Los Angeles the alumni began to grouse about a record that showed three losses and no invitation to a major bowl game.

"ONE MAN'S FAMILY": THE AMAZING BROWNERS

His nickname was "Red," although his eight children loved it when his buddies at the Republic Steel plant in Warren, Ohio, called him the "Strong Man."

Red Browner worked the swing shift at Republic for more than twenty years. He also had a truck and hauled coal, cut firewood, and took on all sorts of moving and hauling jobs, anything to earn an honest dollar. He built his own house on a flat, weedy parcel of land a block outside the city limits, and it was here that three of his older boys helped, pouring concrete, chopping wood, carting away debris.

Red told his boys, "If you work, you eat and you got a home," and he himself worked so hard that no one really knew if his real appetite was food or labor.

Red could neither read nor write. That's why the schooling of his children was an obsession. That's why he worked all those extra hours so he could buy them books, art supplies, whatever they needed to pass those courses in school. And his big dream was that one day he would live to see all his children go on to college.

The boys grew strong and tall and went on to high school, and five of the Browner boys were nominated to the high-school All-America football team. The single exception was Keith, who became an All-State basketball star.

Ross was six feet, three inches and weighed 250 pounds, and from the first day he reported to coach Ara Parseghian in 1973 as a defensive end, he was a star. He was a scourge to enemy backs as they attempted to move into his area, and with his great play he helped the Irish to an 11–0–0 season and the national championship. Ross won both the Lombardi and Outland trophies as "one of the greatest linemen in Notre Dame history."

Brother Jimmy, a mere six-foot, three-inch, 215-pound defensive back for the Irish, was a terror who moved like a big cat and hit like a ton of cement. Few enemy passes or runs were ever successful in Jim's territory from 1975 to 1978.

Willard was "small"—he was only six feet, two inches and weighed 210 pounds, but according to Devine he was one of the hardest-running fullbacks on the 1976 squad, a team that included such outstanding fullbacks as Vagus Ferguson, Jerome Heavens, and Steve Orsini.

Red Browner was delighted, proud as a peacock as he watched his three boys wearing the blue and the gold of Notre Dame in the summer of 1976 as they prepared under coach Dan Devine to battle the best football teams in the land.

But Red suddenly became ill. He began to have trouble with his stomach. He could not keep down a meal and grew thin and worn. Pancreatic cancer, the doctors said. They took Red to surgery, opened him up, then closed him quickly. "Nothing to be done," they said.

Red Browner died in the summer of 1976, but not before he told his eldest, Ross, then a junior at Notre Dame, "Take care of your mother, sisters, and see to it that everyone makes it through college." Ross agreed and that night his dad, tough Red Browner, died.

Dan Devine, his assistants, and several members of the Notre Dame team acted as pallbearers for Red Browner.

Then as a parting tribute to Red Browner, a man who could neither read nor write, a guy who never got his name in the papers, who never made much money, the Notre Dame football squad honored him and his family by electing end Ross Browner, an All-American-to-be, captain of the 1976 football team. At the time the Irish prepared to open the season against the powerful Pitt Panthers, ranked number two in the nation and led by their superstar, Tony Dorsett.

A capacity crowd of more than fifty-nine thousand spectators jammed every inch of Knute Rockne Memorial Stadium as the Panthers rolled into South Bend to open the 1976 season in a renewal of a rivalry that dated back to 1909, when the Irish defeated a strong Pitt team by a 6–0 score. Notre Dame and Pitt had met forty-seven times since that first game and the Irish had won thirty-two games, Pitt fourteen and there was one tie game. Notre Dame had, however, captured eleven of the last twelve games played. But this day the Panthers, with one of the finest teams in their history, were out to win convincingly over their longtime enemy.

Tony Dorsett had a very special reason for wanting to beat Notre Dame.

"I was still in high school and this Notre Dame coach looked me over, watched me play, then reported back to Notre Dame that 'Dorsett is a skinny little kid and will never make it in big-time college football.' "

Tony started running with the kickoff and never stopped until he had gained 185 yards in twenty-two carries; scored a touchdown on a sixty-five-yard jaunt, and was responsible for two additional scores with some of his flashiest breakaway runs as the Panthers buried Notre Dame, 31–10.

Compounding the defeat was the shoulder separation suffered by Joe Montana, the sensational quarterback, who would be out of action for the entire season. It was a bitter blow to the Irish, who had counted on Joe's great passing ability.

"Our big job now is to bounce back," said Devine following Notre Dame's worst opening-game defeat in its history.

Bounce back they did, and in successive weeks they defeated three of their Big Ten opponents: Purdue, 23–0; Northwestern 48–0; and Michigan State, 24–6. Then South Carolina, in the first game between the teams, pushed Notre Dame to the wall as they held the Irish to a 13–6 lead in the final period of their game and were threatening to tie the score at least. Then Al Hunter, Notre Dame's shifty halfback, broke away for a sixty-one yard run to the Fighting Gamecocks' twenty-yard line as the clock ran down and saved the day for the Irish in a hard-fought battle.

Navy passed and passed and passed in their game against Notre Dame at Cleveland on October 30 and almost upset the Irish, who were favored to beat the Middies by four touchdowns; but Notre Dame was exceedingly lucky to win a heart-stopper by a 27–21 score.

Notre Dame had a comfortable 14–3 lead over a scrappy Georgia Tech team going into the third quarter, but then a personal foul was called on cornerback Luther Bradley and the Irish were penalized fifteen yards. Tech was given the ball on the Irish eight-yard line, and then the *Yellow Jackets* scored to cut Notre Dame's lead to a slim 14–10.

Tech added thirteen more points in the third and fourth periods and came away with a 23–14 win. They did not attempt a single pass during the entire game but did manage to run the Irish into the ground as they gained 368 yards rushing to Notre Dame's 107 yards.

The Crimson Tide of Alabama rolled into South Bend for the first regular-season game between the two teams on November 13, and the rivals battled each other furiously while a hometown crowd of over fifty-nine thousand spectators roared on every play.

The second period began as quarterback Rick Slager passed to end Dan Kelleher. The play was good for sixty-five yards, and Notre Dame took a 7–0 lead. The Irish were to score twice more, one on a pass to Ken MacAfee, while Vagus Ferguson, a freshman halfback sensation making his first start, flashed through the 'Bama line for a seventeen-yard touchdown jaunt and a scary 21–18 victory over the Crimson Tide. The Browner brothers, Ross and Jim, were standout performers throughout the long afternoon, but it was Jim who intercepted a Jeff Rutledge pass and broke up a play that had "touchdown" written all over it.

The Miami Hurricanes blew into cold, snowy South Bend on November 20 and made the battle against Notre Dame a most entertaining one as they scored two go-ahead touchdowns in the first half. But once Notre Dame started to move, with Rick Slager passing and Ken MacAfee receiving, the Irish machine scored six times to put the game out of the reach of the visiting Miami eleven, and Notre Dame had racked up its eighth victory of the season by a comfortable 40–27 margin before departing for the warmer climes of Southern California to battle the USC Trojans.

The Irish moved into Los Angeles with an 8–2–0 record and were ranked thirteenth nationally, while the Trojans were ranked number three.

USC, under a new coach, John Robinson, had a remarkable 8–1 record and quickly jumped into the lead as the game began. Quarterback Rob Hertel passed to end Shelly Diggs, who scored for USC. In the third period halfback Vince Evans, a marvelous runner all afternoon, set up a sixty-five-yard scoring play to Randy Simmirin for the second Trojan score and Southern California now had a comfortable 14–0 lead as the fourth quarter began.

But Dan Devine inserted six-foot, four-inch Rusty Lisch at quarterback, and Rusty quickly passed twenty-seven yards to end Kris Haines, and now it was 14–7 as Dan Reeve kicked the extra point. The Trojans hammered back, and at the end of a forty-eight-yard drive Terry Walker kicked a forty-six-yard field goal to give USC a 17–7 lead.

Lisch, playing one of his finest games for the Irish, passed and ran the ball for a couple of big gains and jammed the ball over from the USC ten-yard line to give the Irish their second touchdown. But it was not enough. Time ran out, and Southern California had the edge in a thriller, 17–13, as Dan Devine's second season ended with an 8–3–0 record.

Notre Dame's outstanding play during the second half of the season and strong surge in the second half of the game against Southern California brought an invitation by the Gator Bowl Committee, and Notre Dame agreed to play Penn State in Jacksonville on December 27. The Gator Bowl was the first bowl game for the Irish under Devine and Notre Dame's seventh bowl game.

Penn State, under one of the nation's leading coaches, Joe Paterno, had ended the season with a 7–4 record. But the State team was better than their record indicated, and they were favored to defeat the Irish.

Notre Dame, led by halfback Al Hunter, the first Irish back to rush for more than a thousand yards in a season, scored when Terry Eurick returned a Penn State kick sixty-five yards. Then Hunter banged in for the first Irish score, and Dan Reeve kicked the extra point. In the second period, Jim Browner recovered a State fumble on the Nittany Lions' twenty-three-yard line, and a pass from Slager to Kelleher gave Reeve a chance for a kick from the twenty-three-yard line. Dan made the field goal, and the score was Notre Dame 10, Penn State 3.

Hunter again scored after Slager passed twice to

MacAfee to give Notre Dame a 17–3 lead. Then with just three seconds to play before the half, Reeve kicked another twenty-three-yard field goal, and at the half it was Notre Dame 20, Penn State 3.

Led by linebackers Bob Golic, Doug Becker, Steve Heimkreiter, and Jim Browner, the Irish defense kept Penn State bottled up throughout the second half. State finally was able to score when Bruce Clark blocked a Notre Dame punt with nine minutes left in the game and quarterback Chuck Fusina passed to Matt Suhey for a touchdown as the game ended with Notre Dame out in front, 20–9.

The win gave Dan Devine a 9–3–0 season record.

Ross Browner, Ken MacAfee, Luther Bradley and Willie Fry were named to the All-American team, and with the 1977 season looming and a host of outstanding juniors and sophomores with solid varsity experience, Dan Devine looked forward to an excellent 1977.

Ross Browner, 1977 Irish tri-captain, receives the prestigious Maxwell Award as "the top college player of the year" in 1977. Bob Griese (left) received the Bert Bell Award at the special luncheon in Philadelphia.

COMEBACK PLAYER OF THE YEAR

After Notre Dame thumped Penn State in the 1976 Gator Bowl, Dan Devine knew he'd need to replace his quarterback and split end.

But the offensive unit was otherwise set for his third season at South Bend, and it promised all sorts of rosy things for the harried Notre Dame coach.

When the Irish reassembled in mid-August, Devine's rollcall did not include halfback Al Hunter, Notre Dame's only thousand-yard rusher in history. Hunter was suspended for violation of university rules. "It was a tremendous blow," said Devine. "There aren't many teams in college ball that have a thousand-yard back. Our whole style of attack was built around Hunter."

Willard Browner, another backfield starter, was dropped for scholastic reasons. That too, was a jolt for the six-two Browner had been counted on as a regular.

But loyal legions who live and die with the fortunes of Notre Dame were not shaken. The Irish still were ranked among the leading teams in the nation in '77 pre-season ratings and were listed on anybody's "most likely" major-bowl list. Even the conservative, moody Devine, 17–6–0 for his first two years at Notre Dame, admitted he was thinking national championship, although stipulating, "probably about a hundred other coaches had similar thoughts."

But how many college coaches have ever had their eleven top defensive regulars returning? Devine did, plus two '76 starters injured early that season.

Everything pointed to a truly awesome defensive unit that would include: Ross Browner, six-three, 247 pounds, and Willie Fry, six-three, 242 pounds, defensive ends probably equal or superior to any in college football. Then there was Bob Golic, six-three, 244 pounds; Doug Becker, six feet, 223 pounds; and Steve Heimdreiter, six-two, 228 pounds, perhaps the biggest linebacking unit ever to represent the Irish.

At quarterback Rusty Lisch, a six-four, 200-pound junior, had taken over after Joe Montana was hurt and had led the Irish to the 40–27 win over Miami in his only start in 1976, and he did have impressive relief appearances against several other teams.

In Jerome Heavens and Vagus Ferguson, Notre Dame had two fast, hard-running halfbacks who could break away at any given moment. But the strength of the offense was up front with tight end Ken MacAfee, a six-four, 250-pound senior who had been an All-American for two years. Ken had accounted for over a thousand yards in pass receiving. At center Dave Hoffman, six-five, 241 pounds, had received All-America mention last year. And guard Ernie Hughes, six-three, 248 pounds, looked like another cinch for All-America honors.

From 1974 to 1977, six-foot, five-inch, 235-pound Ken MacAfee, a two-time All-American, was one of college football's greatest tight ends.

No wonder the ordinarily moody Devine was often smiling and humming to himself after practice . . . when he thought nobody was around.

This was the year!

The campaign opened at the home of the 1976 national champions, the Pitt Panthers.

The opening game of the season had been awaited for perhaps as long as a year by a number of the Notre Dame players, for it was just a year earlier that Tony Dorsett and company had humiliated the Irish by pounding out a 31–10 win.

But on Saturday, September 10, when the Panthers went out to defend their first national title in forty years against the Irish, they did so before a sellout crowd of 56,500 who were roaring from the start of the game to the finish.

In the first quarter Rusty Lisch tossed his first pass to Ken MacAfee, but a Panther intercepted the ball. Then quarterback Matt Cavanaugh, who had taken over where Dorsett had left off, passed to Gordon Jones for a score. The kick was good, and Pitt was out in front, 7–0.

However, the touchdown play was a costly one for Cavanaugh and for Pitt. On the play Matt broke to his right and let the ball fly. But at the precise moment that Cavanaugh released the ball, Notre Dame's Willie Fry drove hard into the exposed front part of Cavanaugh, who landed hard on his right wrist. He was injured and through for the afternoon . . . and it was the beginning of the end for both Pitt and the Panthers' title aspirations.

Shortly after Cavanaugh left the game, Notre Dame's Joe Restic came back to punt from his ten-yard line, but he fumbled the center pass and was tackled behind his own goal line for two points. Now it was 9–0 in favor of Pitt.

Most of the capacity crowd settled back in their seats satisfied that Pitt had the game won, and even the hardiest Irish rooter had just about given up all hope.

Then Burgmeier returned a Pitt kick fifteen yards, and Rusty Lisch started to unlimber his great passing arm. He passed to Kris Haines for twenty-seven yards; then two straight tosses to MacAfee; a fifteen-yard scramble by Lisch; another pass to MacAfee, and Ken dashed across the Pitt goal line for the first Irish touchdown. The extra-point try was missed, and the half ended with a Pittsburgh edge, 9–6.

In the third period, Bob Golic, Notre Dame's great linebacker, blocked a Pitt punt and fell on the ball on Pitts's sixteen-yard line. Now the Irish fans were up and screaming for a touchdown.

But Notre Dame was stopped by a tight Pitt defense, and Dan Reeve stepped back and kicked a beautiful thirty-yard field goal. Suddenly it was a 9–9 game.

The Pitt coach, Jackie Sherrill, sent in a freshman quarterback, Steve Yewcic, who fumbled on the first play. Notre Dame recovered the ball and once again Dan Reeve booted a marvelous three-pointer, this one from twenty-six yards out, and Notre Dame had a 12–9 lead.

As the game wound down, Pitt's quarterback Wayne Adams bobbled a pass from center and big Ross Browner, thundering in, crashed into Adams and then fell on the ball for the Irish.

Halfback Terry Eurick quickly took a hand-off from Rusty Lisch and smashed into the tiring Pitt line for a touchdown. And Notre Dame had the most important victory of the season over the former national champions, by a 19–9 score.

The following week, in a game that had all the earmarks of the South's revenge for their loss in the Civil War, the University of Mississippi Rebels upset the Irish, 20–13, at Jackson, Mississippi.

The Irish took the opening kickoff but were unable to mount any sort of offense. Ole Miss took over, marched determinedly some sixty-four yards to Notre Dame's twelve-yard line, and then Hoppy Langley, the Mississippi field-goal specialist, kicked a field goal of twenty-nine yards to give Ole Miss a 3–0 lead.

Notre Dame's attack stalled as Terry Eurick fumbled the ball after a fine thirty-eight-yard dash, and the Rebels recovered the ball. On the following play Bob Garner, the Ole Miss quarterback, attempted a long pass that was intercepted by Jim Browner at the Rebels' twenty-six-yard line.

Eight plays later, Jerome Heavens smashed through the Ole Miss line for two yards and scored for Notre Dame as the Irish captured the lead, 7–3.

On the next series of plays, the Rebels marched seventy-five yards in six plays to score a touchdown that gave them a 10–7 lead. The big play for Ole Miss was a sensational fifty-yard pass from Garner to end Roy Coleman.

With thirteen minutes to play in the final period, Mississippi tailback Ty Richards fumbled, and Jay Case recovered for the Irish on the Rebels' forty-one-yard line. Notre Dame could not advance beyond the twenty-seven-yard line, and once again the reliable Dan Reeve booted a field goal, this one for forty-four yards, to tie the score at 10–10.

On their next possession Ole Miss again fumbled, and the Irish recovered on the Rebels' forty-five-yard stripe. In five plays Notre Dame moved to the eleven-yard line, but on fourth down and eleven to go, Devine sent in Dan Reeve, whose field goal put Notre Dame into a 13–10 lead.

Now there were but 4:53 to play in the game.

Coach Ken Cooper of Mississippi now decided to change quarterbacks and sent in Tim Ellis, who promptly drove the Rebels eighty yards to a touchdown. With Langley's conversion, Ole Miss led 17–13 and the Irish hopes were fading fast.

Notre Dame had but 3:13 to try to pull off a miracle.

Rusty Lisch faded back and tossed a bullet-like pass to Jerome Heavens. But Jerome was hit hard, and just as he was about to break away, he fumbled, and Brian Moreland recovered for Ole Miss.

With fourth down and six yards to go, Langley kicked his second field goal to give the Rebels a 20–13 lead. Now there were less than two minutes to play.

Lisch tried for a "big pass" play but was intercepted, and the game ended shortly thereafter with Notre Dame on the short end of the 20–13 score.

The Irish now had won one and lost one game and did not look at all as if they were of championship caliber.

Coach Devine said, "I remember back at Notre Dame we had a team meeting on the Sunday after the game. I told the players, 'I know we're a better team than we've showed so far. I know that you are a great team and you're good enough to bounce back and win the rest of the games. Now, let's play one game at a time and play tough. Hear me?' " The shouts of the players almost blew the roof off the field house as the squad members, now as enthusiastic as a bunch of freshmen, went about their business.

Quarterback Joe Montana had a lot to look back on in his four years at Notre Dame. He had been a sensation as a freshman and sophomore but had suffered a shoulder separation in the first game of the 1976 season against Pitt and sat on the bench all year long. But on this October afternoon in 1977, though his shoulder had healed, Joe still sat on the sidelines, relegated to the number-three quarterback spot. The great cheers which once surrounded him were now faint memories.

There was no reason to think his situation would change as the Irish prepared to battle the always tough Purdue eleven at Ross-Ade Stadium.

For the third week in a row it appeared that the Irish were simply outmatched, this time by the hard-charging, aggressive Boilermakers of Purdue. Their ace, quarterback Mark Herrmann, a freshman at that, had passed and passed and passed for three touchdowns, and Purdue was out in front by a 24–14 margin going into the last period.

Then Devine sent in Gary Forystek to replace Lisch, and suddenly Gary had the Irish rolling. Two passes to MacAfee and Notre Dame was on the Purdue thirty-yard line. On the next play, Gary rolled right, decided to keep the ball instead of passing, and drove all the way down to the Purdue seventeen, where he was smashed to the turf by a host of Purdue linemen. On the play Gary suffered a broken collarbone and was taken out of the game.

Now the stage was set for the "comeback of the year."

Joe Montana came into the game but could work no immediate miracles, so the Irish had to call on Dan Reeve, who provided a successful field-goal kick from the twenty-four-yard line, and now it was 24–17.

Mark Herrmann resorted to more passes—but one of them was dramatically plucked out of a Purdue receiver's hands by Luther Bradley at Boilermakers' forty-eight-yard line.

Irish quarterback Joe Montana talks over strategy with Coach Dan Devine on the sidelines, during a timeout in the Cotton Bowl battle against Houston, January 1, 1979.

Back in a huddle with teammates, Montana barks out the next play.

Now it was Montana's ball game.

Joe completed a pass to Kris Haines on the sidelines that was good for eleven yards and a first down. Again Montana passed to MacAfee, who smashed to the twenty-five-yard line before he was tackled.

Once again Montana, now cool as ice and faking a run, lofted a high, arching pass to MacAfee, and the six-four tight end simply outjumped three Purdue defenders to grab the ball and fall across the goal line. After a Reeve conversion, it was a 24–24 game with four minutes left to play.

In just four minutes, the once-forgotten Joe Montana had sparked the Irish to new heights, from apparent defeat to new life. He was the spark plug needed for victory.

Joe got the ball on his own thirty-yard line with just three minutes to play, and utilizing Ken MacAfee and Haines as his targets, completed four passes in a row.

Now the ball was on the Purdue ten-yard line.

Montana to Orsini for five yards.

Then it was Dave Mitchell, a big 210-pound full-back, who bulled over from the five-yard line for the touchdown.

The miracle was complete.

Joe Montana had once again returned to the spotlight where he seemed to belong and had led the Irish to a spectacular, last-minute, 31–24 victory over Purdue.

Joe Montana returned to South Bend for his next start, against Michigan State. On the second play of the game, he rolled to his right and heaved a forty-five-yard aerial bomb to Ken MacAfee on the twenty-five-yard line. Then Jerome Heavens and Dave Mitchell pounded the State line to the three-yard

stripe on successive drives; but on the next play Heavens fumbled, and State recovered.

Four plays later the Irish were again threatening the Spartans. Randy Harrison returned a State punt twenty-five yards, but once again the Irish dissipated a scoring threat as Montana's pass was picked off by Jack Anderson of Purdue. Quarterback Ernie Smith, an All-Big Ten star, moved his team to the thirty-eight-yard line, and Hans Mielson of State booted a forty-five-yard field goal to give State a 3–0 lead.

Then Dan Reeve split the uprights from forty-two yards out, and Notre Dame tied the game at 3–3.

With 2:55 left in the second period, Heavens finally tore loose for twenty-eight yards; on the next play, Mitchell broke off-tackle and slammed into the end zone, and Notre Dame had a 10–3 lead at half-time.

In the third period Notre Dame again picked up three points, on a Reeve twenty-eight-yard field goal, and it was 13–3 Notre Dame.

Joe Restic intercepted a State pass at midfield, but the Irish offense stalled, and Dan Reeve was called in to attempt a fifty-one-yard field goal. He calmly booted it home—one of the longest Irish field goals—and Notre Dame had a hard-fought victory over Michigan State by a 16–6 margin.

The Notre Dame–Army game at one time was college football's most glamorous rivalry. In recent years, however, the game had evolved into a mismatch.

In the previous two meetings, the last in 1974, the Irish had outscored the Cadets by a 110–13 margin.

But Army had higher hopes this year, most of them resting on the good right arm of their ace quarterback Leamon Hall, who had passed for twelve touchdowns in the five previous Army games.

On Notre Dame's first possession, Jerome Heavens

carried five times in a row, and just as he was about to break clear on the Army twenty-one-yard line he was hit hard, fumbled, and Army recovered the ball.

But the Cadets' attack stalled and the Irish took over.

Heavens carried the ball for forty-three of the forty-seven yards needed to score and then drove in for a touchdown from the four-yard line.

The first half ended with Notre Dame in front, 7–0.

In the second half Reeve kicked a twenty-nine-yard field goal to boost the Irish lead to 10–0.

Then Mr. Montana started his passing act. He tossed a twenty-yarder to MacAfee. Then Heavens burst out for runs of thirteen and fifteen yards, and then Terry Eurick dove in from the two-yard line. Now the Irish had a 17–0 lead.

Eurick scored the final touchdown with sixteen seconds left in the game after a time-consuming sixty-yard drive. Final score: Notre Dame 24, Army 0.

Southern California had won seven of the past ten games with Notre Dame (with two of the ten games resulting in a tie), including an embarrassing 55–24 beating of the Irish in 1974, and Dan Devine had been preparing his team for months. The preparation even included a "secret" gimmick to psyche up the Irish players by secretly having them wear green jerseys for the USC game. Green jerseys had been worn by some of the Rockne and Leahy teams, and Devine thought it might add the right psychological touch.

At the Friday night rally before the game, Devine spoke to his team.

"I talked to them about the great Irish history and of Rockne and Gipp and of course Leahy and the rest. I spoke of Irish adversity and I talked to our black players and spoke about the great cultural heritage of this great school."

Finally Devine revealed his secret to the three Irish captains for this game, impressing on the three—Ross Browner, Terry Eurick, Willie Fry—that the tradition (wearing the green jerseys) must be maintained.

Notre Dame warmed up wearing the regular blue jerseys before a capacity hometown crowd and the Southern California players. The players then returned to the locker room and discovered a green jersey in each locker. The players quickly put on the new shirts, returned to the field, and the huge crowd roared with approval as they saw the bright green jerseys.

Trojan players stared in astonishment at the sight. "They looked like 'big green monsters,' " said a Trojan player.

Perhaps the "gimmick" worked on USC, for Notre Dame quickly scored a touchdown in eleven plays with Montana, Heavens, and Dave Mitchell providing the spark, and Notre Dame had a 7–0 lead.

USC seemed undaunted by the Irish score and quickly moved to the Notre Dame eleven-yard line on several pass plays, but a tough Irish defense held. Then the Trojans tried a field goal from the twenty-five-yard line but missed.

USC kept the Irish pinned back in their own territory, and when Terry Eurick fumbled, USC's Mario Celotto recovered on the Irish three and dashed into the end zone. The score was tied at 7–7.

USC fumbled and Notre Dame recovered the ball on the Trojans' fourteen-yard line. Then Montana faked a pass, tucked the ball under his arm, and ran for Notre Dame's second score. Burgmeier fumbled the pass on the try for the extra point but quickly shot the ball to Tom Domin, a six-foot, three-inch Irish halfback, who crossed the goal line for a two-point conversion. Now it was 15–7 Notre Dame.

After USC failed to gain, Notra Dame scored again when Montana tossed a perfect strike to Ken Mac-Afee. The kick was good for a 22–7 lead.

The Trojans failed to gain ground, and an attempt to punt was blocked by Bob Golic. Jay Case, a six-foot, three-inch tackle, recovered for the Irish and scampered across from the Trojans' thirty-yard line to score his first touchdown for Notre Dame, giving the Irish a 29–7 lead.

After an exchange of downs, Montana executed a seventy-yard drive with two marvelous passes and short bursts up the middle of the Trojan line, and it was another Irish score. A 35–7 fourth-quarter lead looked pretty safe, but USC pulled themselves up and smashed the length of the field to make the score 35–13.

But Montana, playing the greatest game of his four-year career at Notre Dame, dashed in from the one-yard line to give Notre Dame still another score, and Dan Reeve booted home the conversion.

Rob Hertel filled the air with passes and finally, after a seventy-five-yard drive, scored a touchdown for USC.

Now it was 42–19, with Notre Dame far in the lead.

Then Rusty Lisch came in to replace a tired Joe

Montana at quarterback. Rusty promptly engineered a drive, including three straight passes to MacAfee and then to Kevin Hart for the final tally of the game for a stunning 49–19 victory for the Irish.

It was Devine's first victory over USC as head coach at Notre Dame, and he savored every minute of the win. "By Wednesday we knew we were going to beat them," said Devine. "But we did not know how or who was going to lead us."

One of the most important reasons was Joe Montana, who brought the Irish along to play at their very best. But Joe was not alone as All-American Ken MacAfee registered eight catches for ninety-seven yards and two touchdowns.

For the seniors of the class of 1978, it was their first taste of victory over the Trojans. "Beating Southern California was the biggest, best of my career," said Ted Burgmeier. "They really humiliated us the last three years."

In the forty-ninth meeting between Notre Dame and Navy on October 29 at South Bend, the Middies won the toss of the coin and chose to receive the ball. Navy's fine back Joe Gattuso fumbled the kickoff on his own fifteen-yard line and teammate Phil McConkey recovered the ball. But the Middies could not advance and were forced to kick. The Irish received the ball on their forty-nine-yard line and went to work.

On the very first play from scrimmage, Montana dropped back, sidestepped a pair of Navy tacklers, and fired a bomb—a bulletlike pass some forty-seven yards to split end Kris Haines, who was streaking down the sidelines on a fly pattern. Haines took the ball over his shoulder and was hit on the Navy three-yard line.

"That opening play was the result of a hunch I got that morning," said Devine. "Sometimes a play like that surprises a lot of people, but we did not score a touchdown." Dan Reeve had to drop back for a field goal, but he missed from the twenty-yard line.

Several plays later, Jerome Heavens cracked through the Navy tackle and raced forty-nine yards for a touchdown.

Navy played tough and held the Irish from scoring any further touchdowns in the first half. They did, however, manage to kick three field goals—from the thirty-four-yard line, the twenty-four-yard line, and then from the thirty-two-yard stripe—to give the Irish a 16–0 halftime lead.

In the second half it was all Notre Dame as they rolled over Navy's gritty eleven by scoring four touchdowns; by Montana, a freshman, Steve Stone; Leroy Leopold; and another by Montana, and Notre Dame emerged with a 43–10 win.

And for the second week in a row Notre Dame had executed like a team that had been nationally ranked at the beginning of the season.

The Georgia Tech Yellow Jackets couldn't have selected a worse time to invade South Bend, for the Fighting Irish were ready to spring a trap on them. Notre Dame had prepared for this visit after losing to Tech in 1976 by a 23–14 score.

When the Irish squad left Georgia Tech's Grant Field after their game in 1976, they were abused by the press and by a bottle-throwing group of unruly Tech fans.

Revenge does not aptly describe the performance the Blue and Gold put on this day, November 5, as Georgia Tech was administered the worst defeat ever inflicted on them by a major college. Notre Dame scored early and often as quarterback Joe Montana continued to display the form that would bring him national recognition as he led a charging brigade of Irish players to a 21–7 halftime lead.

Montana's play was near perfect as he passed and ran the team like the well-oiled machine it was, and in the second half of the game, the Irish plowed over, around, and through George Tech's wilting defense for six touchdowns in a complete rout.

Montana, Jim Stone and Vagus Ferguson each scored two touchdowns as Notre Dame rolled in their highest total of points in twenty-five years as they completely routed Tech by a numbing 69–14 score.

The next stop was for a game with another southern rival, the Tigers of Clemson University, and a record-breaking crowd of over fifty-four thousand partisan Tiger fans jammed every inch of the Memorial Stadium in Clemson, South Carolina, to watch the Irish in action. And action it was to the very final moment of the battle.

Notre Dame scored early when Jerome Heavens bucked through the Tigers' line from the five-yard stripe, and the Irish took a 7–0 lead. But Clemson surged back in the second and third periods, scoring seventeen unanswered points to give the Tigers a 17–7 lead as the game entered the final quarter.

But once more Joe Montana's pinpoint passing brought the ball to the Clemson five-yard line, and then Joe, on a bootleg play, spurted in for a touchdown to bring the Irish to within three points.

Going into the final minutes of the game with the Tigers in the lead, 17–14, Mike Calhoun, a six-foot,

Ross Browner tackles Georgia Tech's Danny Meyers (No. 21) for no gain in 1975 game.

five-inch, 235-pound Irish tackle, pounced on a Clemson fumble and Montana drove in from the one-yard line for the winning touchdown. Dave Reeve's extra-point conversion gave the Irish a hard-fought 21–17 win.

The win over Clemson gave the Irish a marvelous 8–1–0 season, with the Air Force Falcons and the Hurricanes of Miami left to play in the regular season.

Although the Air Force game promised to be rather one-sided for Notre Dame, a certain amount of anticipation existed for both teams. The Irish needed a convincing win to assure themselves of a Cotton Bowl invitation, and the Falcons wanted nothing better than to win over the Irish as a final tribute to their retiring coach, Ben Martin. But it became readily apparent that this was not an Air Force day.

On the first play from scrimmage, halfback Vagus Ferguson, who had played magnificently all season long, took a hand-off from Joe Montana and scampered past the Falcons' defense to race fifty-six yards for a touchdown. Montana filled the air with passes to Ferguson, Haines, and then Ferguson again, and the Irish had another score.

At halftime it was 35–0, Coach Devine inserted most of his substitutes and they contributed fourteen additional points in the second half. Dan Reeve etched his name into the record book as he kicked seven successful extra points, while Ferguson rushed for three touchdowns and 128 yards in just eleven carries.

The Irish sojourned to sunny Miami to battle the Miami Hurricanes where they impressed the gathered sportswriters and editors and a small crowd of thirty-five thousand fans at Orange Bowl Stadium with the complete all-around play of both their offense and defense.

The Irish scored two touchdowns within five minutes, took a 20–10 lead at halftime, and then punched over twenty-eight additional points to defeat decisively a tough Miami team by a 48–10 score.

The easy 48–10 win over the Miami Hurricanes so impressed the Cotton Bowl officials that they promptly invited Notre Dame to meet the number-one-ranked unbeaten Texas Longhorns on January 2. Moose Krause, Notre Dame's athletic director, agreed to the game after conferring with Dan Devine.

Now the sports wires carried stories that the contest between Notre Dame and Texas would be no contest at all. Notre Dame was overmatched in this battle and the game would be "a one-sided mismatch," said the Associated Press, and the experts throughout the state of Texas agreed.

The prognostication that the game would be a mismatch proved accurate. Yet Coach Devine was furious to learn that his linebacker Bob Golic had stated the game would be a runaway—for the Irish.

Addressing his team before the game, Devine said, "The Texans are right. The game won't be close. We are going to be blown out. You fellows have come here to Dallas to have a good time, and the workouts

Coach Dan Devine and his quarterback, Joe Montana, discuss a crucial play during a time-out in the 1979 Cotton Bowl game against Texas.

show it. You've gotten careless, and practice the last few days has been just plain lousy."

By kickoff time, Willie Fry, who shared the captaincy with Ross Browner and Terry Eurick, was convinced Notre Dame would win. "Coach Devine's approach and his talk really psyched us up and we were ready to blow them out."

As the game opened, Texas, relying on their great star Heisman Trophy winner-to-be Earl Campbell, marched upfield to their forty-five-yard line on slants into the line. Then Campbell fumbled and Ross Browner fell on the ball for Notre Dame. A Joe Montana pass advanced the ball to the Texas forty-three-yard line, and after failing to gain ground, Devine sent in Dan Reeve for a field-goal attempt. Reeve's kick was good, and the Irish had a 3–0 lead.

That score by the green-shirted Irish team did not faze the Longhorns, for they came right back as quarterback Randy McEachern stuck to the ground game that had given Texas eleven straight wins that season. Handing off to Campbell and halfback Johnny Jones, the Longhorns moved the ball sixty-seven yards to the Irish thirteen-yard line before they were halted. McEachern then switched to the air, was unsuccessful on two passes, and then Texas was forced to settle for a forty-two-yard field goal off the toe of the Longhorns' brilliant kicker, Russ Erxleben. His kick tied the score at 3–3.

Bob Golic and teammates Mike Calhoun and Doug Becker smashed into Johnny Jones after he had taken a McEachern pass. Jones, stunned by the force of the three players driving into him, fumbled the ball, and big Jim Browner, catlike all afternoon, pounced on

the loose ball at the Texas twenty-five-yard line.

Then Captain Terry Eurick smashed through the line on the fifth play of the series, and Notre Dame had its first touchdown to give the Irish a 10–3 lead as the second period began.

On the Longhorns' next possession, tackle Ken Dike stripped the ball from a scrambling Randy McEachern, and an alert Willie Fry recovered for the Irish at the Texas thirty-five-yard line.

Five plays later Eurick carried two Texas tacklers across the goal line as he smashed across the last ten yards for his second score, and Notre Dame had a 17–3 lead.

Doug Becker then intercepted a McEachern pass and raced seventeen yards to the Longhorns' twenty-three-yard line. Then Joe Montana scrambled away from two Texas tacklers and tossed a seventeen-yard pass to Vagus Ferguson, and the Irish had a 24–3 lead, one that seemed to negate any chance of Texas claiming the national championship.

But the Longhorns threw a scare into Notre Dame by moving sixty-eight yards in six plays within twenty-two seconds and scored their first touchdown of the game when McEachern passed thirteen yards to Mike Lockett. At halftime it was 24–10 Notre Dame.

Late in the third period, Notre Dame picked up the game momentum as Steve Heimkreiter intercepted a McEachern pass and Ferguson bulled across the goal line for an Irish score, making it 31–10.

In the final period Heimkreiter recovered a Texas fumble and Ferguson dashed twenty-six yards for his third score of the day. It was 38–10 Notre Dame, and the Irish fans who had traveled to Dallas for the game charged on the field at the final gun and carried the victorious Irish team members off the field.

Hours later, as the AP and UPI wires carried the story of the game around the nation, both wire services tallied the votes of their confreres, and Notre Dame was declared national champions.

For Notre Dame, Vagus Ferguson and Jerome Heavens were the offensive stars—each player had rushed for a hundred or more yards. On defense, it was the play of Bob Golic, Ross Browner, and Willie Fry and of guard Ernie Hughes that stopped Earl Campbell, although he did run for 118 yards. But Notre Dame's defense stopped him cold in the second half, and without his flaming runs, Texas did not have a chance for victory.

At about 2:00 A.M., Coach Devine and Joe Montana got the phone call they had been awaiting and announced to the still celebrating Irish fans that Notre

Dame had just been voted the MacArthur Bowl, symbolic of the national championship.

Ross Browner and Ken MacAfee were unanimously selected for the second straight year on the All-America team. Luther Bradley, Ernie Hughes, Bob Golic, Willie Fry, and Ted Burgmeier also were named to various All-America teams.

Ross Browner won both the coveted Vince Lombardi Award, given to the nations's outstanding lineman, and the Maxwell Trophy as the nation's top college player of the year. Ken MacAfee received the Walter Camp Award, given to the "player of the year."

Upon leaving Notre Dame, Ross Browner, Ernie Hughes, and Luther Bradley played with various NFL teams. Willie Fry took a position with the brokerage firm of Merrill Lynch in New York City.

And a *Chicago Tribune* columnist wrote: "It's about time we gave Dan Devine the accolade he deserves."

Dan Devine did not for a moment sit back and savor the fruits of the national championship, for he was on the go from the second week in January to all parts of the country. His name headed the list of celebrity speakers for football banquets, clinics, and other appearances in Chicago, Detroit, Cleveland, Miami, New Orleans, and New York City and by the time spring practice rolled around, he was delighted just to stay put in South Bend. "These few months were the greatest months of my life," said Dan, "but now I've got to go to work and start all over again."

In 1978, considerably weakened by the loss due to graduation of some of the finest players of the past ten seasons, including such greats as All-Americans Ross Browner, Luther Bradley, Willy Fry, and Ken MacAfee and three-year veterans such as Doug Becker, Ted Burgmeier, Ken Dike, Captain Terry Eurick, Ernie Hughes, Gary Forystek, Dan Reeve, Steve McDaniels, Steve Orsini, and Steve Schmitz, the Irish worked hard under Coach Devine to prepare for the season's three opening games. These were against an experienced Missouri team, then Michigan, and then the Boilermakers of Purdue, who had lost three in a row to the Irish.

The Missouri Tigers lived up their nickname. They held Notre Dame scoreless for the first time in 131 games and won a bitterly fought contest with a last-period thirty-three-yard field goal by their star kicker, Jeff Brockhaus. Final score: Missouri 3, Notre Dame 0.

Notre Dame had not played Michigan since 1943, when the Irish defeated the Wolverines 35–12. It was due mainly to the heroics of halfback Creighton Miller, who scored two touchdowns and had a third called back. Number 37 was unstoppable that afternoon.

This day, September 23, 1978, the Wolverines rolled into South Bend and quickly fell behind in the first period when Joe Montana passed to six-foot, six-inch Dennis Grindinger for a quick score, and the Irish led 7–0. Vagus Ferguson, picking up where he left off in 1977, dashed across on a five-yard slant off-tackle and scored Notre Dame's second touchdown to give the Irish an early 14–0 lead over a supposedly strong Wolverine eleven.

Ricky Leach, Michigan's fine quarterback, evened things up with a touchdown sprint of his own and then a pass covering thirty-five yards for a second touchdown. With fifteen minutes left in the game Leach put Michigan out in front with two spectacular passes that resulted in two touchdowns for a 28–14 Wolverine victory.

Purdue led Notre Dame in the third consecutive home game for the Irish by 6–0 at the half. By this time, the over fifty-nine-thousand fans at the game had forgotten all about the joy and happiness of the 1977 championship season. Here they were in the third game of the 1978 season and already had lost two straight. A third loss this early in the campaign would eliminate any consideration for a bowl game, and suddenly in the stands, one could notice a number of handmade "Dump Devine" signs.

However, in the third period Jerome Heavens dashed off-tackle for twenty-six yards and a touchdown. Then five-foot, eight-inch Joe Unis kicked a field goal to give the Irish their first win of the season by a 10–6 score.

Michigan State trailed 29–13 going into the fourth quarter after Montana and company had ripped the Spartan defenses apart with a series of passes to score four times. But in the final period the Spartans scored twice and almost pulled the game out as they lost by a 29–25 margin.

Pittsburgh seemingly had the game won in their battle against the Irish with a comfortable 17–7 lead in the final period, but Montana fired passes to Kris Haines for a touchdown. Then Joe got to the five-yard line and smashed in for another touchdown, and suddenly Notre Dame was in front by a 19–17 margin. As time ran out, Montana tossed a short pass to Ferguson, who bucked over from the five-yard line. Unis added the extra point, and Notre Dame had pulled the game out of the fire, 26–17.

In the Pitt game, Jerome Heavens ran for 120 yards, erasing George Gipp's career total of 2,341 yards from the record books.

At the Air Force Academy in Colorado Springs, Notre Dame jumped out to an early 3–0 lead on a forty-yard field goal by their great kicker Chuck Male. Then Joe Montana went to work, scored two touchdowns on short runs, and completed passes to Kris Haines and Ferguson for touchdowns. The pass to Haines was a fifty-six-yard play that just about demoralized the entire Air Force team as the Irish easily defeated them 38–15.

The Miami Hurricanes blew into South Bend for the tenth game of a series between the two schools that began back in 1955, when Notre Dame defeated the Hurricanes, 14–0. The game had developed into a number of fierce battles between the two teams, although Miami had won only once and tied one game. This time the Hurricanes were blanked 20–0 as Vagus Ferguson continued his sparkling play by scoring all three Irish touchdowns.

Notre Dame and undefeated Navy collided head-on before a crowd of more than sixty-three-thousand in Cleveland Stadium. Navy came into the game with one of its strongest teams. They had defeated a number of the leading teams in the East, and in so doing had won seven straight games and seemed headed for an undefeated season. The Middies had not won against Notre Dame since 1963 in their annual battle with the Irish. This time they were out for victory. But once again Notre Dame, with Vagus Ferguson at his very best, was simply too fast, and Navy went down to defeat by a 27–7 score.

Time after time in the Navy game, Ferguson brought the huge crowd up on its feet with his sensational running, one of them a sparkling eighty-yard dash for a touchdown that was a picture-perfect play.

The Tennessee Volunteers, ranked as one of the South's top teams, invaded South Bend for the first game ever between the two schools and quickly jumped into a 7–6 lead over the Irish and held on to that precarious lead until the third quarter. Then Notre Dame took over, scored eighteen points, and went on to defeat the bigger, stronger, but slower Southerners by a 31–14 margin.

Georgia Tech was easily beaten in a contest that saw Joe Montana at his brilliant best. Joe passed for two scores and ran for another touchdown as the Irish crushed Tech, 38–21. Immediately after the game, Coach Devine accepted a Cotton Bowl invitation to meet Houston in the annual game at Dallas.

But there still was the final game of the regular season, against Southern California, the third ranked team in the nation.

And the USC-Notre Dame game turned out to be one of the most exciting and dramatic battles between the two bitter rivals in the fifty-two games the two schools had played against each other.

The game began with a series of field-goal attempts, and USC had the advantage as they successfully kicked two, to take a 6–3 lead at the end of the first period. The Trojans scored another field goal and a touchdown, and at the half led Notre Dame, 17–6.

USC further increased their lead to 24–6 early into the final quarter, and it looked as if they would easily defeat the tiring Irish.

Late in that period, however, Joe Montana suddenly uncorked a long pass that traveled some thirty-five yards to Kris Haines, all alone on the USC fifteen-yard line. Kris tore across those last fifteen yards as if he were shot from a cannon. It was the first Notre Dame touchdown. The extra point was missed, and USC still held a commanding 24–12 lead.

After an exchange of downs, Notre Dame took possession of the ball on their three-yard line, and Montana began to move the Irish. He passed to Haines for fifteen yards, then to Dean Masztak for another fifteen. With the ball on the USC forty-nine, Joe faded to pass, then crossed up the Trojans by tucking the ball under his arm and starting upfield. He faked three USC tacklers and got as far as the Trojans' three-yard line before he was brought down.

The crowd of some eighty-four-thousand fans now were screaming.

Notre Dame's Pete Buchanan tried a line buck and scored. Little Joe Unis came in to kick the extra point, and now the score was 24–19, USC.

Now there were only three minutes left in the game. USC failed to gain ground after receiving the kickoff, and Notre Dame took over the ball on their own forty-three-yard line. Once again Montana pulled out all the stops as he passed and ran and passed and got to the USC two-yard line.

Then Montana passed to halfback Pete Holohan, and the big six-foot four-inch Holohan outjumped three Trojans and fell across the goal line for the touchdown.

Now it was Notre Dame 25, USC 24.

And just forty-five seconds left to play.

Montana missed on a two-point conversion, and the Irish fans groaned in anguish.

Paul McDonald, USC's fullback, then fumbled the ball and Jeff Weston of Notre Dame fell on it.

But an official ruled it was not a fumble but an incomplete pass, and USC still had possession of the ball.

Now the Trojans geared up. They passed the ball quickly, got to the Irish twenty-yard line, and then called time.

With the crowd standing and absolutely quiet, USC's Frank Jordan came into the game and calmly kicked a thirty-seven-yard field goal. USC had won a dramatic, last-second, 27–25 victory.

In their fourth appearance at the Cotton Bowl, on January 1, 1979, against an outstanding Houston Cougar squad led by Coach Bill Yeoman, Notre Dame played their finest game of the season to score one of the most unbelievable come-from-behind victories.

An excited Moose Krause, Irish athletic director, said of the game, "This game against Houston beats the Army game of 1932 and it surpasses the win of 1935 against Ohio State. It beats every game we ever played."

The game opened before a sparse crowd of no more than thirty-two-thousand fans. There had been a freezing rain the night before the game, a rainstorm so terrible that it had toppled trees and power wires all over the city of Dallas and made driving and walking hazardous.

But those fans who did brave the elements saw the Irish, determined to prove their ability over the Cougars, quickly jump out to a 12–0 lead in the first period. But just as the Notre Dame fans settled in their seats preparing for an easy victory, the Cougars bared their fangs and struck back.

They completely outplayed and outfought the Irish and scored a touchdown at the end of the first period, two more in the second period, and two more in the third for a commanding 34–12 lead over Notre Dame.

Sportswriters were already preparing to leave the press box for the winners' dressing room when the Irish suddenly struck back.

Quarterback Joe Montana, who had missed part of the second period and all of the third quarter because of below-normal body temperature (he was fed several plates of hot chicken soup to restore his normal body temperature), came back in the fourth period and led the Irish to an amazing finish.

There were but 7:37 to go when freshman reserve fullback Tony Belden, all six feet, three inches of him, blocked a punt by Houston's Jay Wyatt. Steve Cichy, a six-foot-four Irish linebacker, picked up the crazily bouncing ball and thundered thirty-five yards for a score. Notre Dame elected to try for a two-point play, and Montana passed to tailback Vagus Ferguson for those points. The score was now 34–20, Houston.

Houston failed to gain on their possession, and after Wyatt again punted, Montana went to work.

Joe passed three consecutive times—to end Dean Masztak, to Jerome Heavens, and to flanker Pete Holohan. The plays were good for seventeen, thirty-two, and eleven yards, and it was first down for the Irish on the Houston two-yard line. On a bootleg play, Montana swept around his own right end and scored a touchdown, and once again Joe was successful in a two-point pass conversion. Now the score was 34–28, and the fans were hysterical.

Houston gambled on a fourth down and one yard to go, but the Irish defense held, and Notre Dame took over on the Cougars' twenty-nine-yard line. There were twenty-eight seconds left in the game.

Once again Montana took command. He skirted left end for eleven yards and a first down on the eighteen-yard line. A Montana pass to end Kris Haines was good for ten yards.

Now with eight seconds left to play, Montana tried to score with two passes to Kaines, but both missed. With two seconds left in the game, Montana hit Haines for the touchdown.

Now the score was 34–34. And Notre Dame's little Joe Unis kicked the ball right between the uprights for the extra point.

There was no more time remaining. But an official called Notre Dame offside. The Irish were penalized five yards, and Unis had to kick one more.

Unis's kick was good again and Notre Dame had pulled off another miracle victory, 35–34.

In the dressing room after the game, a delighted Father Hesburgh dashed over to Coach Devine, hugged him, and said:

"This is a real Notre Dame victory."

Notre Dame finished the season with a 9–3–0 record, seventh in the Associated Press rating poll.

Bob Golic and Dave Huffman were unanimous All-America selections. Joe Restic, the marvelous place-kicker, won the Academic All-America award and received the prestigious NCAA $2,000 postgraduate award as the top student-athlete of the year.

A KID AND HIS DREAM

If you had submitted the manuscript to Hollywood, it would surely be rejected for being too hokey.

It's all about this kid who grows up in the shadow of the Golden Dome. More than anything else in his life, he wants to attend Notre Dame and play football. But when he applies for admission, he's rejected. His grades are too low.

So he goes to another school, plays ball there, gets three A's and two B's in his subjects, and finally is accepted into Notre Dame.

He goes out for the football team as a "walk-on," which means that he did not get a scholarship. And despite his size, he's five-eight and weighs about 175 pounds—he makes the team as a field-goal kicker.

And a week before the opening game of the 1979 season, the kicker had this dream. He is on the field at Ann Arbor, Michigan, against the University of Michigan, and in his dream he sees himself kicking the winning field goal and over a hundred thousand people are there and the game is on national television and he becomes the big hero.

It didn't happen quite the way Chuck Male dreamed it would.

All Chuck did was kick *four field goals, and his four kicks* were *the only points* for Notre Dame as the Irish eked out a gorgeous 12–10 win over Michigan before over 105,000 fans and millions of television viewers.

And Chuck Male's big dream became a reality.

And he became Notre Dame's big hero that week.

But the following week, against a strong Purdue team, Notre Dame dropped a bitterly fought game by a 28–22 margin.

Purdue's quarterback Mark Herrman played brilliantly and kept the Irish off-balance throughout the game with his unerring pass play.

In their first home game of the season, Notre Dame defeated an aggressive Michigan State eleven, 27–3. Tony Hunter, the Irish six-five end, took a fifteen-yard pass from quarterback Rusty Lisch and scored Notre Dame's first touchdown. Vagus Ferguson continued his magnificent breakaway runs as he dashed for two touchdowns, on runs of twenty-four and forty-eight yards, while Chuck Male kicked two field goals to wrap up the Irish scoring.

Georgia Tech visited South Bend on the rainy

Coach Devine and two of his tri-captains, Dave Waymer (No. 34) and Vagus Ferguson (No. 33), at National Olympic Stadium, Tokyo, in 1979 for game against the University of Miami.

(Left) Notre Dame linebacker Bob Crable (No. 43) leaps onto shoulders of teammates to block a last-second field-goal attempt by Michigan's kicker Bryan Virgil (No. 2). The blocked kick gave the Irish a 12–10 squeaker in the opening game of the 1979 season.

Saturday afternoon of October 6 and took home a 21–13 beating. Notre Dame had a one-point edge in the fourth period before Ferguson dashed for his second touchdown, which gave the Irish the victory.

At the Air Force Academy in Colorado Springs, Notre Dame was so dominant that Coach Devine benched Vagus Ferguson, who had racked up two touchdowns in the first period, as the Irish ran up a 38–13 triumph.

Southern California flew into South Bend and the next day flew back home with an incredible 42–23 trouncing of Notre Dame. Sparked by All-American Charles White, USC simply was too strong for the Irish. White, on his way to the Heisman Trophy that season, splattered the field with Irish bodies as he rushed for four touchdowns and 262 rushing yards. Ferguson ran for seventy-nine yards for Notre Dame in the first period to break the all-time ground-gaining record set by Jerome Heavens.

Next, Navy visited South Bend with a strong attack and a rugged defense but left town quickly on the short end of a 14–0 shutout for their sixteenth consecutive loss to the Irish. The Middies had last defeated Notre Dame in 1961.

One of the largest crowds of the year turned out for a return game against Johnny Majors's Tennessee Volunteers, this time in Tennessee. The crowd was 86,489, and they enjoyed every minute of the game, which saw the Vols rip the Notre Dame line to shreds.

The Volunteers scored on drives of sixty-one, forty-seven, fifty-four, and sixty-six yards the first four times they had the ball. Tennessee led at the half, 30–12. The final score was 40–18 in favor of Tennessee.

Back home in the comforts of South Bend, the Irish played host to their third southern rival in Clemson and received another shock as the Tigers wore them down with a concerted attack in the second half. Notre Dame jumped out to a 10–0 lead on Ferguson's two-yard sprint into the end zone, Male's conversion, followed by a Male field goal. It looked like an Irish walkaway. In the second period, Male missed two field-goal attempts while Rusty Lisch ran for a ten-yard touchdown, then had it called back due to a penalty—and that, according to Devine, "turned the entire game around for us. We lost it right then and there."

Clemson scored on two third-period field goals and a touchdown by quarterback Billy Lott and held Notre Dame in check the rest of the game to eke out a 16–10 upset.

In Tokyo, Japan, on November 24, Notre Dame faced the Miami Hurricanes at National Olympic Stadium and easily defeated the Hurricanes 40–15. Tri-captain Dave Waymer intercepted two Miami passes for touchdowns, while Vagus Ferguson ended his brilliant four-year record-breaking career by dashing for three touchdowns.

Ferguson and Tri-captain Tim Foley were selected on a number of All-America teams, and Coach Dan Devine closed out his fifth season as head coach with a 7–4–0 record.

The wolves who had been after Devine's scalp from day one after his appointment as head coach now broke out in full cry. There were feature stories in the local South Bend paper. In Chicago and across the land, sports broadcasters and writers called for Devine's head, crying for a new coach—*one who would not lose four games a season.*

When Devine took over as head coach following the 1974 season, it was apparent that he was shy, sensitive, moody, and quite often had to fight back tears at disappointments or biting criticism.

"He looks like a college professor, but there's steel inside," explained a former Missouri player.

There was widespread unhappiness and even anger directed at the coach when the Irish barely defeated Boston College in Devine's first game in 1975. After the game, a teary-eyed Devine said, "Such pressure? I wouldn't have taken this job if I thought it was so tough. I thought I'd die until we won this game."

The anti-Devine movement gained ground over the next two seasons as the Irish finished 8–3–0 in 1975 and ended with the same record for the 1976 regular season.

But when Notre Dame defeated a strong Penn State team 20–9 on December 27, 1976, in the Gator Bowl, the wolves' howls momentarily were stilled.

However, in 1977, with an 11–1–0 season and a national championship, Coach Devine seemed headed for a very long run at Notre Dame as the critics melted into the wall.

But 1978 brought another 8–3–0 mark, and when the Irish lost four games in 1979, "Dump Devine" banners appeared all over South Bend, and the wolves now were heard clear and loud.

It was at the regular weekly luncheon of the Notre Dame Quarterback Club that a sullen, moody Dan Devine appeared to say a few words.

Hunched over a plate of uneaten turkey before the speaking began, Devine looked ill at ease. His tie was askew, and his eyes nervously searched the assembled crowd as if he were looking for a friend. Then he arose and began to speak but in a strange, garbled manner.

"I'm kind of at a loss for words," the fifty-five-year-old coach began. "You know this is very hard for me. You know what to say, but . . . ?

"You all know that Joanne, my wife, hasn't been well and . . . it has been very hard for our family . . . all this pressure over the years.

"But first, I thought of saying *sayonara*—that's Japanese. But I'm not going to say *sayonara* because that means 'until we meet again,' and there are a number of guys here I don't care if I ever meet again.

"That first year here was real rough. There were a lot of things said about me then, but if just one person, one player worth anything as a human being had said something critical about me, I think I would have quit. But now, it's been a hard decision.

"I'll be sorry to leave Notre Dame. But this is a decision that I've talked over with my wife, Joanne, and now it's set."

There was a sudden hush around the room. This was not the usual boisterous banter of the regular Quarterback Club lunches. This was different, no laughing matter as the full meaning of Devine's words hit home. Sportswriters and guests finishing their coffee and dessert stopped in midair. And there were those who, having heard the words, did not quite get the true meaning.

Devine went on now slowly, as he looked around the room.

"I've talked this over at great length with Father Hesburgh, and that's that. I am leaving Notre Dame at the end of the season."

The room suddenly was electric with tension as the coach sat down. Not a sound was heard for a full minute.

Then as if on a signal a dozen reporters raced to the phones to break the story of the year. Bedlam broke out as there was a sudden rush to Devine's side. But Dan quickly pushed his way through the crowd and walked over to the locker room to meet with his coaches and players.

Later, in an emotion-packed meeting with the team, Dan repeated much of the same things he had stated at the Quarterback Club. He was tired, there was too much pressure on him and his family, there were too many critics, too many problems.

The next day he was all business as he set about whipping his 1980 team into shape for what would prove to be his greatest season.

Notre Dame had won eight of its past ten games against Purdue, one of their oldest and bitterest rivals, and in the 1980 opening game at South Bend on September 6, before a jam-packed crowd of over fifty-nine-thousand fans, the Irish systematically took Purdue apart in a 31–10 victory.

Michigan was next on the agenda the following week, and a strong Wolverine team coached by Bo Schembechler and led by quarterback John Wangler gave the Irish no quarter. Notre Dame scored twice in the first half on Phil Carter's six-yard smash for a score and Mike Courey's ten-yard pass to Pete Holohan, good for fourteen points.

But the Wolverines came back with two beautiful touchdown passes by Wangler, and the score at half-time was tied, 14–14.

Halfback Tony Carter sent Michigan into the lead in the third quarter with a sixty-seven-yard sprint as the Wolverines surged into the lead by 21–14.

In the third period, Cornerback Johnny Krimm leaped high into the air to intercept a Wangler pass, and then Krimm sent a Notre Dame crowd of over fifty-nine-thousand fans into a frenzy as he scrambled forty-nine yards for another Irish score. Harry Oliver missed the extra point, and Michigan had a 21–20 lead.

With three minutes left to play, flashy Irish half-back, Phil Carter bulled over from the four-yard line, and now Notre Dame was out in front by a 26–21 margin.

Then John Wangler passed to Butch Woolfolk, who tipped the ball, but it was caught by Craig Dunaway, who dove over the line for a Michigan score and a 27–26 lead.

With thirty seconds to play, Devine sent in freshman quarterback Blair Kiel and on the first play Kiel passed to Tony Hunter. Interference was called on the play, and the Irish had the ball on Michigan's forty-eight-yard line. Kiel tried two more passes, both incomplete. But a third one, to Tony Hunter, was good, and Hunter stepped out of bounds on the thirty-five-yard line.

There were four seconds left to play when Devine sent in his left-footed field-goal kicker, Harry Oliver. Oliver's longest field goal had been thirty-eight yards in a JV game. Now he was asked to kick a fifty-one-yard field goal against a stiff fifteen-mile-per-hour wind.

Calmly Oliver stepped into the ball and kicked his way into Notre Dame's Hall of Fame with a fifty-one-yard kick straight as an arrow over the crossbar—just as the final gun sounded for the end of the game and a Notre Dame victory, 29–27.

In the joyous locker-room celebration, Father Hesburgh addressed the team:

"I told you fellows in practice that you're part of the ongoing history here. Today you wrote a great chapter. You did what everybody said was impossible."

Two weeks later, Michigan State was beaten in another tight, hard-fought battle, but the Irish simply outfought the Spartans to win by a 26–21 margin. Then Miami was easily trounced, 32–14; Army was destroyed, 30–3; Arizona was defeated, 20–3; and Navy was shut out, 33–0.

Notre Dame ranked number one nationally, charged into Georgia intent on adding the Georgia Tech team to its string of victories. Perhaps the Irish, inflated with their top ranking and wins over the leading teams in the nation and with seven straight victories, were over confident against Tech; and perhaps, with reason, for Tech had won only one game while losing seven. At any rate, the Yellow Jackets played their best game of the year and at halftime led the Irish 3–0 via a thirty-nine-yard field goal by Jim Smith. In the final period of a very tough game, Notre Dame finally got a forty-seven-yard field goal by Harry Oliver and wound up with a 3–3 tie.

"We almost got beat by a football team that was better coached than ours," said Dan Devine. "We were very lucky this time."

At Tuscaloosa the following week, students and more than seventy-eight-thousand Alabama fans derided Notre Dame's national ranking. This was going to be Alabama's year. On the campus were signs and banners saying, "Notre Dame . . . Notre Who?" Parades and floats whipped the students into a frenzy, and by game time the excitement rippled in the air.

The game matched two of the nations finest coaches: Bear Bryant, Alabama's greatest coach and one of the nation's greatest strategists, and Dan Devine, second highest winner among active coaches.

As the game began, both teams crashed and slashed at each other like packs of snarling tigers. The blocking and tackling were so savage that the sounds of hurtling bodies crashing into each other could be heard throughout the stadium.

Notre Dame's quarterback Blair Kiel moved the ball on a series of short, effective passes and short, savage bursts through the line but then fumbled the ball on the 'Bama one-yard line. Alabama recovered the ball, but on a subsequent play also fumbled, and Notre Dame's fine tackle Scott Zettuck recovered on the Crimson Tide four-yard line. Two plays later, Irish halfback Phil Carter, burst through for Notre Dame's first score. The extra-point conversion was good, and Notre Dame had a 7–0 lead.

For the next three quarters the game turned into a defensive struggle, with neither team having the advantage. Twice Blair Kiel punted on third down to make certain he would not fumble and lose position on the field.

In the final quarter Notre Dame moved the ball to the Alabama one-yard line and then Devine sent in his ace field-goal kicker, Harry Oliver. As Oliver kicked the ball, an Alabama player tore in, blocked the kick, and the Irish scoring threat was gone.

The game ended with no further scoring opportunities for either team, and Notre Dame had its eighth victory of the year by a 7–0 score.

Talking to the press after the game, Bear Bryant said: "Dan Devine had Notre Dame prepared. He did a much better job for this game than I did."

Devine talked with reporters and said that he had accepted an invitation to play Georgia in the Sugar Bowl on January 1.

A week later, with the South Bend campus exhorting the Irish to victory over USC and Georgia,

Notre Dame had to contend with a fired-up Air Force team, and a spirited group of Falcons held the Irish even for two periods. But Notre Dame's offense was too powerful and they defeated Air Force, 24–10.

It was almost impossible to think about Southern California when undefeated Georgia loomed just ahead in the Sugar Bowl, but the Irish's next opponent and last on the regular schedule was USC. And it was a ragged, spiritless Notre Dame team facing the challenge of USC at Los Angeles before a mob of more than eighty-two-thousand, and USC took every advantage, jumping into a 10–0 lead over the Irish at halftime. Notre Dame's play was ragged and uninspired until well into the third period, when Harry Oliver kicked a field goal from the thirty-yard line for Notre Dame's only score of the game as the Trojans pounded out a 20–3 upset over the Irish.

In the locker room after the game, players were sobbing over their poor performances. "We have a winning attitude at Notre Dame," said Phil Carter. "A loss is hard to take."

On January 1, at the Sugar Bowl in New Orleans, undefeated Georgia, with twelve consecutive victories and the great Herschel Walker, their one-man team, ganged up on Dan Devine and the Irish to win a hard-fought battle, 17–10, before a crowd of more than seventy-seven thousand.

What the Bulldogs did, and better than any team Notre Dame faced all season long, was take advantage of Irish mistakes. The most glaring one occurred late in the first quarter with the score tied at 3–3. Rex Robinson's kickoff sailed high and deep. Jim Stone, one of the Notre Dame deep backs, called for Ty Barber, the other deep back, to take the ball. Barber failed to hear him because of the crowd noise, and when he saw Stone moving over to block, assumed Stone was going to take the ball. The ball bounced between them inside the ten-yard line, and Bob Kelly of Georgia fell on the ball. Two plays and Walker dived into the end zone for a touchdown.

A fumble by John Sweeney was recovered by Georgia's Pat McShea on the Irish twenty-two, and then once again Herschel Walker drove in for the touchdown.

Late in the third period, after repeated scoring threats were stopped by a stubborn Georgia defense, Notre Dame rallied, and Tony Hunter leaped into the air to snatch a pass from Blair Kiel for a touchdown. But officials ruled that Kiel's pass was barely out of bounds, and the score was not allowed.

Once again Kiel led a march toward the Bulldogs'

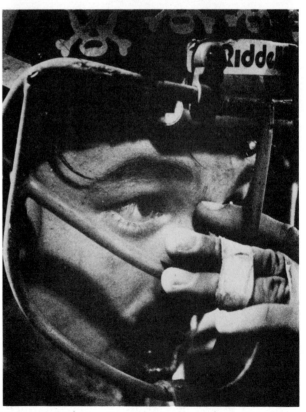

(Top) Coach Devine discusses defensive moves to stop Georgia's great back Herschel Walker in the 1981 Sugar Bowl.

(Above) Bob Crable was a tower of strength on the Irish defensive team in 1980 and 1981, when he was named to All-American Teams.

goal line and tossed a beautiful pass to Pete Holohan, all alone on the two-yard line. But just as Pete was set to catch the ball and go in for a touchdown, Scott Woerner tipped the ball from his hands.

The third time Notre Dame marched downfield, they were not to be denied as Phil Carter and Kiel moved the ball in ten smashing plays for a touchdown. Now the score was 17–10 at the end of the third period.

The Irish, in a determined bid to score once more, marched downfield into Georgia territory. Then a desperate pass, Kiel to Dean Masztak, that had touchdown written all over the ball, was intercepted by pesky Scott Woerner, and Notre Dame's last hope went glimmering as the game ended shortly thereafter.

The Georgia game marked the final one, for Dan Devine as Notre Dame's head coach. His performance in the 1980 season won praise from even his staunchest critics, the sportswriters. He guided a young, inexperienced, injury-riddled team not picked to finish in the top ten in any of the preseason polls to a near-perfect record.

His career at Notre Dame produced six winning seasons, three Bowl victories, and one national championship. But he had never been fully accepted by the alumni, by the press, and by his own players.

The biggest question mark, however, is how Devine will be remembered at Notre Dame. He had many shortcomings; a moody, introspective loner, he made few friends and numerous enemies among some of the more powerful sportswriters, and in his first season an entire group of players threatened to quit the team to go to another school. He could hardly be elevated to the realm of a Rockne, a Leahy, or a Parseghian. But his record is much too good to put him in the mere mortal level of Kuharich, Devore, and Brennan. For now at least, his legacy will be uncertain.

CHAPTER 10

GERRY FAUST: HEAD COACH
(1981–85)

The man chosen to replace Dan Devine as Notre Dame's head coach in 1981, Gerry Faust, was as different from his predecessor as Devine was from Ara Parseghian.

Dan Devine was a modest, quiet, introverted, moody individual, suspicious of people. Gerry Faust was a bouncy, aggressive, outgoing, friendly person. Devine was not a challenging or inspiring speaker; Gerry Faust could mesmerize an audience and command their attention.

This was not to suggest that Gerry Faust was perfect. He did lose seventeen games in eighteen years before coming to Notre Dame. His clothes were always hopelessly out of shape. And he wasn't a good enough quarterback at Chaminade High School in Dayton, where his dad was the head coach, to get a scholarship to Notre Dame, which he desperately wanted. So he ended up playing for a former Notre Dame coach, Hugh Devore, at the University of Dayton, but he says he learned his coaching philosophy—"discipline with compassion"—from his father.

"He was real rough on me," said Gerry. "He didn't want the other kids on the team to think I was playing because I was his son. He really made me make the team."

At Cincinnati's Moeller High School in a career that covered an eighteen-year period, Faust's teams won 174 games, lost seventeen, and tied two. It was a remarkable record.

He was just about the greatest high-school coach in the nation, and when his players graduated from Moeller, a number of them received Notre Dame scholarships and performed very well.

At the time of Faust's signing, the Reverend Edmund Joyce, vice-president and chairman of the Notre Dame Athletic Board, and the man mainly respon-

sible for hiring Faust, said, "Certainly we don't expect Faust to duplicate his high-school record."

But Gerry Faust never even came close at Notre Dame during his five years, struggling through a horrible first year as he won five and lost six games in 1981; he was 6–4–1 in 1982, 7–5–0 in 1983, and 6–6–0 in 1984. In 1985 he ended his tenure with a 5–6–0 season. Faust's five-year totals are thirty wins, twenty-six defeats, and one tie.

Faust was the Notre Dame coach with the most losses. Joe Kuharich is next, with twenty-three losses (from 1959 to 1962).

Instead of reaching the Cotton, Orange, or Sugar bowls, Notre Dame under Gerry Faust backed into such games as the Liberty Bowl and the Aloha Bowl during his five seasons.

"It's been frustrating to both players and coaches not to finish with a better record the past five seasons," said Faust. "But I've always had a philosophy that there's a reason for everything."

Gerry Faust's roller-coaster rookie season in 1981 opened on a tremendously high note with a sensational 27–9 win over a highly rated Louisiana State team. It was a victory that elevated Notre Dame to number one in the national ratings and the forty-nine-year-old coach to a level just below sainthood on the Irish campus.

Faust utilized the services of every able-bodied man on his squad. Seventy Irish players completely overwhelmed the favored Fighting Tiger eleven.

But on September 19, the Wolverines of Michigan outplayed and outmaneuvered Notre Dame before a crowd of more than 105,000 at Ann Arbor and handed the Irish a sound 25–7 defeat. The following week Purdue played host to the Irish squad, and the Boilermakers eked out a last-minute 15–14 squeaker that shocked the Irish and their coach. It was a game they thought they had won. One week later, Michigan State rolled into South Bend intent on scoring revenge. Notre Dame had won the last five games against State, but this time the Spartans were ready for the Irish—or so they thought.

Gerry Faust rallied his troops, led by Irish quarterback Blair Kiel who passed often enough to halfback Phil Carter and end Tony Hunter for three touchdowns and a surprising 20–7 win over Michigan State. The following week Florida State rolled into South Bend with a fine team and came away with a last-period score to win a close battle, 19–13. Now it was time on October 24 for the annual battle with USC, a team that had defeated Notre Dame in the previous three seasons. This day the Trojans made it four in a row as they beat the Irish 14–7 in a hard-fought game at South Bend.

Somehow Gerry Faust rallied his oft-beaten team and they easily defeated a tough Navy eleven by a 38–0 score. Then on the following weeks, Georgia Tech was beaten 35–3, and Air Force succumbed by 35–7, and things looked brighter and cheerier for Faust and his beleaguered Irish, who now were looking at a 5–4–0 season with Penn State and Miami left to play.

But the magic performed by Faust had vanished for the final games. Penn State took a squeaker 24–21, and Miami easily defeated the Irish at the Orange Bowl Stadium by a 37–15 score.

The six losses in 1981 matched the total number of defeats Faust had endured in his last ten seasons at Moeller High. Nonetheless, his tireless efforts, his never-say-die spirit, and his great enthusiasm won him friends and began to pay off as the Irish roared to victories in the first four games of the 1982 season. But then a series of crippling injuries to key players resulted in a disappointing 6–4–1 season in 1982.

Four of Notre Dame's five losses in 1983 were to teams that earned bowl invitations: Miami to the Orange Bowl, Pitt to the Fiesta Bowl, Penn State to the Aloha Bowl, and Air Force to the Independence Bowl—and four of the five defeats suffered by the Irish were by a total of fifteen points.

A series of damaging injuries and three consecutive losses before the home folks at South Bend in the middle of the 1984 season left the Irish with a 3–4–0 record, and "Fire Faust" cards and bumper stickers began to appear all over the campus.

But Faust rallied his battered troops, and Notre Dame defeated the highly rated Penn State and four-

(Top) In 1957 Gerry Faust was a flashy Dayton University quarterback.

(Above) Twenty-four years later he was head coach at Notre Dame on the sidelines in his first game of the 1981 season, against LSU.

teenth-rated USC to finish the regular season with a flourish and four straight victories. The Irish compiled a 7–5–0 mark for the complete season.

"It's bound to turn and get better," said Faust.

Yet for years it had been mostly the leaves that had turned during autumn on the Notre Dame campus. The victories had been special occasions, like anniversaries. Almost every win is proclaimed a turning point by the coach. But Faust detractors, by now all over the country in growing numbers, began to think of them as reprieves.

Moose Krause, Notre Dame's athletic director for more than thirty-five years, a former Irish All-American in football and basketball and known all over America as "Mr. Notre Dame," retired in 1981, and Gene Corrigan, one of the nation's leading athletic directors, was named to the post.

Corrigan had served as director of athletics at the University of Virginia for nine years and during that tenure had developed one of the nation's leading sports programs.

Assessing Gerry Faust, Corrigan said, "Gerry is the most positive thinker in the world. He has so much faith and he will have faith to the end. But when you don't win ball games here at Notre Dame, it affects the entire university."

Gene Corrigan, named director of athletics in 1981, succeeding Moose Krause, who retired.

Corrigan and Faust were neighbors and still are good friends. But it was Corrigan who would be given the job of persuading Faust to resign.

Judgment Day arrived at the start of the 1985 season, in the opinion of numerous sports experts, students, and alumni who became increasingly impatient with the likable coach.

"I think he has put up a good front and concealed his feelings very well," said Ara Parseghian, whose Notre Dame teams compiled a 95–17–4 record in his eleven years as head coach and who now resides in South Bend. (Ara has a busy insurance office and is an outstanding sports commentator for NBC-TV during the football season.)

"I really feel sorry for Gerry," said Ara, "but if I were in Gerry's position, I don't know if I would want to go through all this again. I feel strongly that I would not want to continue."

In 1985 Gerry Faust had a number of outstanding veterans returning. They included Allen Pinkett, Notre Dame's all-time leader in rushing; three-year veteran quarterback Steve Beuerlein, who as a freshman put up the most impressive passing record of any Notre Dame quarterback; Wally Kleine, a six-nine, 275-pound potential All-America tackle; Tony Furjanic, another potential All-American, at linebacker; six-five, 257-pound tackle Greg Dingens; and Eric Dorsey, a six-five, 270-pound tackle. There also were a number of juniors and sophomores with varsity experience, and Notre Dame had high hopes for a return to a national rating in 1985.

But Michigan extinguished those hopes with a one-sided 20–12 beating at Ann Arbor. Michigan State was beaten 27–10, and just when everybody's hopes—including Gerry Faust's—were looking up, Purdue simply ran the Irish ragged, defeating them 35–17.

The following week Air Force compounded that feeling as they upset the Irish, 21–15, and with four games already played, Notre Dame had won but one and lost three.

But four marvelous wins—over Army, USC, Navy, and Mississippi—gave Faust the best record of his five years as coach at Notre Dame. The Irish had a 5–3–0 record with three tough games left to play.

If Faust took all three games, he would have an 8–3–0 season, and it would be a cinch for him to stay on for another year or two.

But Notre Dame lost all three games.

Penn State thoroughly defeated the Irish, 36–6.

Louisiana State eked out a 10–7 win.

Notre Dame's All-America halfback Allen Pinkett (with ball) smashes through the Purdue line and scores in 1984 game.

And Miami University simply ran Notre Dame into the turf in Orange Bowl Stadium with a devastating 58–7 rout.

On November 26, at a hastily called press conference at South Bend, Gerry Faust announced his resignation as Notre Dame's football coach.

"It's best for me to resign now," he said, "in order to give the university an opportunity to get another coach before recruiting starts next week. It's best for the university, best for me, best for my family."

CHAPTER 11

LOU HOLTZ: A NEW ERA BEGINS (1986)

Coach Gerry Faust resigned on the morning of November 26. That afternoon, at about one-thirty, Athletic Director Gene Corrigan placed a call to Coach Lou Holtz at the University of Minnesota.

Holtz had arrived at Minnesota in 1984 after the football fortunes of the once-mighty Minnesota Gophers had fallen to a new low—the football team had not had a winning season in five years, and interest and attendance at football games had reached an all-time nadir. Within two seasons Holtz had completely revitalized and rebuilt the Gophers into a competitive eleven. In 1985 Minnesota won six games and received an invitation to play Clemson in the Independence Bowl.

Suddenly," said Holtz, "sportswriters from all over the country were calling me asking about the Notre Dame job, but I had never heard from them, never talked to anyone at Notre Dame. Then Gene Corrigan called me and said: 'Coach, I don't know if you know it or not, but Gerry Faust has resigned.'

"That was the first I heard from Notre Dame," said Holtz.

"There were a number of reasons why I wanted Lou Holtz as our coach," said Corrigan. "I had been the assistant commissioner of the Atlantic Coast Conference and I was very familiar with Lou's work at William & Mary and particularly at North Carolina State, where he was most successful. I knew and liked Lou's approach to college football and the fact that he had been successful wherever he had coached. Lou had been exposed to the pressures of college football and always handled it well. He is a Rockne sort of a guy. He's glib, clever, and he can recruit and motivate."

"During that first phone call," said Holtz, "Corrigan went over the admissions requirements. He went over the tough schedule, the academics, and after listening to him I asked him a couple of questions and then told him I would be interested in the job at Notre Dame.

"Then Corrigan said he would have Father Joyce call me. Father Joyce was head of the faculty board in charge of athletics.

"Father Joyce called me," said Lou, "and we talked at length, and the next morning I basically made the decision to take the Notre Dame position."

The following day, Holtz conferred with several members of the administration, including the admissions board at Notre Dame; received a reluctant release from his Minnesota contract, which had three more years to run; and then signed a four-year contract with Notre Dame.

As far as Lou Holtz was concerned, the whole slice of life for him was a used Chevrolet and a cushy job in the local steel mill when the miracle of miracles happened: He graduated from high school in 1955. He was number 234 academically in a class that graduated 278 students in East Liverpool, Ohio.

"I looked around town, and what I saw looked pretty good to me," he said. "The fellows my age or a bit older had a car, $5 in their pockets, a girl at their side, and a hamburger in their hand. What more could you want in those days?"

"You, boy, will go to college," said Mother Holtz, "and no matter that it must be a state college, because no school with a right of refusal would have you on its grounds for any reason other than to cut grass or to push a broom."

Thus Lou Holtz, now one of the finest of all college football coaches, the head coach at Notre Dame, trudged off to Kent State.

But not without one last plea for a slice of the good life in East Liverpool.

"I worked the summer before I entered Kent," said

Holtz, "and saved $400. Once again I begged my folks to please allow me to work in the mill and use the money for the Chevvy. But their minds were made up. It was Kent State for me."

And it is astonishing—this story of this very ordinary kid who never had a date in high school. This kid who was just a mediocre high-school football player on his good days, this kid who had to find his way through life without the benefit of a used Chevrolet has become one of the shrewdest, most calculating, crafty, efficient, witty, and one of the winningest college football coaches and certainly one of the most likable in the entire sports world.

And on November 27, 1985, likable Lou Holtz jumped into the most pressure-packed job in all of college football when he accepted the post of head coach at Notre Dame.

As part of his public introduction at Notre Dame, Lou Holtz said, "I hope that I can display the same kind of integrity and strong feelings that Gerry Faust did here for five years. But I want to tell all you folks gathered here for this press meeting, I'm not a miracle worker. I'm not a genius. I wasn't a great athlete. I'm not very impressive. I'm not very smart. Some people are debonair, suave, or great athletes, and their alma matters are maybe going to take them back. My alma mater wouldn't even hire me.

"While we do have a lot of fine athletes here at Notre Dame, other schools have as fine a group as we have here. People expect a minor miracle every Saturday and a major one now and then. You and I both know this is going to be a long, uphill struggle at Notre Dame. But I do believe we are mentally prepared to approach it with an optimistic attitude.

"I'm not looking at Knute Rockne's record," said Holtz, "or Frank Leahy's record or Ara Parseghian's record. I took one look at them and thought it was a misprint. I just want to do the very best I can and in so doing hope to add to the glory and magnificent traditions of Notre Dame."

Gene Corrigan, the athletic director who chose Holtz over seven other candidates, said that he had been told Holtz had exhibited a lower profile in recent

(Left) He dreamed about George Gipp and the Four Horsemen, but never in his most cherished dream did he ever think he would follow in the footsteps of Knute Rockne, Frank Leahy, and Ara Parseghian. But twenty-nine years later, in 1985, Lou Holtz was named head coach.

(Above, left) In 1957 Lou Holtz was a scrappy, aggressive linebacker for Kent State University (he was some forty pounds heavier than he is today).

years. Corrigan said it was important for Holtz to understand procedures that differ from life at state universities with athletic dorms for the players.

"I tried to explain the place to Lou," Corrigan said. "The most important things to understand here is that all our students live together, there is no athletic dorm; they stand in line for their courses and stand in line for their meals, and football players are no different. There is no favoritism here. The players are part of our student body."

Within seventy-two hours of his arrival on the campus, Holtz had found the issue that would help determine his success; the conflict that faces any football coach at Notre Dame is that the amount of time necessary to satisfy the demands off the field can prevent the coach from contributing to the effort to satisfy demands on the field.

Holtz talked at length with Faust and Ara Parseghian, and the two former coaches conveyed the same message: The demands at Notre Dame are difficult to comprehend.

"They said it's impossible to really play a prominent role in the actual coaching of football, that you're involved doing so many things," Holtz said. "I say that cannot happen. That just can't happen."

To Lou Holtz, a football coach has to coach football.

"That's the thing that's an absolute necessity and I enjoy that most. I say all the other activities—the banquets, speeches, appearances on TV, the public-relations stuff—just cannot take up my time."

Holtz had had sixteen years of coaching at places such as William & Mary, North Carolina State, and Arkansas, where his teams had a record of 60–21–2 in seven seasons, including six straight bowl appearances after he arrived. Four of Holtz's Arkansas teams finished in the top ten in the nation, and in his first year at Arkansas, he led the Razorbacks to an astonishing 11–1 season and was selected as coach of the year for 1977.

It was during the 1977 season that Holtz's actions caught the eye of the Reverend Edmund Joyce. A few days before the Arkansas-Oklahoma Orange Bowl game, three star Arkansas players were discovered in a dormitory with a female student. Holtz immediately suspended his stars and refused to budge when some team members threatened a boycott of the Orange Bowl contest. The Razorbacks then went out and crushed the strong Oklahoma eleven, 31–6, without the suspended players.

"I was tremendously impressed with the way Holtz stood up for what he thought was right and then kept his team united and then went out and won the big game of the year," said Joyce.

During his first two weeks at South Bend, Holtz, in a frenzy of activity before the Christmas holidays, hired a staff of ten assistant coaches, raced to Chicago to address more than fifteen hundred cheering members of the Alumni Association, visited half a dozen potential recruits in the Chicago area, held five press conferences, appeared on not less than fifteen national and local sports TV shows, signed contracts for a twice-weekly radio and TV program, met with his coaches to plan and to install a completely new offense and defense for the Irish, and talked with individual team members and the entire varsity squad.

At the first team meeting Holtz cracked down on the entire squad. He walked to the center of the room in front of the slouching, carelessly dressed players; "I don't want to see any of you prop your feet on the stage like you did this morning. If you're tired, well, then go on home. From now on," he said, "when a coach enters a room, I want you to sit up and pay attention.

"This has been a football team that has forgotten the basics," said Lou. "We have to get back to blocking and tackling. We will take nothing for granted.

"We have to be stronger and quicker," said Lou. "I just found out that only four of you fellows can bench-press four hundred pounds. Well, from today on I want every man to be in the training room and work on those weights. And I'm going to test you if I have to do it myself. Each of you has got to be able to press at least four hundred pounds—or else.

"When we're traveling, I want every man with a coat and tie. This is Notre Dame, and you men represent this great university, and I want you to be proud of that."

In an interview with sportswriter Terry Shore, Holtz said, "How good a football team will we be? I don't know the answer to that. All I know is that we've lost a number of quality players, like Allen Pinkett, who broke just about every Notre Dame rushing record. You can't replace him. Then we've lost Tim Scannell, center Ron Plantz, two fine tackles in Mike Perrino and Tom Doerger and Eric Dorsey and Tony Furjanic.

"Our goal is to move the ball, and in Timmy Brown, we have one of the fastest men in college ball today and one of the most intelligent players I've ever known. If we can get the ball to Timmy, I'll guarantee we're going to move the ball. The quarterback situation, with Steve Beuerlein and Terry Andrysiak, is a

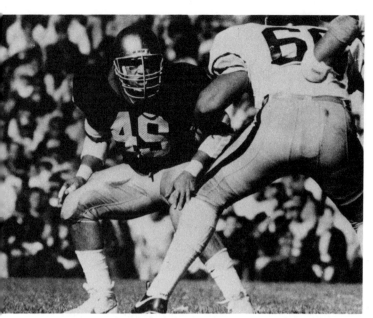

A standout tackle for four years and captain of the 1986 Irish, linebacker Mike Kovaleski will be missed in 1987.

(Above, right) A tense moment in the opening game of the

1986 season against Michigan as Coach Lou Holtz signals for quarterback Steve Beuerlein. Watching the play are Irish players Kurt Zackrison (No. 35), Wally Kleine (No. 96), and Ron Weissenhofer (No. 36) on the sidelines.

key to our future. We've got to get quality performances from one or both of those players. Bobby Banks, Alvin Miller, Mark Green, and Mike Kovaleski all look pretty good. But we'll have to get some support from some of the freshmen this year.

"One reason I would like to have a successful season in 1986," Holtz said, "is because of the seniors on the team. They came here four years ago expecting some big things that just haven't materialized. I would like to have their final year worth remembering.

"We'll be a solid team when we face Michigan next week," said Holtz. "Our objective is to regain respect and to be competitive."

"Competitive" was hardly the word to describe the game against Michigan that marked the beginning of the Lou Holtz Era at Notre Dame on September 13.

In a torrid, tense battle against the nation's number-three football team, the unranked Fighting Irish piled up 455 yards and twenty-seven first downs. They converted eight of twelve third-down situations and lost a 24–23 heartbreaker in one of the most pulsating, come-from-behind surges in recent Irish history, and they came within a single point of toppling the highly ranked Wolverines, losing the game only because Irish kicker John Carney missed an extra-point conversion and then with thirteen seconds remaining missed a forty-five-yard field-goal attempt.

At the end of a gripping afternoon, after Carney's

missed field goal, Lou Holtz strode to his kicker, held up his right hand, and repeatedly bent his index finger toward his face.

Holtz held Carney's head in the crook of his left elbow and patted his helmet with his right hand.

"I told Carney that he's made some great kicks in the past, and he'll make some great ones in the future," Holtz said. "He shouldn't feel too bad at all about it."

The same thought applied to his Irish eleven.

"I think the fight is back at Notre Dame," said Bobby Banks, the senior tackle, who played a marvelous game and made twelve tackles.

"It may very well have been the *best game Notre Dame ever played that it did not win*," said noted *New York Times* sports columnist Dave Anderson in his column.

As the game ended, Notre Dame students saluted the start of the Holtz era with a standing ovation for the new coach, not that it satisfied him.

"Notre Dame," said Lou Holtz, "doesn't have moral victories."

One week later, at East Lansing, Lou Holtz still was looking for his first victory at Notre Dame as the Irish dropped their second straight game in a hard-fought battle against Michigan State University by a 20–15 score. The game marked the twentieth anniversary of the famous 1966 10–10 tie between Notre Dame and Michigan State.

(Top) In 1983 Steve Beuerlein posted the most impressive passing statistics of any freshman quarterback in Irish history. A sophomore star but injured during a good part of his junior year, Steve became the all-time Irish passing star in his last season, 1986.

(Above) A second-team All-America selection in 1985 and 1986, six-foot, three-inch, 235-pound linebacker Cedric Figaro will be one of Lou Holtz's mainstays in 1987.

But this day in 1986 the game featured Todd Krumm, State's slow-moving but fast-thinking quarterback, who twice intercepted Steve Beuerlein's passes—once for a forty-four-yard touchdown runback, and once, with one minute, twenty-six seconds left in the game, to end the Irish's final chance.

The Spartans shut down Notre Dame's running attack and therefore were able to sit back to wait for and stop Beuerlein's passing.

John Carney, Notre Dame's field-goal ace, booted the Irish to a 3–0 lead in the first period, and it appeared that the aggressive play of Beuerlein and Timmy Brown would turn the tables on Michigan State. But Krumm's second score came when Beuerlein was forced to hurry his pass and the ball intended for Brown was short. Krumm dashed in, picked off the ball, and raced in for a State touchdown.

Krumm produced another smart play on a pop-up kickoff by the Irish after Beuerlein had connected with Brown for an Irish score that cut the Spartans' lead to 13–9 late in the third period. Krumm signaled for a fair catch but was hit as he attempted to catch the ball. The Irish were penalized fifteen yards for the personal foul, which brought the ball to the State thirty-five-yard line. A few plays later Dave Yarema connected on a long pass to Mark Ingraham to give the Spartans a 20–9 lead.

Notre Dame scored late in the fourth period when Beuerlein passed to Joel Williams to bring the Irish to within five points, but there was no further scoring.

The following week, Coach Lee Burtnett brought a flashy, pass-oriented Purdue team headed by six-four freshman passing sensation Jeff George to South Bend for its annual battle against the Irish. But Notre Dame smothered George's passing attack under an avalanche of their own and buried the Boilermakers with a devastating attack that brought them six touchdowns and a 41–9 triumph—the first victory for Lou Holtz and the Irish in 1986.

The turning point in the game came late in the first period. With Notre Dame holding a modest 7–0 lead, the Boilermakers twice fumbled the ball, and Notre Dame quickly turned the errors into ten points for a commanding 17–0 lead.

"The important thing in this game," said Holtz, "was that our quarterbacks didn't make any turnovers. I wanted to give my players—all of them—an opportunity to play, and I'm glad we had the opportunity. Skip Holtz, the coach's son, even carried the ball for the first time.

"It's good to win, I'm happy for the players," said

a smiling Lou Holtz. "I didn't doubt that we'd get a win eventually."

The Irish traveled to Birmingham, Alabama, on October 4 for their fourth game of the season, against the Crimson Tide, who were unbeaten and ranked number two nationally, behind the University of Miami. Alabama had lost all four previous games against Notre Dame, including two in bowl games by frustratingly close scores, and were primed for the Irish.

Alabama Coach Ray Perkins, former head coach of the New York Giants, had brought his Crimson Tide eleven along carefully for the all-important game against the Irish, and they were intent on protecting their undefeated season.

All the Crimson Tide really needed on this day, when the temperature on the artificial turf at Legion Field neared the hundred-degree mark, were two big early scoring plays. And they got them.

Alabama's big plays of the game were a sixty-six-yard kick return by Greg Richardson and a fifty-one-yard touchdown pass by Mike Shula for a quick 14–0 lead. Notre Dame never seemed to be in the ball game from that time on before a crowd of more than seventy-nine thousand rabid Alabama fans.

The Irish, still trying to establish a new look under Coach Holtz, played as if they had left back in South Bend all of the spirit and drive they had exhibited in their first three games, for they could do very little against the hard-charging Tide defense.

Alabama's Connie Bennett, an outside linebacker, was all over Irish passer Steve Beuerlein. In the very first period, Bennett drove in from his position and blind-sided Beuerlein with a bone-crushing tackle that nearly crushed him. Later it was found that Steve had suffered a concussion after that smash, and though he reentered the game several times, his passing game was not up to par, and Terry Andrysiak alternated with him without success.

The Irish scored their only touchdown of the game in the second period, when Shula fumbled and Notre Dame recovered the ball. Three plays later, Beuerlein tossed a bullet pass to Tim Brown, and the speedy junior from Dallas, who had played spectacularly in the three previous games, dashed fifteen yards for the score. Notre Dame added a field goal by John Carney on the final play of the first half to trail, 21–10, at halftime. But that was all the scoring for Notre Dame for the afternoon.

"One thing I'll say," said Steve Beuerlein, "that Alabama pass rush gave me fits all afternoon. And that Bennett gave me some pretty good whacks today. Their pass rush was incredible."

The following week a big, beefy Pitt eleven, with a line that averaged nearly 250 pounds per man and spearheaded by a six-foot, three-inch, 260-pound fullback, Craig Heyward, and a fine quarterback in John Congemi, roared into Knute Rockne Memorial Stadium and just managed to squeak by with a one-point victory.

Pitt's only touchdown came on a one-yard quarterback sneak by Congemi in the third period.

Lady Luck once more turned her back on a Notre Dame team that failed to score a single touchdown, yet by virtue of three field goals by John Carney, the Irish managed to hold a 9–7 lead over the Panthers as the game neared its final moments.

There were 1:29 left to play when Pitt's Dave DiTommaso blocked an Irish punt and Pitt managed to wrest possession of the ball from the Irish on the Notre Dame thirty-four-yard line. Jeff Van Horne, Pitt's kicker, entered the game and calmly sent the

"If we can get the ball to Tim Brown," said Coach Holtz, "we will move the ball." And in every one of the eleven games in 1986, Brown broke away for sensational runs. At the end of the season Tim Brown was named to the All-America team and will be a viable candidate for the Heisman Trophy in 1987.

ball squarely between the goalposts for three points and a 10–9 lead.

One minute later, with just twenty-three seconds remaining, Carney tried a forty-four-yard field goal . . . but missed as the game ended, allowing the Panthers to escape with a 10–9 victory.

An outstanding Air Force team, which already had put together five victories in the short season, rolled into South Bend on October 18, heavy favorites to defeat a Notre Dame eleven that had lost four of five games. Instead of another defeat, the Fighting Irish played their best game of the year and routed the number-eleven-ranked Falcons. Notre Dame stunned Air Force with a touchdown in the first minute of the game, then followed with three more touchdowns and left the bewildered Falcons reeling under a 31–3 beating.

As the game opened, Air Force kicked to Tim Brown. It was a long and high kick, and Brown took the ball on the five-yard line and cut up the right sidelines. Momentarily trapped by a horde of Cadet tacklers, Timmy reversed his field, burst through one tackle, and suddenly he was in the clear, all alone, as he sprinted downfield for a remarkable ninety-five-yard touchdown run that gave the Irish a tremendous lift toward their 31–3 victory.

Brown, a six-foot, 195-pound speedster from Woodrow Wilson High in Dallas, sparkled as the leading player on the 1984 Irish freshman team, earned additional honors as the ESPN player of 1985, and in 1986 displayed the elusiveness, speed, and ability to win All-America honors and serious consideration for the Heisman Trophy in 1987.

A two-week respite from the football wars certainly did no harm to the Irish warriors as they roared into Baltimore to battle Navy on November 1.

Quarterback Steve Beuerlein became Notre Dame's career total offense leader as he passed for two touchdowns. Fullback Parnell Taylor added two more rushing touchdowns as the Irish posted their twenty-third consecutive victory over Navy in the nation's longest continuous intersectional rivalry, by a 33–14 score. The Irish lead in the series against the Midshipmen, winning fifty games while Navy has won nine, with one tie in the sixty games between the two rivals.

Beuerlein completed sixteen of twenty-two passes for 248 yards, including seven completions to remarkable Tim Brown for 184 yards. One of the passes to Brown was good for seventy-seven yards as Timmy once more was sensational with his broken-field running each time he caught the ball.

Notre Dame jumped off to a runaway 28–0 lead at the half and it looked as if Navy was in for a tremendous blowout, but just as suddenly, the Irish offense dried up and they scored just five points in the entire second half as Coach Holtz played just about everyone who suited up for the game.

Southern Methodist jetted into South Bend with a strong eleven and a 5–3 record on October 8 but ran into a Notre Dame eleven hungry for another victory after the two sensational wins over Air Force and Navy.

On this particular day, the "luck of the Irish," which had played hide-and-seek with Notre Dame football fortunes all season long, finally came home to roost, for every play the Irish offense tried was successful and they smothered the gallant Mustangs in a 61–29 rout.

Timmy Brown, Notre Dame's outstanding back, scored two touchdowns, including a spectacular eighty-four-yard reception for a score. He rolled up a total of 235 yards rushing as he continuously broke through and around would-be-tacklers, leaving behind a horde of Mustang players. He was a constant threat on offense and a crowd of fifty-nine thousand partisan Irish rooters thundered his name as Coach Lou Holtz removed him from the game in the fourth quarter.

Quarterback Steve Beuerlein was the masterful Notre Dame field general as he directed the Irish attack in one of his finest games in four seasons. Steve passed for a career high 269 yards as the Notre Dame offense rushed for 322 yards and a total of six touchdowns, recording their top point production since 1977, when the Irish drubbed Georgia Tech, 69–14.

The Irish point total was the most allowed by an SMU team since 1916, when the Mustangs dropped a 61–0 blowout to Baylor.

And for the first time in this first heartbreaking season for Lou Holtz, the Irish coach was all smiles as he watched his team in its best performance of the year.

A group of Air Force Academy officers were standing in the lobby of the Morris Inn on the campus of Notre Dame several weeks ago, at a reception for the visiting members of the Air Force Academy's football team. Suddenly a tall, athletic, bespectacled man in a priest's collar approached.

As the officers leaped to their feet to meet the associate provost of the University of Notre Dame, he made his own introduction.

"Hello," he said. "I'm Monk Malloy."

Several days after this introduction and for the first

time in some thirty-five years, Notre Dame had to pick a new president. After five years of searching for and interviewing candidates, the Board of Trustees, headed by President Donald Keough, president of Coca-Cola, chose that same Monk Malloy, the Reverend Edward Malloy who attended Notre Dame on a basketball scholarship and who still likes to mix it up in impromptu games on the campus.

In many ways the Board of Trustees could not have selected anyone more different then the legendary Reverend Theodore Hesburgh who retired in 1987 after ruling over and dramatically changing Notre Dame for so long. Father Hesburgh and the Reverend Edmund Joyce, who also retired, will take a year off to travel and then will come back to Notre Dame "to assist in any way that we can."

Father Malloy, a native of Washington, D.C., was born May 3, 1941. He obtained his undergraduate and graduate degrees from Notre Dame and received a doctorate in Christian ethics from Vanderbilt University.

That same week, amid all the excitement on the campus, the Penn State team rolled into South Bend to battle an aroused Notre Dame team that smelled "upset." Victorious in their past three games, Notre Dame was thirsting for a win over the number-two Nittany Lions, who seemingly were just as concerned over where they might play the University of Miami's Hurricanes in a bowl game.

Referring to the speculation about a Penn State-Miami bowl game, Coach Holtz said, "I wasn't even aware we were going to play Penn State. Everybody's been telling me they're just going to play Miami."

The mark of a great football team is winning the close ones and winning in hostile territory, and that's exactly what Penn State did as they barely escaped with their lives in one of the most thrilling, closely contested games of the season. The Nittany Lions took a 24–19 win over an Irish eleven that made several serious blunders; but time after time the Irish came back and savagely attacked the Penn State defense, for a total of 418 yards.

Just one week after the Penn State heartbreaker, the Irish jetted to Baton Rouge, Louisiana, to tangle with still another bitter rival, eighth-ranked Louisiana State, which had rolled over eight opponents and sported an 8–2 record. A win over the oft-beaten Irish would give LSU a bowl game, and they were determined to get the win.

An equally grim Irish eleven, four of whose five losses had been by five points or less each, were just

as determined to beat LSU and then go on the following week and beat USC in the season's finale. And the two teams played as if a championship were involved.

But it was LSU's Tommy Hudson, a freshman quarterback, who was brilliant as he passed for three touchdowns. And his nose guard, Hank Thomas, helped keep the Irish out of the end zone from scrimmage until the final three minutes of the game as the Fighting Tigers finally prevailed by a 21–19 margin.

With LSU in front 13–0, Notre Dame's Timmy Brown, now one of the most feared broken-field runners in college football, gathered in an LSU kick-off and sped ninety-six yards to give Notre Dame its first score. Two subsequent field goals by John Carney gave the Irish another six points and brought them to within a point of LSU, at 14–13.

In the fourth period the Fighting Tigers drove seventy-nine yards and scored to widen their margin to 21–13.

There were but three minutes to play when Coach Holtz inserted his second-string quarterback, Terry Andrysiak, who led an eighty-yard drive culminating in a fourteen-yard pass to D'Juan Francisco for a touchdown.

The touchdown brought the Irish within two points of LSU, 21–19, and they tried desperately for a two-point conversion to tie the score.

Andrysiak's pass for the two-pointer was right on target to Joel Williams . . . but Williams, so eager to catch the ball, stepped out of bounds as he received it and the play was ruled incomplete as time ran out on the Irish.

Now it was down to the final game of the year, against the Trojans of Southern California at Los Angeles Coliseum. The Irish fought their hearts out in that game to come from behind to win one of the most glorious victories in the one hundred years of Notre Dame football.

Leading by ten points, with several Irish linemen out of the lineup with injuries and with ten minutes to go, USC apparently had the game well in hand, and several thousand spectators started to leave the stadium.

But then the Irish began to move.

A fifteen-yard penalty for unsportsmanlike conduct cost USC as the Irish took the ball over on their own twenty-yard line. Now there were but six minutes to play, and USC was leading, 37–27.

Steve Beuerlein, playing his last game for Notre

Dame and who had been outstanding throughout the seesaw battle, took the pass from center and faded back to throw. He dodged three USC linemen and then saw Timmy Brown dashing downfield all alone. Beuerlein somehow managed to get off the pass to Brown, and Timmy, running as if his life depended on the catch, snared the ball on his fingertips and sprinted to the Trojan twenty-five-yard line before he was brought to earth as the thousands of Irish supporters on hand screamed in a frenzy of excitement. Then Mark Green, a talented tailback from Riverside, California, blasted the Trojan line for successive gains of six, seven, and five yards to bring the ball to the seven-yard line.

On the next play, Beuerlein flipped a short pass to the six-five, 235-pound Bobby Banks, playing his final game for the Irish. Banks would not be denied and crashed through for an Irish touchdown.

Once again the Irish put it all on the line and tried for a two-point conversion. This time Beuerlein shot the ball into the eager hands of six-six, 240-pound Andy Heck, who downed the ball in the end zone for the two points.

And with 4:24 to play, the score was USC 37, Notre Dame 35.

Los Angeles Coliseum was a bedlam as seventy-five thousand fans went crazy.

Notre Dame kicked to USC, but the Trojan attack went nowhere, and they kicked back to Notre Dame.

And then there was Timmy Brown.

The USC kick was high and long and Brown carefully caught the ball, tucked it under his right arm, and started to move upfield as the USC tacklers converged.

A marvelous wall of Irish blockers cleared a path for Timmy, and he dodged and threaded his way fifty-nine yards in as pretty a run as one would ever see on a football field—to the USC sixteen-yard line, where he was tackled from behind by the USC punter, Chris Sperle.

And now the noise in the Coliseum was so loud that the referee held up his arms trying to silence the crowd so the Irish quarterback's signals could be heard.

Fifteen seconds remained on the clock as Mark Green smashed the Trojan line and advanced the ball to the one-yard line, and time was called.

Two seconds remained on the game clock.

The score was USC 37, Notre Dame 35.

Lou Holtz sent in kicker John Carney, and as Carney trotted to his side, Beuerlein said, "John, this kick will make it all worthwhile."

Carney, who earlier in the game had an extra-point kick blocked, replied, "Don't worry, Steve. I got it this time."

Chuck Lanza centered the ball to Beuerlein; who placed it on the turf and Carney calmly stepped in and booted a nineteen-yarder for the winning points.

And the entire Irish coaching staff, including Lou Holtz, rushed onto the field and carried Carney off on their happy shoulders. Final score: Notre Dame 38, USC 37.

"And for 1987," said a smiling Lou Holtz in the locker room, "we'll have a good team. A very good team. Of course, we'll have lost some fine players who had just started to come on, fellows like Steve Beuerlein, who improved tremendously, and Parnell Taylor, Alonzo Jefferson, Milt Jackson, Joe Williams, Alvin Miller, Shawn Heffern, and John Askin. And Notre Dame's all-time-leading place-kicker, John Carney, will be hard to replace. Bob Banks, Mike Griffin, big Wally Kleine, Captain Mike Kovaleski, and Ron Weissenhofer and Mike Haywood, Troy Wilson and Joel Williams—we'll miss all of them.

"But we've got Captain Chuck Lanza, Timmy Brown and Terry Andrysiak, Tony Rice, Mark Green, Brandy Wells, Frank Stams, Jeff Kunz, Andy Heck, Aaron Robb, and a host of outstanding freshmen coming aboard, and those teams that beat us by a point or two last year had better watch out.

"From 1987 on, Notre Dame will be a competitive team with the best of them," said Lou Holtz.

And the year of the Notre Dame football centennial will be one that we won't soon forget!

APPENDIX

STATISTICS AND HIGHLIGHTS

ALL-TIME TEAM RECORD

1887
Coach: None
Captain: Henry Luhn

November 23	L	Michigan	0-8	H
		(0-1-0)		

1888
Coach: None
Captain: Edward Prudhomme

April 20	L	Michigan	6-26	H
April 21	L	Michigan	4-10	H
December 6	W	Harvard School (Chi.)	20-0	H
		(1-2-0)	30-36	

1889
Coach: None
Captain: Edward Prudhomme

November 14	W	Northwestern	9-0	A
		(1-0-0)		

1890–1891—NO TEAM

1892
Coach: None
Captain: Pat Coady

October 19	W	South Bend H.S.	56-0	H
November 24	T	Hillsdale	10-10	H
		(1-0-1)	66-10	

1893
Coach: None
Captain: Frank Keough

October 25	W	Kalamazoo	34-0	H
November 11	W	Albion	8-6	H
November 23	W	DeLaSalle (S)	28-0	H
November 30	W	Hillsdale (S)	22-10	H
January 1	L	Chicago	0-8	A
		(4-1-0)	92-24	

1894
Coach: James L. Morison
Captain: Frank Keough

October 13	W	Hillsdale	14-0	H
October 20	T	Albion	6-6	H
November 15	W	Wabash	30-0	H
November 22	W	Rush Medical	18-6	H
November 29	L	Albion	12-19	H
		(3-1-1)	80-31	

1895
Coach: H. G. Hadden
Captain: Dan Casey

October 19	W	Northwestern Law	20-0	H
November 7	W	Illinois Cycling Club	18-2	H
November 22	L	Indpls. Artillery (S)	0-18	H
November 28	W	Chicago Phys. & Surg.	32-0	H
		(3-1-0)	70-20	

1896
Coach: Frank E. Hering
Captain: Frank E. Hering

October 8	L	Chicago Phys. & Surg.	0-4	H
October 14	L	Chicago	0-18	H
October 27	W	S.B. Commercial A.C.	46-0	H
October 31	W	Albion	24-0	H
November 14	L	Purdue	22-28	H
November 20	W	Highland Views	82-0	H
November 26	W	Beloit (R)	8-0	H
		(4-3-0)	182-50	

1897
Coach: Frank E. Hering
Captain: Jack Mullen

October 13	T	Rush Medical	0-0	H
October 23	W	DePauw	4-0	H
October 28	W	Chicago Dental Surg.	62-0	H
November 6	L	Chicago	5-34	A
November 13	W	St. Viator	60-0	H
November 25	W	Michigan State (R)	34-6	H
		(4-1-1)	165-40	

1898
Coach: Frank E. Hering
Captain: Jack Mullen

October 8	W	Illinois	5-0	A
October 15	W	Michigan State	53-0	H
October 23	L	Michigan	0-23	A
October 29	W	DePauw	32-0	H
November 11	L	Indiana	5-11	H
November 19	W	Albion	60-0	A
		(4-2-0)	155-34	

1899
Coach: James McWeeney
Captain: Jack Mullen

September 27	W	Englewood H.S.	29-5	H
September 30	W	Michigan State	40-0	H
October 4	L	Chicago	6-23	A
October 14	W	Lake Forest	38-0	H
October 18	L	Michigan	0-12	A

October	23	W....Indiana................	17-0	H
October	27	W....Northwestern (R)........	12-0	H
November	4	W....Rush Medical	17-0	H
November	18	T ....Purdue................	10-10	A
November	30	L ....Chicago Phys. & Surg....	0-5	H

(6-3-1) 169-55

1900

Coach: Pat O'Dea
Captain: John Farley

September	29	W....Goshen................	55-0	H
October	6	W....Englewood H.S.	68-0	H
October	13	W....S.B. Howard Park.......	64-0	H
October	20	W....Cincinnati.............	58-0	H
October	25	L ....Indiana...............	0-6	A
November	3	T ....Beloit	6-6	H
November	10	L ....Wisconsin	0-54	A
November	17	L ....Michigan	0-7	A
November	24	W....Rush Medical (R).......	5-0	H
November	29	W....Chicago Phys. & Surg....	5-0	H

(6-3-1) 261-73

1901

Coach: Pat O'Dea
Captain: Al Fortin

September	28	T ....South Bend A.C.	0-0	H
October	5	W....Ohio Medical U.	6-0	A
October	12	L ....Northwestern (R)........	0-2	A
October	19	W....Chicago Medical Col.	32-0	H
October	26	W....Beloit	5-0	A
November	2	W....Lake Forest	16-0	H
November	9	W....Purdue................	12-6	H
November	16	W....Indiana (R)	18-5	H
November	23	W....Chicago Phys. & Surg....	34-0	H
November	28	W....South Bend A.C.	22-6	H

(8-1-1) 145-19

1902

Coach: James F. Faragher
Captain: Louis (Red) Salmon

September	27	W....Michigan State	33-0	H
October	11	W....Lake Forest	28-0	H
October	18	L ....Michigan	0-23	N
October	25	W....Indiana...............	11-5	A
November	1	W....Ohio Medical U.	6-5	A
November	8	L ....Knox	5-12	A
November	15	W....American Medical	92-0	H
November	22	W....DePauw	22-0	H
November	27	T ....Purdue...............	6-6	A

(6-2-1) 203-51

1903

Coach: James F. Faragher
Captain: Louis (Red) Salmon

October	3	W....Michigan State	12-0	H
October	10	W....Lake Forest	28-0	H
October	17	W....DePauw (R)............	56-0	H
October	24	W....American Medical	52-0	H
October	29	W....Chicago Phys. & Surg....	46-0	H
November	7	W....Missouri Osteopaths	28-0	H
November	14	T ....Northwestern	0-0	A
November	21	W....Ohio Medical U.	35-0	A
November	26	W....Wabash	35-0	A

(8-0-1) 292-0

1904

Coach: Louis (Red) Salmon
Captain: Frank Shaughnessy

October	1	W....Wabash	12-4	H
October	8	W....American Medical	44-0	H

October	15	L ....Wisconsin	0-58	N
October	22	W....Ohio Medical U.	17-5	A
October	27	W....Toledo A.A.	6-0	H
November	5	L ....Kansas	5-24	A
November	19	W....DePauw	10-0	H
November	24	L ....Purdue...............	0-36	A

(5-3-0) 94-127

1905

Coach: Henry J. McGlew
Captain: Pat Beacom

September	30	W....N. Division H.S. (Chi.)..	44-0	H
October	7	W....Michigan State	28-0	H
October	14	L ....Wisconsin	0-21	N
October	21	L ....Wabash	0-5	H
October	28	W....American Medical *	142-0	H
November	4	W....DePauw	71-0	H
November	11	L ....Indiana...............	5-22	A
November	18	W....Bennett Med. Col. Chi...	22-0	H
November	24	L ....Purdue...............	0-32	A

(5-4-0) 312-80

* After a twenty-five-minute first half, with Notre Dame leading 121-0, the second half was shortened to only eight minutes to permit the "doctors" time to eat before catching a train to Chicago. Notre Dame scored twenty-seven touchdowns but missed twenty extra points.

1906

Coach: Thomas A. Barry
Captain: Bob Bracken

October	6	W....Franklin..............	26-0	H
October	13	W....Hillsdale.............	17-0	H
October	20	W....Chi. Phys. & Surg.......	28-0	H
October	27	W....Michigan State	5-0	H
November	3	W....Purdue...............	2-0	A
November	10	L ....Indiana...............	0-12	N
November	24	W....Beloit (R).............	29-0	H

(6-1-0) 107-12

1907

Coach: Thomas A. Barry
Captain: Dom Callicrate

October	12	W....Chi. Phys. & Surg. (R) ..	32-0	H
October	19	W....Franklin..............	23-0	H
October	26	W....Olivet...............	22-4	H
November	2	T ....Indiana...............	0-0	H
November	9	W....Knox	22-4	H
November	23	W....Purdue...............	17-0	H
November	28	W....St. Vincent's (Chi.)......	21-12	A

(6-0-1) 137-20

KEY TO ABBREVIATIONS

W-L-T—game won, lost, or tied
H—home game
A—away game, played at opponent's home stadium
N—game played at a neutral site
Nt—night game
YS—game played at Yankee Stadium, New York
HC—homecoming game
TH—game played on Thanksgiving Day
R—game played in rain
S—game played in snow
U—major upset

SCORING VALUES

SEASONS	TOUCHDOWN	FIELD GOAL	POINT AFTER	SAFETY
1887–1897	4 points	5 points	2 points	2 points
1898–1903	5 points	5 points	1 point	2 points
1904–1908	5 points	4 points	1 point	2 points
1909–1911	5 points	3 points	1 point	2 points
1912–1957	6 points	3 points	1 point	2 points
1958 to date	6 points	3 points	1 point for kick	2 points
			2 points for run or pass	

1908

Coach: Victor M. Place
Captain: Harry Miller

October	3	W....Hillsdale	39-0	H
October	10	W....Franklin	64-0	H
October	17	L ....Michigan	6-12	A
October	24	W....Chicago Phys. & Surg.	88-0	H
October	29	W....Ohio Northern	58-4	H
November	7	W....Indiana	11-0	N
November	13	W....Wabash	8-4	A
November	18	W....St. Viator	46-0	H
November	26	W....Marquette	6-0	A

(8-1-0)   326-20

1909 *

Coach: Frank C. Longman
Captain: Howard Edwards

October	9	W....Olivet	58-0	H
October	16	W....Rose Poly	60-11	H
October	23	W....Michigan State	17-0	H
October	30	W....Pittsburgh	6-0	A
November	6	W....Michigan (U)	11-3	A
November	13	W....Miami (Ohio)	46-0	H
November	20	W....Wabash	38-0	H
November	25	T ....Marquette	0-0	A

(7-0-1)   236-14

* "The Notre Dame Victory March" was introduced this season.

1910

Coach: Frank C. Longman
Captain: Ralph Dimmick

October	8	W....Olivet	48-0	H
October	22	W....Butchel (Akron)	51-0	H
November	5	L ....Michigan State	0-17	A
November	12	W....Rose Poly	41-3	A
November	19	W....Ohio Northern	47-0 *	H
November	24	T ....Marquette	5-5	A

(4-1-1)   192-25

* Notre Dame's 100th victory.

1911

Coach: John L. Marks
Captain: Luke Kelly

October	7	W....Ohio Northern	32-6	H
October	14	W....St. Viator	43-0	H
October	21	W....Butler (R)	27-0	H
October	28	W....Loyola (Chi.)	80-0	H
November	4	T ....Pittsburgh	0-0	A
November	11	W....St. Bonaventure	34-0	H
November	20	W....Wabash	6-3	A
November	30	T ....Marquette	0-0	A

(6-0-2)   222-9

1912

Coach: John L. Marks
Captain: Charles (Gus) Dorais

October	5	W....St. Viator	116-7	H
October	12	W....Adrian	74-7	H
October	19	W....Morris Harvey	39-0	H
October	26	W....Wabash	41-6	H
November	2	W....Pittsburgh (S)	3-0	A
November	9	W....St. Louis	47-7	A
November	28	W....Marquette	69-0	N

(7-0-0)   389-27

1913

Coach: Jesse Harper
Captain: Knute Rockne

October	4	W....Ohio Northern	87-0	H
October	18	W....South Dakota	20-7	H
October	25	W....Alma	62-0	H
November	1	W....Army (U)	35-13	A
November	7	W....Penn State (R)	14-7	A
November	22	W....Christian Bros. (St. Louis)	20-7	A
November	27	W....Texas	30-7	A

(7-0-0)   268-41

1914

Coach: Jesse Harper
Captain: Keith Jones

October	3	W....Alma	56-0	H
October	10	W....Rose Poly	103-0	H
October	17	L ....Yale	0-28	A
October	24	W....South Dakota	33-0	N
October	31	W....Haskell	20-7	H
November	7	L ....Army	7-20	A
November	14	W....Carlisle	48-6	N
November	26	W....Syracuse	20-0	A

(6-2-0)   287-61

1915

Coach: Jesse Harper
Captain: Freeman Fitzgerald

October	2	W....Alma	32-0	H
October	9	W....Haskell	34-0	H
October	23	L ....Nebraska	19-20	A
October	30	W....South Dakota	6-0	H
November	6	W....Army	7-0	A
November	13	W....Creighton	41-0	A
November	25	W....Texas	36-7	A
November	27	W....Rice	55-2	A

(7-1-0)   230-29

1916

Coach: Jesse Harper
Captain: Stan Cofall

September	30	W....Case Tech	48-0	H
October	7	W....Western Reserve	48-0	A
October	14	W....Haskell	26-0	H
October	28	W....Wabash	60-0	H
November	4	L ....Army	10-30	A
November	11	W....South Dakota	21-0	N
November	18	W....Michigan State	14-0	A
November	25	W....Alma	46-0	H
November	30	W....Nebraska	20-0	A

(8-1-0)   293-30

1917

Coach: Jesse Harper
Captain: Jim Phelan

October	6	W....Kalamazoo	55-0	H
October	13	T ....Wisconsin	0-0	A
October	20	L ....Nebraska	0-7	A
October	27	W....South Dakota (R)	40-0	H
November	3	W....Army (U)	7-2	A
November	10	W....Morningside	13-0	A
November	17	W....Michigan State	23-0	H
November	24	W....Wash. & Jefferson	3-0	A

(6-1-1)   141-9

1918

Coach: Knute Rockne
Captain: Leonard Bahan

September	28	W....Case Tech	26-6	A
November	2	W....Wabash	67-7	A
November	9	T ....Great Lakes	7-7	H
November	16	L ....Michigan State (U) (R)	7-13	A
November	23	W....Purdue	26-6	A
November	28	T ....Nebraska (S)	0-0	A

(3-1-2)   133-39

1919

Coach: Knute Rockne
Captain: Leonard Bahan

October	4	W....Kalamazoo	14-0	H
October	11	W....Mount Union	60-7	H
October	18	W....Nebraska	14-9	A
October	25	W....Western Michigan	53-0	H
November	1	W....Indiana (R)	16-3	N
November	8	W....Army	12-9	A
November	15	W....Michigan State	13-0	H
November	22	W....Purdue	33-13	A
November	27	W....Morningside (S)	14-6	A

(9-0-0) 229-47

1920

Coach: Knute Rockne
Captain: Frank Coughlin

October	2	W....Kalamazoo	39-0	H
October	9	W....Western Michigan	42-0	H
October	16	W....Nebraska	16-7	A
October	23	W....Valparaiso	28-3	H
October	30	W....Army	27-17	A
November	6	W....Purdue (HC)	28-0	H
November	13	W....Indiana	13-10	N
November	20	W....Northwestern	33-7 *	A
November	25	W....Michigan State	25-0	A

(9-0-0) 251-44

* George Gipp's last game. He contracted a strep throat and died from complications of the disease on December 14 at age twenty-five.

1921

Coach: Knute Rockne
Captain: Eddie Anderson

September	24	W....Kalamazoo	56-0	H
October	1	W....DePauw	57-10	H
October	8	L....Iowa (U)	7-10	A
October	15	W....Purdue	33-0	A
October	22	W....Nebraska (HC)	7-0	H
October	29	W....Indiana	28-7	N
November	5	W....Army	28-0	A
November	8	W....Rutgers	48-0	N
November	12	W....Haskell	42-7	H
November	19	W....Marquette	21-7	A
November	24	W....Michigan State	48-0	H

(10-1-0) 375-41

1922

Coach: Knute Rockne
Captain: Glenn Carberry

September	20	W....Kalamazoo	46-0	H
October	7	W....St. Louis	26-0	H
October	14	W....Purdue	20-0	A
October	21	W....DePauw	34-7	H
October	28	W....Georgia Tech	13-3	A
November	4	W....Indiana (HC)	27-0	H
November	11	T....Army	0-0	A
November	18	W....Butler	31-3	A
November	25	W....Carnegie Tech	19-0	A
November	30	L....Nebraska	6-14	A

(8-1-1) 222-27

1923

Coach: Knute Rockne
Captain: Harvey Brown

September	29	W....Kalamazoo	74-0	H
October	6	W....Lombard	14-0	H
October	13	W....Army	13-0	N
October	20	W....Princeton	25-2	A
October	27	W....Georgia Tech	35-7	H
November	3	W....Purdue (HC)	34-7	H
November	10	L....Nebraska	7-14	A

November	17	W....Butler	34-7	H
November	24	W....Carnegie Tech	26-0	A
November	29	W....St. Louis	13-0	A

(9-1-0) 275-37

1924

Coach: Knute Rockne
Captain: Adam Walsh

October	4	W....Lombard	40-0	H
October	11	W....Wabash	34-0	H
October	18	W....Army	13-7	N
October	25	W....Princeton	12-0	A
November	1	W....Georgia Tech	34-3 *	H
November	8	W....Wisconsin	38-3	A
November	15	W....Nebraska	34-6	H
November	22	W....Northwestern	13-6	N
November	29	W....Carnegie Tech	40-19	A

(9-0-0) 258-44

ROSE BOWL

January	1	W....Stanford	27-10	N

* Notre Dame's 200th victory.

1925

Coach: Knute Rockne
Captain: Clem Crowe

September	26	W....Baylor	41-0	H
October	3	W....Lombard	69-0	H
October	10	W....Beloit	19-3	H
October	17	L....Army	0-27	YS
October	24	W....Minnesota	19-7	A
October	31	W....Georgia Tech	13-0	A
November	7	T....Penn State	0-0	A
November	14	W....Carnegie Tech (HC)	26-0	H
November	21	W....Northwestern	13-10	H
November	26	L....Nebraska	0-17	A

(7-2-1) 200-64

1926

Coach: Knute Rockne
Co-captains: Gene Edwards and Tom Hearden

October	2	W....Beloit	77-0	H
October	9	W....Minnesota	20-7	A
October	16	W....Penn State	28-0	H
October	23	W....Northwestern	6-0	A
October	30	W....Georgia Tech	12-0	H
November	6	W....Indiana	26-0	H
November	13	W....Army	7-0	YS
November	20	W....Drake (HC)	21-0	H
November	27	L....Carnegie Tech	0-19	A
December	4	W....USC	13-12	A

(9-1-0) 210-38

1927

Coach: Knute Rockne
Captain: John Smith

October	1	W....Coe	28-7	H
October	8	W....Detroit	20-0	A
October	15	W....Navy	19-6	N
October	22	W....Indiana	19-6	A
October	29	W....Georgia Tech	26-7	H
November	5	T....Minn.	7-7	H
November	12	L....Army	0-18	YS
November	19	W....Drake	32-0	A
November	26	W....USC	7-6	N

(7-1-1) 158-57

1928

Coach: Knute Rockne
Captain: Fred Miller

September	29	W....Loyola	12-6	H
October	6	L....Wisconsin	6-22	A

October	13	W....Navy..................	7-0	N
October	20	L ....Georgia Tech...........	0-13	A
October	27	W....Drake	32-6	H
November	3	W....Penn State	9-0	N
November	10	W....Army (U)...............	12-6	YS
November	17	L ....Carnegie Tech..........	7-27 *	H
December	1	L ....USC..................	14-27	A
		(5-4-0)	99-107	

* First defeat at home since 1905.

1929 *

Coach: Knute Rockne
Captain: John Law

October	5	W....Indiana	14-0	A
October	12	W....Navy	14-7	N
October	19	W....Wisconsin	19-0	N
October	26	W....Carnegie Tech..........	7-0	A
November	2	W....Georgia Tech	26-6	A
November	9	W....Drake	19-7	N
November	16	W....USC	13-12	N
November	23	W....Northwestern	26-6	A
November	30	W....Army	7-0	YS
		(9-0-0)	145-38	

* No home games; Notre Dame Stadium was under construction.

1930

Coach: Knute Rockne *
Captain: Tom Conley

October	4	W....SMU	20-14	H
October	11	W....Navy †	26-2	H
October	18	W....Carnegie Tech..........	21-6	H
October	25	W....Pittsburgh.............	35-19	A
November	1	W....Indiana	27-0	H
November	8	W....Pennsylvania	60-20	A
November	15	W....Drake	28-7	H
November	22	W....Northwestern	14-0	A
November	29	W....Army (R-S).............	7-6	N
December	6	W....USC (U)	27-0	A
		(10-0-0)	265-74	

* Coach Knute Rockne, forty-three, and seven other persons were killed in a plane crash near Bazaar, Kansas, on March 31, 1931.
† Dedication of Notre Dame Stadium.

1931

Coach: Heartley (Hunk) Anderson
Captain: Tommy Yarr

October	3	W....Indiana	25-0	A
October	10	T ....Northwestern (R)........	0-0	N
October	17	W....Drake	63-0	H
October	24	W....Pittsburgh.............	25-12	H
October	31	W....Carnegie Tech..........	19-0	A
November	7	W....Pennsylvania	49-0	H
November	14	W....Navy	20-0	N
November	21	L ....USC (U)	14-16	H
November	28	L ....Army (U)...............	0-12	YS
		(6-2-1)	215-40	

1932

Coach: Heartley (Hunk) Anderson
Captain: Paul Host

October	8	W....Haskell	73-0	H
October	15	W....Drake	62-0	H
October	22	W....Carnegie Tech..........	42-0	H
October	29	L ....Pittsburgh (U)	0-12	A
November	5	W....Kansas	24-6	A
November	12	W....Northwestern	21-0	H
November	19	W....Navy	12-0	N
November	26	W....Army	21-0	YS
December	10	L ....USC	0-13	A
		(7-2-0)	255-31	

1933

Coach: Heartley (Hunk) Anderson
Co-captains: Hugh Devore and Tom Gorman

October	7	T ....Kansas	0-0	H
October	14	W....Indiana	12-2	A
October	21	L ....Carnegie Tech (U)	0-7	A
October	28	L ....Pittsburgh.............	0-14	H
November	4	L ....Navy	0-7	N
November	11	L ....Purdue	0-19	H
November	18	W....Northwestern	7-0	A
November	25	L ....USC	0-19	H
December	2	W....Army (U)...............	13-12	YS
		(3-5-1)	32-80	

1934

Coach: Elmer Layden
Captain: Dom Vairo

October	6	L ....Texas	6-7	H
October	13	W....Purdue	18-7	H
October	20	W....Carnegie Tech (R)	13-0	H
October	27	W....Wisconsin	19-0	H
November	3	L ....Pittsburgh.............	0-19	A
November	10	L ....Navy (R)	6-10	N
November	17	W....Northwestern	20-7	A
November	24	W....Army	12-6	YS
December	8	W....USC	14-0	A
		(6-3-0)	108-56	

1935

Coach: Elmer Layden
Captain: Joe Sullivan *

September	28	W....Kansas	28-7	H
October	5	W....Carnegie Tech..........	14-3	A
October	12	W....Wisconsin	27-0	A
October	19	W....Pittsburgh.............	9-6	H
October	26	W....Navy	14-0	N
November	2	W....Ohio State (U)..........	18-13	A
November	9	L ....Northwestern (R) (U)	7-14	H
November	16	T ....Army	6-6	YS
November	23	W....USC	20-13	H
		(7-1-1)	143-62	

* Died from complications of pneumonia, March 1935.

1936

Coach: Elmer Layden
Captain: Bill Smith—John Lautar *

October	3	W....Carnegie Tech..........	21-7	H
October	10	W....Washington	14-6	H
October	17	W....Wisconsin (R)	27-0	H
October	24	L ....Pittsburgh.............	0-26	A
October	31	W....Ohio State (R)..........	7-2	H
November	7	L ....Navy (U)	0-3	N
November	14	W....Army	20-6	YS
November	21	W....Northwestern (U)	26-6	H
December	5	T ....USC	13-13	A
		(6-2-1)	128-69	

* Captain-elect Smith resigned his captaincy because of illness, and Lautar was elected acting captain.

1937

Coach: Elmer Layden
Captain: Joe Zwers

October	2	W....Drake	21-0	H
October	9	T ....Illinois	0-0	A
October	16	L ....Carnegie Tech (U)	7-9	A
October	23	W....Navy (S)	9-7	H
October	30	W....Minnesota (U)	7-6	A
November	6	L ....Pittsburgh.............	6-21	H
November	13	W....Army (R)	7-0	YS
November	20	W....Northwestern	7-0	A
November	27	W....USC	13-6	H
		(6-2-1)	77-49	

1938

Coach: Elmer Layden
Captain: Jim McGoldrick

October	1	W....Kansas	52-0	H
October	8	W....Georgia Tech	14-6	A
October	15	W....Illinois	14-6	H
October	22	W....Carnegie Tech	7-0	H
October	29	W....Army	19-7	YS
November	5	W....Navy (R)	15-0	N
November	12	W....Minnesota	19-0*	H
November	19	W....Northwestern	9-7	A
December	3	L....USC (U)	0-13	A
		(8-1-0)	149-39	

*Notre Dame's 300th victory.

1939

Coach: Elmer Layden
Captain: Johnny Kelly

September	30	W....Purdue	3-0	H
October	7	W....Georgia Tech	17-14	H
October	14	W....SMU	20-19	H
October	21	W....Navy	14-7	N
October	28	W....Carnegie Tech (S)	7-6	A
November	4	W....Army	14-0	YS
November	11	L....Iowa (U)	6-7	A
November	18	W....Northwestern	7-0	H
November	25	L....USC	12-20	H
		(7-2-0)	100-73	

1940

Coach: Elmer Layden
Captain: Milt Piepul

October	5	W....Col. of Pacific	25-7	H
October	12	W....Georgia Tech	26-20	H
October	19	W....Carnegie Tech	61-0	H
October	26	W....Illinois	26-0	A
November	2	W....Army (R)	7-0	YS
November	9	W....Navy	13-7	N
November	16	L....Iowa	0-7	H
November	23	L....Northwestern	0-20	A
December	7	W....USC	10-6	A
		(7-2-0)	168-67	

1941

Coach: Frank Leahy
Captain: Paul Lillis

September	27	W....Arizona	38-7	H
October	4	W....Indiana (R)	19-6	H
October	11	W....Georgia Tech	20-0	A
October	18	W....Carnegie Tech (R)	16-0	A
October	25	W....Illinois	49-14	H
November	1	T....Army (R)	0-0	YS
November	8	W....Navy	20-13	N
November	15	T....Northwestern	7-6	A
November	22	W....USC	20-18	H
		(8-0-1)	189-64	

1942

Coach: Frank Leahy
Captain: George Murphy

September	26	T....Wisconsin	7-7	A
October	3	L....Georgia Tech (U)	6-13	H
October	10	W....Stanford	27-0	H
October	17	W....Iowa Pre-Flight (U)	28-0	H
October	24	W....Illinois	21-14	A
October	31	W....Navy (R)	9-0	N
November	7	W....Army	13-0	YS
November	14	L....Michigan	20-32	H
November	21	W....Northwestern	27-20	H
November	28	W....USC	13-0	A
December	5	T....Great Lakes (S)	13-13	N
		(7-2-2)	184-99	

1943

Coach: Frank Leahy
Captain: Pat Filley

September	25	W....Pittsburgh	41-0	A
October	2	W....Georgia Tech	55-13	H
October	9	W....Michigan	35-12	A
October	16	W....Wisconsin	50-0	A
October	23	W....Illinois (R)	47-0	H
October	30	W....Navy	33-6	N
November	6	W....Army	26-0	YS
November	13	W....Northwestern	25-6	A
November	20	W....Iowa Pre-Flight	14-13	H
November	27	L....Great Lakes (U)	14-19	A
		(9-1-0)	340-69	

1944

Coach: Ed McKeever
Captain: Pat Filley

September	30	W....Pittsburgh	58-0	A
October	7	W....Tulane	26-0	H
October	14	W....Dartmouth (R)	64-0	N
October	21	W....Wisconsin	28-13	H
October	28	W....Illinois	13-7	A
November	4	L....Navy	13-32	N
November	11	L....Army	0-59	YS
November	18	W....Northwestern	21-0	H
November	25	W....Georgia Tech	21-0	A
December	2	W....Great Lakes	28-7	H
		(8-2-0)	272-118	

1945

Coach: Hugh Devore
Captain: Frank Dancewicz

September	29	W....Illinois	7-0	H
October	6	W....Georgia Tech	40-7	A
October	13	W....Dartmouth	34-0	H
October	20	W....Pittsburgh	39-9	A
October	27	W....Iowa	56-0	H
November	3	T....Navy	6-6	N
November	10	L....Army	0-48	YS
November	17	W....Northwestern	34-7	A
November	24	W....Tulane	32-6	A
December	1	L....Great Lakes	7-39	A
		(7-2-1)	255-122	

1946

Coach: Frank Leahy
Game Captains

September	28	W....Illinois	26-6	A
October	5	W....Pittsburgh	33-0	H
October	12	W....Purdue	49-6	H
October	26	W....Iowa	41-6	A
November	2	W....Navy	28-0	N
November	9	T....Army	0-0	YS
November	16	W....Northwestern (R)	27-0	H
November	23	W....Tulane	41-0	H
November	30	W....USC	26-6	H
		(8-0-1)	271-24	

1947

Coach: Frank Leahy
Captain: George Connor

October	4	W....Pittsburgh	40-6	A
October	11	W....Purdue	22-7	A
October	18	W....Nebraska	31-0	H
October	25	W....Iowa	21-0	H
November	1	W....Navy	27-0	N
November	8	W....Army	27-7	H
November	15	W....Northwestern (R)	26-19	A
November	22	W....Tulane	59-6	H
December	6	W....USC	38-7	A
		(9-0-0)	291-52	

1948

Coach: Frank Leahy
Captain: Bill Fischer

September 25	W	Purdue	28-27	H
October 2	W	Pittsburgh	40-0	A
October 9	W	Michigan State	26-7	H
October 16	W	Nebraska	44-13	A
October 23	W	Iowa	27-12	A
October 30	W	Navy	41-7	N
November 6	W	Indiana (R)	42-6	A
November 13	W	Northwestern	12-7	H
November 27	W	Washington	46-0	H
December 4	T	USC	14-14	A
		(9-0-1)	320-93	

1949

Coach: Frank Leahy
Co-captains: Leon Hart and Jim Martin

September 24	W	Indiana	49-6	H
October 1	W	Washington	27-7	A
October 8	W	Purdue	35-12	A
October 15	W	Tulane	46-7	H
October 29	W	Navy	40-0	N
November 5	W	Michigan State	34-21	A
November 12	W	North Carolina	42-6	YS
November 19	W	Iowa	28-7	H
November 26	W	USC	32-0	H
December 3	W	SMU	27-20	A
		(10-0-0)	360-86	

1950

Coach: Frank Leahy
Captain: Jerry Groom

September 30	W	No. Carolina	14-7	H
October 7	L	Purdue	14-28	H
October 14	W	Tulane	13-9	A
October 21	L	Indiana	7-20	A
October 28	L	Michigan State	33-36	H
November 4	W	Navy	19-10	N
November 11	W	Pittsburgh	18-7	H
November 18	T	Iowa	14-14	A
December 2	L	USC	7-9	A
		(4-4-1)	139-140	

1951

Coach: Frank Leahy
Captain: Jim Mutscheller

September 29	W	Indiana	48-6	H
October 5	W	Detroit	40-6	N
October 13	L	SMU	20-27	H
October 20	W	Pittsburgh	33-0	A
October 27	W	Purdue	30-9	H
November 3	W	Navy	19-0	N
November 10	L	Michigan State	0-35	A
November 17	W	North Carolina	12-7 *	A
November 24	T	Iowa	20-20	H
December 1	W	USC	19-12	A
		(7-2-1)	241-122	

* Notre Dame's 400th victory.

1952

Coach: Frank Leahy
Captain: Jack Alessandrini

September 27	T	Pennsylvania	7-7	A
October 4	W	Texas (U)	14-3	A
October 11	L	Pittsburgh (U)	19-22	H
October 18	W	Purdue	26-14	A
October 25	W	North Carolina	34-14	H
November 1	W	Navy	17-6	N
November 8	W	Oklahoma (U)	27-21	H

November 15	L	Michigan State	3-21	A
November 22	W	Iowa	27-0	A
November 29	W	USC (U)	9-0	H
		(7-2-1)	183-108	

1953

Coach: Frank Leahy
Captain: Don Penza

September 26	W	Oklahoma	28-21	A
October 3	W	Purdue	37-7	A
October 17	W	Pittsburgh	23-14	H
October 24	W	Georgia Tech	27-14	H
October 31	W	Navy	38-7	H
November 7	W	Pennsylvania	28-20	A
November 14	W	North Carolina	34-14	H
November 21	T	Iowa	14-14	H
November 28	W	USC	48-14	A
December 5	W	SMU	40-14	H
		(9-0-1)	317-139	

1954

Coach: Terry Brennan
Co-captains: Paul Matz and Dan Shannon

September 25	W	Texas	21-0	H
October 2	L	Purdue (U)	14-27	H
October 9	W	Pittsburgh	33-0	A
October 16	W	Michigan State (R)	20-19	H
October 30	W	Navy	6-0	N
November 6	W	Pennsylvania	42-7	A
November 13	W	North Carolina	42-13	H
November 20	W	Iowa	34-18	A
November 27	W	USC (R)	23-17	H
December 4	W	SMU	26-14	A
		(9-1-0)	261-115	

1955

Coach: Terry Brennan
Captain: Ray Lemek

September 24	W	SMU	17-0	H
October 1	W	Indiana	19-0	H
October 7	W	Miami (Fla.) (Nt)	14-0	A
October 15	L	Michigan State	7-21	A
October 22	W	Purdue	22-7	A
October 29	W	Navy (R)	21-7	H
November 5	W	Pennsylvania	46-14	A
November 12	W	North Carolina	27-7	A
November 19	W	Iowa	17-14	H
November 26	L	USC (U)	20-42	A
		(8-2-0)	210-112	

1956

Coach: Terry Brennan
Captain: Jim Morse

September 22	L	SMU (U) (Nt)	13-19	A
October 6	W	Indiana	20-6	H
October 13	L	Purdue	14-28	H
October 20	L	Michigan State	14-47	H
October 27	L	Oklahoma	0-40	H
November 3	L	Navy (R)	7-33	N
November 10	L	Pittsburgh	13-26	A
November 17	W	No. Carolina	21-14	H
November 24	L	Iowa	8-48	A
December 1	L	USC	20-28	A
		(2-8-0)	130-289	

1957

Coach: Terry Brennan
Co-captains: Dick Prendergast and Ed Sullivan

| September 28 | W | Purdue | 12-0 | A |
| October 5 | W | Indiana | 26-0 | H |

October	12	W....Army	23-21	N
October	26	W....Pittsburgh............	13-7	H
November	2	L ....Navy	6-20	H
November	9	L ....Michigan State	6-34	A
November	16	W....Oklahoma	7-0	A
November	23	L ....Iowa	13-21	H
November	30	W....USC (S)	40-12	H
December	7	W....SMU	54-21	A

(7-3-0)   200-136

1958

Coach: Terry Brennan
Co-captains: Al Ecuyer and Chuck Puntillo

September	27	W....Indiana................	18-0	H
October	4	W....SMU	14-6	A
October	11	L ....Army	2-14	H
October	18	W....Duke	9-7	H
October	25	L ....Purdue	22-29	H
November	1	W....Navy	40-20	N
November	8	L ....Pittsburgh............	26-29	A
November	15	W....North Carolina	34-24	H
November	22	L ....Iowa	21-31	A
November	29	W....USC	20-13	A

(6-4-0)   206-173

1959

Coach: Joe Kuharich
Captain: Ken Adamson

September	26	W....North Carolina (R)	28-8	H
October	3	L ....Purdue	7-28	A
October	10	W....California.............	28-6	A
October	17	L ....Michigan State	0-19	A
October	24	L ....Northwestern	24-30	H
October	31	W....Navy.................	25-22	H
November	7	L ....Georgia Tech	10-14	H
November	14	L ....Pittsburgh............	13-28	A
November	21	W....Iowa	20-19	H
November	28	W....USC (U)	16-6	H

(5-5-0)   171-180

1960

Coach: Joe Kuharich
Captain: Myron Pottios

September	24	W....California.............	21-7	H
October	1	L ....Purdue	19-51	H
October	8	L ....North Carolina (R)	7-12	A
October	15	L ....Michigan State	0-21	H
October	22	L ....Northwestern	6-7	A
October	29	L ....Navy (R)	7-14	N
November	5	L ....Pittsburgh............	13-20	H
November	12	L ....Miami (Nt)	21-28	A
November	19	L ....Iowa	0-28	H
November	26	W....USC (U) (R)	17-0	A

(2-8-0)   111-188

1961

Coach: Joe Kuharich
Co-captains: Norb Roy and Nick Buoniconti

September	30	W....Oklahoma	19-6	H
October	7	W....Purdue	22-20	A
October	14	W....USC	30-0	H
October	21	L ....Michigan State	7-17	A
October	28	L ....Northwestern	10-12	H
November	4	L ....Navy	10-13	H
November	11	W....Pittsburgh.............	26-20	A
November	18	W....Syracuse	17-15	H
November	25	L ....Iowa	21-42	A
December	2	L ....Duke	13-37	A

(5-5-0)   175-182

1962

Coach: Joe Kuharich
Captain: Mike Lind

September	29	W....Oklahoma	13-7	A
October	6	L ....Purdue	6-24	H
October	13	L ....Wisconsin	8-17	A
October	20	L ....Michigan State (R)	7-31	H
October	27	L ....Northwestern	6-35	A
November	3	W....Navy (R)	20-12	N
November	10	W....Pittsburgh............	43-22	H
November	17	W....North Carolina	21-7	H
November	24	W....Iowa	35-12	H
December	1	L ....USC	0-25	A

(5-5-0)   159-192

1963

Coach: Hugh Devore
Captain: Bob Lehmann

September	28	L ....Wisconsin	9-14	H
October	5	L ....Purdue	6-7	A
October	12	W....USC (U)	17-14	H
October	19	W....UCLA	27-12	H
October	26	L ....Stanford (U)..........	14-24	H
November	2	L ....Navy	14-35	H
November	9	L ....Pittsburgh............	7-27	H
November	16	L ....Michigan State	7-12	A
November	23		......Iowa *	...	A
November	28	L ....Syracuse	7-14	YS

(2-7-0)   108-159

* Game canceled because of the death of President Kennedy.

1964

Coach: Ara Parseghian
Captain: Jim Carroll

September	26	W....Wisconsin (R)	31-7	A
October	3	W....Purdue	34-15	H
October	10	W....Air Force	34-7	A
October	17	W....UCLA	24-0	H
October	24	W....Stanford	28-6	H
October	31	W....Navy	40-0	N
November	7	W....Pittsburgh............	17-15	A
November	14	W....Michigan State	34-7	H
November	21	W....Iowa	28-0	H
November	28	L ....USC (U)	17-20	A

(9-1-0)   287-77

1965

Coach: Ara Parseghian
Captain: Phil Sheridan

September	18	W....California.............	48-6	A
September	25	L ....Purdue	21-25	A
October	2	W....Northwestern	38-7	H
October	9	W....Army (Nt)	17-0	N
October	23	W....USC (R).............	28-7	H
October	30	W....Navy	29-3	H
November	6	W....Pittsburgh............	69-13	A
November	13	W....North Carolina	17-0	H
November	20	L ....Michigan State	3-12	H
November	27	T ....Miami (Nt)	0-0	A

(7-2-1)   270-73

1966

Coach: Ara Parseghian
Captain: Jim Lynch

September	24	W....Purdue	26-14	H
October	1	W....Northwestern	35-7	A
October	8	W....Army	35-0	H
October	15	W....North Carolina	32-0	H
October	22	W....Oklahoma	38-0	A
October	29	W....Navy.................	31-7	N

November	5	W	Pittsburgh	40-0	H
November	12	W	Duke	64-0	H
November	19	T	Michigan State	10-10	A
November	26	W	USC	51-0	A

(9-0-1)   362-38

1967

Coach: Ara Parseghian
Captain: Bob (Rocky) Bleier

September	23	W	California	41-8	H
September	30	L	Purdue	21-28	A
October	7	W	Iowa	56-6	H
October	14	L	USC	7-24	H
October	21	W	Illinois	47-7	A
October	28	W	Michigan State	24-12	H
November	4	W	Navy	43-14	H
November	11	W	Pittsburgh	38-0	A
November	18	W	Georgia Tech	36-3*	A
November	24	W	Miami (Nt)	24-22	A

(8-2-0)   337-124

*Notre Dame's 500th victory.

1968

Coach: Ara Parseghian
Co-captains: George Kunz and Bob Olson

September	21	W	Oklahoma	45-21	H
September	28	L	Purdue	22-37	H
October	5	W	Iowa	51-28	A
October	12	W	Northwestern	27-7	H
October	19	W	Illinois	58-8	H
October	26	L	Michigan State	17-21	A
November	2	W	Navy	45-14	N
November	9	W	Pittsburgh	56-7	H
November	16	W	Georgia Tech	34-6	H
November	30	T	USC	21-21	A

(7-2-1)   376-170

1969

Coach: Ara Parseghian
Co-captains: Bob Olson and Mike Oriard

September	20	W	Northwestern	35-10	H
September	27	L	Purdue	14-28	A
October	4	W	Michigan State	42-28	H
October	11	W	Army	45-0	N
October	18	T	USC	14-14	H
October	25	W	Tulane (Nt)	37-0	A
November	1	W	Navy	47-0	H
November	8	W	Pittsburgh	49-7	A
November	15	W	Georgia Tech (Nt)	38-20	A
November	22	W	Air Force	13-6	H

(8-1-1)   334-113

COTTON BOWL

January	1	L	Texas	17-21	N

1970

Coach: Ara Parseghian
Co-captains: Larry DiNardo and Tim Kelly

September	19	W	Northwestern	35-14	A
September	26	W	Purdue	48-0	H
October	3	W	Michigan State	29-0	A
October	10	W	Army	51-10	H
October	17	W	Missouri	24-7	A
October	31	W	Navy	56-7	N
November	7	W	Pittsburgh	46-14	H
November	14	W	Georgia Tech	10-7	H
November	21	W	Louisiana State	3-0	H
November	28	L	USC	28-38	A

(9-1-0)   330-97

COTTON BOWL

January	1	W	Texas	24-11	N

1971

Coach: Ara Parseghian
Co-captains: Walt Patulski and Tom Gatewood

September	18	W	Northwestern	50-7	H
September	25	W	Purdue	8-7	A
October	2	W	Michigan State	14-2	H
October	9	W	Miami	17-0	A
October	16	W	North Carolina	16-0	H
October	23	L	USC	14-28	H
October	30	W	Navy	21-0	H
November	6	W	Pittsburgh	56-7	A
November	13	W	Tulane	21-7	H
November	20	L	Louisiana State	8-28	A

(8-2-0)   225-86

1972

Coach: Ara Parseghian
Co-captains: John Dampeer and Greg Marx

September	23	W	Northwestern	37-0	A
September	30	W	Purdue	35-14	H
October	7	W	Michigan State	16-0	A
October	14	W	Pittsburgh	42-16	H
October	21	L	Missouri (U) (R)	26-30	H
October	28	W	TCU	21-0	H
November	4	W	Navy	42-23	N
November	11	W	Air Force	21-7	A
November	18	W	Miami	20-17	H
December	2	L	USC	23-45	A

(8-2-0)   283-152

ORANGE BOWL

January		L	Nebraska	6-40	N

1973

Coach: Ara Parseghian
Tri-captains: Dave Casper, Frank Pomarico, and Mike Townsend

September	22	W	Northwestern	44-0	H
September	29	W	Purdue	20-7	A
October	6	W	Michigan State	14-10	H
October	13	W	Rice	28-0	A
October	20	W	Army	62-3	A
October	27	W	USC	23-14	H
November	3	W	Navy	44-7	H
November	10	W	Pittsburgh	31-10	H
November	22	W	Air Force	48-15	H
December	1	W	Miami	44-0	A

(10-0-0)   358-66

SUGAR BOWL

December	31	W	Alabama (Nt)	24-23	N

1974

Coach: Ara Parseghian
Co-captains: Tom Clements and Greg Collins

September	9	W	Georgia Tech (Nt)	31-7	A
September	21	W	Northwestern	49-3	A
September	28	L	Purdue (U) (R)	20-31	H
October	5	W	Michigan State	19-14	A
October	12	W	Rice	10-3	H
October	19	W	Army	48-0	H
October	26	W	Miami	38-7	H
November	2	W	Navy	14-6	N
November	16	W	Pitt (R)	14-10	H
November	23	W	Air Force	38-0	H
November	30	L	USC	24-55	A

(9-2-0)   305-136

ORANGE BOWL

January	1	W	Alabama (U)	13-11	N

1975

Coach: Dan Devine
Co-captains: Ed Bauer and Jim Stock

September 15	W	Boston College (Nt)	17-3	N
September 20	W	Purdue	17-0	A
September 27	W	Northwestern	31-7	H
October 4	L	Michigan State	3-10	H
October 11	W	No. Carolina	21-14	A
October 18	W	Air Force	31-30	A
October 25	L	USC	17-24	H
November 1	W	Navy	31-10	H
November 8	W	Georgia Tech	24-3	H
November 15	L	Pittsburgh	20-34	A
November 22	W	Miami	32-9	A

(8-3-0) 244-144

1976

Coach: Dan Devine
Co-captains: Mark McLane and Willie Fry

September 11	L	Pittsburgh	10-31	H
September 18	W	Purdue	23-0	H
September 25	W	Northwestern	48-0	A
October 2	W	Michigan State	24-6	A
October 16	W	Oregon	41-0	H
October 23	W	South Carolina	13-6	A
October 30	W	Navy	27-21	N
November 6	W	Georgia Tech	14-23	A
November 13	W	Alabama	21-18	H
November 20	W	Miami	40-27	H
November 27	L	USC	13-17	A

(8-3-0) 274-149

GATOR BOWL

December 27	W	Penn State	20-9	N

1977

Coach: Dan Devine
Tri-captains: Ross Browner, Terry Eurick, and Willie Fry

September 10	W	Pittsburgh	19-9	A
September 17	L	Mississippi	13-20	N
September 24	W	Purdue	31-24	A
October 1	W	Michigan State	16-6	H
October 15	W	Army	24-0	N
October 22	W	USC	49-19	H
October 29	W	Navy	43-10	H
November 5	W	Georgia Tech	69-14	H
November 12	W	Clemson	21-17	A
November 19	W	Air Force	49-0	H
December 3	W	Miami	48-10	A

(10-1-0) 382-129

COTTON BOWL

January 2	W	Texas (U)	38-10	N

1978

Coach: Dan Devine
Tri-captains: Bob Golic, Jerome Heavens, and Joe Montana

September 9	L	Missouri	0-3	H
September 23	L	Michigan	14-28	H
September 30	W	Purdue	10-6	H
October 7	W	Michigan State	29-25	A
October 14	W	Pittsburgh	26-17	H
October 21	W	Air Force	38-15	A
October 28	W	Miami (Fla.)	20-0	H
November 4	W	Navy	27-7	N
November 11	W	Tennessee	31-14	H
November 18	W	Georgia Tech	38-21	A
November 25	L	USC	25-27	A

(8-3-0) 258-163

COTTON BOWL

January 1	W	Houston	35-34*	N

*Notre Dame's 600th victory.

1979

Coach: Dan Devine
Tri-captains: Vagus Ferguson, Tim Foley, and Dave Waymer

September 15	W	Michigan	12-10	A
September 22	L	Purdue	22-28	A
September 29	W	Michigan State	27-3	H
October 6	W	Georgia Tech	21-13	H
October 13	W	Air Force	38-13	A
October 20	L	USC	23-42	H
October 27	W	South Carolina	18-17	H
November 3	W	Navy	14-0	H
November 10	L	Tennessee	18-40	A
November 17	L	Clemson	10-16	H
November 24	W	Miami	40-15	N

(7-4-0) 243-197

1980

Coach: Dan Devine
Tri-captains: Bob Golic, Tom Gibbons, and John Scully

September 6	W	Purdue	31-10	H
September 20	W	Michigan	29-27	H
October 4	W	Michigan State	26-21	A
October 11	W	Miami	32-14	H
October 18	W	Army	30-3	H
October 25	W	Arizona	20-3	A
November 1	W	Navy	33-0	N
November 8	T	Georgia Tech	3-3	A
November 15	W	Alabama	7-0	A
November 22	W	Air Force	24-10	H
December 6	L	USC	3-20	A

(9-1-1) 238-111

SUGAR BOWL

January 1	L	Georgia	10-17	N

1981

Coach: Gerry Faust
Co-captains: Bob Crable and Phil Carter

September 12	W	LSU	27-9	H
September 19	L	Michigan	7-25	A
September 26	L	Purdue	14-15	A
October 3	W	Michigan State	20-7	H
October 10	L	Florida State	13-19	H
October 24	L	USC	7-14	H
October 31	W	Navy	38-0	H
November 7	W	Georgia Tech	35-3	H
November 14	W	Air Force	35-7	A
November 21	L	Penn State	21-24	A
November 27	L	Miami	15-37	A

(5-6-0) 232-160

1982

Coach: Gerry Faust
Tri-captains: Phil Carter, Dave Duerson, and Mark Zavagnin

September 18	W	Michigan	23-17	H
September 25	W	Purdue	28-14	H
October 2	W	Michigan State	11-3	A
October 9	W	Miami	16-14	H
October 16	L	Arizona	13-16	H
October 23	T	Oregon	13-13	A
October 30	W	Navy	27-10	N
November 6	W	Pittsburgh (U)	31-16	A
November 13	L	Penn State	14-24	H
November 20	L	Air Force	17-30	A
November 27	L	USC	13-17	A

(6-4-1) 206-174

1983

Coach: Gerry Faust
Co-captains: Blair Kiel and Stacey Toran

September 10	W	Purdue	52-6	A
September 17	L	Michigan State	23-28	H

September 24	L	Miami	0-20	A	
October 1	W	Colorado	27-3	A	
October 8	W	South Carolina	30-6	A	
October 15	W	Army	42-0	N	
October 22	W	USC	27-6	H	
October 29	W	Navy	28-12	H	
November 5	L	Pittsburgh	16-21	H	
November 12	L	Penn State	30-34	A	
November 19	L	Air Force	22-23	H	

(6-5-0)   297-159

LIBERTY BOWL

December 29 W....Boston College 13   19-18   N

1984

Coach: Gerry Faust
Tri-captains: Mike Golic, Joe Johnson, and Larry Williams

September 8	L	Purdue	21-23	N
September 15	W	Michigan State	24-20	A
September 22	W	Colorado	52-6	H
September 29	W	Missouri	16-14	A
October 6	L	Miami	13-31	H
October 13	L	Air Force	7-21	H
October 20	L	South Carolina	32-36	H
October 27	W	LSU (U)	30-22	A
November 3	W	Navy	18-17	N
November 17	W	Penn State	44-7	H
November 24	W	USC	19-7	A

(7-4-0)   279-212

ALOHA BOWL

December 29 L....SMU   20-27   N

ALL-TIME TEAM SCORING RECORD

YEAR	OPPONENTS	SCORE	ND
1905	American Medical	0	142
1912	St. Viator	7	116
1914	Rose Poly Tech	0	103
1913	Ohio Northern	0	87
1911	Olivet	0	80
1925	Lombard	0	69
1977	Georgia Tech	14	69
1965	Pittsburgh	13	69
1930	Pennsylvania	20	60
1986	SMU	29	61

LONGEST KICKOFF RETURNS

YEAR	PLAYER	OPPONENT	YARDS
1911	Dutch Bergman	Loyola	105*
1930	Joe Savoldi	SMU	100
1981	Greg Bell	Miami	98
1932	George Melinkovich	Northwestern	98
1919	Dutch Bergman	Nebraska	97
1947	Terry Brennan	Army	97
1966	Nick Eddy	Purdue	96
1986	Tim Brown	LSU	96
1907	Dom Callicrate	Olivet	95
1922	Paul Castner	Kalamazoo	95
1922	Don Miller	St. Louis	95
1922	Bill Cerney	DePauw	95
1956	Paul Hornung	USC	95
1986	Tim Brown	Air Force	95

* The playing field was 110 yards long in 1911. Bergman was downed on the Loyola five-yard line.

1985

Coach: Gerry Faust
Captain: Tony Furjanic

September 14	L	Michigan	12-20	A
September 21	W	Michigan State	27-10	H
September 28	L	Purdue	17-35	A
October 5	L	Air Force	15-21	A
October 19	W	Army	24-10	H
October 26	W	USC	37-3	A
November 2	W	Navy	41-17	A
November 9	W	Mississippi	37-14	A
November 16	L	Penn State	6-36	A
November 23	L	LSU	7-10	A
November 30	L	Miami	7-58	A

(5-6-0)   229-234

1986

Coach: Lou Holtz
Captain: Mike Kovaleski

September 13		Michigan	23-24	H
September 20		Michigan State	15-20	A
September 27		Purdue	41-9	H
October 4		Alabama	10-28	A
October 11		Pittsburgh	9-10	H
October 18		Air Force	31-3	H
November 1		Navy	33-14	N
November 8		SMU	61-29	H
November 15		Penn State	19-24	H
November 22		LSU	19-21	A
November 29		USC	38-37	A

(5-6-0)   229-221

SINGLE-SEASON ALL-TIME SCORING LEADERS

YEAR	PLAYER	TD	X PT	FG	TOTAL PTS.
1983	Allen Pinkett	18	2	0	110
1984	Allen Pinkett	18	0	0	108
1979	Vagus Ferguson	17	0	0	102
1944	Bob Kelly	13	6	0	84
1968	Bob Gladieux	14	0	0	84
1976	Al Hunter	13	0	0	78
1943	Creighton Miller	13	0	0	78
1982	Mike Johnson	0	19	19	76
1975	Dan Reeve	0	39	12	75
1980	Harry Oliver	0	19	18	73
1921	John Mohardt	12	0	0	72
1974	Wayne Bullock	12	0	0	72
1924	Jimmy Crowley	9	17	0	71
1973	Bob Thomas	0	43	9	70
1941	Fred Evans	11	1	0	67

SINGLE-SEASON TOP RECEIVERS

YEAR	PLAYER	CAUGHT	YDS.	TD
1970	Tom Gatewood	77	1,123	7
1964	Jack Snow	60	1,114	9
1977	Ken MacAfee	54	797	6
1968	Jim Seymour	53	736	4
1966	Jim Seymour	48	862	8
1969	Tom Gatewood	47	743	8
1974	Pete Demmerle	43	667	6
1982	Tony Hunter	42	507	0
1962	Jim Kelly	41	523	4
1967	Jim Seymour	37	515	4

LONGEST INDIVIDUAL RUSHING PLAYS

YEAR	PLAYER	OPPONENT	YARDS
1947	Bob Livingstone	USC	92
1949	Larry Coutre	Navy	91
1954	Joe Heap	SMU	89
1908	Ulric Ruel	Ohio	85
1907	Paul McDonald	St. Vincent	85
1937	Jack McCarthy	Drake	85
1944	Bob Kelly	Pittsburgh	85
1973	Eric Penick	USC	85
1938	Lou Zontini	Minnesota	84
1946	Emil Sitko	Illinois	83
1942	Corwin Clatt	Great Lakes	81
1949	Larry Coutre	Tulane	81

ALL-TIME TOP PUNTERS

YEAR	PLAYER	OPPONENT	YARDS
1935	Bill Shakespeare	Pittsburgh	86
1935	Bill Shakespeare	Navy	81
1922	Ed DeGree	Nebraska	74
1934	Bill Shakespeare	Pittsburgh	72
1957	Nick Pietrosante	Navy	72
1924	Elmer Layden	Wabash	71
1971	Jim Yoder	Texas	71
1964	Jack Snow	Purdue	70

ALL-TIME TOP FIELD-GOAL KICKS

YEAR	PLAYER	OPPONENT	YARDS
1976	Dan Reeve	Pittsburgh	53
1984	John Carney	SMU	51
1980	Harry Oliver	Michigan	51
1977	Dan Reeve	Michigan State	51
1980	Harry Oliver	Georgia	50
1980	Harry Oliver	Navy	50
1983	Mike Johnston	South Carolina	49
1980	Harry Oliver	Army	49
1979	Chuck Male	Michigan State	49
1961	Joe Perkowski	USC	49
1986	John Carney	Purdue	49

SINGLE-SEASON ALL-TIME PASSING LEADERS

YEAR	PLAYER	ATT.	COMP.	YDS.	TD
1970	Joe Theismann	268	155	2,429	16
1964	John Huarte	205	114	2,062	16
1978	Joe Montana	260	141	2,010	10
1984	Steve Beuerlein	232	140	1,920	7
1979	Rusty Lisch	208	108	1,781	4
1977	Joe Montana	189	99	1,604	11
1974	Tom Clements	215	122	1,549	8
1969	Joe Theismann	192	108	1,531	13
1968	Terry Hanratty	197	116	1,466	10
1967	Terry Hanratty	206	110	1,439	9

INDIVIDUAL SINGLE-GAME RUSHING RECORDS

PLAYER	OPPONENT	YEAR	CARRIES	YARDS
Vagus Ferguson	Georgia Tech	1978	30	255
Phil Carter	Michigan State	1980	40	254
Jim Stone	Miami	1980	38	224
Vagus Ferguson	Navy	1978	18	219
Allen Pinkett	Penn State	1983	36	217
Jim Stone	Navy	1980	33	211
Jerome Heavens	Army	1977	34	200
Allen Pinkett	Air Force	1983	27	197
Allen Pinkett	Penn State	1984	34	189
Emil Sitko	Michigan State	1948	24	186
Vagus Ferguson	USC	1979	25	185
Marchy Schwartz	Carnegie Tech	1931	18	185
George Gipp	Kalamazoo	1920	16	183
Phil Carter	Air Force	1980	29	181
Al Hunter	South Carolina	1976	32	181

CAREER INDIVIDUAL RUSHING RECORDS

YEARS	PLAYER	CARRIES	YARDS	TD	AVG.
1976–79	Vagus Ferguson	673	3,472	32	5.2
1982–84	Allen Pinkett	634	3,031	38	4.8
1975–78	Jerome Heavens	590	2,682	15	4.5
1979–82	Phil Carter	557	2,409	14	4.3
1917–20	George Gipp	369	2,341	16	6.3
1946–49	Emil Sitko	362	2,226	25	6.1
1951–53	Neil Worden	476	2,039	29	4.3
1929–31	Marchy Schwartz	335	1,945	16	5.8

1922–24	Don Miller	283	1,933	17	6.8
1922–24	Jim Crowley	294	1,841	15	6.3
1925–27	Christie Flanagan	285	1,822	15	6.4
1973–76	Al Hunter	382	1,766	23	4.6
1972–74	Wayne Bullock	392	1,730	22	4.2
1951–53	John Lattner	350	1,724	18	4.9
1964–66	Nick Eddy	293	1,615	17	5.5

LONGEST INDIVIDUAL PASS PLAYS

YEAR	PASSER	RECEIVER	OPPONENT	YARDS
1981	Blair Kiel	Joe Howard	Georgia Tech	96
1964	John Huarte	Nick Eddy	Pittsburgh	91
1966	Terry Hanratty	Jim Seymour	Purdue	84
1986	Steve Beuerlein	Timmy Brown	SMU	84
1975	Joe Montana	Ted Burgmeier	North Carolina	80
1971	Joe Theismann	Mike Creaney	Pittsburgh	78
1955	Paul Hornung	Jim Morse	USC	78
1979	Rusty Lisch	Tony Hunter	Air Force	75
1924	Harry Stuhldreher	Jim Crowley	Nebraska	75
1958	Bob Williams	Gary Meyers	Navy	75
1984	Steve Beuerlein	Reggie Ward	Missouri	74
1957	George Izo	Aubrey Lewis	Pittsburgh	74
1964	John Huarte	Nick Eddy	Navy	74

NOTRE DAME ALL-AMERICANS

1913
Gus Dorais, QB
Ray Eichenlaub, FB

1916
Stan Cofall, HB
Charlie Bachman, G

1917
Frank Rydzewski, C

1920
George Gipp, HB
Roger Kiley, E

1921
Roger Kiley, E
Eddie Anderson, E
Hunk Anderson, G
Johnny Mohardt, HB
Paul Castner, HB
Buck Shaw, T

1922
Ed DeGree, G

1923
Don Miller, HB
Elmer Layden, FB
Harvey Brown, G

1924
Harry Stuhldreher, QB
Jim Crowley, HB
Elmer Layden, FB
Adam Walsh, C

1926
Art Boeringer, C
Christie Flanagan, HB

1927
Christie Flanagan, HB
John Smith, G
John Polisky, T

1928
Fred Miller, T

1929
Frank Carideo, QB
Jack Cannon, G
Ted Twomey, T

1930
Frank Carideo, QB
Marchy Schwartz, HB
Marty Brill, HB
Joe Savoldi, FB
Bert Metzger, G
Tom Conley, E
Al Culver, T

1931
Marchy Schwartz, HB
Joe Kurth, T
Tommy Yarr, C
Nordy Hoffmann, G

1932
Joe Kurth, T
Ed Krause, T
George Melinkovich, FB
Ed Kosky, E

1934
Jack Robinson, C

1935
Bill Shakespeare, HB
Wayne Millner, E
Andy Pilney, HB

1936
John Lautar, G

1937
Chuck Sweeney, E
Joe Beinor, T

1938
Joe Beinor, T
Earl Brown, E
Jim McGoldrick, G

1939
Bud Kerr, E
Milt Piepul, FB

1940
Milt Piepul, FB

1941
Bob Dove, E
Bernie Crimmins, G

1942
Angelo Bertelli, QB
Bob Dove, E
Harry Wright, G

1943
Angelo Bertelli, QB
Creighton Miller, HB
John Yonakor, E
Jim White, T
Pat Filley, G
Herb Coleman, C

1944
Bob Kelly, HB
Pat Filley, G

1945
John Mastrangelo, G
Frank Dancewicz, QB

1946
John Lujack, QB
George Connor, T
John Mastrangelo, G
George Strohmeyer, C

1947
John Lujack, QB
George Connor, T
Bill Fischer, G
Ziggy Czarobski, T
Leon Hart, E

1948
Bill Fischer, G
Leon Hart, E
Emil Sitko, FB
Marty Wendell, G

1949
Emil Sitko, FB
Leon Hart, E
Bob Williams, QB
Jim Martin, T

1950
Bob Williams, QB
Jerry Groom, C

1951
Bob Toneff, T
Jim Mutscheller, E

1952

John Lattner, HB
Bob O'Neill, DE

1953

John Lattner, HB
Art Hunter, T
Don Penza, E

1954

Ralph Guglielmi, QB
Frank Varrichione, T
Dan Shannon, E

1955

Paul Hornung, HB
Don Schaefer, FB
Pat Bisceglia, G

1956

Paul Hornung, QB

1957

Al Ecuyer, G

1958

Nick Pietrosante, FB
Al Ecuyer, G
Monty Stickles, E

1959

Monty Stickles, E

1960

Myron Pottios, G

1961

Nick Buoniconti, G

1962

Jim Kelly, E

1963

Jim Kelly, E
Bob Lehmann, G

1964

John Huarte, QB
Jack Snow, E
Jim Carroll, LB
Tony Carey, DB

1965

Dick Arrington, G
Nick Rassas, DB
Tom Regner, G
Jim Lynch, LB

1966

Nick Eddy, HB
Jim Lynch, LB
Tom Regner, G
Alan Page, DE
Pete Duranko, DT
Kevin Hardy, DT
Jim Seymour, E
Paul Seiler, T
George Goeddeke, C
Tom Schoen, DB

1967

Tom Schoen, DB
Kevin Hardy, DE

Jim Seymour, E
Mike McGill, LB
John Pergine, LB
Dick Swatland, G
Jim Smithberger, DB

1968

George Kunz, T
Terry Hanratty, QB
Jim Seymour, E

1969

Mike McCoy, DT
Jim Reilly, T
Larry DiNardo, G
Bob Olson, LB
Mike Oriard, C

1970

Larry DiNardo, G
Tom Gatewood, E
Clarence Ellis, DB
Joe Theismann, QB

1971

Walt Patulski, DE
Clarence Ellis, DB
Tom Gatewood, E
Mike Kadish, DT

1972

Greg Marx, DT
John Dampeer, OT

1973

Dave Casper, TE
Mike Townsend, DB

1974

Pete Demmerle, SE
Mike Fanning, DT
Gerry DiNardo, G
Tom Clements, QB
Greg Collins, LB
Steve Niehaus, DT

1975

Steve Niehaus, T
Ken MacAfee, TE
Luther Bradley, DB

1976

Ross Browner, DE
Ken MacAfee, TE
Luther Bradley, DB
Willie Fry, DE

1977

Ross Browner, DE
Ken MacAfee, TE
Luther Bradley, DB
Ernie Hughes, G
Bob Golic, MG
Willie Fry, DE
Ted Burgmeier, DB

1978

Bob Golic, LB
Dave Huffman, C

1979

Vagus Ferguson, HB
Tim Foley, OT

1980

John Scully, C
Bob Crable, LB
Scott Zettek, DE

1981

Bob Crable, LB
John Krimm, CB

1982

Dave Duerson, FS
Tony Hunter, TE
Mark Zavagnin, LB

1983

Allen Pinkett, TB
Larry Williams, OT

1984

Mark Bavaro, TE
Larry Williams, OG
Mike Gann, DT
Mike Kelley, C

1985

Allen Pinkett, TB

1986

Tim Brown, TB

NOTRE DAME NATIONAL CHAMPIONSHIPS

YEAR	TEAM	RECORD	COACH	SELECTOR
1919	Harvard	9-0-1	Bob Fisher	Unanimous
	Notre Dame	9-0	Knute Rockne	Davis (tie)
	Illinois	6-1	Bob Zuppke	Davis (tie)
1920	California	9-0	Andy Smith	Helms
	Notre Dame	9-0	Knute Rockne	Davis (tie)
	Princeton	6-0-1	Bill Roper	Davis (tie)
1924	Notre Dame	10-0	Knute Rockne	DS, Helms, IFA
	Pennsylvania	9-1-1	Lou Young	Davis
1927	Illinois	7-0-1	Bob Zuppke	DS, Davis, Helms
	Yale	7-1	T.A.D. Jones	IFA
	Notre Dame	7-1-1	Knute Rockne	TFT
1929	Notre Dame	9-0	Knute Rockne	DS, Dunkel, IFA, Helms
	Pittsburgh	9-1	Jock Sutherland	Davis
	USC	10-2	Howard Jones	TFT
1930	Notre Dame	10-0	Knute Rockne	Unanimous
	Alabama	10-0	Wallace Wade	Davis (tie)
1938	Tennessee	11-0	Bob Neyland	Dunkel, LS, IFA, TFT
	TCU	11-0	Dutch Meyer	AP, WS, Helms
	Notre Dame	8-1	Elmer Layden	DS

1943	Notre Dame	9-1	Frank Leahy	Unanimous
1946	Notre Dame	8-0-1	Frank Leahy	AP, Dunkel, LS
	Army	9-0-1	Red Blaik	Helms, TFT
	Georgia	11-0	Wally Butts	WS
1947	Notre Dame	9-0	Frank Leahy	AP, WS, Helms
	Michigan	10-0	Fritz Crisler	Dunkel, LS, TFT
1949	Notre Dame	10-0	Frank Leahy	Unanimous
1953	Notre Dame	9-0-1	Frank Leahy	All but AP, UPI
	Maryland	10-1	Jim Tatum	AP, UPI
1964	Alabama	10-1	Bear Bryant	AP, UPI, LS
	Arkansas	11-0	Frank Broyles	FWAA, Helms
	Notre Dame	9-1	Ara Parseghian	NFFHF
	Michigan	9-1	Bump Elliott	Dunkel
1966	Notre Dame	9-0-1	Ara Parseghian	Unanimous
	Michigan State	9-0-1	Duff Daugherty	Helms, NFFHF (tie)
1967	USC	10-1	John McKay	All but Dunkel
	Notre Dame	8-2	Ara Parseghian	Dunkel
1973	Notre Dame	11-0	Ara Parseghian	All but UPI, Dunkel
	Alabama	10-1	Bear Bryant	UPI
	Oklahoma	10-0-1	Barry Switzer	Dunkel
1977	Notre Dame	11-1	Dan Devine	Unanimous

RATING SYSTEMS

AP — *Associated Press (1936–current); poll of sportswriters and broadcasters

Davis — Park H. Davis Ratings (1889–1935); chosen by Davis, a player at Princeton in 1889 and a former coach at Wisconsin, Amherst, and Lafayette, and first published in the 1934 *Spalding's Football Guide*

DS — Dickinson System (1924–40); chosen by University of Illinois economics professor Frank G. Dickinson; based on system that awarded various point totals for wins over teams with winning or non-winning records

Dunkel — Dunkel System (1929–current); a power index rating system devised by Dick Dunkel and syndicated to newspapers around the nation

FWAA — Football Writers Association of America (1954–current); chosen by five-man committee representing membership

Helms — First Interstate Bank Athletic Foundation (1899–current); originally founded in 1936 as Helms Athletic Foundation and changed in early 1970s to Citizen Savings Athletic Foundation before current name was adopted in 1981

IFA — *Illustrated Football Annual* (1924–41); an "azzi ratem" system published in this highly regarded fan magazine by William F. Boand

LS — Litkenhous System (1934–current); a "differ-ence-by-score" method syndicated by Fred Litkenhous and his brother Edward

NFFHF — National Football Foundation and Hall of Fame (1959–current); chosen annually by committee representing membership

TFT — *The Football Thesaurus* (1927–58); system devised by Duke Houlgate and published in book of same title

UPI — United Press International (1950–current); poll of 35 college coaches

WS — Williamson System (1932–63); system of syndicated power ratings chosen by Paul Williamson, a geologist and member of the Sugar Bowl committee

* The evolution of the Associated Press national championship began with the awarding of the Rissman Trophy starting in 1924. It was retired in 1930 after Notre Dame won the award for the third time ('24, '29 and '30). Notre Dame's Four Horsemen—Elmer Layden, Jim Crowley, Don Miller, and Harry Stuhldreher—then donated the Knute Rockne Trophy which was awarded beginning in 1931. The AP began its poll in 1936, but it continued to award the Rockne Trophy to its national champion until 1940 when Minnesota retired it by winning for the third time ('34, '36, and '40). Minnesota put up the Dr. Henry L. Williams Trophy which Notre Dame retired in 1947 ('43, '46, and '47). A group of Notre Dame alumni then put up the Father O'Donnell Trophy which Oklahoma retired in 1956 ('50, '55, and '56). Beginning with the 1957 season, the award has been known as the AP Trophy.

NOTRE DAME COACHES AND PLAYERS IN NFF HALL OF FAME

The National Football Foundation each year honors former college football players and coaches who rank among the greats in the game and inducts them into its Hall of Fame.

Since inductions began in 1951, twenty-eight former Notre Dame players and five former coaches have been honored as Hall of Fame enshrinees.

In addition, three individuals who played at Notre Dame have been inducted for their coaching excellence—Charlie Bachman (played guard 1914–16, coached at Great Lakes, Northwestern, Kansas State, Florida, Michigan State, and Hillsdale), Frank Thomas (played quarterback 1920–22, coached at Chattanooga and Alabama), and Eddie Anderson (played end 1918–21, coached at Loras, DePaul, Holy Cross, and Iowa).

COACHES

1951	Knute Rockne	105-12-5	1918–30
1970	Frank Leahy	87-11-9	1941–43, 46–53
1971	Jesse Harper	34-5-1	1913–17
1980	Ara Parseghian	95-17-4	1964–74
1985	Dan Devine	53-16-1	1975–80

PLAYERS

1951	George Gipp	HB	1917–20
1951	Elmer Layden	FB	1922–24
1954	Frank Carideo	QB	1928–30
1958	Harry Stuhldreher	QB	1922–24
1960	John Lujack	QB	1943, 46–47
1963	George Connor	OT	1946–47
1965	Jack Cannon	QB	1927–29
1966	Edgar (Rip) Miller	OT	1922–24
1966	Jim Crowley	HB	1922–24
1968	Adam Walsh	C	1922–24
1970	Don Miller	HB	1922–24
1971	Louis (Red) Salmon	FB	1900–03
1972	Angelo Bertelli	QB	1941–43
1972	Ray Eichenlaub	FB	1911–14
1973	Leon Hart	TE	1946–49
1974	Marchy Schwartz	HB	1929–31
1974	Heartley (Hunk) Anderson	OG	1918–21
1975	John (Clipper) Smith	OG	1925–27
1976	Creighton Miller	HB	1941–43
1977	Zygmont (Ziggy) Czarobski	OT	1942–43, 46–47
1978	Frank (Nordy) Hoffmann	OG	1930–31
1979	John Lattner	HB	1951–53
1982	Bert Metzger	OG	1928–30
1983	Bill (Moose) Fischer	OG	1945–48
1983	Bill Shakespeare	HB	1933–35
1984	Emil (Red) Sitko	HB	1946–49
1985	Paul Hornung	QB	1954–56
1985	Fred Miller	T	1926–28

HEISMAN TROPHY WINNERS

Since the inception of the Heisman Trophy in 1935, six Notre Dame players have won the award, more than from any other university:

1943	Angelo Bertelli, QB
1947	John Lujack, QB
1949	Leon Hart, E
1953	John Lattner, HB
1956	Paul Hornung, QB
1964	John Huarte, QB

Notre Dame has had a player finish among the top ten in the Heisman voting in twenty-eight of the fifty years the award has been presented. In addition to the six winners, the Irish have had two players finish second: Bertelli in 1941 and Joe Theismann in 1970.

Five players finished in third place: Bill Shakespeare in 1935, Lujack in 1946, Nick Eddy in 1966, Terry Hanratty in 1968, and Ken MacAfee in 1977. Three Irish stars finished in fourth place: Creighton Miller in 1943, Ralph Guglielmi in 1954, and Tom Clements in 1974. Six players finished in sixth place: Bob Williams in 1949, Lattner in 1952, Hornung in 1955, Jack Snow in 1964, Ross Browner in 1977, and Vagus Ferguson in 1979.

FUTURE SCHEDULES POST THE SCORES

1987

Sept. 12 — at Michigan
Sept. 19 — Michigan State
Sept. 26 — at Purdue
Oct. 10 — at Pittsburgh
Oct. 17 — at Air Force
Oct. 24 — USC
Oct. 31 — Navy
Nov. 7 — Boston College
Nov. 14 — Alabama
Nov. 21 — at Penn State
Nov. 28 — at Miami

1988

Sept. 10 — Michigan
Sept. 17 — at Michigan State
Sept. 24 — Purdue
Oct. 1 — Stanford
Oct. 8 — at Pittsburgh
Oct. 15 — Miami
Oct. 22 — Air Force
Oct. 29 — at Navy
Nov. 5 — at SMU
Nov. 19 — Penn State
Nov. 26 — at USC

1989

Sept. 16 — at Michigan
Sept. 23 — Michigan State
Sept. 30 — at Purdue
Oct. 7 — at Stanford
Oct. 14 — at Air Force
Oct. 21 — USC
Oct. 28 — Pittsburgh
Nov. 4 — Navy
Nov. 11 — SMU
Nov. 18 — at Penn State
Nov. 25 — at Miami

1990

Sept. 15 — Michigan
Sept. 22 — at Michigan State
Sept. 29 — Purdue
Oct. 6 — Stanford
Oct. 13 — Air Force
Oct. 20 — Miami
Oct. 27 — at Pittsburgh
Nov. 3 — at Navy
Nov. 10 — at Tennessee
Nov. 17 — Penn State
Dec. 1 — at USC

1991

Sept. 7 — Indiana
Sept. 14 — at Michigan
Sept. 21 — Michigan State
Sept. 28 — at Purdue
Oct. 5 — at Stanford
Oct. 12 — Pittsburgh
Oct. 19 — at Air Force
Oct. 26 — USC
Nov. 2 — Navy
Nov. 9 — Tennessee
Nov. 16 — at Penn State
Nov. 30 — at Hawaii

INDEX

(Italicized page numbers indicate photographs)